650 best selling
Home Plans

table of contents

the Garlinghouse company

W9-DBK-965

Bradford J. Kidney

Staff Writers
Debra Cochran/Susan Barile

Cover Design
Marla Gladstone

Library of Congress No.: 99-76700
ISBN: 0-938708-90-2

cover photography from top to bottom:
94644 photography by M & A Studios pg. 269
99844 photography by Jon Riley, Riley & Riley Photography pg. 205
32063 photography supplied by The Meredith Corporation pg. 6
32291 photography supplied by The Meredith Corporation pg. 172

Warm Welcome

Price Code: C

PLAN NO. 24245

- This plan features:
— Three bedrooms
— Two full and one half baths
- Formal areas flanking the entry hall
- A Living Room that includes a wonderful fireplace
- Direct access from the formal Dining Room to the Kitchen
- A U-shaped Kitchen including a breakfast bar, built-in pantry and planning desk and a double sink
- A Mudroom entry that will help keep the dirt from play or muddy shoes away from the rest of the home
- An expansive Family Room with direct access to the rear deck
- A Master Suite highlighted by a walk-in closet and a private Master Bath
- Two additional bedrooms, one with a built-in desk, share a full hall bath with a double vanity

FIRST FLOOR — 1,113 SQ. FT.
SECOND FLOOR — 970 SQ. FT.
GARAGE — 480 SQ. FT.
BASEMENT — 1,113 SQ. FT.

TOTAL LIVING AREA:
2,083 SQ. FT.

ZIP QUOTE
HOME COST CALCULATOR
see order pages for details

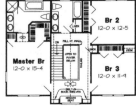

FIRST FLOOR

74'-0"
41'-6"

Garage
21-5 x 21-5

Mud Room

Kitchen
12-0 x 12-5

Deck

Nook

Family
23-1 x 12-5

Dining
13-1 x 14-2

Living
13-1 x 14-2

Porch

SECOND FLOOR

Master Br
12-0 x 15-4

Br 2
12-0 x 12-5

Br 3
12-0 x 11-4

CRAWL SPACE/SLAB OPTION

1

Colonial Styling

Price Code: C

■ This plan features:

— Four bedrooms

— Two full, one three quarter, and one half baths

■ The Dining Room has a built-in hutch and a wetbar

■ The Parlor may be used for formal entertaining space or a quiet repose

■ The Great Room has a rear wall fireplace with windows set to ether side

■ The Kitchen has a smart arrangement and shares a snack bar with the Nook

■ The Breakfast Nook has a bay with windows and transoms above

■ The Master Bedroom is located on the first floor for privacy

FIRST FLOOR — 1,865 SQ. FT.

SECOND FLOOR — 774 SQ. FT.

TOTAL LIVING AREA:
2,639 SQ. FT.

FIRST FLOOR

SECOND FLOOR

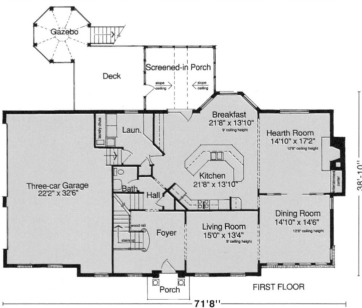

Gazebo

Deck

Screened-in Porch
slope ceiling · slope ceiling

Laun.

Breakfast
21'8" x 13'10"
9' ceiling height

Hearth Room
14'10" x 17'2"
12'8" ceiling height

Three-car Garage
22'2" x 32'6"

Kitchen
21'8" x 13'10"

Bath

Hall

Foyer

Living Room
15'0" x 13'4"
9' ceiling height

Dining Room
14'10" x 14'6"
12'8" ceiling height

38'-10"

Porch

FIRST FLOOR

71'8"

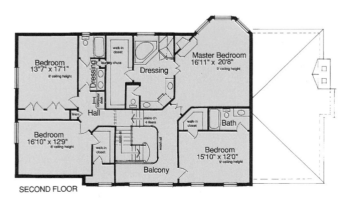

Bedroom
13'7" x 17'1"
8' ceiling height

Dressing

laundry chute

Dressing

Master Bedroom
16'11" x 20'8"
9' ceiling height

Hall

Bedroom
16'10" x 12'9"
8' ceiling height

Bath

Bedroom
15'10" x 12'0"
9' ceiling height

Balcony

SECOND FLOOR

Two Story Brick Colonial

Price Code: F

■ This plan features:

— Four bedrooms

— Three full and one half baths

■ A covered front Porch and Foyer with lovely staircase greet you

■ The Living Room flows freely into the Dining Room for carefree entertaining

■ The Hearth Room has a twelve foot ceiling, fireplace, and entertainment center

■ The unique Kitchen design is a cook's delight and it adjoins the Breakfast Nook and a screen Porch

■ Upstairs find four large Bedrooms with ample closet space, and three full Baths

■ No materials list available for this plan

FIRST FLOOR — 1,666 SQ. FT.
SECOND FLOOR — 1,036 SQ. FT.
MID FLOOR — 743 SQ. FT.

TOTAL LIVING AREA:
3,445 SQ. FT.

Old-Fashioned Porch

Price Code: B

- This plan features:
— Three bedrooms
— Two full and one half baths

- A Traditional front Porch, with matching dormers above and a Garage hidden below, leading into a open, contemporary layout

- A Living Area with a cozy fireplace visible from the Dining Room for warm entertaining

- A U-shaped, efficient Kitchen including a pass-thru to the Dining Room

- A convenient half Bath/Laundry center on the first floor

- A spacious Master Suite with a lavish Master Bath including a double vanity, walk-in closet and an oval, corner window tub

FIRST FLOOR — 1,057 SQ. FT.
SECOND FLOOR — 611 SQ. FT.
BASEMENT — 511 SQ. FT.
GARAGE — 546 SQ. FT.

TOTAL LIVING AREA:
1,668 SQ. FT.

ZIP QUOTE
HOME COST CALCULATOR
see order pages for details

SECOND FLOOR

Bdrm. 2
15-8 x 13-4

Bdrm. 3
15-6 x 11-0

Bath 2

Sundeck
16-0 x 12-0

Brkfst.
9-0 x 8-0

Kit.
9-0 x 9-6

Dining
9-10 x 11-4

Lav.

M.Bath

Living Area
18-0 x 13-6

Master Bdrm.
15-6 x 13-6

Porch

©1983, Jannis Vann & Associates, Inc.

38-0

40-4

FIRST FLOOR

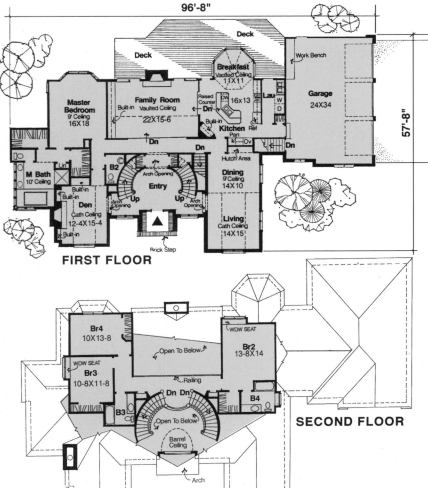

FIRST FLOOR

SECOND FLOOR

Unusual and Dramatic

Price Code: F

- ■ This plan features:
  - — Four bedrooms
  - — Three full and one half baths
- ■ Elegant Entry with arched openings and a double curved staircase
- ■ Cathedral ceilings crown arched windows in the Den and Living Room
- ■ Spacious Family Room with a vaulted ceiling and a large fireplace
- ■ Hub Kitchen with a work island/serving counter, Breakfast alcove
- ■ Secluded Master Suite with a lovely bay window, two walk-in closets and a plush bath
- ■ Three second floor bedrooms, one with a private bath, offer ample closets

FIRST FLOOR — 2,646 SQ. FT.
SECOND FLOOR — 854 SQ. FT.

TOTAL LIVING AREA:
3,500 SQ. FT.

Photography Supplied By The Meredith Corporation

Forest Cottage

Price Code: F

- This plan features:
— Four Bedrooms
— Four full and one half baths
- The bow shaped front Deck mirrors the eyebrow dormer and large arched window
- Kitchen with an island and a built-in Pantry
- The Great Room is highlighted by a fireplace and access to the screened Porch
- The second floor Master Suite has two walk-in closets and is pampered by a five-piece Bath
- The lower level contains a Media Room, a Play Room, and a Guest Suite

FIRST FLOOR — 1,642 SQ. FT.
SECOND FLOOR — 1411 SQ. FT.
LOWER LEVEL — 1,230 SQ. FT.
BASEMENT — 412 SQ. FT.

TOTAL LIVING AREA:
4283 SQ. FT.

Traditional Cape Cod

Price Code: C

- This plan features:
  - Three bedrooms
  - Two full and one half baths
- With easy access from the Foyer, there is a Library with built-in shelves
- The formal Dining Room has columns and a dramatic view through the Great Room to the fireplace and rear windows
- The spacious Kitchen offers an island with seating which opens into a roomy Breakfast Area surrounded by windows
- A Master Bedroom Suite with deluxe Bath and a spacious walk-in closet
- No materials list is available for this plan

FIRST FLOOR — 1,710 SQ. FT.
SECOND FLOOR — 733 SQ. FT.
BONUS ROOM — 181 SQ. FT.

TOTAL LIVING AREA:
2,443 SQ. FT.

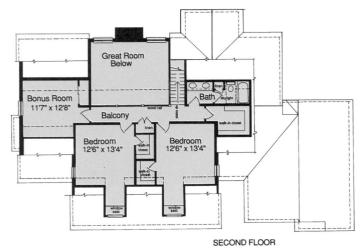

Porch

Breakfast
10' x 10'

Kitchen
9'2" x 11'8"

Master
Bedroom
14' x 13'

Great Room
16'9" x 17'6"

pantry

Dressing

Library
11' x 13'4"

Foyer

Dining Room
11'4" x 13'5"

Laun.

Two-car
Garage
20'4" x 26'4"

walk-in closet

47'8"

78'4"

FIRST FLOOR

Great Room
Below

Bonus Room
11'7" x 12'8"

Bath

Balcony

Bedroom
12'6" x 13'4"

Bedroom
12'6" x 13'4"

walk-in closet

linen

window seat

window seat

SECOND FLOOR

Convenient Country

Price Code: B

- This plan features:
  — Three bedrooms
  — Two full and one half baths
- Full front Porch provides a sheltered entrance
- Expansive Living Room with an inviting fireplace opens to bright Dining Room and Kitchen
- U-shaped Kitchen with peninsula serving counter, Dining Room and nearby Pantry, Laundry and Garage entry
- Secluded Master Bedroom with two closets and a double vanity Bath
- Two second floor Bedrooms with ample closets and dormer windows, share a full Bath
- No materials list is available for this plan

FIRST FLOOR — 1,108 SQ. FT.
SECOND FLOOR — 659 SQ. FT.
BASEMENT — 875 SQ. FT.

TOTAL LIVING AREA:
1,767 SQ. FT.

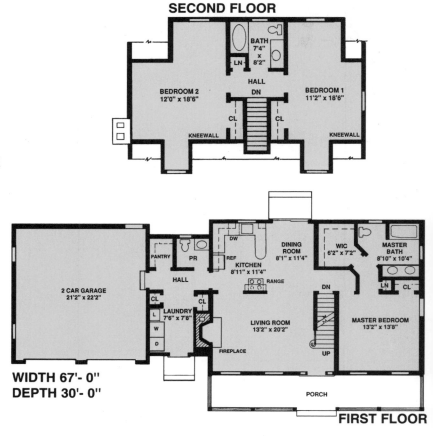

SECOND FLOOR

BATH
7'4"
x
8'2"

LN

HALL
DN

BEDROOM 2
12'0" x 18'6"

BEDROOM 1
11'2" x 18'6"

CL   CL

KNEEWALL   KNEEWALL

PANTRY   PR   DW

DINING ROOM
8'1" x 11'4"

WIC
6'2" x 7'2"

MASTER BATH
8'10" x 10'4"

REF

KITCHEN
8'11" x 11'4"

HALL

RANGE

DN

LN   CL

2 CAR GARAGE
21'2" x 22'2"

CL

CL

LAUNDRY
7'6" x 7'8"

L

W

D

LIVING ROOM
13'2" x 20'2"

MASTER BEDROOM
13'2" x 13'8"

FIREPLACE

UP

WIDTH 67'- 0"
DEPTH 30'- 0"

PORCH

FIRST FLOOR

FIRST FLOOR

Great Room
16' x 19'6"

Breakfast
10'8" x 11'2"

Kitchen
13'5" x 14'

Laun.

Dressing

walk-in closet

Master Bedroom
14' x 14'1"

Foyer

Porch

Dining Room
12' x 13'10"

Two-car Garage
21' x 20'4"

Sitting Area
11'2" x 9'4"

48'

63'4"

SECOND FLOOR

high glass

Bath

Bedroom
11'4" x 12'6"

Great Room
Below
high ceiling

Hall

linen

Bedroom
10' x 13'10"

Bath

walk-in closet

Bedroom
12' x 10'6"

slope ceiling   slope ceiling

TOTAL LIVING AREA:
2,403 SQ. FT.

Dynamic Two-Story

Price Code: D

■ This plan features:

— Four bedrooms

— Three full and one half baths

■ Sheltered entry surrounded by glass leads into open Foyer and Great Room with high ceiling, hearth fireplace and atrium door to back yard

■ Columns frame entrance to conveniently located Dining Room

■ Efficient Kitchen with built-in pantry, work island and bright Breakfast area accesses Laundry, backyard and Garage

■ Master Bedroom wing with sitting area, walk-in closet and private bath with corner window tub and double vanity

■ Three additional bedrooms, one with a private bath, located on second floor

■ No materials list available for this plan

FIRST FLOOR — 1,710 SQ. FT.
SECOND FLOOR — 693 SQ. FT.
BASEMENT — 1,620 SQ. FT.
GARAGE — 467 SQ. FT.

Southern Traditional

Price Code: B

■ This plan features:

— Three bedrooms

— Two full baths

■ A varied roof line with dormers and a charming colonnaded front Porch

■ Living Room enhanced by nine foot ceilings and a bookcase flanked fireplace

■ Two mullioned French doors leading from the Dining Room to the rear terrace

■ A bayed area in the wrap-around Kitchen

■ Laundry area serving as a Mudroom between the Garage and Kitchen

■ A Master Suite with a walk-in closet, a compartmented Bath with a whirlpool tub, double basin vanity and linen closet

■ Second floor to be finished for future use

FIRST FLOOR — 1,567 SQ. FT.
SECOND FLOOR ´BONUS SPACE — 462 SQ. FT.
BASEMENT — 1,567 SQ. FT.
GARAGE — 504 SQ. FT.

TOTAL LIVING AREA:
1,567 SQ. FT.

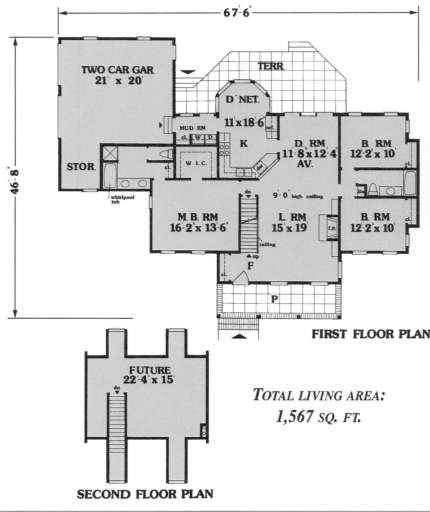

FIRST FLOOR PLAN

SECOND FLOOR PLAN

TOTAL LIVING AREA:
1,567 SQ. FT.

A Touch of Old World Charm

Price Code: D

■ This plan features:

— Four bedrooms

— Two full and one half baths

■ Authentic balustrade railings and front courtyard greet one and all

■ High ceiling in Great Room tops corner fireplace and French doors with arched window

■ Formal Dining Room enhanced by a decorative window and furniture alcove

■ Country Kitchen with work island, two Pantries, Breakfast Area with French door to rear yard, Laundry and Garage Entry

■ Master Bedroom wing offers a sloped ceiling, plush Bath and a huge walk-in closet

■ Three additional Bedrooms share second floor, balcony and double vanity Bath

■ No materials list available for this plan

FIRST FLOOR — 1,595 SQ. FT.
SECOND FLOOR — 725 SQ. FT.
GARAGE — 409 SQ. FT.

SECOND FLOOR

TOTAL LIVING AREA:
2,320 SQ. FT.

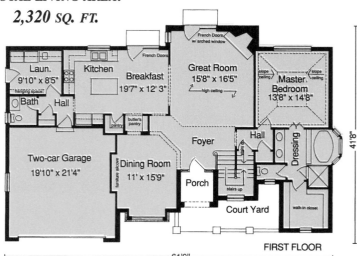

FIRST FLOOR

Neat and Tidy

Price Code: A

■ This plan features:

— Two bedrooms

— Two full baths

■ A two-story Living Room and Dining Room with a handsome stone fireplace

■ A well-appointed Kitchen with a peninsula counter

■ A Master Suite with a walk-in closet and private Master Bath

■ A large utility room with laundry facilities

■ An optional basement or crawl space foundation — please specify when ordering

FIRST FLOOR — 952 SQ. FT.
SECOND FLOOR — 297 SQ. FT.

TOTAL LIVING AREA:
1,249 SQ. FT.

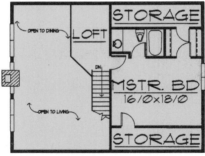

ZIP QUOTE
HOME COST CALCULATOR
see order pages for details

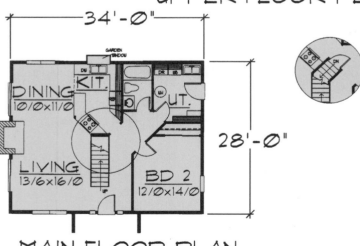

UPPER FLOOR PLAN

MAIN FLOOR PLAN

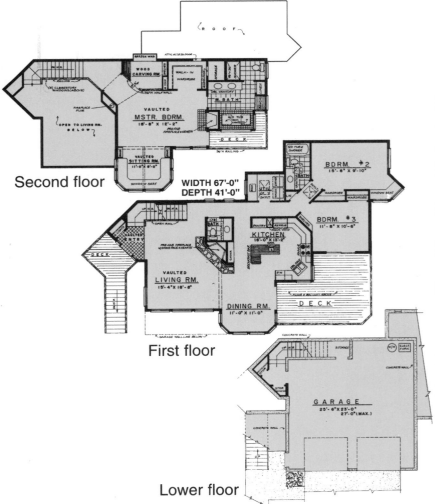

Second floor

WIDTH 67'-0"
DEPTH 41'-0"

First floor

Lower floor

Customized for Sloping View Site

Price Code: C

■ This plan features:

— Three bedrooms

— Two full and one half baths

■ A stone-faced fireplace and vaulted ceiling in the Living Room

■ An island food preparation center with a sink and a Breakfast bar in the Kitchen

■ Sliding glass doors leading from the Dining Room to the adjacent deck

■ A Master Suite with a vaulted ceiling, a sitting room, and a lavish Master Bath with a whirlpool tub, skylights, double vanity, and a walk-in closet

FIRST FLOOR — 1,338 SQ. FT.
SECOND FLOOR — 763 SQ. FT.
LOWER FLOOR — 61 SQ. FT.

TOTAL LIVING AREA:
2,162 SQ. FT.

© 1996 Donald A. Gardner Architects, Inc.

Charm and Personality

Price Code: D

ZIP QUOTE
HOME COST CALCULATOR
see order pages for details

■ This plan features:

— Three bedrooms

— Two full baths

■ Interior columns dramatically open the Foyer and Kitchen to the spacious Great Room

■ Drama is heightened by the Great Room cathedral ceiling and fireplace

■ Master Suite with a tray ceiling combines privacy with access to the rear Deck with spa, while the skylight Bath has all the amenities expected in a quality home

■ Tray ceilings with round-top picture windows bring a special elegance to the Dining Room and the front Swing Room

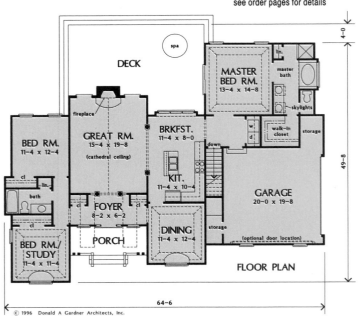

MAIN FLOOR — 1,655 SQ. FT.
GARAGE — 434 SQ. FT.

TOTAL LIVING AREA:
1,655 SQ. FT.

14

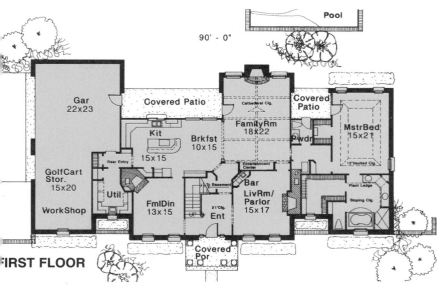

FIRST FLOOR

Gar 22x23

Covered Patio

Covered Patio

Kit

FamilyRm 18x22

MstrBed 15x21

Brkfst 10x15

GolfCart Stor. 15x20

Pwdr

WorkShop

Util

FmlDin 13x15

Bar LivRm/ Parlor 15x17

Ent

Covered Por

90' - 0"

Pool

Grand Entrance
Price Code: F

■ This plan features:

— Four bedrooms

— Two full, one three-quarter and one half baths

■ Covered Porch with columns leads to entry hall with a graceful landing staircase

■ Fireplaces highlight both the Living Room/Parlor and formal Dining Room

■ An efficient Kitchen with an island cooktop, built-in Pantry and open Breakfast Area

■ Cathedral ceiling crowns expansive Family Room, accented by a fireplace and a built-in entertainment center

■ Lavish Master Bedroom wing

■ Three additional Bedrooms, one with a private Bath, on the second floor

■ A Garage with Workshop and rear entry to Kitchen and Utility Area

■ No materials list is available for this plan

FIRST FLOOR — 2,432 SQ. FT.
SECOND FLOOR — 903 SQ. FT.
BASEMENT — 2,432 SQ. FT.
GARAGE — 742 SQ. FT.

TOTAL LIVING AREA: 3,335 SQ. FT.

SECOND FLOOR

Bed#4 13x11

Balcony

Bed#3 13x14

Bed#2 15x11

Ent Below

Opulent Luxury

Price Code: F

■ This plan features:

— Four bedrooms

— Three full and one half baths

■ Columns frame elegant two-story Entry with a graceful banister staircase

■ A stone hearth fireplace and built-in book shelves enhance the Living Room

■ Comfortable Family Room with a huge fireplace, cathedral ceiling and access to Covered Veranda

■ Spacious Kitchen with cooktop island/ snackbar, built-in pantry and Breakfast Room

■ Lavish Master Bedroom wing with a pullman ceiling, sitting area, private Covered Patio and a huge bath with two walk-in closets and a whirlpool tub

■ Three additional bedrooms on second floor with walk-in closets and private access to a full bath

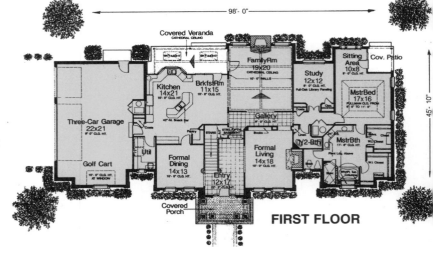

FIRST FLOOR

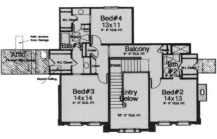

SECOND FLOOR

FIRST FLOOR — 2,804 SQ. FT.
SECOND FLOOR — 979 SQ. FT.
BASEMENT — 2,804 SQ. FT.
GARAGE — 802 SQ. FT.

TOTAL LIVING AREA:
3,783 SQ. FT.

© 1990 design basics inc.

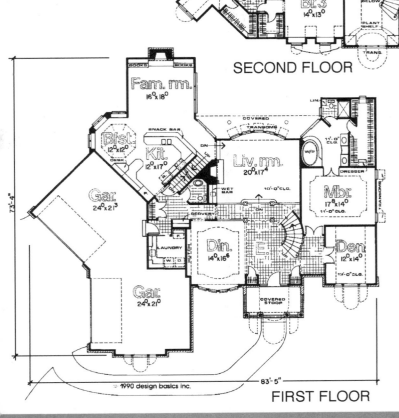

SECOND FLOOR

FIRST FLOOR

© 1990 design basics inc.

Spectacular Voluminous Entry

Price Code: E

■ This plan features:

— Four bedrooms

— Three full, two three-quarter, one half baths

■ The spectacular entry of this home has a curving staircase and defining columns leading into the sunken Living Room

■ Dramatic Kitchen is equipped with a large snack bar, Pantry and desk

■ Double doors introduce the Master Suite with private back patio door, oval whirlpool and large walk-in closet

■ A beautiful arched window in each secondary Bedroom adds natural light and elegance

FIRST FLOOR — 2,617 SQ. FT.
SECOND FLOOR — 1,072 SQ. FT.

TOTAL LIVING AREA: 3,689 SQ. FT.

Distinguished Dwelling

Price Code: E

■ This plan features:

— Four bedrooms

— Two full and one half baths

■ Grand two-story Entry into Foyer

■ Formal Living Room with a decorative window and a vaulted ceiling extending into Family Room with cozy fireplace

■ Beautiful bay window in formal Dining Room

■ Convenient Kitchen with cooktop work island, pantry, octagon Dining area, and nearby Study, Laundry and Garage entry

■ Luxurious Master Bedroom offers a glass alcove, walk-in closet and pampering bath with a corner tub

■ Three additional bedrooms with decorative windows, share a full bath

■ No materials list is available

FIRST FLOOR — 1,514 SQ. FT.
SECOND FLOOR — 1,219 SQ. FT.

TOTAL LIVING AREA:
2,733 SQ. FT.

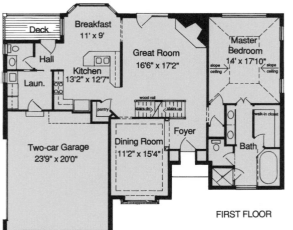

Breakfast 11' x 9'

Deck

Hall

Kitchen 13'2" x 12'7"

Laun.

Great Room 16'6" x 17'2"

Master Bedroom 14' x 17'10" slope ceiling slope ceiling

walk-in closet

wood rail

stairs dn. stairs up

pantry

Two-car Garage 23'9" x 20'0"

Dining Room 11'2" x 15'4"

Foyer

Bath

46'8"

54'8"

FIRST FLOOR

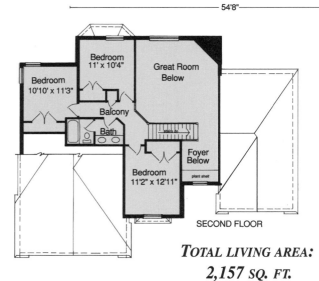

Bedroom 11' x 10'4"

Bedroom 10'10" x 11'3"

Great Room Below

Balcony

Bath

Bedroom 11'2" x 12'11"

Foyer Below

plant shelf

SECOND FLOOR

TOTAL LIVING AREA:
2,157 SQ. FT.

A Traditional Two-Story with Character

Price Code: C

■ This plan features:

— Four bedrooms

— Two full and one half baths

■ Front entrance into two-story Foyer with a plant shelf and lovely railing staircase

■ Expansive Great Room with corner fireplace and access to rear yard topped by two-story ceiling

■ Efficient Kitchen with peninsula counter, walk-in pantry, Breakfast bay and access to Deck, Laundry, Garage entry and formal Dining Room

■ Secluded Master Bedroom offers a sloped ceiling and lavish bath with walk-in closet

■ Three additional bedrooms on second floor share a double vanity bath

■ No materials list available for this plan

FIRST FLOOR — 1,511 SQ. FT.
SECOND FLOOR — 646 SQ. FT.
BASEMENT — 1,479 SQ. FT.
GARAGE — 475 SQ. FT.

Luxurious Elegance

Price Code: E

■ This plan features:

— Four bedrooms

— Three full and one half baths

■ Double door leads into two-story entry with an exquisite curved staircase

■ Formal Living Room features a marble hearth fireplace, triple window and built-in book shelves

■ Formal Dining Room defined by columns and a lovely bay window

■ Efficient Kitchen offers cooktop/work island, Utility/Garage entry and serving counter for informal Dining area

■ Expansive Great Room with entertainment center, fieldstone fireplace, cathedral ceiling and access to Covered Patio

■ Vaulted ceiling crowns Master Bedroom suite offering a plush bath and two walk-in closets

■ Three second floor bedrooms, one with a private bath, have walk-in closets

■ No materials list available for this plan

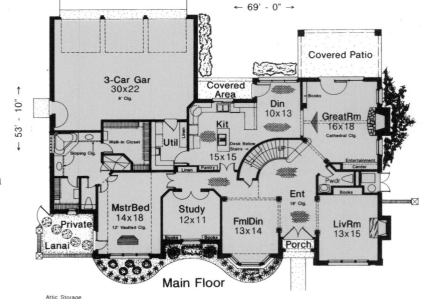

Main Floor

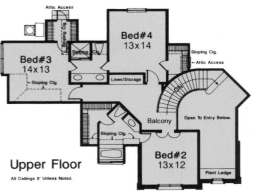

Upper Floor

All Ceilings 8' Unless Noted.

MAIN FLOOR —
2,190 SQ. FT.
UPPER FLOOR —
920 SQ. FT.
GARAGE — 624 SQ. FT.

TOTAL LIVING AREA:
3,110 SQ. FT.

Luxury is Always Popular

Price Code: F

■ This plan features:

— Three bedrooms

— Three full and one half bath

■ A sunken Great Room, a spectacular Breakfast Nook, and a bridge-like balcony on the second floor

■ A Master Suite highlighted by two huge walk-in closets, a five-piece Bath, and a Sitting Room with bay window

■ A Great Room accented by a bar, fireplace, and built-in cabinets for the television and stereo

■ Cathedral ceilings in the Dining Room and Foyer

FIRST FLOOR — 2,579 SQ. FT.
SECOND FLOOR — 997 SQ. FT.
BASEMENT — 2,579 SQ. FT.
GARAGE & STORAGE — 1,001 SQ. FT.

TOTAL LIVING AREA:
3,576 SQ. FT.

FIRST FLOOR

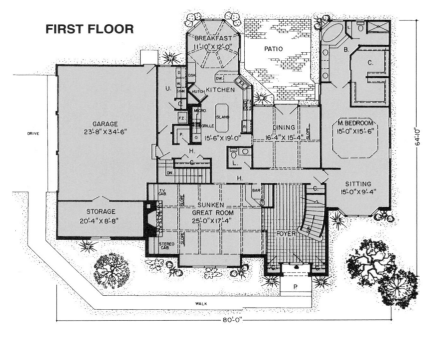

SECOND FLOOR

Simple Lines Enhanced by Elegant Window Treatment

Price Code: A

■ This plan features:

— Two bedrooms (optional third)

— Two full baths

■ A huge, arched window that floods the front room with natural light

■ A homey, well-lit Office or Den

■ Compact, efficient use of space

■ An efficient Kitchen with easy access to the Dining Room

■ A fireplaced Living Room with a sloping ceiling and a window wall

■ A Master Bedroom sporting a private master Bath with a roomy walk-in closet

MAIN FLOOR — 1,492 SQ. FT.
BASEMENT — 1,486 SQ. FT.
GARAGE — 462 SQ. FT.

TOTAL LIVING AREA:
1,492 SQ. FT.

ZIP QUOTE
HOME COST CALCULATOR
see order pages for details

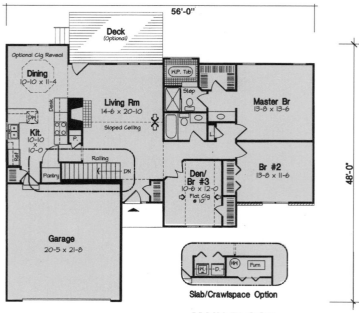

MAIN FLOOR

ZIP QUOTE
HOME COST CALCULATOR
see order pages for details

Deck

Great Room Below

Bedroom
15 x 10-8

Bath

Bedroom
14 x 10-6

Foyer Below

Second floor

WIDTH 59'-0"
DEPTH 60'-8"

Breakfast
9-2 x 16

Sunken
Great Room
16-10 x 21

Kitchen
8 x 13-4

Bath

Walk-in closet

Dining Room
16 x 11-8

Foyer

Master Bedroom
14 x 17-4

Bath

Hall

Laundry

Slope ceiling   Slope ceiling

Two-car Garage
21 x 20-8

First floor

Unique Turret Master Bedroom

Price Code: C

■ This plan features:

— Three bedrooms

— Two full and one half baths

■ Curved glass entry into two-story Foyer with graceful, apron staircase

■ Sunken Great Room with focal point fireplace and atrium door to Deck

■ Efficient U-shaped Kitchen with work island, built-in Pantry, breakfast alcove

■ Sloped ceiling accents window alcove in Master Bedroom suite offering a plush Bath and walk-in closet

■ No materials list is available for this plan

FIRST FLOOR — 1,626 SQ. FT.
SECOND FLOOR — 475 SQ. FT.
BASEMENT — 1,512 SQ. FT.
GARAGE — 438 SQ. FT.

TOTAL LIVING AREA:
2,101 SQ. FT.

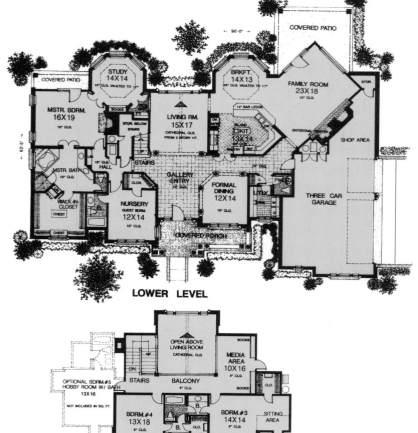

Magnificent Stature

Price Code: F

■ This plan features:

— Four bedrooms

— Three full and one half baths

■ A two-story cathedral ceiling crowns the Living Room of this manor-styled home

■ The main level Master Suite features a private, octagonal Study with a wetbar

■ The upper level includes a Media Area and a Bonus space

■ The expansive Family Room opens on to the covered Patio

■ No materials list is available for this plan

LOWER LEVEL — 3,168 SQ. FT.
UPPER LEVEL — 998 SQ. FT.
BONUS — 320 SQ. FT.
GARAGE — 810 SQ. FT.

TOTAL LIVING AREA:
4,166 SQ. FT.

LOWER LEVEL

UPPER LEVEL

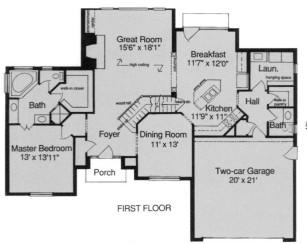

FIRST FLOOR

- Great Room 15'6" x 18'1" — high ceiling
- Breakfast 11'7" x 12'0"
- Laun. — hanging space
- Bath
- walk-in closet
- Kitchen 11'9" x 11'
- Hall
- walk-in pantry
- Bath
- Master Bedroom 13' x 13'11"
- Foyer
- Dining Room 11' x 13'
- wood rail / stairs dn
- Porch
- Two-car Garage 20' x 21'

58'6" 49'

TOTAL LIVING AREA:
2,209 SQ. FT.

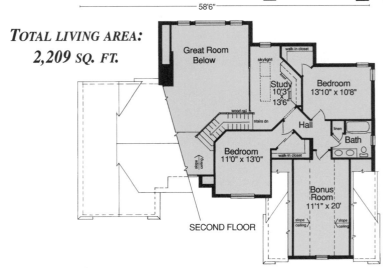

SECOND FLOOR

- Great Room Below
- skylight
- Study 10'3" x 13'6"
- walk-in closet
- Bedroom 13'10" x 10'8"
- wood rail / stairs dn
- Hall
- linen
- Bath
- Bedroom 11'0" x 13'0"
- slope ceiling
- walk-in closet
- Bonus Room 11'1" x 20' — slope ceiling

Exciting Impact
Price Code: D

■ This plan features:
— Three bedrooms
— Two full and one half baths

■ Keystone arch accents entrance into open Foyer with lovely angled staircase and sloped ceiling

■ Great Room with entertainment center, hearth fireplace and a wall of windows overlooks the back yard

■ Efficient, angled Kitchen offers work island/snackbar, Breakfast area next to Dining Room, Laundry, and Garage entry

■ Master Bedroom wing features a lavish Bath with two vanities, large walk-in closet and corner window tub

■ Two second floor bedrooms with walk-in closets share a skylit Study, double vanity bath and a Bonus Room

■ No materials list is available

FIRST FLOOR — 1,542 SQ. FT.
SECOND FLOOR — 667 SQ. FT.
BONUS ROOM — 236 SQ. FT.
GARAGE — 420 SQ. FT.

Country Styled Home

Price Code: C

■ This plan features:
— Three bedrooms
— Two full and one half baths

■ A Country-styled front Porch provides a warm welcome

■ The Family Room is highlighted by a fireplace and front windows

■ The Dining Room is separated from the U-shaped Kitchen by only an extended counter

■ The first floor Master Suite pampers it's owners with a walk-in closet and a five-piece Bath

■ There are two additional Bedrooms with a convenient Bath in the hall

FIRST FLOOR — 1,288 SQ. FT.
SECOND FLOOR — 545 SQ. FT.
GARAGE — 540 SQ. FT.

TOTAL LIVING AREA: 1,833 SQ. FT.

SECOND FLOOR

WIDTH 50'-8"
DEPTH 74'-0"

FIRST FLOOR

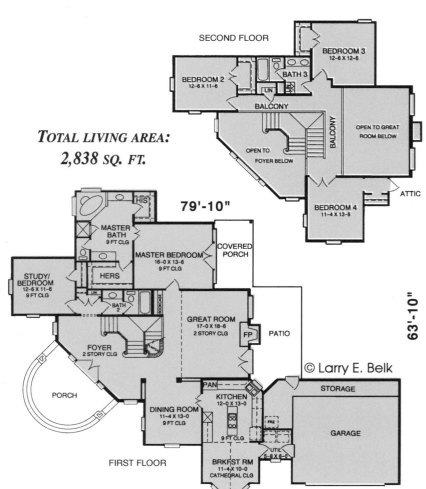

SECOND FLOOR

BEDROOM 2
12-6 X 11-6

BEDROOM 3
12-6 X 12-6

BATH 3

LIN

BALCONY

OPEN TO GREAT
ROOM BELOW

BALCONY

OPEN TO
FOYER BELOW

ATTIC

BEDROOM 4
11-4 X 13-6

TOTAL LIVING AREA:
2,838 SQ. FT.

79'-10"

HIS

MASTER
BATH
9 FT CLG

COVERED
PORCH

MASTER BEDROOM
16-0 X 13-6
9 FT CLG

HERS

STUDY/
BEDROOM
12-6 X 11-6
9 FT CLG

LIN

BATH
2

BOOKCASE

GREAT ROOM
17-0 X 18-6
2 STORY CLG

FP

PATIO

63'-10"

FOYER
2 STORY CLG

PORCH

© Larry E. Belk

PAN

KITCHEN
12-0 X 13-0

STORAGE

DINING ROOM
11-4 X 13-0
9 FT CLG

FRZ

9 FT CLG

GARAGE

FIRST FLOOR

BRKFST RM
11-4 X 10-0
CATHEDRAL CLG

UTIL
5-8 X 6-0

Towering Windows Enhance Elegance

Price Code: E

- ■ This plan features:
- — Four bedrooms
- — Three full baths
- ■ Designed for a corner or pie-shaped lot
- ■ Spectacular split staircase highlights Foyer
- ■ Expansive Great Room with hearth fireplace opens to formal Dining Room and Patio
- ■ Quiet Study easily another Bedroom or Home Office
- ■ Secluded Master Bedroom suite offers private Porch, two walk-in closets, vanity, and a corner whirlpool tub
- ■ Three second floor Bedrooms with walk-in closets, share a balcony and double vanity Bath
- ■ No materials list is available for this plan

FIRST FLOOR — 1,966 SQ. FT.
SECOND FLOOR — 872 SQ. FT.
GARAGE — 569 SQ. FT.

Impressive Two-Story

Price Code: E

- This plan features:
  — Four bedrooms
  — Two full and one half baths
- Two-story Foyer highlighted by lovely, angled staircase and decorative window
- Bay windows enhance Dining and Living rooms
- Efficient Kitchen with work island and an open Breakfast area with back yard access
- Spacious, yet cozy Family Room with a fireplace and Future Sunroom access
- Private Master Suite offers a walk-in closet and pampering bath
- Three additional bedrooms share a double vanity bath and large Study

FIRST FLOOR — 1,497 SQ. FT.
SECOND FLOOR — 1,460 SQ. FT.
FUTURE SUNROOM — 210 SQ. FT.
GARAGE — 680 SQ. FT.

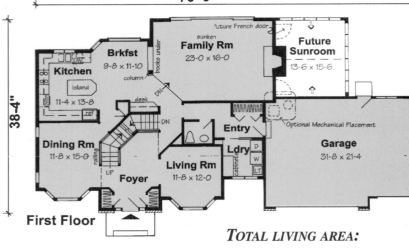

First Floor

TOTAL LIVING AREA:
2,957 SQ. FT.

ALTERNATE FOUNDATION OPTION

Second Floor

ZIP QUOTE
HOME COST CALCULATOR
see order pages for details

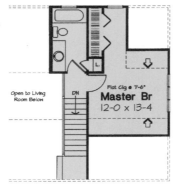

Open to Living
Room Below

DN

Flat Clg @ 7'-6"
Master Br
12-0 x 13-4

Upper Floor

Rustic Exterior;
Complete Home

Price Code: A

■ This plan features:

— Three bedrooms

— Two full baths

■ A two-story, fireplaced Living Room with exposed beams adds to the rustic charm

■ An efficient, modern Kitchen with ample work and storage space

■ Two first floor bedrooms with individual closet space share a full bath

■ A Master Bedroom secluded on the second floor with its own full bath

■ A welcoming front Porch adding to the living space

MAIN FLOOR — 1,013 SQ. FT.
UPPER FLOOR — 315 SQ. FT.
BASEMENT — 1,013 SQ. FT.

TOTAL LIVING AREA:
1,328 SQ. FT.

38'-0"

36'-0"

REF   DW

Kitchen & Dining
17-4 x 10-8

Br 2
12-0 x 10-4
8' Flat Clg

16'-3" Flat Clg

DN

Living Rm
19-4 x 16-8

UP

Br 3
12-0 x 13-0
8' Flat Clg

Porch

Main Floor

FURN   HH

Crawl
Space
Access

Crawl Space / Slab Plan

Stately Presence

Price Code: E

■ This plan features:

— Four bedrooms

— Three full and one half baths

■ The Patio and covered Patio expand living space to the outdoors

■ The cathedral ceiling in the Living Room gives added volume to the room

■ The future Playroom on the second floor has a perfect location for keeping peace and quiet on the first floor

■ An optional basement, crawl space or slab foundation — please specify when ordering

■ No materials list available for this plan

LOWER LEVEL — 2,115 SQ. FT.
UPPER LEVEL — 947 SQ. FT.
BONUS ROOM — 195 SQ. FT.
GARAGE — 635 SQ. FT.
DECK — 210 SQ. FT.

TOTAL LIVING AREA: 3,062 SQ. FT.

Photography Supplied By The Meredith Corporation

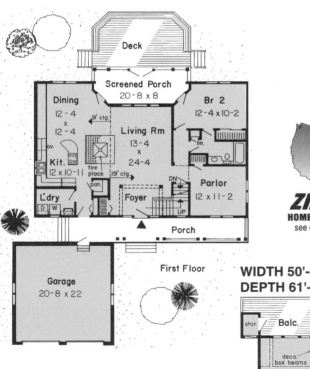

Deck

Screened Porch
20-8 x 8

Dining
12-4
x
12-4

9' clg.

Living Rm
13-4
x
24-4

Br 2
12-4 x 10-2

ov.

Kit.
12 x 10-11

fire place

9' clg.

lin.

L'dry
D   W

pan.

Foyer

DN

UP

Parlor
12 x 11-2

Porch

First Floor

Garage
20-8 x 22

TOTAL LIVING AREA:
1,695 SQ. FT.

ZIP QUOTE
HOME COST CALCULATOR
see order pages for details

WIDTH 50'-8"
DEPTH 61'-8"

stor.   Balc.

seat

deco.
box beams

MBr
15-8 x 11-9

make-up

beams @
foyer below

DN

Second Floor   deco. beam

Master Retreat Crowns Spacious Home

Price Code: B

■ This plan features:

— Two bedrooms

— Two full baths

■ An open Foyer leading up a landing staircase with windows above and into a two-story Living Room

■ A unique four-sided fireplace separates the Living Room, Dining Area and Kitchen

■ A well-equipped Kitchen featuring a cook island, a walk-in Pantry and access to Dining Area and Laundry Room

■ A three season Screened Porch and Deck beyond adjoining Dining Room, Living Room, and second Bedroom

■ A private second floor Master Suite offering a dormer window seat, private balcony, and relaxing window tub

FIRST FLOOR — 1,290 SQ. FT.
SECOND FLOOR — 405 SQ. FT.
SCREENED PORCH — 152 SQ. FT.
GARAGE — 513 SQ. FT.

Photography Supplied by The Meredith Corporation

Traditional Exterior

Price Code: B

■ This plan features:

— Three bedrooms

— Two full and one half baths

■ The Master Bedroom includes a private balcony

■ The two secondary Bedrooms are identical in size

■ A see-through fireplace warms two rooms

■ Relax with a cup of coffee in the Morning Room

■ A Studio Apartment is located over the Garage

MAIN LEVEL — 1,546 SQ. FT.
UPPER LEVEL — 1,218 SQ. FT.
BONUS — 403 SQ. FT.
GARAGE — 624 SQ. FT.

TOTAL LIVING AREA: 2,764 SQ. FT.

ZIP QUOTE
HOME COST CALCULATOR
see order pages for details

UPPER LEVEL

- BEDROOM 11x12
- BEDROOM 11x12
- OPEN TO GREAT-ROOM
- OPEN
- DN
- BALC
- W D
- MASTER BEDROOM 13x21
- CLOS
- BATH
- ATTIC
- STUDIO 22x14
- DN

MAIN LEVEL

- FIRESIDE 13x12
- LIBRARY 13x12
- FP TV
- GREAT-ROOM 21x16
- ENTRY
- UP
- DINING 13x10
- KITCHEN 13x10
- R
- COVERED TERRACE
- MORNING ROOM 19x12
- DN
- BREEZE-WAY
- UP
- GARAGE 25x24

WIDTH 89'-0"
DEPTH 63'-8"

Breakfast 10'8" x 11'

Great Room 14'10" x 17'1"

Laun.
hanging space
Bath

10'6" x 13'6" **Kitchen**

pantry

French doors w/ arched window above

high ceiling

wood rail
stairs up
stairs dn.

Foyer

furniture alcove

Dining Room 11' x 13'7"

Two-car Garage 20' x 21'

38'

48'

FIRST FLOOR

walk-in closet

Master Bedroom 12' x 14'11"

Bedroom 10'6" x 11'2"

Great Room Below

computer desk

Bath

Bath

Balcony

Bedroom 11' x 12'

stairs dn.
window seat

SECOND FLOOR

ZIP QUOTE
GARLINGHOUSE
HOME COST CALCULATOR
see order pages for details

Detail and Design

Price Code: C

■ This plan features:

— Three bedrooms

— Two full and one half baths

■ Impressive entry into open Foyer with landing staircase highlighted by decorative windows

■ Great Room accented by hearth fireplace and French doors with arched window above and topped by a high ceiling

■ Formal Dining Room enhanced by furniture alcove and decorative window

■ Efficient, L-shaped Kitchen with work island, walk-in Pantry, bright Breakfast Area, adjoining Laundry, half Bath and Garage Entry

■ Quiet Master Bedroom offers a walk-in closet, and plush Bath with two vanities and whirlpool tub

FIRST FLOOR — 1,036 SQ. FT.
SECOND FLOOR — 861 SQ. FT.
GARAGE — 420 SQ. FT.

TOTAL LIVING AREA:
1,897 SQ. FT.

Impressive Plan

Price Code: E

■ This plan features:

— Four bedrooms

— Two full and one half baths

■ A see-through fireplace straddles the Living and Hearth rooms

■ The U-shaped Kitchen has an island in its center

■ A tray ceiling graces the Dining Room

■ The Master Suite is in its own wing

■ Four Bedrooms are on the second floor

■ No materials list is available for this plan

FIRST FLOOR — 1,893 SQ. FT.
SECOND FLOOR — 893 SQ. FT.
GARAGE — 632 SQ. FT.

TOTAL LIVING AREA:
2,786 SQ. FT.

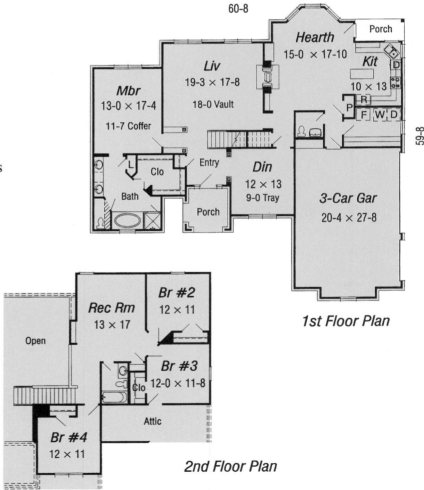

1st Floor Plan

2nd Floor Plan

46'-8"

35'-8"

Dining
12-1 x 11-4

Kitchen
13 x 11-4

W
D

pantry

DN

Great Rm
14 x 21-8

UP

Garage
22 x 23-4

open to above

First Floor

ZIP QUOTE
HOME COST CALCULATOR
see order pages for details

Br 2
11-6 x 11-4

linen

Br 3
11 x 11-4

DN

open to below

1/2 wall

railing

Mstr Br
13-4 x 15

Second Floor

Second Floor Balcony Overlooks Great Room

Price Code: B

■ This plan features:

— Three bedrooms

— Two full and one half baths

■ A Great Room with a focal point fireplace and a two-story ceiling

■ An efficient Kitchen with an island, double sinks, built-in Pantry and ample storage and counter space

■ A convenient first floor Laundry Room

■ A Dining Room with easy access to both the Kitchen and the outside

■ A Master Suite with a private Master Bath and a walk-in closet

■ Two additional Bedrooms with ample closet space that share a full hall Bath

FIRST FLOOR — 891 SQ. FT.
SECOND FLOOR — 894 SQ. FT.
GARAGE — 534 SQ. FT.
BASEMENT — 891 SQ. FT.

TOTAL LIVING AREA:
1,785 SQ. FT.

A Home of Distinction

Price Code: E

■ This plan features:

— Four bedrooms

— Three full and one half baths

■ The Dining room and the Study are to either side of the Entry

■ The Study entrance is at an angle with a double door Entry

■ The two-story Family Room includes a fireplace and a highly windowed rear wall

■ The Breakfast Room is open to the Kitchen

■ The first floor Master Suite includes a whirlpool tub

■ An optional basement or slab foundation — please specify when ordering

FIRST FLOOR — 1,844 SQ. FT.
SECOND FLOOR — 794 SQ. FT.

TOTAL LIVING AREA: 2,638 SQ. FT.

FIRST FLOOR

© design basics, Inc.

65'-6"

56'-10"

SECOND FLOOR

Ideal Family Home

Price Code: C

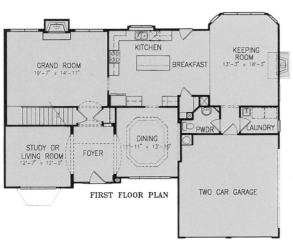

WIDTH 54'-0"
DEPTH 45'-4"

FIRST FLOOR PLAN

GRAND ROOM
19'-7" x 14'-11"

KITCHEN

BREAKFAST

KEEPING ROOM
13'-3" x 18'-3"

STUDY OR LIVING ROOM
12'-7" x 12'-0"

FOYER

DINING
11'-11" x 13'-10"

PWDR

LAUNDRY

TWO CAR GARAGE

OPTION KITCHEN

KITCHEN

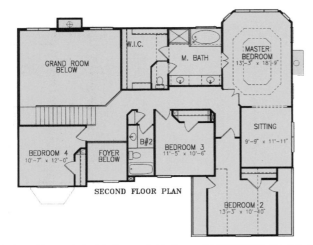

SECOND FLOOR PLAN

GRAND ROOM BELOW

W.I.C.

M. BATH

MASTER BEDROOM
13'-3" x 18'-9"

BEDROOM 4
10'-7" x 12'-0"

FOYER BELOW

B#2

BEDROOM 3
11'-5" x 10'-6"

SITTING
9'-9" x 11'-11"

BEDROOM 2
13'-3" x 10'-10"

■ This plan features:
— Four bedrooms
— Two full and one half baths

■ Inside, from the two-story Foyer enter either the Living Room or the Dining Room

■ In the rear of the home there is the Grand Room and the Keeping Room both with fireplaces

■ The L-shaped Kitchen has a center island and is open to the Breakfast Nook

■ Upstairs the Master Bedroom has a decorative ceiling and a huge walk-in closet

■ An optional basement or slab foundation — please specify when ordering

■ No materials list is available for this plan

FIRST FLOOR — 1,534 SQ. FT.
SECOND FLOOR — 1,236 SQ. FT.
GARAGE — 418 SQ. FT.

TOTAL LIVING AREA:
2,770 SQ. FT.

Brick and Stone

Price Code: E

- This plan features:
— Four bedrooms
— Three full and one half baths
- Beautiful front Entry on this exciting two-story begins at the covered Porch
- Great Room with a gas fireplace and built-in bookcases
- First floor Master Suite with deluxe Dressing Area and spacious walk-in closet
- No materials list is available for this plan

FIRST FLOOR — 1,978 SQ. FT.
SECOND FLOOR — 958 SQ. FT.
GARAGE — 651 SQ. FT.
DECK — 181 SQ. FT.
PORCH — 72 SQ. FT.

TOTAL LIVING AREA:
2,936 SQ. FT.

Traditional That Has it All

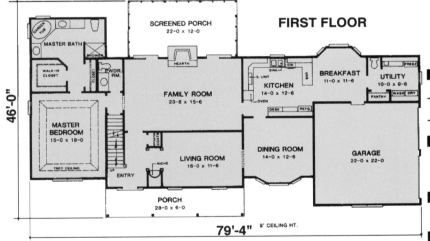

FIRST FLOOR

SCREENED PORCH
22-0 x 12-0

MASTER BATH
WALK-IN CLOSET
GARDEN TUB
SHOWER
PWDR. RM.
CLOSET
HEARTH

FAMILY ROOM
23-8 x 15-6

KITCHEN
14-0 x 12-6
S. UNIT
SINK
DW
BAR
OVEN

BREAKFAST
11-0 x 11-6

UTILITY
10-0 x 9-6
PANTRY
WASH DRY
FREEZ

MASTER BEDROOM
15-0 x 18-0
TREY CEILING

46'-0"

LIVING ROOM
16-0 x 11-6

UP
ENTRY
COATS
NICHE

DESK
REFG.

DINING ROOM
14-0 x 12-6

GARAGE
22-0 x 22-0

PORCH
28-0 x 6-0

79'-4"   9' CEILING HT.

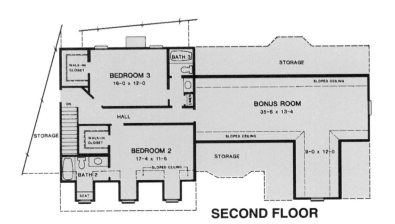

WALK-IN CLOSET

BEDROOM 3
16-0 x 12-0

BATH 3

STORAGE

SLOPED CEILING

BONUS ROOM
35-6 x 13-4

DN
HALL
STORAGE
WALK-IN CLOSET

SLOPED CEILING

BEDROOM 2
17-4 x 11-6
SLOPED CEILING

STORAGE

9-0 x 12-0

BATH 2
SEAT

SECOND FLOOR

Price Code: E

■ This plan features:
— Three bedrooms
— Three full and one half baths

■ A Master Suite with two closets and a private Bath with separate shower, corner tub and dual vanity

■ A large Dining Room with a bay window, adjacent to the Kitchen

■ A formal Living Room for entertaining and a cozy Family Room with fireplace for informal relaxation

■ A Bonus Room to allow the house to grow with your needs

■ An optional basement, slab, or crawl space foundation — please specify when ordering

FIRST FLOOR — 1,927 SQ. FT.
SECOND FLOOR — 832 SQ. FT.
BONUS ROOM — 624 SQ. FT.
BASEMENT — 1,674 SQ. FT.

TOTAL LIVING AREA:
2,759 SQ. FT.

Sprawling Farmhouse

Price Code: E

■ This plan features:

— Four bedrooms

— Three full and one half baths

■ The Kitchen opens past a snack bar to the Family Room with a fireplace and access to the rear deck and side Porch

■ The Master Bedroom enjoys direct access to the rear Deck

■ The front Music Room has a bayed windowed area

■ An optional basement or slab foundation — please specify when ordering

■ No material list is available for this plan

LOWER LEVEL — 2,023 SQ. FT.
UPPER LEVEL — 749 SQ. FT.
BONUS — 450 SQ. FT.
GARAGE — 546 SQ. FT.

TOTAL LIVING AREA:
2,772 SQ. FT.

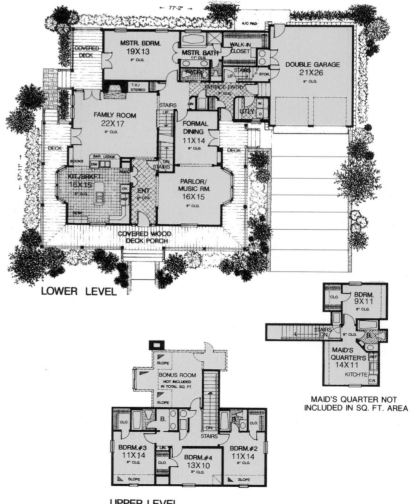

Second floor

© design basics, inc.

First floor

66'-8"

Arched and Bayed Windows

Price Code: E

- This plan features:
  - Three bedrooms
  - Two full and one half baths
- The Entry is dominated by a T-shaped staircase and accented by tile flooring
- The casual Family Room boasts a wetbar, see-through fireplace and a view of the outdoors through the large rear window
- French doors reveal a dramatic tiered ceiling of the Master Suite
- A skylight enhances the sloped ceiling over the whirlpool tub in the Master Bath
- The second floor Laundry adds the convenience of being on the same floor the Laundry originates

FIRST FLOOR — 1,392 SQ. FT.
SECOND FLOOR — 1,335 SQ. FT.
BASEMENT — 1,392 SQ. FT.
GARAGE — 738 SQ. FT.
BONUS — 111 SQ. FT.

TOTAL LIVING AREA:
2,727 SQ. FT.

Dignified Family Home

Price Code: D

- This plan features:
- — Three bedrooms
- — Two full and one half baths
- The Living Room adjoins the formal Dining Room
- A U-shaped Kitchen equipped with a built-in Pantry
- A large Family Room flows from the Kitchen
- A second floor Master Suite topped by a decorative ceiling
- A Bonus Room for future needs
- No materials list is available for this plan

FIRST FLOOR — 1,245 SQ. FT.
SECOND FLOOR — 1,333 SQ. FT.
BONUS ROOM — 192 SQ. FT.
GARAGE — 650 SQ. FT.

TOTAL LIVING AREA:
2,578 SQ. FT.

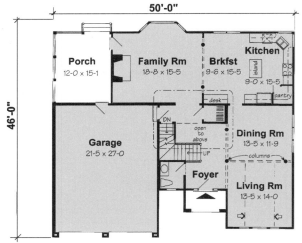

First Floor

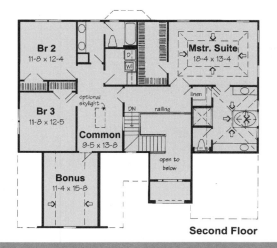

Second Floor

Crawl Space/ Slab Option

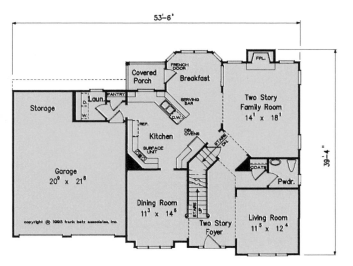

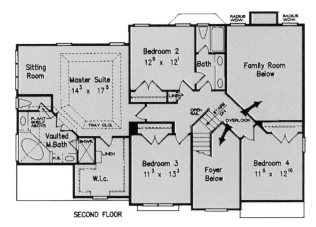

Grand Styling

Price Code: D

■ This plan features:

— Four bedrooms

— Two full and one half baths

■ The Family Room, Breakfast Room, and Kitchen are laid out so the open feeling prevails through-out

■ There is a fireplace in the Family Room

■ The Master Suite includes a walk-in closet a cozy Sitting Room

■ The Master Bedroom is topped by a tray ceiling

■ An optional basement or crawl space foundation — please specify when ordering

■ No materials list is available for this plan

FIRST FLOOR — 1,205 SQ. FT.
SECOND FLOOR — 1,277 SQ. FT.
BASEMENT — 1,128 SQ. FT.
GARAGE — 528 SQ. FT.

TOTAL LIVING AREA:
2,482 SQ. FT.

B. NATHAN

© 1997 Donald A. Gardner Architects, Inc.

Stature and Dignity

Price Code: F

■ This plan features:

— Four bedrooms

— Three full baths

■ Multiple columns and gables add appeal to traditional style

■ Foyer and Great Room both have two-story ceilings and clerestory windows

■ Great Room highlighted by fireplace, built-in shelves and French doors to back Porch

■ Bright Breakfast bay accesses efficient Kitchen and back stairway to Bedrooms and Bonus Room

■ Bedroom/Study and full Bath near Master Bedroom offers multiple uses

FIRST FLOOR — 2,067 SQ. FT.
SECOND FLOOR — 615 SQ. FT.
BONUS ROOM — 433 SQ. FT.
GARAGE & STORAGE — 729 SQ. FT.

TOTAL LIVING AREA:
2,682 SQ. FT.

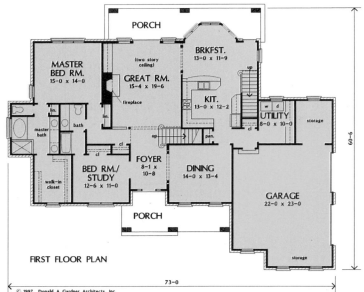

FIRST FLOOR PLAN

© 1997 Donald A Gardner Architects, Inc.

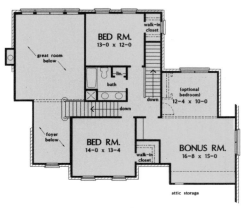

SECOND FLOOR PLAN

© 1995 Donald A Gardner Architects, Inc.

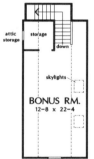

attic storage

storage

down

skylights

BONUS RM.
12-8 x 22-4

Classic Country Farmhouse

Price Code: D

■ This plan features:

— Three bedrooms

— Two full baths

■ Dormers, arched windows and multiple columns give this home Country charm

■ Foyer, expanded by vaulted ceiling, accesses Dining Room, Bedroom/Study and Great Room

■ Expansive Great Room, with hearth fireplace topped by cathedral ceiling, opens to rear Porch and efficient Kitchen

■ Tray ceiling adds volume to private Master Bedroom with plush Bath and walk-in closet

■ Extra room for growth offered by Bonus Room with skylight

MAIN FLOOR — 1,832 SQ. FT.
BONUS ROOM — 425 SQ. FT.
GARAGE & STORAGE — 562 SQ. FT.

TOTAL LIVING AREA:
1,832 SQ. FT.

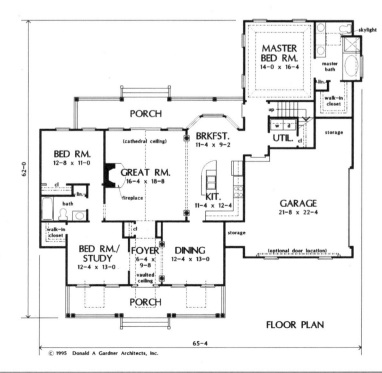

FLOOR PLAN

© 1995 Donald A Gardner Architects, Inc.

Elegant Living

Price Code: D

- This plan features:
- — Three bedrooms
- — Two full and one half baths

- The spacious Great Room has a two-story ceiling, a fireplace and naturally illuminating rear windows

- The Den features built-in cabinetry located immediately off the Great Room

- The formal Dining Room located at the front of the house provides a quiet place for entertaining

- The first floor Laundry is located just off the three-car Garage

- The Master suite with generous windows to the rear, also has a private Bath and an extra large walk-in closet

- No materials list is available for this plan

FIRST FLOOR — 1,408 SQ. FT.
SECOND FLOOR — 1,184 SQ. FT.
BASEMENT — 1,408 SQ. FT.

TOTAL LIVING AREA:
2,592 SQ. FT.

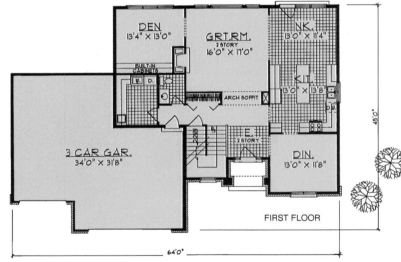

DEN
13'4" X 13'0"

GRT.RM.
2 STORY
16'0" X 17'0"

NK.
13'0" X 11'4"

BUILT-IN CABINETS

W. D.

ARCH SOFFIT

KIT.
13'0" X 13'8"

3 CAR GAR.
34'0" X 31'8"

E.
2 STORY

DIN.
13'0" X 11'8"

45'0"

FIRST FLOOR

64'0"

MBR.
13'4" X 16'10"

OPEN TO
GRT.RM.

BR.#2
13'0" X 14'6"

LINEN

DOWN

OPEN TO
E.

BRICK ARCH

BR.#3
13'0" X 14'0"

SECOND FLOOR

Photography Supplied by The Meredith Corporation

BATH

MASTER BEDROOM 20x19

DRESSING

DECK

DECK

BREAKFAST 12x12

LIVING 19x18

UP

R

KIT 13x13

DN

FAMILY 18x16

GARAGE 21x34

GALLERY

STUDY 15x15

UP

DINING 19x14

ENTRY

W D

LAUN

PORCH

MAIN LEVEL

PORCH

WIDTH 111'-2"
DEPTH 66'-2"

BEDROOM 12x12

OPEN TO LIVING

PLAYROOM 18x12

AU PAIR SUITE 12x16

CLOSET

DN

DN

BEDROOM 16x12

BEDROOM 16x12

OPEN TO ENTRY

UPPER LEVEL

Country Manor

Price Code: F

■ This plan features:

— Four Bedrooms

— Four full and one half baths

■ Combined with the Study, Master Suite occupies entire wing of the first floor

■ Living Room and Dining Room with adjacent locations for ease in entertaining

■ Kitchen, Breakfast Nook and Family Room create large informal area

■ Three Bedrooms, Au Pair Suite, three baths and playroom complete the upper level

■ Upper level balcony connects the Bedroom wings and overlooks Living Room above Foyer

MAIN LEVEL — 3,322 SQ. FT.
UPPER LEVEL — 1,966 SQ. FT.

TOTAL LIVING AREA:
5,288 SQ. FT.

GARLINGHOUSE

ZIP QUOTE
HOME COST CALCULATOR
see order pages for details

Lasting Impression

Price Code: D

- ■ This plan features:
- — Four bedrooms
- — Three full and one half baths
- ■ The two-story Foyer is enhanced by a cascading staircase with an open rail
- ■ The Living Room is topped by a 12′ tray ceiling
- ■ Double doors lead from the Dining Room to the covered Porch
- ■ The Master Suite includes a Sitting Area and a five-piece Bath
- ■ Three additional Bedrooms have access to a full Bath
- ■ An optional basement, crawl space or slab foundation — please specify when ordering

FIRST FLOOR — 2,044 SQ. FT.
SECOND FLOOR — 896 SQ. FT.

TOTAL LIVING AREA:
2,940 SQ. FT.

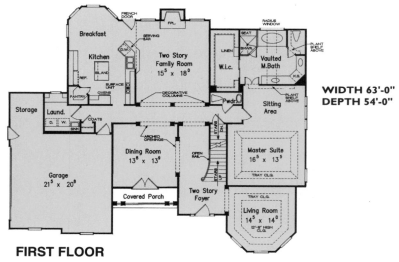

WIDTH 63'-0"
DEPTH 54'-0"

FIRST FLOOR

SECOND FLOOR

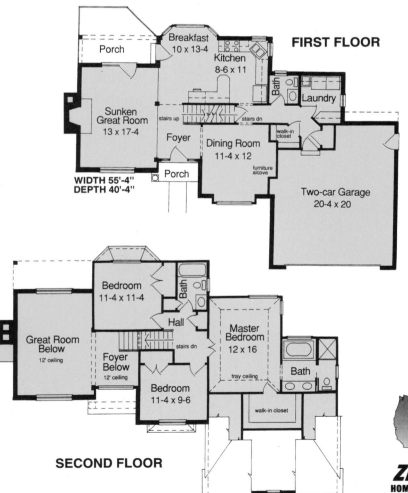

FIRST FLOOR

Porch

Breakfast
10 x 13-4

Kitchen
8-6 x 11

Bath

Laundry

Sunken
Great Room
13 x 17-4

stairs up

stairs dn

walk-in
closet

Foyer

Dining Room
11-4 x 12

furniture
alcove

Porch

Two-car Garage
20-4 x 20

WIDTH 55'-4"
DEPTH 40'-4"

Bedroom
11-4 x 11-4

Bath

Hall

Master
Bedroom
12 x 16

Great Room
Below
12' ceiling

stairs dn

Foyer
Below
12' ceiling

Bath

Bedroom
11-4 x 9-6

tray ceiling

walk-in closet

SECOND FLOOR

A Little Drama

Price Code: B

- This plan features:
— Three bedrooms
— Two and one half baths
- A 12' high Entry with transom and side-lights, multiple gables and a box window
- A sunken Great Room with a fireplace and access to a rear Porch
- A Breakfast Bay and Kitchen flowing into each other and a rear Porch
- A Master Bedroom with a tray ceiling, walk-in closet and a private Master Bath
- No materials list is available for this plan

FIRST FLOOR — 960 SQ. FT.
SECOND FLOOR — 808 SQ. FT.

TOTAL LIVING AREA:
1,768 SQ. FT.

ZIP QUOTE
HOME COST CALCULATOR
see order pages for details

A Splendid Porch

Price Code: D

- This plan features:
  — Four bedrooms
  — Two full and one half baths
- A stylish front Porch enhances this attractive home
- Dual closets and an attractive staircase greet you upon entering
- There is a room devoted to a Home Office or a Media Center
- The Great Room is open to the Kitchen and they share a serving bar
- The Breakfast Nook overlooks the rear Deck
- Upstairs find the Bedrooms and a Reading Nook
- No materials is available for this plan

FIRST FLOOR — 1,305 SQ. FT.
SECOND FLOOR — 1,121 SQ. FT.
BASEMENT — 1,194 SQ. FT.
GARAGE — 576 SQ. FT.

TOTAL LIVING AREA:
2,426 SQ. FT.

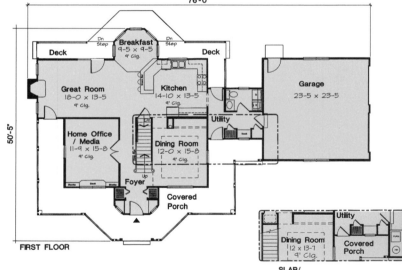

76'-0"

Breakfast
9-5 x 9-5
9' Clg.

Deck   Deck

Great Room
18-0 x 13-5
9' Clg.

Kitchen
14-10 x 13-5
9' Clg.

Garage
23-5 x 23-5

50'-5"

Home Office / Media
11-9 x 15-8
9' Clg.

Dining Room
12-0 x 15-8
9' Clg.

Utility

Foyer   Covered Porch

FIRST FLOOR

Utility

Dining Room
12 x 13-7
9' Clg.

Covered Porch

SLAB/
CRAWLSPACE OPTION

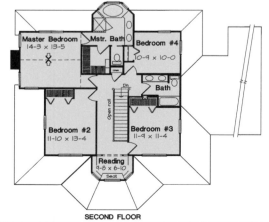

Master Bedroom
14-3 x 13-5

Mstr. Bath

Bedroom #4
10-9 x 10-0

Bath

Bedroom #2
11-10 x 13-4

Open rail

Bedroom #3
11-9 x 11-4

Reading
4-8 x 6-10
Seat

SECOND FLOOR

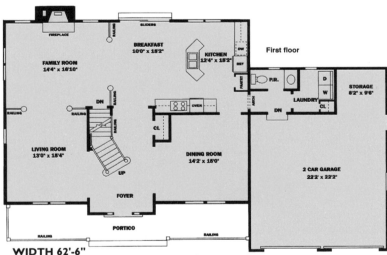

WIDTH 62'-6"
DEPTH 38'-6"

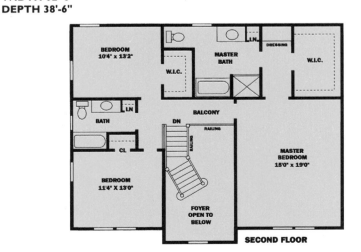

Cascading Gable Roofs
Price Code: D

■ This plan features:
— Three bedrooms
— Two full and one half baths

■ A well-designed exterior with clean lines, cascading gable roofs, covered Porch and clap board siding

■ An open floor plan on the first floor for a feeling of more space

■ Wood columns define the Living Room from the Family Room and the Family Room form the Breakfast Room

■ The Kitchen has an angled island and abundant counter space

■ No materials list is available for this plan

FIRST FLOOR — 1,354 SQ. FT.
SECOND FLOOR — 1,072 SQ. FT.
BASEMENT — 1,354 SQ. FT.

TOTAL LIVING AREA:
2,426 SQ. FT.

Rewards of Success

Price Code: F

■ This plan features:

— Four bedrooms

— Three full and one half baths

■ An open Foyer flanked by formal areas, left to the Dining Room, right to the Living Room

■ An expansive Den with a large fireplace with a flat tiled hearth warming the room

■ Built-in cabinets and shelves providing an added convenience in the Den

■ A well-appointed Kitchen serving the formal Dining Room and the informal Kitchen with equal ease and providing a snack bar for meals on the run

■ A Master Bedroom with a lavish Bath and a walk-in closet

■ An optional crawl space or slab foundation — please specify when ordering

FIRST FLOOR — 2,019 SQ. FT.
SECOND FLOOR — 946 SQ. FT.
GARAGE — 577 SQ. FT.

TOTAL LIVING AREA: 2,965 SQ. FT.

FIRST FLOOR

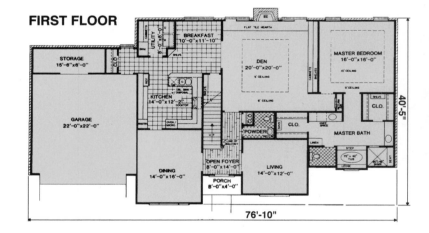

SECOND FLOOR

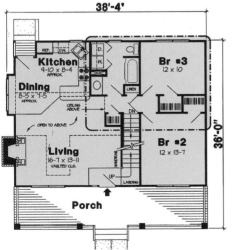

38'-4'

First Floor floor plan:
- Kitchen 9-10 x 8-4 APPROX.
- Dining 8-5 x 7-5 APPROX.
- REF. / D.W.
- D.
- PL.
- LINEN
- Br #3 12 x 10
- CEILING ABOVE
- OPEN TO ABOVE
- DN
- HANDRAIL
- Br #2 12 x 13-7
- Living 16-7 x 13-11 VAULTED CLG.
- UP
- LANDING
- **36'-0"**
- **Porch**

First Floor

Crawl Space Option:
- MXH.
- F
- LINEN
- Br #3 12 x 10
- W/D
- CRAWL ACCESS

Crawl Space Option

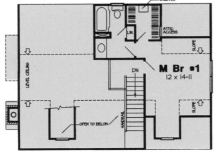

Second Floor plan:
- SHELVES
- LIN
- ATTIC ACCESS
- LEVEL CEILING
- SLOPE
- M Br #1 12 x 14-11
- DN
- HANDRAIL
- OPEN TO BELOW
- SLOPE
- O

Second Floor

ZIP QUOTE
HOME COST CALCULATOR
see order pages for details

Country Touch

Price Code: A

■ This plan features:

— Three bedrooms

— Two full baths

■ A Country-styled front Porch

■ Vaulted ceiling in the Living Room which includes a fireplace

■ An efficient Kitchen with double sinks and peninsula counter that may double as an eating bar

■ Two first floor Bedrooms with ample closet space

■ A second floor Master Suite with sloped ceiling, walk-in closet and private Master Bath

FIRST FLOOR — 1,007 SQ. FT.
SECOND FLOOR — 408 SQ. FT.

TOTAL LIVING AREA:
1,415 SQ. FT.

©1993 Donald A. Gardner Architects, Inc.

Impressive Spaces Prevail

Price Code: G

- ■ This plan features:
- — Four bedrooms
- — Three full and one half baths
- ■ Two-level Foyer with a clerestory window and a curved balcony above the Great Room
- ■ Family Kitchen is convenient to the Breakfast Bay, rear Porch, Dining Room and the Utility/Garage
- ■ Master Bedroom retreat offers a Sitting Area, walk-in closet and a double vanity Bath
- ■ The Bonus Room and ample storage space provide additional space for a growing family

FIRST FLOOR — 2,357 SQ. FT.
SECOND FLOOR — 995 SQ. FT.
BONUS ROOM — 545 SQ. FT.
GARAGE & STORAGE — 975 SQ. FT.

TOTAL LIVING AREA:
3,352 SQ. FT.

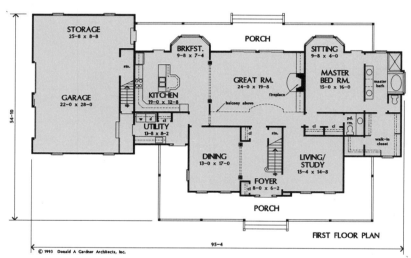

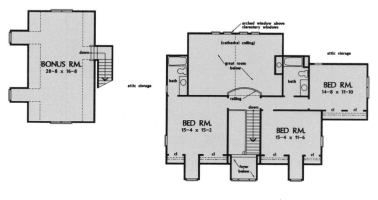

© design basics, inc.

First floor

Second floor

Grandeur Within

Price Code: F

■ This plan features:

— Four bedrooms

— Two full, one three-quarter, and one half baths

■ Bright and cheerful Den has a bay window and built-in bookcases

■ The Living and Dining Rooms both have ten-foot ceilings and access a screen Porch

■ The Family Room, Nook, and Kitchen contain all of the immunities that you expect

■ The upstairs Master Suite has built-ins, a Sitting Area and a wonderful Bath

FIRST FLOOR — 1,923 SQ. FT.
SECOND FLOOR — 1,852 SQ. FT.
BASEMENT — 1,923 SQ. FT.
GARAGE — 726 SQ. FT.

TOTAL LIVING AREA:
3,775 SQ. FT.

©1997 Donald A. Gardner Architects, Inc

Spacious Farmhouse

Price Code: F

■ This plan features:

— Three bedrooms

— Two full and one half baths

■ Bold, front facing gables, bay windows, and a generous front and back Porches accent the elevation

■ The Master Suite is privately located on the first floor and includes a tray ceiling, his and her walk-in closets and a splendid Bath with every amenity

■ The loft overlooks both the two-story Family Room and the Foyer

■ The Bonus Room allows for future expansion

First floor — 1,914 sq. ft.
Second floor — 597 sq. ft.
Bonus — 487 sq. ft.
Garage — 580 sq. ft.

Total living area:
2,511 sq. ft.

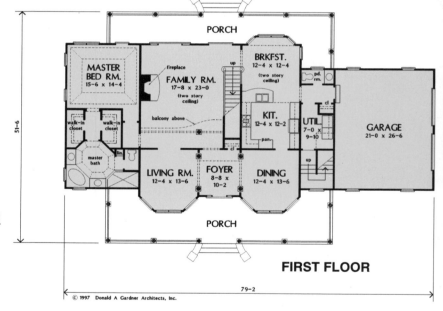

FIRST FLOOR

© 1997 Donald A Gardner Architects, Inc.

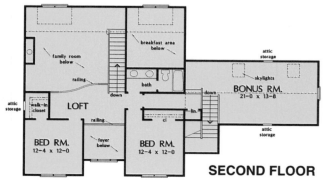

SECOND FLOOR

SECOND FLOOR

Master Br
16-0 x 11-11

DN

Br 2
11-8 x 10-8

linen

Br 3
11-4 x 10-7

Country Influence

Price Code: B

- This plan features:
  — Three bedrooms
  — Two full and one half baths

- Open Living Room enhanced by palladium window, focal point fireplace and atrium door to Deck

- Bay window brightens formal Dining Room conveniently located between Living Room and Kitchen

- Efficient L-shaped Kitchen with bay window eating area, Laundry closet and handy Garage entrance

- Plush Master Bedroom offers another bay window crowned by tray ceiling and private Bath with double vanity

FIRST FLOOR — 806 SQ. FT.
SECOND FLOOR — 748 SQ. FT.
GARAGE — 467 SQ. FT.

TOTAL LIVING AREA:
1,554 SQ. FT.

50'-0"

40'-0"

Deck

Living
13-4 x 17-4

1/2 wall

Dining
11-0 x 12-2

Kitchen
14-5 x 11-10

UP

W D

Sun
Rm

Garage
21-4 x 21-8

FIRST FLOOR

Streaming Natural Light

Price Code: B

■ This plan features:

— Three bedrooms

— Two full and one half baths

■ An outstanding, two-story Great Room with an unusual floor-to-ceiling, corner front window and cozy, hearth fireplace

■ A formal Dining Room opening from the Great Room makes entertaining easy

■ An efficient Kitchen with a work island, Pantry, a corner, double sink opening to the Great Room, and a bright, bay window eating Nook

■ A quiet, Master Suite with a vaulted ceiling and a plush Bath with a double vanity, spa tub and walk-in closet

■ On the second floor, two additional Bedrooms share a full hall Bath and a Bonus Area for multiple uses

FIRST FLOOR — 1,230 SQ. FT.
SECOND FLOOR — 477 SQ. FT.
BONUS — 195 SQ. FT.

TOTAL LIVING AREA:
1,707 SQ. FT.

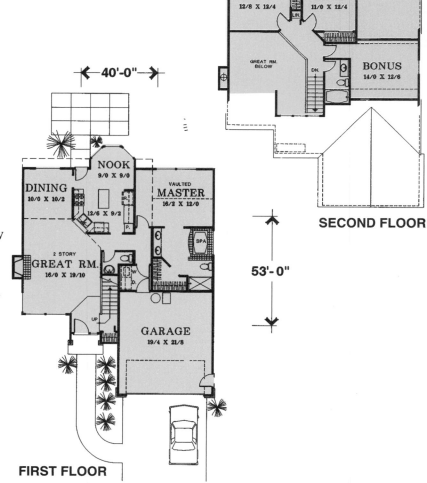

MAIN FLOOR

Fam. rm.
18⁸ x 15⁰

Bfst.
11⁰ x 13⁰

Kit.
10⁰ x 14⁰

Din.
12⁰ x 14³

Liv. rm.
13⁰ x 15⁰
12'-0" CEILING

Gar.
32⁰ x 23⁴

Den
11⁰ x 13⁴

COVERED STOOP

TRANSOMS

© design basics inc.

65' - 4"

SECOND FLOOR

Mbr.
18⁸ x 16⁰
10'-0" CEILING

Br. 4
12⁷ x 12⁰

Br. 3
12⁰ x 13⁷

WHIRLPOOL

KITCHEN-ETTE

Br. 2
11⁰ x 13⁴
10'-0" CLG.

OPEN TO BELOW

UNFINISHED BONUS ROOM
8⁴ x 15⁰

Striking Brick Detailing

Price Code: E

■ This plan features:

— Four bedrooms

— Three full and one half baths

■ The formal Living Room has oak flooring and a twelve-foot high ceiling

■ There is a decorative ceiling and hutch space in the formal Dining Room

■ The gourmet Kitchen includes a central island, a roomy Pantry and a Lazy Susan

■ The comfortable Family Room is enhanced by a brick fireplace

■ The Master Suite contains a vaulted ceiling and a built-in Kitchenette

MAIN FLOOR — 1,561 SQ. FT.
SECOND FLOOR — 1,458 SQ. FT.
BONUS ROOM — 160 SQ. FT.
BASEMENT — 1,561 SQ. FT.
GARAGE — 748 SQ. FT.

TOTAL LIVING AREA:
3,019 SQ. FT.

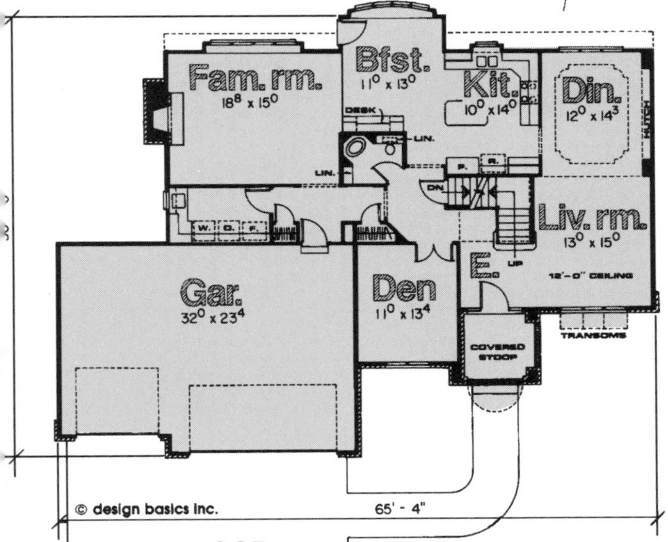

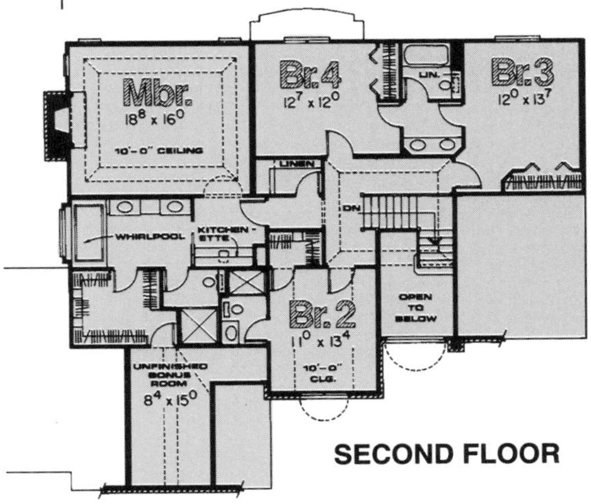

© Donald A. Gardner Architects, Inc.

Stone and Stucco

Price Code: E

■ This plan features:

— Three bedrooms

— Two full and one half baths

■ The Family Room is two stories high and accented by a fireplace, and an overlooking balcony

■ The Kitchen/Breakfast Area has easy access to the formal Dining Room

■ An elegant tray ceiling highlights the Dining Room

■ The Bonus Room stands ready for future expansion

■ No materials list is available for this plan

FIRST FLOOR — 1,904 SQ. FT.
SECOND FLOOR — 645 SQ. FT.
BONUS ROOM — 434 SQ. FT.
GARAGE — 646 SQ. FT.

TOTAL LIVING AREA: 2,549 SQ. FT.

FIRST FLOOR PLAN

© 1996 Donald A Gardner Architects, Inc.

SECOND FLOOR PLAN

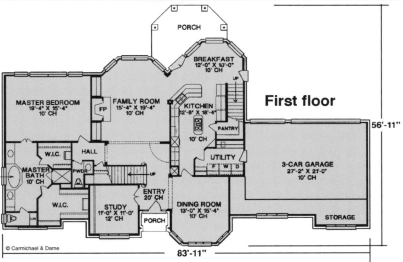

First floor

PORCH

BREAKFAST
12'-0" X 10'-0"
10' CH

MASTER BEDROOM
19'-4" X 15'-4"
10' CH

FAMILY ROOM
15'-4" X 19'-4"
10' CH

FP

KITCHEN
12'-8" X 18'-4"

W.I.C.

HALL

PANTRY
10' CH

UP

MASTER BATH
10' CH

PWDR

UTILITY
F W D

3-CAR GARAGE
27'-2" X 21'-0"
10' CH

56'-11"

W.I.C.

STUDY
11'-0" X 11'-0"
12' CH

ENTRY
20' CH

UP

DINING ROOM
13'-0" X 15'-4"
10' CH

PORCH

STORAGE

© Carmichael & Dame

83'-11"

Optional Basement Access

KITCHEN
12'-8" X 18'-4"

PANTRY
10' CH

UTILITY

DOWN TO BASEMENT

F W D

SUN DECK

BEDROOM 3
14'-0" X 12'-4"
9' CH

W.I.C.

GAME ROOM
15'-0" X 19'-8"
9' CH

BATH

W.I.C.

BEDROOM 4
13'-4" X 11'-4"
9' CH

DN

BATH

LIN

HALL

DN

W.I.C.

Second floor

OPEN TO BELOW

BEDROOM 2
13'-0" X 13'-4"
9' CH

Eye Catching Tower
Price Code: E

■ This plan features:

— Four bedrooms

— Four full and one half baths

■ Dining Room with bay perfect for special dinner parties

■ Study with high ceiling and windows

■ Family Room with fireplace is open to the Breakfast Bay and gourmet Kitchen

■ First floor Master Bedrooms spans the width of the home and contains every luxury imaginable

■ Upstairs find three Bedrooms, a Game Room, a Sun Deck and two full Baths

■ This plan has a three-car Garage with Storage Space

FIRST FLOOR — 2,117 SQ. FT.
SECOND FLOOR — 1,206 SQ. FT.
GARAGE — 685 SQ. FT.

TOTAL LIVING AREA:
3,323 SQ. FT

© 1994 Donald A. Gardner Architects, Inc.

Four Dramatic Gables

Price Code: F

- This plan features:
- — Three bedrooms
- — Two full and one half baths

- Four dramatic gables lend curb appeal to this impressive executive home

- Two fireplaces add warmth to this home, one in the two-story Family Room, the other in the Study/Living Room

- Vaulted and nine-foot ceilings create maximum volume

- First floor Master Suite, with an angled hall entrance for privacy, features a sitting bay, whirlpool tub, a double vanity and a separate shower

- Extra room is added on the second floor by a skylight Bonus Room and attic storage

FIRST FLOOR — 2,162 SQ. FT.
SECOND FLOOR — 671 SQ. FT.

TOTAL LIVING AREA:
2,833 SQ. FT.

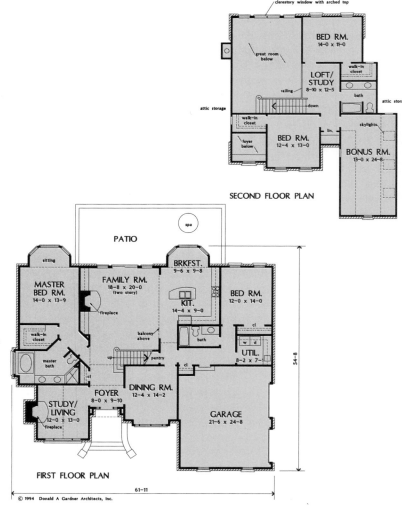

SECOND FLOOR PLAN

FIRST FLOOR PLAN

© 1994 Donald A Gardner Architects, Inc.

Photography Supplied by The Meredith Corporation

WIDTH 64'-0"
DEPTH 65'-0"

PORCH

BRKFST
9x9

PORCH

PLAYROOM
14x12

FAMILY
21x15

KITCHEN
14x11

UP   MUDRM

MECH

GARAGE
21x26

R

P

UP

LIVING
14x15

ENTRY

DINING
14x16

PORCH

MAIN LEVEL

MASTER
BEDROOM
16x21

DRESSING

BATH

BEDROOM
12x12

CLOS   CLOS

BATH

DN   HALL   DN

BEDROOM
12x12

BEDROOM
14x13

LDRY
W
D

BEDROOM
14x13

BATH

UPPER LEVEL

Luxurious Country

Price Code: F

■ This plan features:

— Five bedrooms

— Four full and one half baths

■ A welcoming front Porch adds style to this luxurious Country home

■ The Living room and the Dining Room are located in the front of the home

■ The Family Room in the rear has a fireplace and doors to the rear Porch

■ A Playroom is located behind the Garage for the kids

■ The Kitchen is designed in a convenient U-shape

■ Upstairs find the Master Bedroom which comprises half of the space

■ Also upstairs are four secondary Bedrooms

MAIN LEVEL — 1,928 SQ. FT.
UPPER LEVEL — 2,364 SQ. FT.
GARAGE — 578 SQ. FT.

TOTAL LIVING AREA:
4,292 SQ. FT.

Touch of Country

Price Code: E

- This plan features:
- — Three or four bedrooms
- — Three full baths

- A Study/Guest Room with convenient access to a full, hall Bath

- An elegant Dining Room topped by a decorative ceiling treatment

- An expansive Family Room equipped with a massive fireplace with built-in bookshelves

- An informal Breakfast Room conveniently enhanced by a built-in planning desk

- A cathedral ceiling crowning the Master Suite

FIRST FLOOR — 1,378 SQ. FT.
SECOND FLOOR — 1,269 SQ. FT.
BASEMENT — 1,378 SQ. FT.
GARAGE — 717 SQ. FT.

TOTAL LIVING AREA: 2,647 SQ. FT.

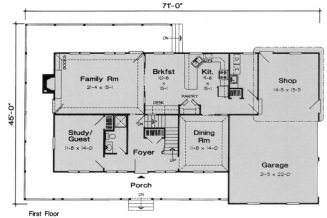

First Floor

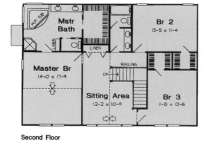

Second Floor

Optional Second Floor

Crawl Space/Slab Option

ZIP QUOTE
HOME COST CALCULATOR
see order pages for details

ZIP QUOTE
HOME COST CALCULATOR
see order pages for details

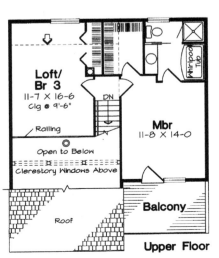

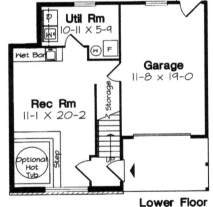

Util Rm
10-11 X 5-9

Wet Bar

Garage
11-8 x 19-0

Rec Rm
11-1 X 20-2

Storage

Step

Optional
Hot
Tub

UP

Lower Floor

**Loft/
Br 3**
11-7 X 16-6
Clg @ 9'-6"

DN

Railing

Mbr
11-8 X 14-0

Open to Below

Clerestory Windows Above

Roof

Balcony

Upper Floor

28'-0"

DN

Broom

Linen

Ref

Kitchen
11-1 X 7-7

Flue

Brkfst Bar

Dining
11-11 X 8-7

DN

Railing

Br 1
12-0 X 11-3

Loft
Above

Fireplace

UP

Living
15-1 X 14-10

DN

32'-0"

Deck

Main Floor

Home With Many Views

Price Code: B

■ This plan features:

— Three bedrooms

— Two full baths

■ Large Decks and windows taking full advantage of the view

■ A fireplace that divides the Living Room from the Dining Room

■ A Kitchen flowing into the Dining Room

■ A Master Bedroom with full Master Bath

■ A Recreation Room sporting a whirlpool tub and a bar

MAIN FLOOR — 728 SQ. FT.
UPPER FLOOR — 573 SQ. FT.
LOWER FLOOR — 409 SQ. FT.
GARAGE — 244 SQ. FT.

TOTAL LIVING AREA:
1,710 SQ. FT.

Zoned for Harmony
PRICE CODE: D

■ This plan features:
— Three bedrooms
— Two full and one half baths
■ A lofty vaulted ceiling over the entire living level
■ A spacious, efficient Kitchen with a peninsula counter separating it from the Breakfast Room
■ A formal Living and Dining Room that efficiently flow into each other for ease in entertaining
■ A Family Room with a fireplace and built-in bookshelves
■ A Master Suite with a romantic window seat, a large walk-in closet and a lavish Master Bath
■ Two additional Bedrooms, with walk-in closets, that share a full hall Bath

MAIN FLOOR — 1,861 SQ. FT.
LOWER FLOOR — 526 SQ. FT.
BASEMENT — 874 SQ. FT.
GARAGE — 574 SQ. FT.

TOTAL LIVING AREA:
2,387 SQ. FT.

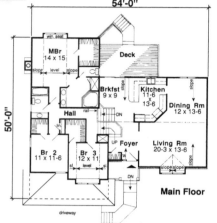

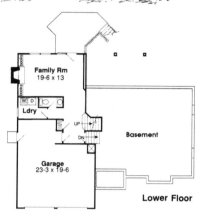

Two Fireplaces Adding Warmth and Atmosphere
PRICE CODE: A

■ This plan features:
— Three bedrooms
— Two full baths
■ The terrific Great Room has a ten foot boxed ceiling and a gas fireplace
■ The secondary bedrooms share a full bath located in close proximity
■ The Master Suite enjoys a boxed ceiling and a luxurious private bath
■ The informal Hearth Room has an optional gas fireplace and access to the Grilling Porch
■ An optional basement, slab or crawl space foundation — Please specify when ordering
■ No materials list is available for this plan

MAIN FLOOR — 1,425 SQ. FT.
GARAGE — 353 SQ. FT.
PORCH — 137 SQ. FT.

TOTAL LIVING AREA
1,425 SQ. FT.

MAIN FLOOR

To order your Blueprints, call 1-800-235-5700

Split-Bedroom Ranch
PRICE CODE: C

■ This plan features:
— Three bedrooms
— Two full baths
■ The formal Foyer opens into the Great Room which features a vaulted ceiling and a hearth fireplace
■ The U-shaped Kitchen is located between the Dining Room and the Breakfast Nook
■ The secluded Master Bedroom is spacious and includes amenities such as walk-in closets and a full Bath
■ Two secondary Bedrooms have ample closet space and share a full Bath
■ The covered front Porch and rear Deck provide additional space for entertaining
■ An optional basement, slab or a crawl space foundation — please specify when ordering

MAIN FLOOR — 1,804 SQ. FT.
BASEMENT — 1,804 SQ. FT.
GARAGE — 506 SQ. FT.

TOTAL LIVING AREA:
1,804 SQ. FT.

MAIN AREA

A Home for Today and Tomorrow
PRICE CODE: B

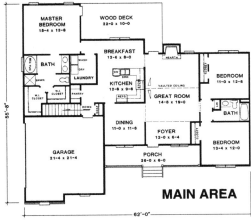

■ This plan features:
— Three bedrooms
— Two full baths
■ An intriguing Breakfast Nook off the Kitchen
■ A wide open, fireplaced Living Room with glass sliders to an optional Deck
■ A step-saving Kitchen with a Pantry
■ A handsome Master Bedroom with skylit compartmentalized Bath

MAIN AREA — 1,583 SQ. FT.
BASEMENT — 1,573 SQ. FT.
GARAGE — 484 SQ. FT.

TOTAL LIVING AREA:
1,583 SQ. FT.

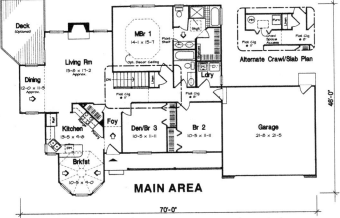

MAIN AREA

To order your Blueprints, call 1-800-235-5700

Traditionally Styled

Price Code: C

■ This plan features:

— Three bedrooms

— Two full and one half baths

■ There are Porches both in the front and the rear

■ The Kitchen is conveniently appointed and located

■ A fireplace warms the Great Room

■ The Master Bedroom is located on the first floor

■ The secondary Bedrooms are located upstairs

■ No materials list is available for this plan

FIRST FLOOR — 1,432 SQ. FT.
SECOND FLOOR — 585 SQ. FT.
BASEMENT — 1,432 SQ. FT.

TOTAL LIVING AREA: 2,017 SQ. FT.

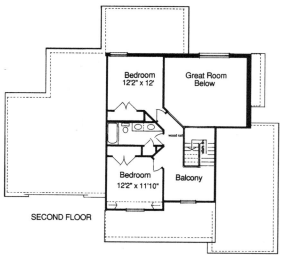

To order your Blueprints, call 1-800-235-5700

©1995 Donald A. Gardner Architects, Inc.

B. NATHAN

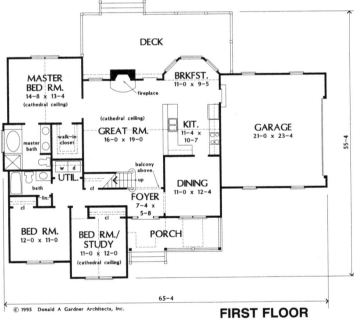

MASTER BED RM. 14-8 x 13-4 (cathedral ceiling)

DECK

BRKFST. 11-0 x 9-5

fireplace

master bath

walk-in closet

GREAT RM. 16-0 x 19-0 (cathedral ceiling)

KIT. 11-4 x 10-7

GARAGE 21-0 x 23-4

w d

bath

UTIL.

cl

lin:

cl

BED RM. 12-0 x 11-0

BED RM./ STUDY 11-0 x 12-0 (cathedral ceiling)

cl

FOYER 7-4 x 5-8

balcony above
up

DINING 11-0 x 12-4

PORCH

55-4

65-4

© 1995 Donald A Gardner Architects, Inc.

FIRST FLOOR
No. 96463

(unfinished)
BONUS 14-8 x 17-0

down

great room below

railing

balcony (optional)

(unfinished)
BONUS 11-0 x 12-4

attic storage

SECOND FLOOR

Your Family Will Grow In Style

Price Code: D

■ This plan features:

— Three bedrooms

— Two full baths

■ Open Great Room and Kitchen enlarged by a cathedral ceiling

■ Wooden rear Deck expand entertaining to the outdoors

■ Cathedral ceiling adding volume and drama to the Master Suite

■ Flexible Bedroom/Study includes a cathedral ceiling and an arched double window

■ Second floor bonus space may be finished with two more Bedrooms

FIRST FLOOR — 1,633 SQ. FT.
GARAGE & STORAGE — 512 SQ. FT.
SECOND FLOOR BONUS SPACE — 595 SQ. FT.

TOTAL LIVING AREA:
1,633 SQ. FT.

Covered Front Porch
PRICE CODE: B

- This plan features:
— Three bedrooms
— Two full and one half baths
- The Great Room has columns at its entrance and the options for a fireplace and a media center.
- There is a first floor Master Suite tucked into the rear for privacy and topped by a boxed ceiling.
- The Kitchen has easy access to the formal Dining Room, the Garage and the Grilling Porch.
- There is Storage Space in the attic, in the Garage and if you choose a basement foundation plan that would expand your Storage Space
- An optional basement, crawl space or slab foundation — please specify when ordering
- No materials list is available for this plan

FIRST FLOOR — 1,112 SQ. FT.
SECOND FLOOR — 483 SQ. FT.
GARAGE — 342 SQ. FT.

TOTAL LIVING AREA:
1,595 SQ. FT.

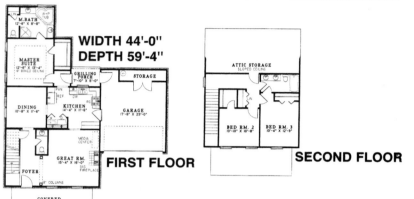

WIDTH 44'-0"
DEPTH 59'-4"

FIRST FLOOR

SECOND FLOOR

Multiple Gables
and Double Dormer
PRICE CODE: C

- This plan features:
— Three bedrooms
— Two full baths
- Distinguished details inside and out make this modest home very appealing
- Cathedral ceiling, cozy fireplace, built-in shelves and a wall of windows with Porch access enhance the Great Room, Dining Area and open Kitchen
- Quiet corner Master Bed Room features a cathedral ceiling, walk-in closet and and plush Bath
- Two additional Bedrooms, with ample closets, share a hall Bath and Laundry facilities
- Bonus Room over Garage provides options for growing family

MAIN FLOOR — 1,377 SQ. FT.
BONUS ROOM — 383 SQ. FT.
GARAGE & STORAGE — 597 SQ. FT.

TOTAL LIVING AREA:
1,377 SQ. FT.

To order your Blueprints, call 1-800-235-5700

Secluded Master Suite

PRICE CODE: C

■ This plan features:
— Three bedrooms
— Two full baths
■ A convenient one-level design with an open floor plan between the Kitchen, Breakfast Area and Great Room
■ A vaulted ceiling and a cozy fireplace in the spacious Great Room
■ A well-equipped Kitchen using a peninsula counter as an eating bar
■ A Master Suite with a luxurious Master Bath
■ Two additional Bedrooms having use of a full hall Bath
■ An optional crawl space or slab foundation—please specify when ordering

MAIN AREA — 1,680 SQ. FT.
GARAGE — 538 SQ. FT.

TOTAL LIVING AREA:
1,680 SQ. FT.

MAIN AREA

A Grand Entrance

PRICE CODE: E

■ This plan features:
— Five bedrooms
— Three full baths
■ The arched window above the front door provides a grand entrance
■ Inside the two-story Foyer find the first of two open rail staircases in this home
■ The formal Living and Dining rooms are only separated by a set of boxed columns
■ The U-shaped Kitchen has a walk-in Pantry and a wall oven
■ A serving bar services the Breakfast Nook
■ The Family Room has a fireplace as well as a vaulted ceiling
■ Rounding out the first floor is a Den/Bedroom with a Bath located off of it
■ Upstairs find the family sleeping quarters and Baths
■ An optional basement or crawl space foundation — please specify when ordering

FIRST FLOOR — 1,424 SQ. FT.
SECOND FLOOR — 1,256 SQ. FT.
BASEMENT — 1,424 SQ. FT.
GARAGE — 494 SQ. FT.

TOTAL LIVING AREA:
2,680 SQ. FT.

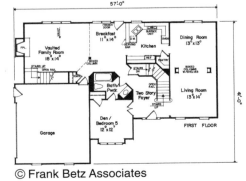

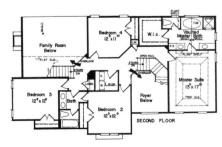

© Frank Betz Associates

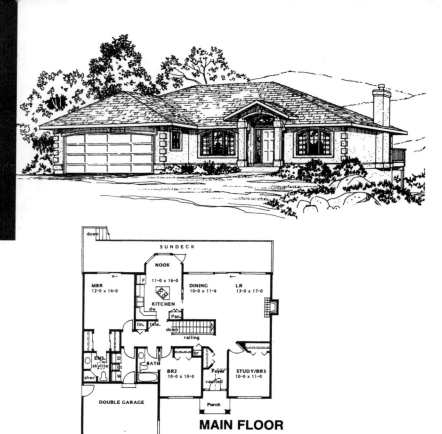

Comfort and Style
PRICE CODE: A

■ This plan features:
— Two or three bedrooms
— One full and one three-quarter baths
■ An unfinished daylight basement, providing possible space for family recreation
■ A Master Suite complete with private Bath and skylight
■ A large Kitchen including an Eating Nook
■ A Sundeck that is easily accessible from the Master Suite, Nook and the Living/Dining Area

MAIN FLOOR — 1,423 SQ. FT.
BASEMENT — 1,423 SQ. FT.
GARAGE — 399 SQ. FT.
WIDTH — 46'-0"
DEPTH — 52'-0"

TOTAL LIVING AREA:
1,423 SQ. FT.

MAIN FLOOR

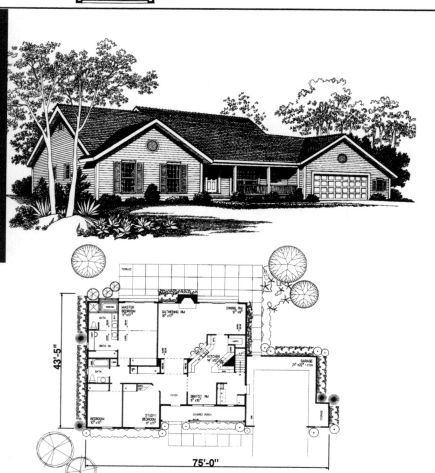

Cozy Traditional with Style
PRICE CODE: C

■ This plan features:
— Three bedrooms
— Two full baths
■ A convenient one-level design
■ A galley-style Kitchen that shares a snack bar with the spacious Gathering Room
■ A focal point fireplace making the Gathering Room warm and inviting
■ An ample Master Suite with a luxury Bath which includes a whirlpool tub and separate Dressing Room
■ Two additional Bedrooms, one that could double as a Study, located at the front of the house

MAIN FLOOR — 1,830 SQ. FT.
BASEMENT — 1,830 SQ. FT.

TOTAL LIVING AREA:
1,830 SQ. FT.

MAIN FLOOR

To order your Blueprints, call 1-800-235-5700

Roof Angles And Window Arches

PRICE CODE: A

■ This plan features
– Three bedrooms
– Two full baths
  Positioned for privacy, the Master Suite has double doors leading to the Bath
  Dining Room conversation flows easily into the Great Room
■ The Great Room includes a cozy fireplace
  Bedroom three can easily convert into a Home Office space
■ An optional basement, slab or crawl space foundation — please specify when ordering
  No materials list is available for this plan

MAIN FLOOR — 1,383 SQ. FT.
BASEMENT — 1,460 SQ. FT.
GARAGE — 416 SQ. FT.
DECK — 120 SQ. FT.
PORCH — 29 SQ.FT.

TOTAL LIVING AREA:
1,383 SQ. FT.

WIDTH 50'-0"
DEPTH 40'-0"   **MAIN FLOOR**

On A Budget

PRICE CODE: C

© 1998 Donald A. Gardner, Inc.

■ This plan features:
— Three bedrooms
— Two full baths
■ A front and side Porches add outdoor living space
■ The Great Room has a fireplace set between built-ins
■ Columns separate the Dining Room from the Great Room
■ The Kitchen is conveniently set up for the family cook
■ The Master Bedroom has a tray ceiling
■ Ample Storage and Bonus Space are provided
■ No materials list is available for this plan

MAIN FLOOR — 1,428 SQ. FT.
BONUS — 313 SQ. FT.
GARAGE — 453 SQ. FT.

TOTAL LIVING AREA:
1,428 SQ. FT.

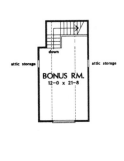

FLOOR PLAN

© 1998 Donald A Gardner, Inc.

To order your Blueprints, call 1-800-235-5700

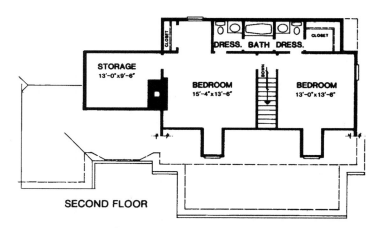

SECOND FLOOR

Country Living in Any Neighborhood

Price Code: C

- This plan features:
— Three bedrooms
— Two full and two half baths
- An expansive Family Room with fireplace
- A Dining Room and Breakfast Nook lit by flowing natural light from bay windows
- A first floor Master Suite with a double vanitied Bath that wraps around his-n-her closets
- An optional basement, slab or crawl space foundation — please specify when ordering

FIRST FLOOR — 1,477 SQ. FT.
SECOND FLOOR — 704 SQ. FT.
BASEMENT — 1,374 SQ. FT.
GARAGE — 528 SQ. FT.

TOTAL LIVING AREA:
2,181 SQ. FT.

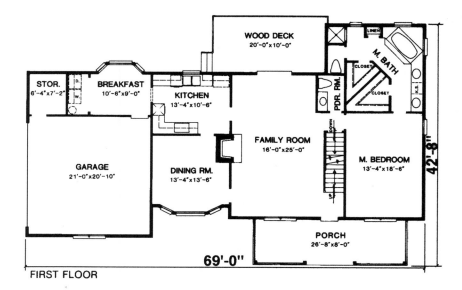

FIRST FLOOR

To order your Blueprints, call 1-800-235-5700

Eyebrow Window
PRICE CODE: E

This plan features:
- Four bedrooms
- Three full baths

Porches and a Deck complement this home

The Dining Room is highlighted by a bay window

A lovely staircase is central to the Foyer

The Master Suite is privately located

An additional Bedroom on the first floor could also be a study

The Kitchen has plenty of working space

No materials list is available for this plan

FIRST FLOOR — 1,743 SQ. FT.
SECOND FLOOR — 555 SQ. FT.
BONUS — 350 SQ. FT.
GARAGE — 518 SQ. FT.

TOTAL LIVING AREA:
2,298 SQ. FT.

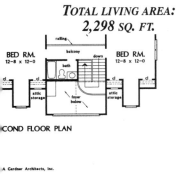

SECOND FLOOR PLAN

A Gardner Architects, Inc.

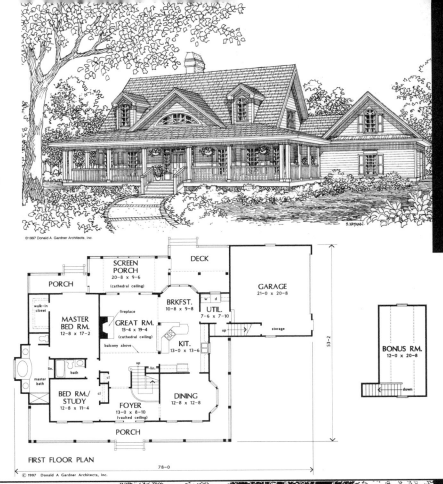

©1997 Donald A. Gardner Architects, Inc.

FIRST FLOOR PLAN

© 1997 Donald A Gardner Architects, Inc.

Cozy Front Porch
PRICE CODE: A

- This plan features:
  — Three bedrooms
  — Two full baths
- The Great Room, located in the center of the home, has a boxed ceiling and a gas fireplace
- The Kitchen includes a peninsula counter/snack bar perfect for meals on the go
- The Dining Area has direct access to the Grilling Porch
- Entrance from the Garage is into the Laundry Room, creating a Mud Room arrangement cutting down on tracked in dirt
- An optional basement, slab or crawl space foundation— please specify when ordering
- No materials list is available for this plan

MAIN FLOOR — 1,289 SQ. FT.
GARAGE — 342 SQ. FT.
PORCH — 198 SQ. FT.

TOTAL LIVING AREA:
1,289 SQ. FT.

MAIN FLOOR

Private Master Suite
PRICE CODE: B

■ This plan features:
— Three bedrooms
— Two full baths
■ A spacious Great Room enhanced by a vaulted ceiling and fireplace
■ A well-equipped Kitchen with windowed double sink
■ A secluded Master Suite with decorative ceiling, private Master Bath, and walk-in closet
■ Two additional Bedrooms sharing hall Bath
■ An optional crawlspace or slab foundation — please specify when ordering

MAIN AREA — 1,293 SQ. FT.
GARAGE — 433 SQ. FT.

TOTAL LIVING AREA:
1,293 SQ. FT.

WIDTH 51'-10"
DEPTH 40'- 4"

mbr 12⁶ x 12⁶
sto 5⁶ x 6
kit 9 x 10
dining 11⁴ x 10
br 3 11⁸ x 11
garage 20 x 20
den 19 x 17
br 2 12 x 11
porch 19 x 4
MAIN AREA

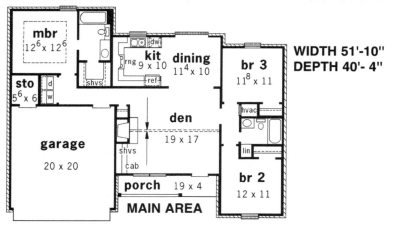

© Donald A. Gardner Architects, Inc.

Splendid Country Home
PRICE CODE: E

■ This plan features:
— Three bedrooms
— Two full and one half baths
■ The arched clerestory window in the center dormer casts natural light into the vaulted Foyer and second floor Bath
■ The Great Room is open to both the Breakfast room and the Kitchen and is topped by a cathedral ceiling and access to the rear deck
■ The Master Suite includes a lavish Bath and a walk-in closet
■ The two secondary Bedrooms have walk-in closest and separate vanities with a shared Bath

FIRST FLOOR — 1,569 SQ. FT.
SECOND FLOOR — 682 SQ. FT.
BONUS — 332 SQ. FT.
GARAGE — 492 SQ. FT.

TOTAL LIVING AREA:
2,251 SQ. FT.

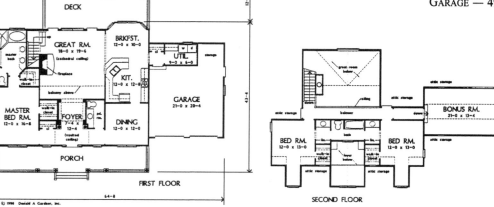

To order your Blueprints, call 1-800-235-5700

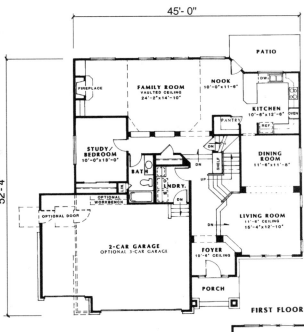

45'- 0"

52'- 4"

PATIO

FIREPLACE

FAMILY ROOM
VAULTED CEILING
24'-2"x14'-10"

NOOK
10'-0"x11'-6"

DW

KITCHEN
10'-6"x12'-6"

OVEN

PANTRY

REF

**STUDY/
BEDROOM**
10'-0"x13'-0"

BATH

SHELF

DN

DN

UP

**DINING
ROOM**
11'-6"x11'-8"

OPTIONAL
WORKBENCH

D LNDRY.
W

DN

LIVING ROOM
11'-6" CEILING
15'-4"x12'-10"

OPTIONAL DOOR

DN

2-CAR GARAGE
OPTIONAL 3-CAR GARAGE

FOYER
10'-6" CEILING

PORCH

FIRST FLOOR

OPEN TO BELOW

BEDROOM
11'-8"x12'-0"

LIN

BATH

OPTIONAL
FIREPLACE

DN

MASTER BEDROOM
VAULTED CEILING
17'-0"x16'-0"

HIS

OPEN
TO
BELOW

BEDROOM
11'-6"x15'-0"

MASTER BATH

HERS

LINEN

SECOND FLOOR

Comfortable Living

Price Code: E

■ This plan features:

— Three or Four Bedrooms

— Three full baths

■ Easy access between Living Room and Dining Room for ease in entertaining

■ Modern Kitchen with double sink, built-in Pantry and peninsula counter

■ Vaulted ceiling in the Family Room which also features a fireplace

■ A Master Suite with vaulted ceiling, optional fireplace, his and her walk-in closets and lavish Master Bath

FIRST FLOOR — 1,574 SQ. FT.
SECOND FLOOR — 1,098 SQ. FT.

TOTAL LIVING AREA:
2,672 SQ. FT.

Photography Supplied by The Meredith Corporation

Prairie Style Retreat

Price Code: C

- This plan features:
- — Three bedrooms
- — Two full and one half baths
- Shingle siding, tall expanses of glass and wrapping decks accent the exterior
- The octagonal shaped Living Room has a two-story ceiling and French doors
- The Kitchen is enhanced by a cooktop island
- The main level Master Suite offers a private Bath
- Two additional, second floor Bedrooms share the full Bath in the hall

First floor — 1,213 sq. ft.
Second floor — 825 sq. ft.
Basement — 1,213 sq. ft.

Total living area:
2,038 sq. ft.

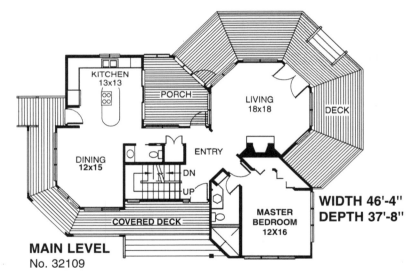

KITCHEN
13x13

PORCH

LIVING
18x18

DECK

DINING
12x15

ENTRY

DN

UP

COVERED DECK

MASTER
BEDROOM
12X16

WIDTH 46'-4"
DEPTH 37'-8"

MAIN LEVEL
No. 32109

ZIP QUOTE
HOME COST CALCULATOR
see order pages for details

BEDROOM
12x16

OPEN TO
LIVING

DN

OPEN

BEDROOM
12x16

UPPER LEVEL

To order your Blueprints, call 1-800-235-5700

A Compact Home
PRICE CODE: A

- This plan features:
  - Three bedrooms
  - Two full baths
- Siding with brick wainscoting distinguishing the elevation
- A large Family Room with a corner fireplace and direct access to the outside
- An arched opening leading to the Breakfast Area
- A bay window illuminating the Breakfast Area with natural light
- An efficiently designed, U-shaped Kitchen with ample cabinet and counter space
- A Master Suite with a private Master Bath
- Two additional Bedrooms that share a full hall Bath
- No materials list is available for this plan

MAIN FLOOR — 1,142 SQ. FT.
GARAGE — 428 SQ. FT.

TOTAL LIVING AREA:
1,142 SQ. FT.

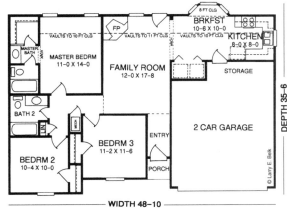

MAIN FLOOR

WIDTH 48–10

Studious Stucco
PRICE CODE: E

- This plan features:
  - Four bedrooms
  - Three full baths
- Columns delineate the Dining Room
- There is a huge walk in closet in the Master Suite
- The Great Room has a fireplace flanked by built-ins
- A covered Porch is located off the Nook
- Storage and bonus space can be found upstairs
- No materials list is available for this plan

FIRST FLOOR — 2,167 SQ. FT.
SECOND FLOOR — 891 SQ. FT.
BONUS — 252 SQ. FT.
GARAGE — 725 SQ. FT.

TOTAL LIVING AREA:
3,058 SQ. FT.

WIDTH 64'-0"
DEPTH 73'-7"

FIRST FLOOR

SECOND FLOOR

© Larry E. Belk

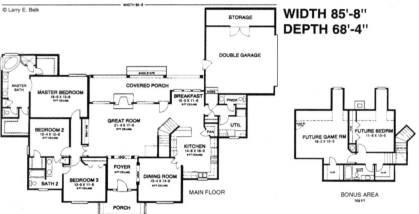

WIDTH 85'-8"
DEPTH 68'-4"

Stately Elegance
PRICE CODE: D

■ This plan features:
— Three bedrooms
— Two full and one half baths

■ Elegant columns frame entry into Foyer and expansive Great Room beyond

■ Efficient Kitchen ideal for busy cook with walk-in Pantry, Breakfast Area and access to formal Dining Room, Laundry and Garage

■ A private Master Suite boasts a plush Bath with two huge, walk-in closets, a double vanity and whirlpool tub

■ Two secondary Bedrooms with large closets, share a double vanity Bath

■ Staircase in Kitchen area leads to expandable second floor

■ An optional slab or crawl space foundation — please specify when ordering

MAIN FLOOR — 2,409 SQ. FT.
GARAGE — 644 SQ. FT.
BONUS — 709 SQ. FT.W

TOTAL LIVING AREA:
2,409 SQ. FT.

© Frank Betz Associates, Inc.

Stucco & Stone
PRICE CODE: E

■ This plan features:
— Three bedrooms
— Two full and one half baths

■ Vaulted Great Room unfolds directly in front of the entry, this room is highlighted by a fireplace and French doors to the rear yard

■ Decorative columns define the Dining Room adding elegance

■ A built-in Pantry and a radius window above the double sink in the Kitchen add style

■ The Breakfast Bay is crowned by a vaulted ceiling

■ There is a tray ceiling over the Master Bedroom and Sitting Area, while a vaulted ceiling crowns the Master Bath

■ Two additional Bedrooms, each with a walk-in closet, share the full, double vanity Bath in the hall

■ An optional basement, slab or crawl space foundation — please specify when ordering

■ No material list is available for this plan

FIRST FLOOR — 1,796 SQ. FT.
SECOND FLOOR — 629 SQ. FT.
BONUS ROOM — 208 SQ. FT.
BASEMENT — 1,796 SQ. FT.
GARAGE — 588 SQ. FT.

TOTAL LIVING AREA:
2,425 SQ. FT.

TOTAL LIVING AREA:
2,250 SQ. FT.

BED RM.
12-0 x 12-8

great room
below

walk-in
closet

bath

bath

linen

foyer
below

BED RM.
12-4 x 12-8

walk-in
closet

down

down

cl

storage

down

skylights

BONUS RM.
15-6 x 21-8

SECOND FLOOR PLAN

SCREEN
PORCH
12-0 x 11-0

PORCH

GREAT RM.
17-4 x 17-9

BRKFST.
12-0 x 11-0

master
bath

fireplace

walk-in
closet

walk-in
closet

KITCHEN
12-4 x 13-11

pan.

MASTER
BED RM.
13-0 x 14-0

pd. rm.

up

FOYER
11-4 x 6-5

DINING
12-4 x 12-8

up

w d

UTILITY
10-6 x 6-10

storage

PORCH

67-4

GARAGE
22-4 x 21-8

FIRST FLOOR PLAN

61-7

Traditional Two-Story Home

Price Code: E

■ This plan features:

— Three bedrooms

— Two full and two half baths

■ Facade handsomely accented by multiple gables, keystone arches and transom windows

■ Arched clerestory window lights two-story Foyer for dramatic entrance

■ Two-story Great Room exciting with inviting fireplace, wall of windows and back Porch access

■ Cooks will enjoy open Kitchen and easy access to screen Porch and Dining Room

■ Private Master Bedroom Suite offers two walk-in closets and deluxe Bath

FIRST FLOOR — 1,644 SQ. FT.
SECOND FLOOR — 606 SQ. FT.
BONUS ROOM — 548 SQ. FT.
GARAGE & STORAGE — 657 SQ. FT.

The Ultimate Kitchen

Price Code: C

■ This plan features:

— Three bedrooms

— Two full and one half baths

■ Front Porch invites visiting and leads into an open entry with an angled staircase

■ Living Room with a wall of windows and an island fireplace, opens to Dining Room with a bright, bay window

■ Large and efficient Kitchen with a work island, walk-in Pantry, garden window over sink, skylit Nook and nearby Deck

■ Corner Master Suite enhanced by Deck access, vaulted ceiling, a large walk-in closet and Spa Bath

■ Guest/Utility Room offers a pullman bed and Laundry

■ Two second floor Bedrooms with large closets, share a full Bath

FIRST FLOOR —1,472 SQ. FT.
SECOND FLOOR — 478 SQ. FT.
GARAGE — 558 SQ. FT.

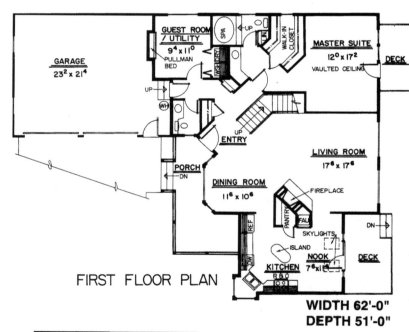

FIRST FLOOR PLAN

WIDTH 62'-0"
DEPTH 51'-0"

SECOND FLOOR PLAN

TOTAL LIVING AREA:
1,950 SQ. FT.

Especially Unique
PRICE CODE: E

■ This plan features:
— Four bedrooms
— Three full baths and on half baths
■ An arch covered Entry and arched windows add a unique flair to the home
■ From the 11-foof Entry turn left in to the Study/Media Room
■ The formal Dining Room is open to the Gallery, and the Living Room beyond
■ The Family Room has a built-in entertainment center, fireplace and access to the rear Patio
■ The Master Bedroom is isolated, and has a fireplace, a private Bath, and a walk-in closet
■ Three additional Bedrooms on the opposite side of the home share two full Baths
■ No materials list is available for this plan

MAIN FLOOR — 2,748 SQ. FT.
GARAGE — 660 SQ. FT.

TOTAL LIVING AREA:
2,748 SQ. FT.

ZIP QUOTE
HOME COST CALCULATOR
see order pages for details

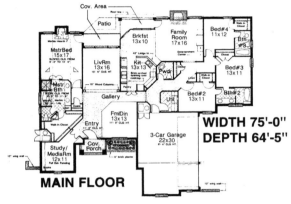

WIDTH 75'-0"
DEPTH 64'-5"

MAIN FLOOR

For A Narrow Lot
PRICE CODE: D

■ This plan features:
— Three bedrooms
— Two full baths
■ A wrap-around front Porch, triple gable and arched window add curb appeal to this charming home
■ Columns, a vaulted ceiling and inviting fireplace accent the Great Room
■ Unusual octagon Dining Area with Porch access provides elegant setting
■ Open Kitchen easily serves Dining area, Breakfast Alcove and screened Porch
■ Master Bedroom suite offers privacy, two walk-in closets and skylit Bath
■ Two more Bedrooms, with ample closets, share a skylit Bath
■ Bonus Room upstairs could be a future fourth Bedroom
■ No materials list is available for this plan

MAIN FLOOR — 1,918 SQ. FT.
BONUS ROOM — 307 SQ. FT.
GARAGE — 552 SQ. FT.

TOTAL LIVING AREA:
1,918 SQ. FT.

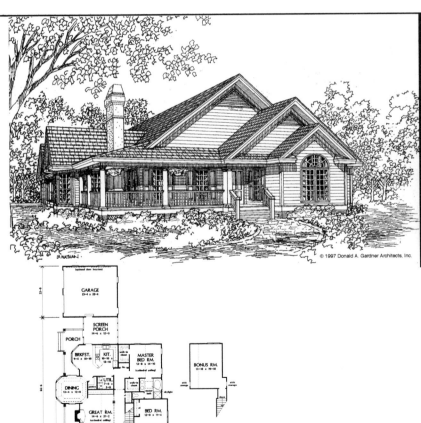

© 1997 Donald A. Gardner Architects, Inc.

Luxurious Living
PRICE CODE: E

- This plan features:
  — Four bedrooms
  — Three full and one half baths
- A covered Portico greets your entry
- The bay shape of the Dining Room adds expanse
- The Kitchen has an island and a walk-in Pantry
- Access the rear Deck from the open living space
- The Master Suite is located for privacy
- A large Multi-purpose Room is located upstairs
- No materials list is available for this plan

FIRST FLOOR — 1,725 SQ. FT.
SECOND FLOOR — 1,317 SQ. FT.
GARAGE — 435 SQ. FT.

TOTAL LIVING AREA:
3,042 SQ. FT.

FIRST FLOOR

SECOND FLOOR

WIDTH 45'-10"
DEPTH 59'-2"

Character and Charm
PRICE CODE: C

- This plan features:
  — Three bedrooms
  — Two full and one half baths
- Dining Room with direct access to the Kitchen, yet can be made private by the pocket door
- Kitchen made efficient by a cooktop island, an abundance of counter space and a built-in Pantry
- Sun room adjoining Kitchen and the Family Room.
- Fireplace and a fourteen-foot ceiling highlighting the Family Room
- Master Suite with a five-piece Bath and a walk-in closet
- No materials list is available for this plan

FIRST FLOOR — 1,626 SQ. FT.
SECOND FLOOR — 522 SQ. FT.
BONUS — 336 SQ. FT.
GARAGE — 522 SQ. FT.

TOTAL LIVING AREA:
2,148 SQ. FT.

WIDTH 54'-7"
DEPTH 62'-8"

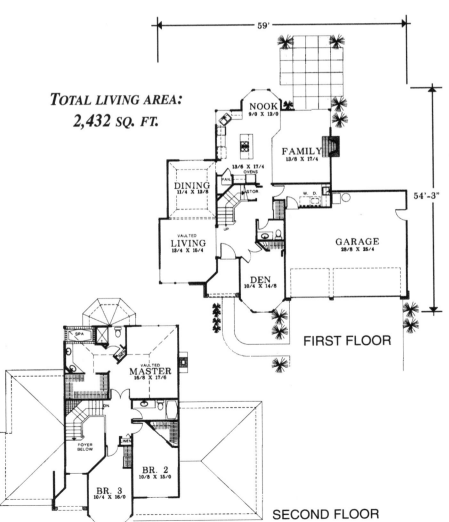

59'

TOTAL LIVING AREA:
2,432 SQ. FT.

NOOK
9/0 X 12/0

FAMILY
13/8 X 17/4

DINING
11/4 X 13/8

13/6 X 17/4
OVENS

PAN.

MSTOR

VAULTED
LIVING
13/4 X 15/4

UP

W. D.

GARAGE
28/8 X 25/4

DEN
10/4 X 14/8

54'-3"

FIRST FLOOR

SPA

VAULTED
MASTER
16/8 X 17/6

FOYER
BELOW

LINEN

BR. 2
10/8 X 15/0

BR. 3
10/4 X 16/0

SECOND FLOOR

Designed for Today's Busy Lifestyle

Price Code: D

■ This plan features:

— Three bedrooms

— Two full and one half baths

■ Open lay-out between the Kitchen, Family Room and Eating Nook giving a feeling of spaciousness

■ A fireplace in both the Family Room and the Living Room

■ An efficient Kitchen that easily accesses the Eating Nook as well as the Formal Dining Room

■ A large triple window provides view of the front yard from the Den

■ A Master Suite with decorative ceiling, large walk-in closet and private Master Bath

■ Two additional bedrooms share a full hall bath

FIRST FLOOR — 1,408 SQ. FT.
SECOND FLOOR — 1,024 SQ. FT.

Vaulted Ceilings Make Every Room Special

PRICE CODE: F

- This plan features:
  - Five bedrooms
  - Five full baths
- An enjoyable view from the island Kitchen which is separated from the Morning Room by only a counter
- Access to the pool from the covered patio or from the Living and Family Rooms
- The Living and Family Rooms with beamed ten-foot ceilings and massive fireplaces
- A Master Suite with a raised tub, built-in dressing tables and a fireplaced Sitting Room with vaulted ceiling

FIRST FLOOR — 4,014 SQ. FT.
SECOND FLOOR — 727 SQ. FT.
GARAGE — 657 SQ. FT.

TOTAL LIVING AREA: 4,741 SQ. FT.

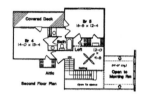

Quaint and Cozy

PRICE CODE: B

- This plan features:
  - Three bedrooms
  - Two full and one half baths
- The Dining Room is defined at its corner by an elegant column
- The Kitchen includes a work island and a peninsula counter/snack bar separating it from the Breakfast Room
- The Breakfast Room has direct access to the rear covered Porch
- An optional basement, crawl space or slab foundation — Please specify when ordering
- No materials list is available for this plan

FIRST FLOOR — 1,334 SQ. FT.
SECOND FLOOR — 437 SQ. FT.
GARAGE — 342 SQ. FT.

TOTAL LIVING AREA 1,771 SQ. FT.

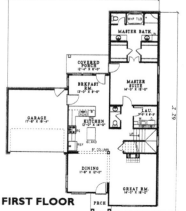

FIRST FLOOR

SECOND FLOOR

To order your Blueprints, call 1-800-235-5700

Classical Style
PRICE CODE: C

■ This plan features:
— Three bedrooms
— Two full baths
■ There are ten-foot ceilings in many of the rooms
■ This home has plenty of Storage Space
■ The Dining Room is open to the Foyer and Living Room
■ A fireplace is set between built in cabinets in the Living Room
■ The Kitchen is well planned and executed
■ No materials list is available for this plan

MAIN FLOOR — 1,890 SQ. FT.
GARAGE — 565 SQ. FT.

TOTAL LIVING AREA: 1,890 SQ. FT.

WIDTH 65–10

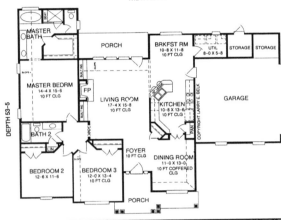

Easy Living Plan
PRICE CODE: D

■ This plan features:
— Three bedrooms
— Two full baths
■ Sunlit Foyer flows easily into the generous Great Room
■ Great Room crowned in a cathedral ceiling and accented by a fireplace
■ Accent columns define the open Kitchen and Breakfast Bay
■ Master Bedroom topped by a tray ceiling and highlighted by a well-appointed Master Bath
■ Two additional Bedrooms, sharing a skylit Bath in the hall, create the children's wing

FIRST FLOOR—1,864 SQ. FT.
BONUS ROOM—319 SQ. FT.
GARAGE—503 SQ. FT.

TOTAL LIVING AREA: 1,864 SQ. FT.

©1996 Donald A. Gardner Architects, Inc.

© 1996 Donald A Gardner Architects, Inc.

Luxury and Style
PRICE CODE: E

■ This plan features:
— Three bedrooms
— Two full and one half baths
■ A two story Foyer setting the tone for grandeur
■ A two story ceiling and two-way fireplace in the formal Living Room and the Family Room
■ A terrific family living area created by the Family Room, Breakfast Nook and Kitchen designed in an open layout
■ A first floor Master Suite crowned by a tray ceiling and enhanced by a lavish Bath and walk-in closet
■ Two additional Bedrooms, one with a sloped ceiling and built-in desk, on the second floor
■ No materials list is available for this plan

FIRST FLOOR — 1,979 SQ. FT.
SECOND FLOOR — 948 SQ. FT.

**TOTAL LIVING AREA:
2,927 SQ. FT.**

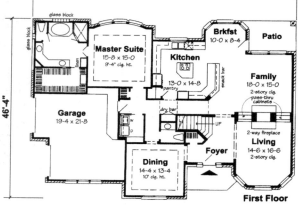

First Floor

Second Floor

©1997 Donald A. Gardner Architects, Inc.

Dormer Delight
PRICE CODE: D

■ This plan features:
— Three bedroom
— Two full baths
■ Tray ceilings can be found in the Dining Room and the Master Suite
■ Skylights brighten the Master Bath and the Screened Porch
■ Columns mark the openings of the Dining Room
■ The Great Room has a voluminous cathedral ceiling
■ A Bonus Room is located over the Garage
■ No materials list is available for this plan

MAIN FLOOR — 1,652 SQ. FT.
BONUS — 367 SQ. FT.
GARAGE — 507 SQ. FT.

**TOTAL LIVING AREA:
1,652 SQ. FT.**

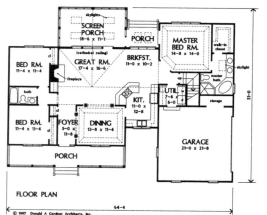

FLOOR PLAN

© 1997 Donald A. Gardner Architects, Inc.

To order your Blueprints, call 1-800-235-5700

© 1995 Donald A. Gardner Architects, Inc.

B. NATHAN

Beautiful From Front to Back

Price Code: D

■ This plan features:

— Three bedrooms

— Two full baths

■ Porches front and back, gables and dormers providing special charm

■ Central Great Room with a cathedral ceiling, fireplace, and a clerestory window which bringing natural light

■ Columns dividing the open Great Room from the Kitchen and the Breakfast Bay

■ A tray ceiling and columns dressing up the formal Dining Room

■ Skylit Master Bath with shower, whirlpool tub, dual vanity and spacious walk-in closet

MAIN FLOOR — 1,632 SQ. FT.
GARAGE & STORAGE — 561 SQ. FT.

TOTAL LIVING AREA:
1,632 SQ. FT.

Floor Plan

PORCH

MASTER BED RM.
13-4 x 16-4

skylight

master bath

walk-in closet

lin.

storage

BRKFST.
10-4 x 8-8

cl

w
d

UTIL.

BED RM.
11-4 x 11-0

(cathedral ceiling)

GREAT RM.
15-4 x 18-6

fireplace

KIT.
11-4 x 12-10

GARAGE
21-0 x 21-8

cl

lin.

bath

walk-in closet

55-2

BED RM./ STUDY
11-0 x 11-8

cl

FOYER
6-0 x 8-4

DINING
11-0 x 11-8

storage

(optional door location)

PORCH

62-4

FLOOR PLAN

© 1995 Donald A Gardner Architects, Inc.

Covered Porch
PRICE CODE: B

- This plan features:
  — Three bedrooms
  — Two full baths
- A welcoming covered Porch and dormer windows provide an old-fashioned appeal to this home
- The Great Room includes a fireplace to gather around on colder evenings
- The Master Bedroom is located on the first floor with two walk-in closets and a whirlpool tub
- The Kitchen is efficiently arranged and includes a Pantry for easy storage
- The Breakfast Room has access to the rear Grilling Porch
- An optional basement, slab or crawl space foundation — please specify when ordering
- No materials list is available for this plan

FIRST FLOOR — 980 SQ. FT.
SECOND FLOOR — 561 SQ. FT.
GARAGE — 342 SQ. FT.

TOTAL LIVING AREA:
1,541 SQ. FT.

FIRST FLOOR

WIDTH 47'-0"
DEPTH 55'-2"

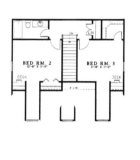

© 1996 Donald A. Gardner, Inc.

Stately Traditional
PRICE CODE: E

- This plan features:
  — Three bedrooms
  — Two full and one half baths
- An amiable balance of formal and informal space provides flexibility
- Special ceiling treatments cap the Living Room, Study, Family Room, and Master Bedroom for added spaciousness
- The second floor Loft has a curved railing and overlooks the Foyer and the Family Room
- No materials list is available for this plan

FIRST FLOOR — 1,701 SQ. FT.
SECOND FLOOR — 534 SQ. FT.
BONUS ROOM — 274 SQ. FT.
GARAGE — 574 SQ. FT.

TOTAL LIVING AREA:
2,235 SQ. FT.

WIDTH 65'-11"
DEPTH 43'-5"

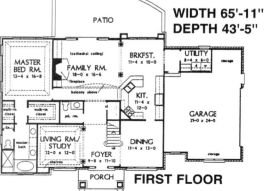

FIRST FLOOR

SECOND FLOOR

© Donald A. Gardner Architects, Inc.

To order your Blueprints, call 1-800-235-5700

Striking Traditional
PRICE CODE: D

©1998 Donald A. Gardner, Inc.

This plan features:
- Three bedrooms
- Two full baths

A cathedral ceiling expands the Great Room, Dining Room, and Kitchen; all are open to one another for a casual atmosphere

The efficient, U-shaped Kitchen positions sink, stove and refrigerator in perfect proximity

The front Bedroom and the Master Bedroom have cathedral ceilings for added spaciousness

Both the Great Room and the Master Bedroom allow access to an optional rear deck or patio

FIRST FLOOR — 1,658 SQ. FT.
GARAGE & STORAGE — 522 SQ. FT.
BONUS — 359 SQ. FT.

TOTAL LIVING AREA:
1,658 SQ. FT.

PLAN NO. 98062

Easy Living
PRICE CODE: A

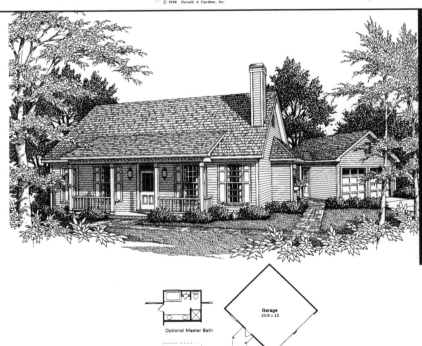

This plan features:
- Three bedrooms
- Two full baths

- A covered front Porch shelters the entry to this home
- The Family Room is enlarged by a vaulted ceiling and also has a fireplace
- The Kitchen is L-shaped and includes a center island
- The Dining Room is open to the Kitchen for maximum convenience
- A covered walkway leads to the two-car Garage
- The Master Bedroom has a private Bath, which has two building options
- Both of the secondary Bedrooms have walk-in closets
- No materials list is available for this plan

MAIN FLOOR — 1,474 SQ. FT.
GARAGE — 454 SQ. FT.

TOTAL LIVING AREA:
1,474 SQ. FT.

MAIN FLOOR

PLAN NO. 93447

To order your Blueprints, call 1-800-235-5700

© 1996 Donald A. Gardner Architects, Inc.

Polished & Poised
PRICE CODE: E

- This plan features:
  — Three bedrooms
  — Two full and one half baths
- Hip roof, gables and brick accents add poise and polish to this Traditional home
- Curved transom window and sidelights illuminate the gracious Foyer
- A curved balcony overlooks the Great Room which has a cathedral ceiling, fireplace and a wall of windows overlooking the Patio
- Hub Kitchen easily serves the Dining Room, Breakfast area and the Patio beyond
- Master Bedroom wing is enhanced by a tray ceiling, walk-in closet and a deluxe Bath

FIRST FLOOR — 1,577 SQ. FT.
SECOND FLOOR — 613 SQ. FT.
BONUS ROOM — 390 SQ. FT.
GARAGE & STORAGE — 634 SQ. FT

TOTAL LIVING AREA:
2,190 SQ. FT.

FIRST FLOOR PLAN

SECOND FLOOR PLAN

© 1996 Donald A Gardner Architects, Inc.

Classic Home
PRICE CODE: F

- This plan features:
  — Four bedrooms
  — Three full and one half baths
- Space and light connect the Entry, Gallery, Dining Room, and Living Room
- A Butler's Pantry connects the Kitchen to the Dining Room
- The Master Suite encompasses a whole wing on the first floor
- Up the curved staircase find three Bedrooms all with walk in closets
- Also upstairs is a Game Room with built-in cabinets
- A three car Garage completes this home
- An optional basement or a slab foundation — please specify when ordering
- No materials list is available for this plan

FIRST FLOOR — 2,688 SQ. FT.
SECOND FLOOR — 1,540 SQ. FT.
BASEMENT — 2,688 SQ. FT.
GARAGE — 635 SQ. FT.

TOTAL LIVING AREA:
4,228 SQ. FT.

Optional Basement Access

WIDTH 84'-3"
DEPTH 80'-1"

Second floor

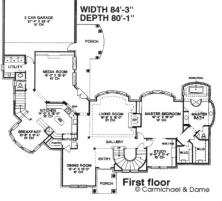

First floor

© Carmichael & Dame

To order your Blueprints, call 1-800-235-5700

Sprawling Four Bedroom
PRICE CODE: E

PLAN NO. 98060

■ This plan features:
– Four bedrooms
– Three full baths
  A trio of dormers and a gracious front Porch adorn the facade of this home
  The spacious Great Room sports a cathedral ceiling a fireplace and built-in shelves
■ A split Bedroom layout provides privacy for homeowners
  A generous Master Suite with a tray ceiling, private Bath with a corner tub and a walk-in closet pamper the owner
  No material list is available for this plan

MAIN FLOOR — 2,487 SQ. FT.
GARAGE & STORAGE — 606 SQ. FT.

TOTAL LIVING AREA:
2,487 SQ. FT.

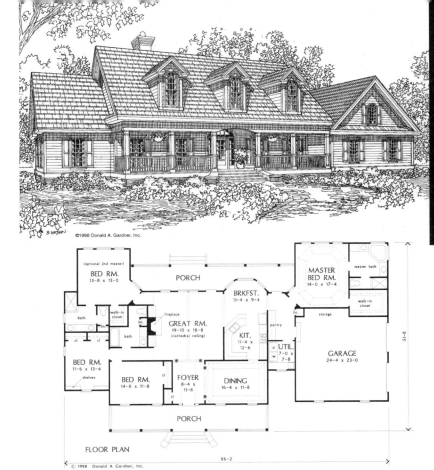

©1998 Donald A. Gardner, Inc.

FLOOR PLAN

Kitchen Island
PRICE CODE: B

PLAN NO. 96925

■ This plan features:
– Three bedrooms
– Two full   and one half baths
■ This private Master Suite is entered through double doors, and boasts an oversized walk-in closet
■ The Dining Room conversation easily flows to the open Great-Room in this layout
■ A huge Bonus Room is included with this plan.
■ An optional slab or a crawl space foundation — please specify when ordering
■ No materials list is available for this plan

FIRST FLOOR — 1,251 SQ. FT.
SECOND FLOOR — 505 SQ. FT.
BONUS — 447 SQ. FT.
GARAGE — 463 SQ. FT.
DECK — 120 SQ. FT.

TOTAL LIVING AREA:
1,756 SQ. FT.

FIRST FLOOR

WIDTH 50'-0"
DEPTH 39'-0"

SECOND FLOOR

To order your Blueprints, call 1-800-235-5700

Timeless Appeal
PRICE CODE: A

- This plan features:
  — Three bedrooms
  — Two full baths
- Ten-foot ceilings giving the living room an open feel
- A cozy corner fireplace and access to the rear yard highlight the Living Room
- The Dining Area is enhanced by a sunny bay window and is open to the Kitchen
- Bedrooms are conveniently grouped and include roomy closets
- The Master Bedroom features a private Bath
- The Garage is located in the rear, leaving the curb appe intact
- An optional crawl space or slab foundation — please specify when ordering
- No materials list is available for this plan

MAIN FLOOR — 1,170 SQ. FT.
GARAGE — 478 SQ. FT.

TOTAL LIVING AREA:
1,170 SQ. FT.

Width 51'-10"
Depth 53'-6"

GARAGE

STORAGE

MSTR BDRM
11-0 x 13-8
10 FT CLG

LIVING
13-0 x 17-8
10 FT CLG

DINING
11-0 x
9-2

MSTR BATH

BATH 2

STOR

FOYER

KITCH
11-6 x
8-0

BDRM 2
10-4 x 10-2

BDRM 3
10-10 x 11-6

COVERED PORCH

MAIN FLOOR

Innovative Floor Plan
PRICE CODE: E

- This plan features:
  — Three bedrooms
  — Two full and one half baths
- This plan is designed so that the main living areas can l quickly closed off
- The Family Room to the rear makes a great relaxed family hangout
- The Master Suite features a private Bath with a walk-in closet, separate shower and garden tub and an enclosed toilet area
- A Bonus Room stands ready for future expansion

FIRST FLOOR — 1,816 SQ. FT.
SECOND FLOOR — 650 SQ. FT.
BONUS ROOM — 447 SQ. FT.

TOTAL LIVING AREA:
2,466 SQ. FT.

living room below

plant shelf

linen below

bath

down

railing

BED RM.
11-0 x 12-8

BED RM.
12-0 x 13-0
(vaulted ceiling)

walk-in closet

sto.

sto.

walk-in closet

foyer below

attic storage

down

SECOND FLOOR PLAN

BONUS RM.
13-4 x 22-0

attic storage

PORCH

FAMILY RM.
15-0 x 15-10
(cathedral ceiling)

MASTER BED RM.
15-4 x 14-0

LIVING RM.
15-0 x 15-8
(vaulted ceiling)

BRKFST.
13-0 x 12-0

fireplace

walk-in closet

storage

KIT.
11-4 x 13-0

master bath
(cathedral ceiling)

FOYER
6-0 x
11-0
(two story)

DINING
12-0 x 13-0

pd. rm.

pan.

UTILITY
11-0 x 6-0

shelves

workshop

GARAGE
24-8 x 22-0

PORCH

storage

FIRST FLOOR PLAN

61-8

To order your Blueprints, call 1-800-235-5700

Brick Home with Four Bedrooms

PRICE CODE: C

■ This plan features:
— Four bedrooms
— Two full and one half baths
■ Four roomy Bedrooms, including the Master Bedroom
■ A centrally located Family Room including a fireplace, wetbar, and access to the Patio
■ A large Dining Room at the front of the home for entertaining
■ An interesting Kitchen and Nook with an adjoining Utility Room

MAIN FLOOR — 2,070 SQ. FT.
GARAGE — 474 SQ. FT.

TOTAL LIVING AREA: 2,070 SQ. FT.

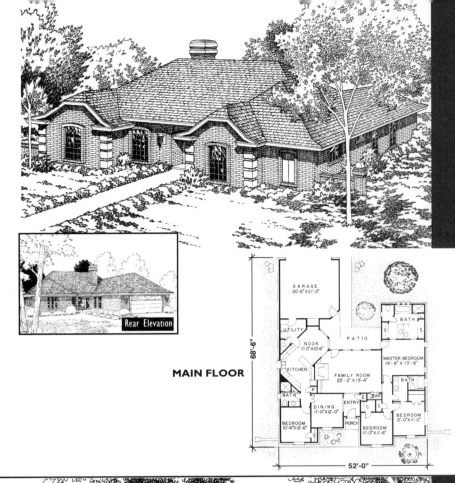

Rear Elevation

MAIN FLOOR

Easy One Floor Living

PRICE CODE: B

■ This plan features:
—Three bedrooms
—Two full baths
■ A spacious Family Room topped by a vaulted ceiling and highlighted by a large fireplace and a French door to the rear yard
■ A serving bar open to the Family Room and the Dining Room, a Pantry and a peninsula counter adding more efficiency to the Kitchen
■ A crowning tray ceiling over the Master Bedroom and a vaulted ceiling over the Master Bath
■ A vaulted ceiling over the cozy Sitting Room in the Master Suite
■ Two additional Bedrooms, roomy in size sharing the full Bath in the hall
■ An optional basement, slab, or crawl space foundation — please specify when ordering

MAIN FLOOR — 1,671 SQ. FT.
BASEMENT — 1,685 SQ. FT.
GARAGE — 400 SQ. FT.

TOTAL LIVING AREA: 1,671 SQ. FT.

WIDTH 50'-0"
DEPTH 51'-0"

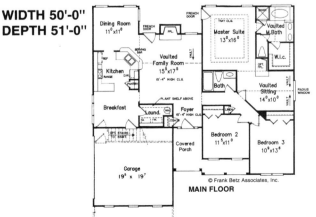

© Frank Betz Associates, Inc.

MAIN FLOOR

Comfortable Country Ease
PRICE CODE: C

■ This plan features:
— Three or four bedrooms
— Two full and two half baths
■ A sprawling front porch giving way to a traditional Foyer area with a half bath and a graceful staircase
■ A tray ceiling adding elegance to the Dining Room which directly accesses the Kitchen
■ A large country Kitchen with a center work island including plenty of storage and work space
■ A tray ceiling accenting the Family Room, also highlighted by a fireplace
■ A vaulted ceiling and a private bath enhancing the Master Suite
■ Two additional bedrooms served by a full hall Bath
■ An optional fourth Bedroom

FIRST FLOOR — 1,104 SQ. FT.
SECOND FLOOR — 960 SQ. FT.

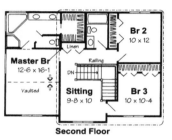

TOTAL LIVING AREA:
2,064 SQ. FT.

ZIP QUOTE
HOME COST CALCULATOR
see order pages for details

Very Versatile
PRICE CODE: A

■ This plan features:
— Three bedrooms
— Two full baths
■ The Great Room has a boxed ceiling and a gas fireplace
■ An efficient U-shaped design in the Kitchen allows all the appliances to be convenient to each other
■ The Breakfast Room has direct access to the Grilling Porch, as does the Master Suite
■ The Master Suite includes a ten foot boxed ceiling and a luxurious Master Bath
■ The study could easily be converted into a third Bedroom
■ An optional slab or crawl space foundation — please specify when ordering
■ No materials list is available for this plan

FIRST FLOOR — 1,447 SQ. FT.
GARAGE — 491 SQ. FT.

TOTAL LIVING AREA
1,447 SQ. FT.

FIRST FLOOR

To order your Blueprints, call 1-800-235-5700

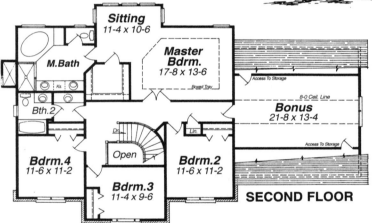

Sitting
11-4 x 10-6

Master Bdrm.
17-8 x 13-6

Boxed Tray

M.Bath

Kit.

Access To Storage

Bth.2

8-0 Ceil. Line

Bonus
21-8 x 13-4

Dr.

Lin.

Bdrm.4
11-6 x 11-2

Open

Bdrm.2
11-6 x 11-2

Access To Storage

Bdrm.3
11-4 x 9-6

SECOND FLOOR

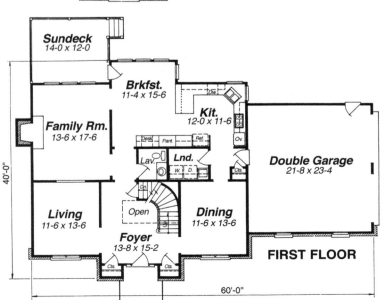

Sundeck
14-0 x 12-0

Brkfst.
11-4 x 15-6

Dw.

Kit.
12-0 x 11-6

Family Rm.
13-6 x 17-6

Desk Pant. Ref.

Ov.

40'-0"

Lav.

Lnd.

W. D.

Cts.

Double Garage
21-8 x 23-4

Dn.

Living
11-6 x 13-6

Open

Dining
11-6 x 13-6

Foyer
13-8 x 15-2

FIRST FLOOR

Cts.   Cts.

60'-0"

Elegant Master Suite

Price Code: E

- ■ This plan features:
- — Four bedrooms
- — Two full and one half baths
- ■ Comfortable Family Room with a fireplace
- ■ Efficient Kitchen with built-in Pantry and serving counter
- ■ Master Suite with decorative ceiling, Sitting Room and a plush Bath
- ■ An optional basement, slab, or crawl space foundation — please specify when ordering

FIRST FLOOR — 1,307 SQ. FT.
SECOND FLOOR — 1,333 SQ. FT.
BONUS — 308 SQ. FT.
BASEMENT — 1,307 SQ. FT.
GARAGE — 528 SQ. FT.

TOTAL LIVING AREA:
2,640 SQ. FT.

ZIP QUOTE
HOME COST CALCULATOR
see order pages for details

97

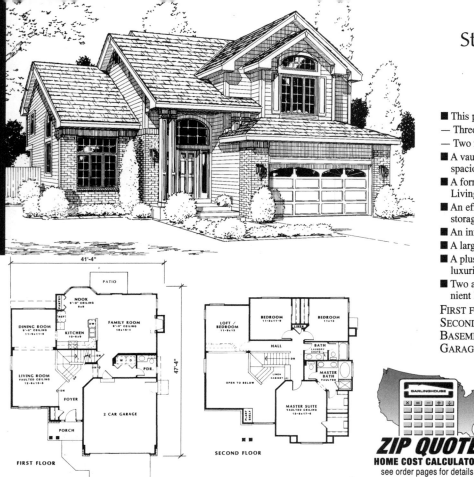

Stately Entrance Adds to Home's Exterior
PRICE CODE: D

■ This plan features:
— Three or four bedrooms
— Two full and one half baths
■ A vaulted ceiling in the Living Room adding to its spaciousness
■ A formal Dining Room with easy access to both the Living Room and the Kitchen
■ An efficient Kitchen with double sinks, and ample storage and counter space
■ An informal Eating Nook with a built-in Pantry
■ A large Family Room with a fireplace
■ A plush Master Suite with a vaulted ceiling and luxurious Master Bath plus two walk-in closets
■ Two additional Bedrooms share a full Bath with a convenient laundry chute

FIRST FLOOR — 1,115 SQ. FT.
SECOND FLOOR — 1,129 SQ. FT.
BASEMENT — 1,096 SQ. FT.
GARAGE — 415 SQ. FT.

ZIP QUOTE
HOME COST CALCULATOR
see order pages for details

TOTAL LIVING AREA:
2,244 SQ. FT.

PLAN NO. 98083

Craftsman Character
PRICE CODE: D

■ This plan features:
— Three bedrooms
— Two full baths
■ The Great Room is the heart of this home and includes a cathedral ceiling, a fireplace, and convenient built-ins
■ A trio of skylights let the sun shine into the Great Room
■ The Master Suite has Deck access and a cathedral ceiling
■ An oversized Garage allows for ample storage
■ A large Bonus Room above the Garage stands ready for future expansion

FIRST FLOOR — 1,511 SQ. FT.
GARAGE — 655 SQ. FT.
BONUS — 549 SQ. FT.

TOTAL LIVING AREA:
1,511 SQ. FT.

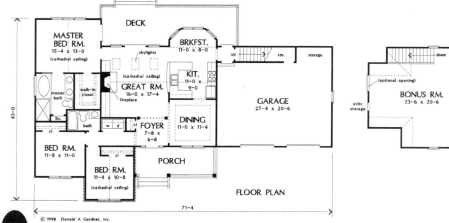

© 1998 Donald A. Gardner, Inc.

To order your Blueprints, call 1-800-235-5700

Charming Brick Home

PRICE CODE: C

■ This plan features:

— Three bedrooms

— Two full baths

■ A covered entrance leading into a spacious Living Room with a fireplace and an airy Dining Room with access to the Patio

■ An island Kitchen, open to the Dining Room, offering ample storage and easy access to the Laundry area and the Garage

■ A Master Bedroom with a walk-in closet, access to the Patio and a plush Bath offering a window tub, a step-in shower and a double vanity

■ Two additional Bedrooms, with decorative windows, sharing a full hall Bath

■ No materials list is available for this plan

MAIN FLOOR — 1,868 SQ. FT.
BASEMENT — 1,868 SQ. FT.

TOTAL LIVING AREA:
1,868 SQ. FT.

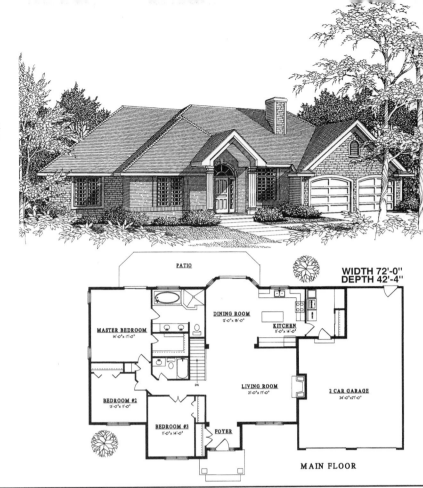

WIDTH 72'-0"
DEPTH 42'-4"

MAIN FLOOR

Eye-Catching Glass Turrets

PRICE CODE: D

■ This plan features:

— Three bedrooms

— Three full baths

■ Two-story Foyer with a curved staircase, opens to a unique Living Room with an alcove of windows and inviting fireplace

■ Alcove of glass and a vaulted ceiling in the open Dining Area

■ Kitchen with built-in Pantry and desk, cooktop island/snackbar and a Nook with double door

■ Comfortable Family Room highlighted by another fireplace and wonderful outdoor views

■ Vaulted Master Suite offers a plush Dressing Area with walk-in closet and spa tub

■ Two additional Bedrooms, one with a glass alcove, share a double vanity Bath

■ Bonus Room

FIRST FLOOR — 1,592 SQ. FT.
SECOND FLOOR — 958 SQ. FT.
BONUS ROOM — 194 SQ. FT.
GARAGE — 956 SQ. FT.

TOTAL LIVING AREA:
2,550 SQ. FT.

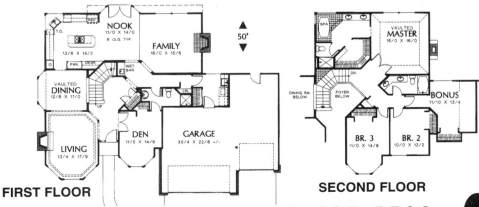

FIRST FLOOR

SECOND FLOOR

To order your Blueprints, call 1-800-235-5700

MAIN AREA

Hip Roof Ranch
PRICE CODE: B

- This plan features:
  — Three bedrooms
  — Two full baths
- Cozy front Porch leads into Entry with vaulted ceiling and sidelights
- Open Living Room enhanced by a cathedral ceiling, a wall of windows and corner fireplace
- Large and efficient Kitchen with an extended counter and a bright Dining Area with access to a screen Porch
- Convenient Utility Area with access to Garage and Storage Area
- Spacious Master Bedroom with a walk-in closet and private Bath
- Two additional Bedrooms with ample closets, share a full Bath

MAIN AREA — 1,540 SQ. FT.
BASEMENT — 1,540 SQ. FT.

TOTAL LIVING AREA:
1,540 SQ. FT.

ZIP QUOTE
HOME COST CALCULATOR
see order pages for details

© Frank Betz Associates

Small, Yet Lavishly Appointed
PRICE CODE: C

- This plan features:
  — Three bedrooms
  — Two full and one half baths
- The Dining Room, Living Room, Foyer and Master Bath all topped by high ceilings
- Master Bedroom includes a decorative tray ceiling and a walk-in closet
- Kitchen open to the Breakfast Room enhanced by a serving bar and a Pantry
- Living Room with a large fireplace and a French door to the rear yard
- Master Suite located on opposite side from secondary Bedrooms, allowing for privacy
- An optional basement or crawl space foundation — please specify when ordering

MAIN FLOOR — 1,845 SQ. FT.
BONUS — 409 SQ. FT.
BASEMENT — 1,845 SQ. FT.
GARAGE — 529 SQ. FT.

TOTAL LIVING AREA:
1,845 SQ. FT.

To order your Blueprints, call 1-800-235-5700

Delightful

PRICE CODE: C

- This plan features:
  — Three bedrooms
  — Three full baths
- A bonus second floor has a Game Room and a full Bath
- The secondary Bedrooms each have a vanity, but share the rest of the Bath
- The Master Suite has a large walk-in closet and a Bath with a clawfoot tub
- The Living Room features a fireplace with a built-in media center to its left
- Porches and Decking wrap this home for outdoor options
- Another fireplace can be found in the Hearth/Dining Room
- An optional basement, a slab, or a crawl space foundation — please specify when ordering
- No materials list is available for this plan

MAIN LEVEL — 1,921 SQ. FT.
BONUS — 812 SQ. FT.
GARAGE — 505 SQ. FT.

TOTAL LIVING AREA:
1,921 SQ. FT.

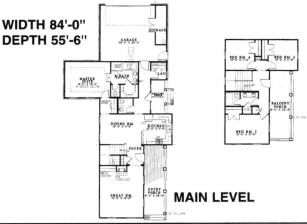

WIDTH 84'-0"
DEPTH 55'-6"

MAIN LEVEL

Front & Rear Porches

PRICE CODE: C

- This plan features:
  — Three bedrooms
  — Two full baths
- The Master Bedroom is located in the rear of this plan for optimum privacy
- The Master Bedroom has a cathedral ceiling and access to the rear Porch
- A large walk-in closet spans the entire width of the room
- The Dining Room features a decorative tray ceiling and lovely arches supported by columns
- No materials list is available for this plan

MAIN FLOOR — 1,469 SQ. FT.
GARAGE — 481 SQ. FT.
BONUS — 383 SQ. FT.

TOTAL LIVING AREA:
1,469 SQ. FT.

©1999 Donald A. Gardner, Inc.

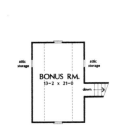

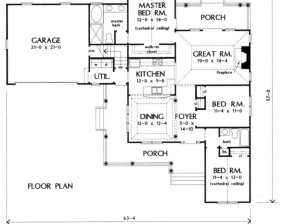

FLOOR PLAN

© 1999 Donald A. Gardner, Inc. All rights reserved

Photography Supplied by The Meredith Corporation

Mansion Mystique

Price Code: F

- This plan features:
  — Four bedrooms
  — Four full and one half baths
- A beautiful exterior includes multiple rooflines and a covered porch
- The Entry includes a curved staircase
- Multi purpose rooms include a Guest Room/Study and an upstairs Office
- Both the Family Room and the Great Room have fireplaces
- The L-shaped Kitchen opens to the Breakfast Nook
- Upstairs find multiple Bedrooms, Baths, and a bonus space

MAIN LEVEL — 2,727 SQ. FT.
UPPER LEVEL — 1,168 SQ. FT.
BONUS — 213 SQ. FT.
BASEMENT — 2,250 SQ. FT.
GARAGE — 984 SQ. FT.

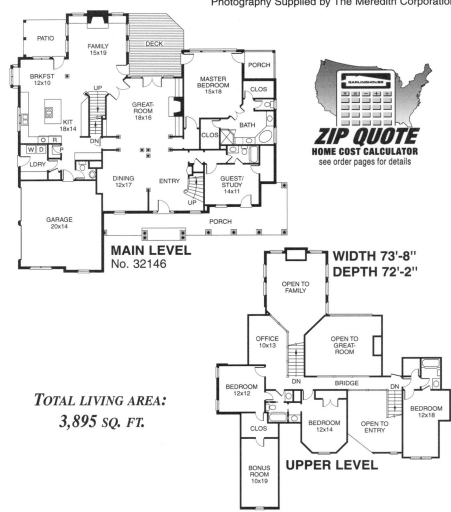

TOTAL LIVING AREA:
3,895 SQ. FT.

WIDTH 73'-8"
DEPTH 72'-2"

To order your Blueprints, call 1-800-235-5700

Functional Contemporary

PRICE CODE: D

- This plan features:
— Three bedrooms
— Two full and one half baths
- Exciting contemporary exterior design for an abundance of curb appeal
- Great Room topped by a vaulted ceiling accessing the Sun Room and Deck through sliding glass doors
- U-shaped Kitchen with a garden window, Breakfast Bar, and ample cabinet space
- Master Suite privately located on the first floor with cathedral ceiling, fireplace and Sun Room access

FIRST FLOOR — 1,338 SQ. FT.
SECOND FLOOR — 545 SQ. FT.
GARAGE & STORAGE — 454 SQ. FT.

TOTAL LIVING AREA:
1,883 SQ. FT.

©1984 Donald A. Gardner Architects, Inc.

FIRST FLOOR PLAN

SECOND FLOOR PLAN

© Donald A. Gardner Architects, Inc.

Perfect Hillside Haven

PRICE CODE: F

- This plan features:
— Four bedrooms
— Three full baths
- The lower floor of this plan provides for a walk-out Patio
- There is a lower floor Rec Room where the ground acts as a natural air conditioner, and guests can enjoy the Patio
- The first floor offers a private Master Bedroom with a decorative tray ceiling

FIRST FLOOR — 2,105 SQ. FT.
LOWER FLOOR — 798 SQ. FT.
GARAGE — 596 SQ. FT.
BONUS — 453 SQ. FT.

TOTAL LIVING AREA:
2,903 SQ. FT.

© Donald A. Gardner Architects, Inc.

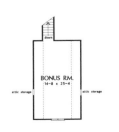

FIRST FLOOR PLAN

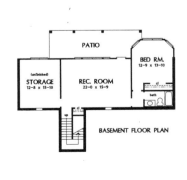

BASEMENT FLOOR PLAN

© 1999 Donald A. Gardner, Inc. All rights reserved

A Must See Design

Price Code: D

■ This plan features:
— Three bedrooms
— Two full baths

■ Attractive, arched entrance leads into Great Room with a wall of windows and expansive cathedral ceiling above a cozy fireplace

■ Convenient Kitchen easily accesses Nook and Dining areas, Laundry and Garage

■ Corner Master Bedroom enhanced by two large, walk-in closets, cathedral ceiling and private, double vanity Bath

■ Two secondary Bedrooms with large closets share a double vanity Bath

■ No materials list is available for this plan

MAIN FLOOR — 2,229 SQ. FT.
BASEMENT — 2,229 SQ. FT.
GARAGE — 551 SQ. FT.

TOTAL LIVING AREA:
2,229 SQ. FT.

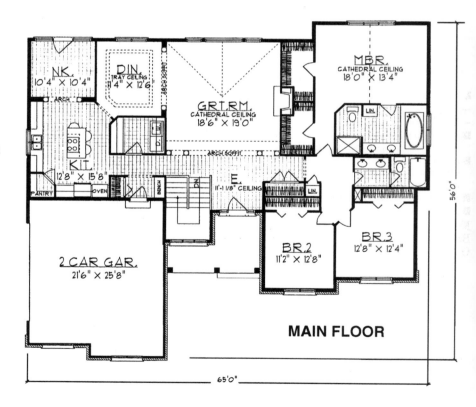

MAIN FLOOR

To order your Blueprints, call 1-800-235-5700

Warmth and Charm

PRICE CODE: E

This plan features:
- Four bedrooms
- Three full and one half baths

A space-enhancing cathedral ceiling tops the Great Room where convenient built-ins, positioned on either side of the fireplace

The Master Suite has a built-in entertainment center as well as dual walk-in closets and a private Bath

The secondary Bedrooms all have easy access to a full Bath, one having a private Bath

■ A Bonus Room stands ready for future expansion

FIRST FLOOR — 1,575 SQ. FT.
SECOND FLOOR — 788 SQ. FT.
BONUS — 251 SQ. FT.
GARAGE & STORAGE — 524 SQ. FT.

TOTAL LIVING AREA: 2,363 SQ. FT.

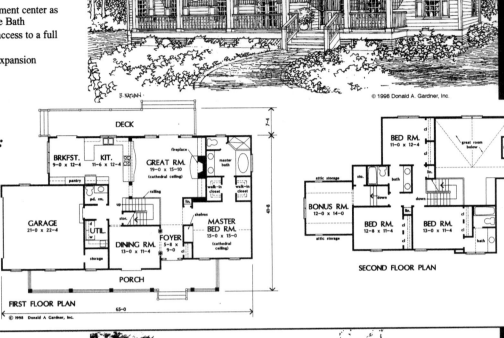

© 1998 Donald A. Gardner, Inc.

Large Living in a Small Space

PRICE CODE: A

■ This plan features:
- Three bedrooms
- Two full baths

■ A sheltered entrance leads into an open Living Room with a corner fireplace and a wall of windows

■ A well-equipped Kitchen features a peninsula counter with a Nook, a Laundry and clothes closet, and a built-in Pantry

■ A Master Bedroom with a private Bath

■ Two additional Bedrooms that share full hall Bath

MAIN FLOOR — 993 SQ. FT.
BASEMENT — 987 SQ. FT.
GARAGE — 390 SQ. FT.

TOTAL LIVING AREA: 993 SQ. FT.

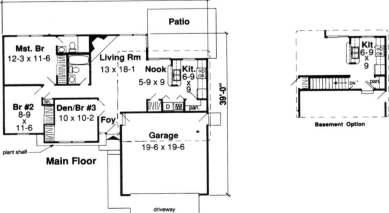

To order your Blueprints, call 1-800-235-5700

PLAN NO. 93165

MAIN FLOOR PLAN

48'-0"

Brick Details Add Class
PRICE CODE: A

■ This plan features:
— Three bedrooms
— Two full baths
■ Keystone entrance leads into easy care, tile Entry with plant ledge and convenient closet
■ Expansive Great Room with cathedral ceiling over triple window and a corner gas fireplace
■ Hub Kitchen accented by arches and columns serving Great Room and Dining Area, near Laundry Area and Garage
■ Adjoining Dining Area with large windows, access to rear yard and screen Porch
■ Private Master Suite with a walk-in closet and plush Bath with corner whirlpool tub
■ Two additional Bedrooms share a full Bath
■ No materials list is available for this plan
■ This plan is not to be built within a 20 mile radius of Iowa City, IA

MAIN FLOOR — 1,472 SQ. FT.
BASEMENT — 1,472 SQ. FT.
GARAGE — 424 SQ. FT.

TOTAL LIVING AREA:
1,472 SQ. FT.

PLAN NO. 83000

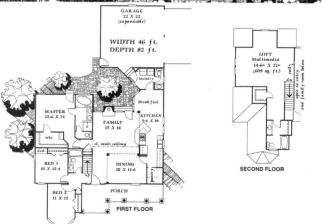

WIDTH 46 ft.
DEPTH 82 ft.

FIRST FLOOR

SECOND FLOOR

Cottage Characteristics
PRICE CODE: D

■ This plan features:
— Three bedrooms
— Two full and one half baths
■ The Garage is located in the rear for aethestic purposes
■ The Bedrooms are all located in one wing of the home
■ Columns separate the space in the active areas of the home
■ A large walk-in Pantry complements the galley Kitchen
■ A fireplace warms the Family Room
■ Upstairs find a loft with a full Bath
■ No materials list is available for this plan

FIRST FLOOR — 1,854 SQ. FT.
SECOND FLOOR — 609 SQ. FT.
GARAGE — 484 SQ. FT.

TOTAL LIVING AREA:
2,463 SQ. FT.

To order your Blueprints, call 1-800-235-5700

Simple Foot Print

PRICE CODE: D

This plan features:
- Three bedrooms
- Two full baths

The dimensions of this home gear it toward a narrow lot

The wrapping porch gives a Country appeal to the elevation

The Great Room is crowned in a cathedral ceiling and accented by a fireplace

A rear Deck extends living space to the outdoors

FIRST FLOOR — 1,099 SQ. FT.

SECOND FLOOR — 601 SQ. FT.

PORCH — 347 SQ. FT.

TOTAL LIVING AREA:
1,700 SQ. FT.

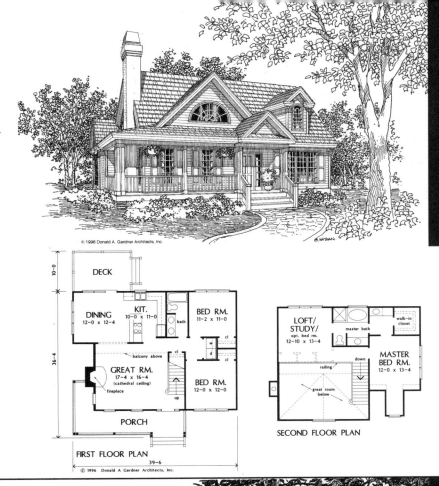

© 1996 Donald A. Gardner Architects, Inc.

FIRST FLOOR PLAN

- DECK
- DINING 12-0 x 12-4
- KIT. 10-0 x 11-0
- bath
- BED RM. 11-2 x 11-0
- balcony above
- GREAT RM. 17-4 x 16-4 (cathedral ceiling) fireplace
- BED RM. 12-0 x 12-0
- PORCH
- 10-0
- 36-4
- 39-6

© 1996 Donald A Gardner Architects, Inc.

SECOND FLOOR PLAN

- LOFT/ STUDY/ opt. bed rm. 12-10 x 13-4
- master bath
- walk-in closet
- MASTER BED RM. 12-0 x 13-4
- great room below
- railing

Stately Colonial Home

PRICE CODE: E

This plan features:
- Four bedrooms
- Three full and one half baths

Stately columns and arched windows project luxury and quality that is evident throughout this home

The entry is highlighted by a palladian window, a plant shelf and an angled staircase

The formal Living and Dining Rooms located off the Entry for ease in entertaining

The comfortable Great Room has an inviting fireplace and opens to Kitchen/Breakfast area and the Patio

The Master Bedroom wing offers Patio access, a luxurious Bath and a walk-in closet

No materials list is available for this plan

FIRST FLOOR — 1,848 SQ. FT.

SECOND FLOOR — 1,111 SQ. FT.

GARAGE & SHOP — 722 SQ. FT.

TOTAL LIVING AREA:
2,959 SQ. FT.

ZIP QUOTE
HOME COST CALCULATOR
see order pages for details

WIDTH 73'-4"
DEPTH 44'-0"

SECOND FLOOR

- BDRM.#2 13X11
- BDRM.#3 13X12
- BALCONY
- STAIRS DOWN
- ENTRY BELOW
- LOFT AREA 13X14
- BDRM.#4 13X12
- PLANT LEDGE
- PORCH BELOW

FIRST FLOOR

- PATIO AREA
- COVERED AREA
- PATIO
- BREAKFAST 13X12
- GREAT ROOM 19X16
- MSTR. BDRM. 18X14
- THREE CAR TANDEM GARAGE 22X40
- KITCHEN 13X13
- UTLY
- PWDR
- MSTR. BATH
- WALK-IN CLOSET
- HALL
- SHOP AREA
- FORMAL DINING 13X13
- ENT
- STAIRS
- FORMAL LIVING 13X13
- PORCH

© E. NATHAN

To order your Blueprints, call 1-800-235-5700

107

PLAN NO. 98088

PLAN NO. 98534

© Frank Betz Associates, Inc.

Split Bedroom Plan
PRICE CODE: C

- This plan features:
  — Three bedrooms
  — Two full baths
- Dining Room is crowned by a tray ceiling
- Living Room/Den privatized by double doors at its entrance, and is enhanced by a bay window
- The Kitchen includes a walk-in pantry and a corner double sink
- The vaulted Breakfast Room flows naturally from the Kitchen
- The Master Suite is topped by a tray ceiling, and contains a compartmental bath plus two walk-in closets
- Two roomy additional Bedrooms share a full Bath in the hall
- An optional basement or crawl space foundation — please specify when ordering

MAIN FLOOR — 2,051 SQ. FT.
BASEMENT — 2,051 SQ. FT.
GARAGE — 441 SQ. FT.

TOTAL LIVING AREA:
2,051 SQ. FT.

WIDTH 56'-0"
DEPTH 60'-6"

Bedroom 2
11⁹ x 11¹

Bath

Vaulted Breakfast

Vaulted Master Bath

W.i.c. W.i.c.

Bedroom 3
11⁰ x 12⁴⁰

Kitchen

Serving Bar

Family Room
16⁰ x 22⁰
(12'-0" CLG. HEIGHT)

Master Suite
13' x 17⁰

Radius Window Above

Pantry

W.i.c.

Laund.

Stor.

Stairs Down

Tray Clg.

Dining Room
12⁰ x 13⁸
(9'-0" CLG. HEIGHT)
Tray Clg.

Foyer
(12'-0" CLG. HEIGHT)

Opt. Doors

Living Room/Den
13' x 13⁸

Garage

MAIN FLOOR

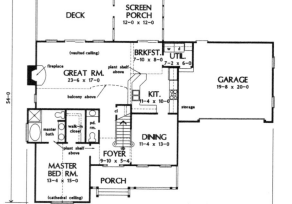

© 1994 Donald A. Gardner Architects, Inc.

Sunny Two-Story Foyer
PRICE CODE: D

- This plan features:
  — Three bedrooms
  — Two full and one half baths
- The two-story Foyer off the formal Dining Room sets an elegant mood
- The Great Room and Breakfast Area are both topped by a vaulted ceiling
- The screened porch has a relaxing atmosphere
- The Master Suite includes a cathedral ceiling and an elegant Bath
- There is plenty of storage space available

FIRST FLOOR — 1,335 SQ. FT.
SECOND FLOOR — 488 SQ. FT.
GARAGE & STORAGE — 465 SQ. FT.

TOTAL LIVING AREA:
1,823 SQ. FT.

DECK

SCREEN PORCH
12-0 x 12-0

BRKFST.
7-10 x 8-0

UTIL.
7-2 x 6-0

(vaulted ceiling)

GREAT RM.
23-6 x 17-0

fireplace

plant shelf above

balcony above

KIT.
11-4 x 10-0

GARAGE
19-8 x 20-0

storage

cl

54-0

master bath

walk-in closet

pd. rm.

plant shelf above

DINING
11-4 x 13-0

MASTER BED RM.
13-4 x 15-0

FOYER
9-10 x 5-4

PORCH

(cathedral ceiling)

© Donald A. Gardner Architects, Inc.

FIRST FLOOR PLAN

61-6

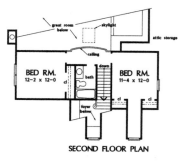

great room below

skylight

attic storage

railing

BED RM.
12-2 x 12-0

down

bath

BED RM.
11-4 x 12-0

cl

cl

foyer below

SECOND FLOOR PLAN

Great Starter or Empty Nester

Price Code: A

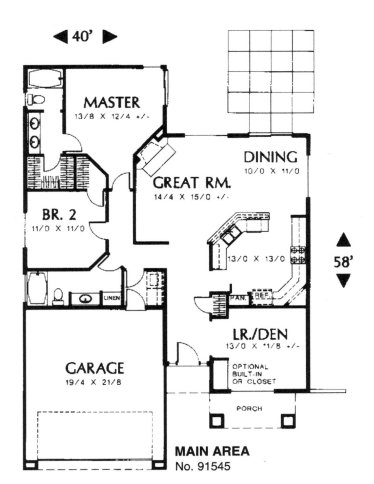

◄ 40' ►

MASTER
13/8 X 12/4 +/-

DINING
10/0 X 11/0

GREAT RM.
14/4 X 15/0 +/-

BR. 2
11/0 X 11/0

13/0 X 13/0

58'

LINEN

LR./DEN
13/0 X 11/8 +/-

PAN. REF.

GARAGE
19/4 X 21/8

OPTIONAL
BUILT-IN
OR CLOSET

PORCH

MAIN AREA
No. 91545

■ This plan features:

— Two bedrooms

— Two full baths

■ A formal Living Room or a cozy Den, the front room to the right of the Entry Hall adapts to your lifestyle

■ An efficient Kitchen with ample counter and storage space

■ A formal Dining Room situated next to the Kitchen and flowing from the Great Room

■ A corner fireplace highlighting the Great Room

■ A walk-in closet and a private double vanity Bath in the Master Suite

■ An additional Bedroom that easily accesses the full hall Bath

■ This home cannot be built in Clark County, Washington

MAIN AREA — 1,420 SQ. FT.

TOTAL LIVING AREA:
1,420 SQ. FT.

© 1997 Donald A. Gardner Architects, Inc.

B. NATHAN

Relaxed Country Living

Price Code: E

■ This plan features:

— Three bedrooms

— Two full baths

■ Comfortable Country home with deluxe Master Suite, front and back Porches and dual-sided fireplace

■ Vaulted Great Room brightened by two clerestory dormers and fireplace shared with Breakfast Bay

■ Dining Room and front Bedroom/Study dressed up with tray ceilings

■ Master Bedroom features vaulted ceiling, back Porch access, and luxurious Bath with over-sized, walk-in closet

■ Skylit bonus room over Garage provides extra room for family needs

MAIN FLOOR — 2,027 SQ. FT.
BONUS ROOM — 340 SQ. FT.
GARAGE & STORAGE — 532 SQ. FT.

TOTAL LIVING AREA:
2,027 SQ. FT.

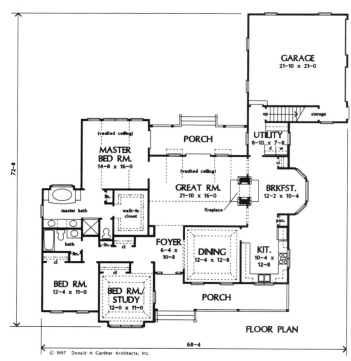

© 1997 Donald A Gardner Architects, Inc.

FLOOR PLAN

Fashionable Country Style

PRICE CODE: E

- This plan features:
  - Four bedrooms
  - Two full, one three-quarter and one half baths
- The large covered front Porch adds old-fashioned appeal to this modern floor plan
- The Dining Room features a decorative ceiling and a built-in hutch
- The Kitchen has a center island and is adjacent to the gazebo-shaped Nook
- The Great Room is accented by transom windows and a fireplace with bookcases on either side of it
- The Master Bedroom has a cathedral ceiling, a door to the front porch, and a large Bath with a whirlpool tub
- Upstairs are three additional Bedrooms and two full Baths
- An optional basement or slab foundation — please specify when ordering

FIRST FLOOR — 1,881 SQ. FT.
SECOND FLOOR — 814 SQ. FT.
GARAGE — 534 SQ. FT.

TOTAL LIVING AREA: 2,695 SQ. FT.

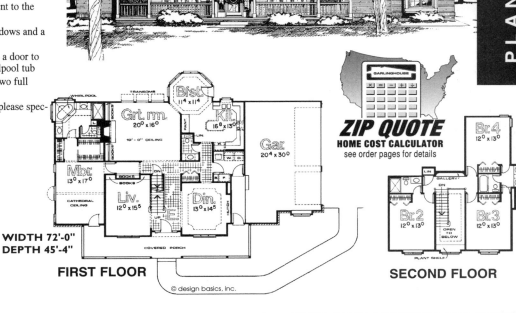

WIDTH 72'-0"
DEPTH 45'-4"

FIRST FLOOR

SECOND FLOOR

© design basics, inc.

Country Flair

PRICE CODE: A

- This plan features:
  - Three bedrooms
  - Two full baths
- An inviting front Porch leads into a tiled Entry and Great Room with focal point fireplace
- Open layout of Great Room, Dining Area, Wood Deck and Kitchen easily accommodates a busy family
- Master Bedroom set in a quiet corner, offers a huge walk-in closet and double vanity Bath
- Two additional Bedrooms, one an optional Den, share a full hall Bath
- No materials list is available for this plan

MAIN FLOOR — 1,461 SQ. FT.
BASEMENT — 1,461 SQ. FT.
GARAGE — 458 SQ. FT.

TOTAL LIVING AREA: 1,461 SQ. FT.

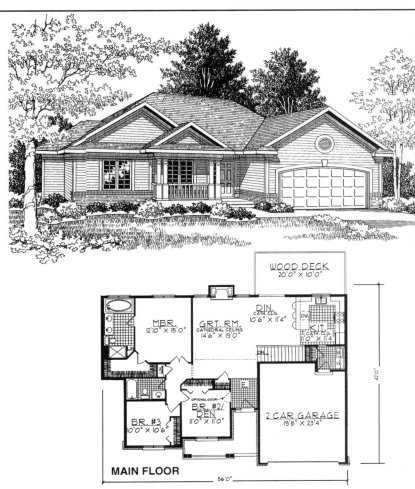

MAIN FLOOR

To order your Blueprints, call 1-800-235-5700

© 1997 Donald A. Gardner Architects, Inc.

An Exciting Mixture
PRICE CODE: E

FLOOR PLAN

© 1997 Donald A. Gardner Architects, Inc.

■ This plan features:
— Four bedrooms
— Two full and one half baths
■ The exterior is an exciting mixture of brick, and siding
■ The Dining Room has five windows that view the wrapping front Porch
■ A fireplace with built-ins set between it adds character to the Great Room
■ The U-shaped Kitchen is the ultimate for cooking convenience
■ There is a rear-covered Porch and a breezeway that leads to the Garage
■ The walk-in closet in the Master Bedroom is a delight
■ Lovely windows brighten all of the secondary Bedrooms
■ There is a bonus room over the Garage awaiting your finishing touches

MAIN FLOOR — 2,273 SQ. FT.
BONUS — 342 SQ. FT.
GARAGE — 528 SQ. FT.

TOTAL LIVING AREA:
2,273 SQ. FT.

Tremendous Appeal
PRICE CODE: F

■ This plan features:
— Four bedrooms
— Two full and one half baths
■ A European Country exterior with a modern American interior
■ The circular stairway highlights the entry
■ The formal Dining Room has a bay window and easy access to the Kitchen
■ A private Study with a double door entry
■ Formal Living Room has a fireplace and elegant columns
■ The large Family Room boasts a large brick fireplace and a built-in TV cabinet
■ An angled Kitchen contains all the conveniences that the cook demands, including a built-in Pantry and ovens
■ A large informal Dining Area that is adjacent to the Kitchen
■ The Master Suite occupies one wing of the house with a Bath and a huge walk-in closet
■ No material list is available for this plan

MAIN FLOOR — 2,658 SQ. FT.
UPPER FLOOR — 854 SQ. FT.
GARAGE — 660 SQ. FT.

TOTAL LIVING AREA:
3,512 SQ. FT.

Upper Floor

Main Floor

Small, But Not Lacking

Price Code: C

- This plan features:
- —Three bedrooms
- — One full and one three-quarter baths
- Great Room adjoining the Dining Room for ease in entertaining
- Kitchen highlighted by a peninsula counter/snack bar extending work space and offering convenience in serving informal meals or snacks
- Split-bedroom plan allowing for privacy for the Master Bedroom with a private Bath and a walk-in closet
- Two additional Bedrooms share the full family Bath in the hall
- Garage entry convenient to the kitchen

MAIN FLOOR — 1,546 SQ. FT.
BASEMENT — 1,530 SQ. FT.
GARAGE — 440 SQ. FT.

TOTAL LIVING AREA:
1,546 SQ. FT.

MAIN FLOOR
No. 94116

BR2
10'6 x 12'

WI Closet

GREAT RM
13'10 x 14'6

DIN
11'2 x 10'2

MBATH

MBR
14' x 14'10

WI Closet

SNACK BAR

FOYER

KIT
11'2 x 13'2

Entry

Laun

DIN RM
10'4 x 12'8

BR3
10'11 x 10'8

Covered Entry

GARAGE

43'

60'

Fan-lights Highlight Facade
PRICE CODE: A

■ This plan features:
— Three bedrooms
— Two full baths
■ Front Porch entry leads into an open Living Room, accented by a hearth fireplace below a sloped ceiling
■ Efficient Kitchen with a peninsula counter convenient to the Laundry, Garage, Dining area and Deck
■ Master Bedroom accented by a decorative ceiling, a double closet and a private Bath
■ Two additional Bedrooms with decorative windows and ample closets share a full Bath

MAIN FLOOR — 1,312 SQ. FT.
BASEMENT — 1,293 SQ. FT.
GARAGE — 459 SQ. FT.

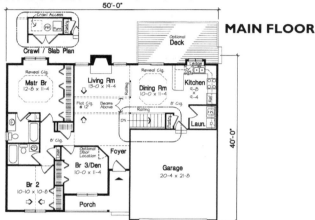

MAIN FLOOR

TOTAL LIVING AREA:
1,312 SQ. FT.

ZIP QUOTE
HOME COST CALCULATOR
see order pages for details

Traditional Stucco and Stone
PRICE CODE: F

■ This plan features:
— Four bedrooms
— Three full and one half baths
■ There is a Study, complete with fireplace and cathedral ceiling
■ The terrific Bonus Room could become a fifth Bedroom
■ The Master Suite has an expansive walk-in closet, tray ceiling and private Bath containing a whirlpool tub, double sinks, and a dressing table
■ The Great Room is complimented by soffits upon entry and a central fireplace flanked on both side by built-in cabinets
■ No materials list is available for this plan

FIRST FLOOR — 2,639 SQ. FT.
SECOND FLOOR — 1,570 SQ. FT.

TOTAL LIVING AREA:
4,209 SQ. FT.

To order your Blueprints, call 1-800-235-5700

A Country Estate

PRICE CODE: F

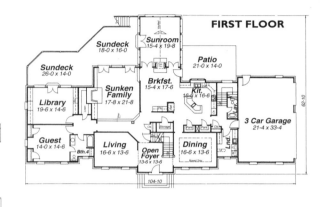

- This plan features:
— Four bedrooms
— Four full and one half baths
- A formal Living Room and Dining Room located at opposite sides of the Foyer
- A Library tucked into a corner of the house for quiet study
- A sunken Family Room highlighted by a fireplace and built-in shelves
- A Breakfast Room warmed by a see-through fireplace that is shared with the Sun Room
- A gourmet Kitchen with two built-in pantries, generous counter and storage space and an island with a vegetable sink
- No materials list is available for this plan

FIRST FLOOR — 3,199 SQ. FT.
SECOND FLOOR — 2,531 SQ. FT.
BASEMENT — 3,199 SQ. FT.
GARAGE — 748 SQ. FT.
BONUS — 440 SQ. FT.

TOTAL LIVING AREA: 5,730 SQ. FT.

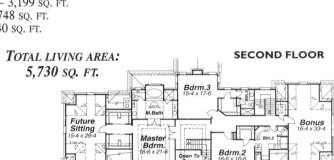

Growing Families Take Note

PRICE CODE: D

- This plan features:
— Three bedrooms
— Two full baths
- Unlimited options on the second floor Bonus Area
- Columns accenting the Dining Room, adjacent to the Foyer
- Great Room, open to the Kitchen and Breakfast Room, enlarged by a cathedral ceiling
- Living and entertaining space expands to the Deck
- Master Suite topped by a tray ceiling and including a walk-in closet skylit Bath with garden tub and a double vanity
- Flexible Bedroom/Study share a Bath with another Bedroom

FIRST FLOOR — 1,803 SQ. FT.
SECOND FLOOR — 80 SQ.FT.
GARAGE & STORAGE — 569 SQ. FT.
BONUS SPACE — 918 SQ. FT.

TOTAL LIVING AREA: 1,883 SQ. FT.

© 1995 Donald A. Gardner Architects, Inc.

To order your Blueprints, call 1-800-235-5700

©1998 Donald A. Gardner, Inc.

Innovative Floor Plan
PRICE CODE: D

■ This plan features:
— Three bedrooms
— Two full and one half baths
■ Elegant columns divide the home's Foyer from its formal Dining Room, which is separated from the Kitchen by a sizable pantry.
■ The Great Room is topped by a cathedral ceiling and accented by a fireplace with built-ins and a wall of windows that overlooks the back Porch.
■ The Master Suite is crowned in a cathedral ceiling and includes a private Bath and a walk-in closet.
■ Two more Bedrooms upstairs share a hall bath, large linen closet, and access to the Bonus Room.

FIRST FLOOR — 1,454 SQ. FT.
SECOND FLOOR — 533 SQ. FT.
GARAGE — 537 SQ. FT.

TOTAL LIVING AREA:
1,987 SQ. FT.

FIRST FLOOR PLAN

© 1998 Donald A Gardner, Inc.

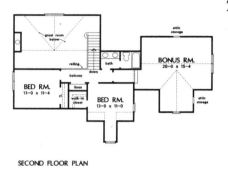

SECOND FLOOR PLAN

Open Family Living Area
PRICE CODE: E

■ This plan features:
— Four bedrooms
— Two full and one half baths
■ An immediate spacious feeling created by a two-story foyer
■ Formal Living Room topped by a vaulted ceiling
■ Pocket doors between the Family Room and the Living Room
■ Open layout between the Family Room, Dinette and Kitchen
■ Efficient Kitchen with an island, pantry and snack bar
■ A bayed window enhancing elegant formal Dining Room
■ Secluded Master Suite with a double door entry and plush Master Bath
■ No materials list is available for this plan

FIRST FLOOR — 1,861 SQ. FT.
SECOND FLOOR — 598 SQ. FT.
BASEMENT — 1,802 SQ. FT.
GARAGE — 523 SQ. FT.

TOTAL LIVING AREA:
2,459 SQ. FT.

FIRST FLOOR

SECOND FLOOR

To order your Blueprints, call 1-800-235-5700

© design basics inc.

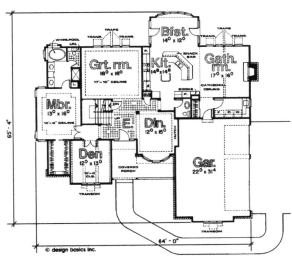

FIRST FLOOR
No. 99452

SECOND FLOOR

ZIP QUOTE
HOME COST CALCULATOR
see order pages for details

Traditional Home
Price Code: E

■ This plan features:

— Four bedrooms

— Two full, one three-quarter and one half baths

■ Dining Room has a built-in hutch and a bay window

■ Cozy Den and Great Room have high ceilings and transom windows

■ Conveniently arranged Kitchen adjoins the Breakfast Nook

■ The warm Gathering Room features a fireplace and a cathedral ceiling

■ The secluded Master Bedroom is a world away from the busy areas of the home

■ Upstairs are three Bedrooms and two full Baths

FIRST FLOOR — 2,158 SQ. FT.
SECOND FLOOR — 821 SQ. FT.
BASEMENT — 2,158 SQ. FT.
GARAGE — 692 SQ. FT.

TOTAL LIVING AREA:
2,979 SQ. FT.

American Gothic
PRICE CODE: F

- This plan features:
  — Four bedrooms
  — Three full and two half baths
- High ceilings add space and volume to the Dining and Family Rooms
- A rear staircase accesses the Guestroom/Maids Room
- Three secondary Bedrooms are located on the second floor
- The Master Suite on the first floor includes a walk-in closet
- The Kitchen is smartly arranged for the family cook
- An optional basement or a crawl space foundation — please specify when ordering
- No materials list is available for this plan

MAIN LEVEL — 1,752 SQ. FT.
UPPER LEVEL — 1,453 SQ. FT.
BASEMENT — 1,575 SQ. FT.
GARAGE — 532 SQ. FT.

TOTAL LIVING AREA:
3,205 SQ. FT.

PLAN NO. 99452

FIRST FLOOR

ROOM 14 X 18 cathedral ceiling
breakfast
MASTER 13-6 X 16-6
KITCHEN 12 X 14
utility
GARAGE 22 X 22 (plus offset)
up
wic
open to above
DINING 11-9 X 18-9 (plus offset) vaulted
WIDTH 72 ft.
DEPTH 56 ft.

SECOND FLOOR

BED 3 11 X 12
open to below
BED 2 11-6 X 15-6 (plus offset)
dn
Guestroom Maid's room
BED 4 11 X 12
open to below
sitting area

Contemporary Simplicity
PRICE CODE: A

- This plan features:
  — Two bedrooms
  — Two full baths
- A tile entrance leading into a two-story, beamed Living Room with a circular, center fireplace
- An efficient, U-shaped Kitchen, with plenty of counter and Storage Space opens into the Dining Area with sliding glass doors to an optional Deck
- Two Bedrooms, one with a private shower, both with ample closet space
- A second floor Loft overlooking the Living Area

MAIN FLOOR — 866 SQ. FT.
LOFT — 172 SQ. FT.

TOTAL LIVING AREA:
1,038 SQ. FT

PLAN NO. 24307

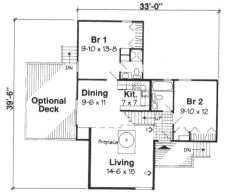

LOFT

Loft 14-6 x 10
railing DN
beam above
open to below

MAIN FLOOR

33'-0"
39'-6"
Br 1 9-10 x 13-8
DN
Dining 9-6 x 11
Kit. 7 x 7
Br 2 9-10 x 12
Optional Deck
UP
fireplace
DN
Living 14-6 x 15

Irresistible Craftsman Style

PRICE CODE: E

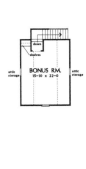

©1998 Donald A. Gardner, Inc.

■ This plan features:
— Four bedrooms
— Two full baths
■ The Dining Room enjoys a graceful tray ceiling and multiple columns
■ A cathedral ceiling expands the Great Room and the Kitchen
■ A duo of double doors connects the Great Room to the back porch
■ The Master Suite has a tray ceiling, his and her walk-in closets, and a linen closet and Bath with dual sink vanity

MAIN FLOOR — 2,342 SQ. FT.
GARAGE & STORAGE — 575 SQ. FT.
BONUS ROOM — 353 SQ. FT.

TOTAL LIVING AREA: 2,342 SQ. FT.

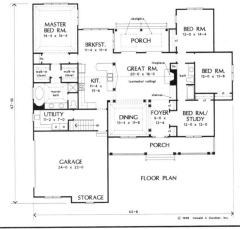

© 1998 Donald A. Gardner, Inc.

Country Cottage Charm

PRICE CODE: F

■ This plan features:
— Four bedrooms
— Two full and one half baths
■ Vaulted Master Bedroom has a private skylight Bath and large walk-in closet with a built in chest of drawers
■ Three more Bedrooms (one possibly a Study) have walk-in closets and share a full Bath
■ A loft and Bonus Room above the Living Room
■ Family Room has built-in book shelves, a fireplace, and overlooks the covered Verandah in the backyard
■ The huge three-car Garage has a separate shop area
■ An optional slab or crawl space foundation — please specify when ordering
■ No materials list is available for this plan

FIRST FLOOR — 2,787 SQ. FT.
SECOND FLOOR — 636 SQ. FT.

TOTAL LIVING AREA: 3,423 SQ. FT.

ZIP QUOTE
HOME COST CALCULATOR
see order pages for details

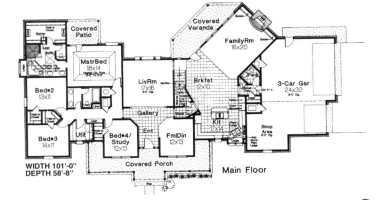

Upper Floor
Optional Bonus Room & Loft

WIDTH 101'-0"
DEPTH 58'-8"

Main Floor

To order your Blueprints, call 1-800-235-5700

With All the Amenities
PRICE CODE: C

- This plan features:
  — Three bedrooms
  — Two full and one half baths
- A sixteen-foot high ceiling over the Foyer
- Arched openings highlight the hallway accessing the Great Room which is further enhanced by a fireplace
- A French door to the rear yard and decorative columns at its arched entrance
- Another vaulted ceiling topping the Dining Room, convenient to both the Living Room and the Kitchen
- An expansive kitchen features a center work island, a built-in Pantry and a Breakfast Area defined by a tray ceiling
- A Master Suite also has a tray ceiling treatment and includes a lavish private Bath and a huge walk-in closet
- Secondary Bedrooms have private access to a full Bath
- An optional basement, slab, or crawl space foundation — please specify when ordering

MAIN FLOOR — 1,884 SQ. FT.
BASEMENT — 1,908 SQ. FT.
GARAGE — 495 SQ. FT.

TOTAL LIVING AREA:
1,884 SQ. FT.

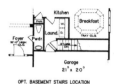

OPT. BASEMENT STAIRS LOCATION

© Frank Betz Associates

Main floor

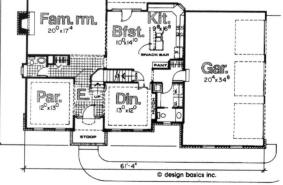

© design basics inc.

Captivating Colonial
PRICE CODE: D

- This plan features:
  — Four bedrooms
  — Two full and one half baths
- Decorative windows and brick detailing
- Dining Room highlighted by decorative ceiling, French doors, and hutch space
- The Family Room has a fireplace and a bow window
- The Breakfast Nook and Kitchen are perfectly set up for meals on the run
- Upstairs find the Master Bedroom and Bath fully complemented
- Three more Bedrooms and a Bath completed the second floor plan
- An optional basement or slab foundation — please specify when ordering

FIRST FLOOR — 1,362 SQ. FT.
SECOND FLOOR — 1,223 SQ. FT.
GARAGE — 734 SQ. FT.
BASEMENT — 1,362 SQ. FT.

TOTAL LIVING AREA:
2,585 SQ. FT.

© design basics inc.

FIRST FLOOR   **SECOND FLOOR**

To order your Blueprints, call 1-800-235-5700

Adding Ease to Busy Lifestyles
PRICE CODE: E

This plan features:
- Three bedrooms
- Two full and one half baths

An elegant two-story Foyer leads the way to the spacious Family Room.

The Family Room has built-in cabinets surrounding the comforting fireplace

A Den with a built-in desk off the Family Room.

An open Kitchen with ample counter space, a walk-in Pantry, an island Breakfast Bar, and a sunny Nook for family meals.

A formal Dining Room and a Living Room provide an elegant atmosphere for entertaining

The second floor Master Suite has a private Bath with a garden spa tub, and a large walk-in closet

No materials list is available for this plan

FIRST FLOOR — 1,533 SQ. FT.

SECOND FLOOR — 1,255 SQ. FT.

BASEMENT — 1,533 SQ. FT.

TOTAL LIVING AREA:
2,788 SQ. FT.

FIRST FLOOR

SECOND FLOOR

Distinctive Ranch
PRICE CODE: C

This plan features:
- Three bedrooms
- Two full baths

This hipped roofed ranch has an exterior that mixes brick and siding

The cozy front Porch leads into a recessed Entry with sidelights and transoms

The Great Room has a cathedral ceiling, and a rear wall fireplace

The Kitchen has a center island and opens into the Nook

The Dining Room features a high ceiling and a bright front window

The Bedroom wing has three large Bedrooms and two full Baths

The two-car Garage could easily be expanded to three with a door placed in the rear Storage Area

No materials list is available for this plan

MAIN FLOOR — 1,802 SQ. FT.

BASEMENT — 1,802 SQ. FT.

TOTAL LIVING AREA:
1,802 SQ. FT.

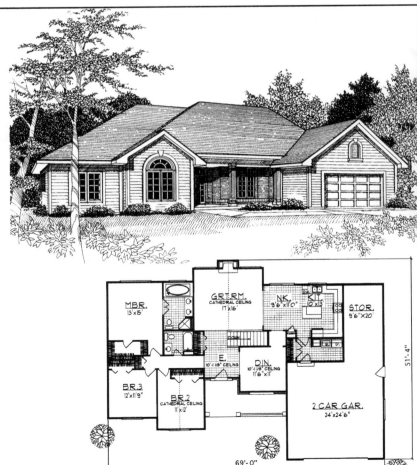

MAIN FLOOR PLAN

121

To order your Blueprints, call 1-800-235-5700

Let the Sun Shine In

Price Code: E

- This plan features:
- — Four bedrooms
- — Two full and one three-quarter baths
- Two-story entrance with a second floor window
- Den with windows on two sides including a corner window
- Family Room, Nook and Kitchen are open to each other for a spacious feeling
- Cooktop island/snack bar built-in desk and a pantry highlight the efficient Kitchen
- Family Room enhanced by a second fireplace
- Lavish Master Suite with a decorative ceiling in the Bedroom and a private, plush Bath
- No materials list is available for this plan

FIRST FLOOR — 1,575 SQ. FT.
SECOND FLOOR — 1,338 SQ. FT.
GARAGE — 864 SQ. FT.

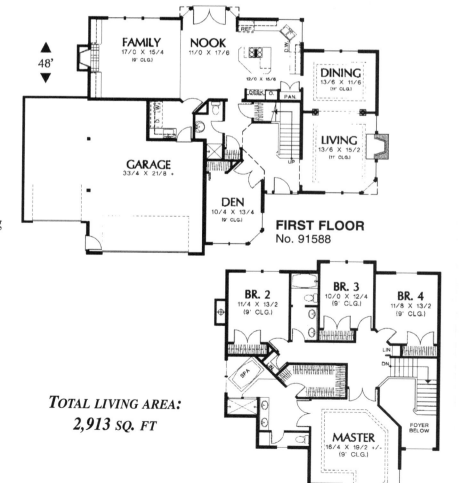

◀ 66' ▶

48'

FAMILY
17/0 X 15/4
(9' CLG.)

NOOK
11/0 X 17/6

REF.

P.W.

DINING
13/6 X 11/6
(11' CLG.)

12/0 X 15/6

DESK O. PAN.

GARAGE
33/4 X 21/8 +

LIVING
13/6 X 15/2
(11' CLG.)

UP

DEN
10/4 X 13/4
(9' CLG.)

FIRST FLOOR
No. 91588

BR. 2
11/4 X 13/2
(9' CLG.)

BR. 3
10/0 X 12/4
(9' CLG.)

BR. 4
11/8 X 13/2
(9' CLG.)

LIN.

DN.

SPA

FOYER
BELOW

TOTAL LIVING AREA:
2,913 SQ. FT

MASTER
16/4 X 19/2 +/-
(9' CLG.)

SECOND FLOOR

To order your Blueprints, call 1-800-235-5700

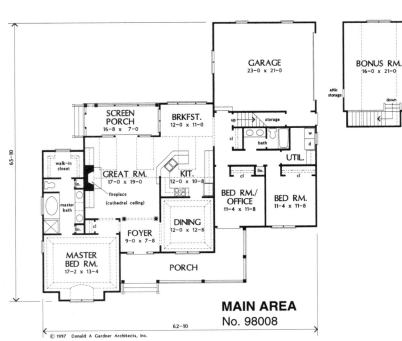

MAIN AREA
No. 98008

MAIN FLOOR — 1,911 SQ. FT.
BONUS — 406 SQ. FT.
GARAGE — 551 SQ. FT.

TOTAL LIVING AREA:
1,911 SQ. FT.

Pretty as a Picture

Price Code: D

■ This plan features:

— Three bedrooms

— Two full baths

■ Picture perfect this Country style plan offers space and flexibility

■ The wrapping front Porch is beautiful and functional at the same time

■ Inside the Great Room has a cathedral ceiling and a fireplace

■ The Dining Room has windows that overlook the front Porch, plus a tray ceiling

■ The Kitchen has a convenient layout with a good work triangle

■ The Master Bedroom is isolated and features a galley Bath that leads into the walk-in closet

■ Two additional bedrooms are located in their own wing with a full Bath

■ The two-car Garage is conveniently located in the rear of the home

■ There is a Bonus Room over the Garage waiting to be finished to suit your needs

B. NATHAN

© 1995 Donald A. Gardner Architects, Inc.

Comfort and Charm

Price Code: D

■ This plan features:

— Three bedrooms

— Two full and one half baths

■ The Foyer opens into the dormers vaulted ceiling

■ A cathedral ceiling in the Great Room soars up to a palladian window

■ The Kitchen is equipped with an angled island peninsula

■ Bay windows accent the formal Dining Room and Breakfast Nook

■ The Master Suite accesses the Deck and includes a private Bath

■ Upstairs find two Bedrooms and a balcony that overlooks the Great Room

FIRST FLOOR — 1,480 SQ. FT.
SECOND FLOOR — 511 SQ. FT.
BONUS ROOM — 363 SQ. FT.
GARAGE — 621 SQ. FT.

TOTAL LIVING AREA: 1,991 SQ. FT.

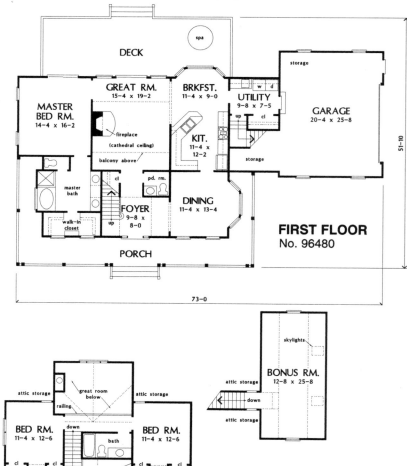

FIRST FLOOR
No. 96480

SECOND FLOOR

To order your Blueprints, call 1-800-235-5700

Stucco Accents

PRICE CODE: E

■ This plan features:
— Four bedrooms
— Two full, one three-quarter and one half baths

■ Stucco accents and graceful window treatments enhance the front of this home

■ Double doors open to the private Den which features brilliant bayed windows

■ French doors open to a large screened-in verandah ideal for outdoor entertaining

■ The open Living Room and handsome curved staircase add drama to the entry area

■ The gourmet Kitchen, Breakfast bay and Family Room flow together for easy living

■ The elegant Master Bedroom has a ten-foot vaulted ceiling

■ Two walk-in closets, his and her vanities and a whirlpool tub highlight the Master Bath

■ Three additional Bedrooms have private access to full Baths

FIRST FLOOR — 1,631 SQ. FT.
SECOND FLOOR — 1,426 SQ. FT.
BASEMENT — 1,631 SQ. FT.
GARAGE — 681 SQ. FT.

TOTAL LIVING AREA:
3,057 SQ. FT.

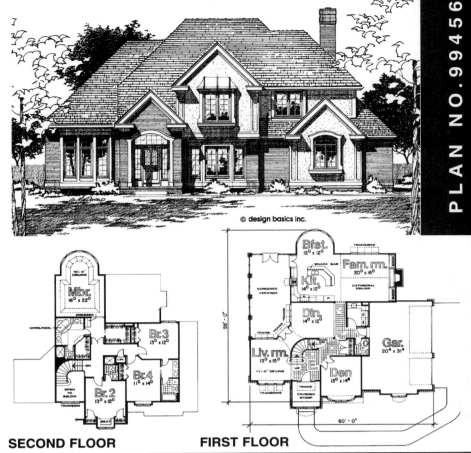

© design basics inc.

SECOND FLOOR   **FIRST FLOOR**

PLAN NO. 99456

Exceptional Family Living

PRICE CODE: F

■ This plan features:
— Four bedrooms
— Three full and one half baths

■ A decorative dormer, a bay window and an eyebrow arched window provide for a pleasing Country farmhouse facade

■ The cozy Study has its own fireplace and a bay window

■ The large formal Living Room has a fireplace and built-in bookcases

■ The huge island Kitchen is open to the Breakfast Bay and the Family Room

■ The Master Suite includes a large Bath with a unique closet

■ Three more Bedrooms located at the other end of the home each have private access to a full Bath

■ No materials list is available for this plan

MAIN FLOOR — 4,082 SQ. FT.
GARAGE — 720 SQ. FT.

TOTAL LIVING AREA:
4,082 SQ. FT.

PLAN NO. 98538

Floor Plan

To order your Blueprints, call 1-800-235-5700

With Room to Expand
PRICE CODE: B

■ This plan features:
— Three bedrooms
— Two full and one half baths
■ An impressive two-story Foyer
■ The Kitchen is equipped with ample cabinet and counter space
■ Spacious Family Room flows from the Breakfast Bay and is highlighted by a fireplace and a French door to the rear yard
■ The Master Suite is topped by a tray ceiling and is enhanced by a vaulted, five-piece Master Bath
■ An optional basement, slab, or crawl space foundation — please specify when ordering

FIRST FLOOR — 882 SQ. FT.
SECOND FLOOR — 793 SQ. FT.
BONUS ROOM — 416 SQ. FT.
BASEMENT — 882 SQ. FT.
GARAGE — 510 SQ. FT.

TOTAL LIVING AREA:
1,675 SQ. FT.

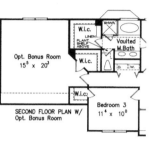

© Frank Betz Associates

FIRST FLOOR PLAN

SECOND FLOOR PLAN

SECOND FLOOR PLAN W/ Opt. Bonus Room

Secluded Master Suite
PRICE CODE: B

■ This plan features:
— Three bedrooms
— Two full baths
■ The centrally located Great Room is crowned in an eleven-foot box ceiling and includes a fireplace
■ The Kitchen and Breakfast Room flow into each other with a center island doubling as a snack bar
■ The formal Dining Room has direct access to the Kitchen and a ten-foot boxed ceiling
■ This home has a split-bedroom set up affording more privacy to the Master Suite
■ No materials list is available for this plan
■ An optional basement, crawl space or slab foundation – please specify when ordering

MAIN FLOOR — 1,746 SQ. FT.
GARAGE — 491 SQ. FT.

TOTAL LIVING AREA:
1,746 SQ. FT.

MAIN FLOOR

To order your Blueprints, call 1-800-235-5700

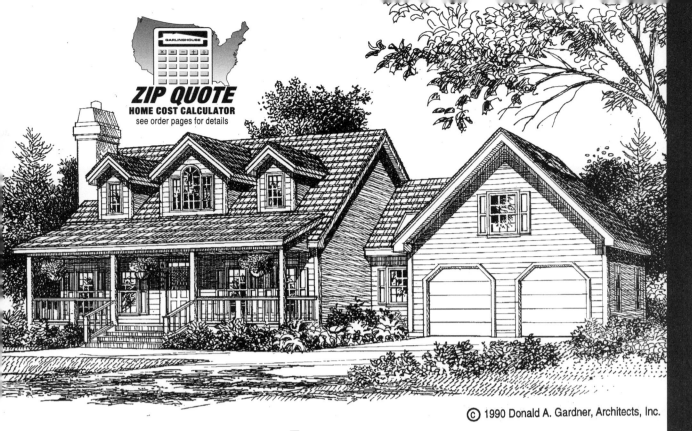

PLAN NO. 99859

© 1990 Donald A. Gardner, Architects, Inc.

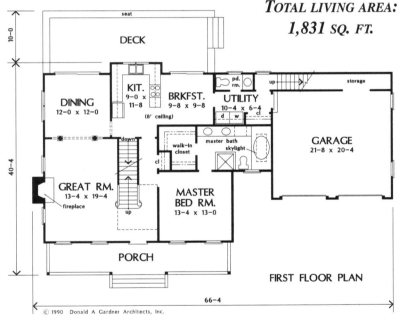

TOTAL LIVING AREA: 1,831 SQ. FT.

DECK

seat

KIT.
9-0 x 11-8
(8' ceiling)

BRKFST.
9-8 x 9-8

UTILITY
10-4 x 6-4

pd. rm.

up

storage

DINING
12-0 x 12-0

down

walk-in closet

master bath
skylight

d w

cl

GARAGE
21-8 x 20-4

GREAT RM.
13-4 x 19-4

fireplace

up

MASTER
BED RM.
13-4 x 13-0

PORCH

FIRST FLOOR PLAN

10-0

40-4

66-4

© 1990 Donald A Gardner Architects, Inc.

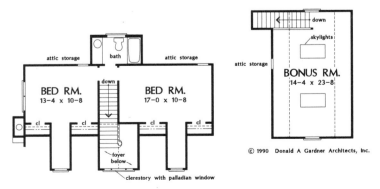

attic storage

bath

attic storage

attic storage

down

skylights

BED RM.
13-4 x 10-8

BED RM.
17-0 x 10-8

cl   cl   cl   cl

foyer
below

clerestory with palladian window

SECOND FLOOR PLAN

BONUS RM.
14-4 x 23-8

© 1990 Donald A Gardner Architects, Inc.

Flexibility to Expand

Price Code: D

- ■ This plan features:
- — Three bedrooms
- — Two full and one half baths
- ■ Three Bedroom country cottage has lots of room to expand
- ■ Two-story Foyer contains palladian window in a clerestory dormer
- ■ Efficient Kitchen opens to Breakfast Area and Deck for outdoor dining
- ■ Columns separating the Great Room and the Dining Room that have nine foot ceilings
- ■ Master Bedroom Suite is on the first level and features a skylight above the whirlpool tub

FIRST FLOOR — 1,289 SQ. FT.
SECOND FLOOR — 542 SQ. FT.
BONUS ROOM — 393 SQ. FT.
GARAGE & STORAGE — 521 SQ. FT.

© 1996 Donald A Gardner Architects, Inc.

Cathedral Ceiling
Enlarges Great Room

Price Code: D

■ This plan features:

— Three bedrooms

— Two full baths

■ Two dormers add volume to the Foyer

■ Great Room, topped by a cathedral ceiling, is open to the Kitchen and Breakfast Area

■ Accent columns define the Foyer, Great Room, Kitchen, and Breakfast Area

■ Private Master Suite crowned in a tray ceiling and highlighted by a skylit Bath

■ The front Bedroom is topped by a tray ceiling

MAIN FLOOR — 1,699 SQ. FT.
BONUS — 336 SQ. FT.
GARAGE — 498 SQ. FT.

TOTAL LIVING AREA:
1,699 SQ. FT.

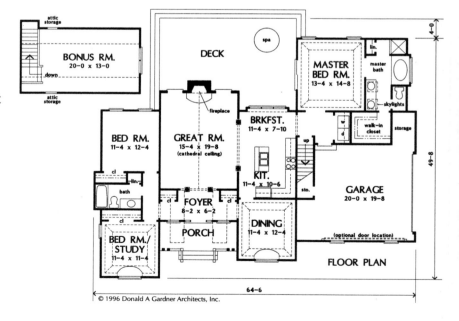

© 1996 Donald A Gardner Architects, Inc.

To order your Blueprints, call 1-800-235-5700

© design basics inc.

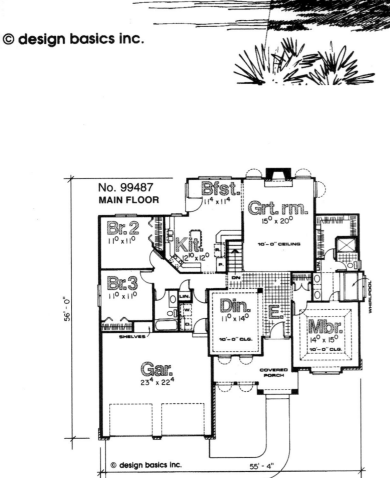

No. 99487
MAIN FLOOR

Br. 2
11⁰ x 11⁰

Br. 3
11⁰ x 11⁰

Kit.
12¹⁰ x 12⁰

Bfst.
11⁴ x 11⁴

Grt. rm.
15⁰ x 20⁰
10'-0" CEILING

DN

Din.
11⁰ x 14⁰
10'-0" CLG.

E.

Mbr.
14⁰ x 15⁰
10'-0" CLG.

LIN

SHELVES

LIN

W.

WHIRLPOOL

Gar.
23⁴ x 22⁴

COVERED
PORCH

56'-0"

55'-4"

© design basics inc.

Columns and Arched Windows

Price Code: C

■ This plan features:

— Three bedrooms

— Two full baths

■ Ten-foot entry with formal views of the Dining Room and the Great Room

■ A brick fireplace and arched windows in the Great Room

■ Large island Kitchen with an angled range and a built-in Pantry

■ Master Suite with a whirlpool Bath and a sloped ceiling

■ An optional basement or slab foundation — please specify when ordering

MAIN FLOOR — 1,806 SQ. FT.
GARAGE — 548 SQ. FT.

TOTAL LIVING AREA:
1,806 SQ. FT.

S. NATHAN

© 1990 Donald A. Gardner Architects, Inc.

Compact Three Bedroom

Price Code: C

- This plan features:
- — Three bedrooms
- — Two full baths
- Contemporary interior punctuated by elegant columns
- Dormers above the covered Porch light the Foyer leading to the dramatic Great Room crowned in a cathedral ceiling and enhanced by a fireplace
- Great Room opens to the island Kitchen with Breakfast Area and access to a spacious rear Deck
- Tray ceilings adding interest to the Bedroom/Study, Dining Room and the Master Bedroom
- Luxurious Master Bedroom Suite highlighted by a walk-in closet and a Bath with dual vanity, separate shower and a whirlpool tub

MAIN FLOOR — 1,452 SQ. FT.
GARAGE & STORAGE — 427 SQ. FT.

ZIP QUOTE
HOME COST CALCULATOR
see order pages for details

TOTAL LIVING AREA:
1,452 SQ. FT.

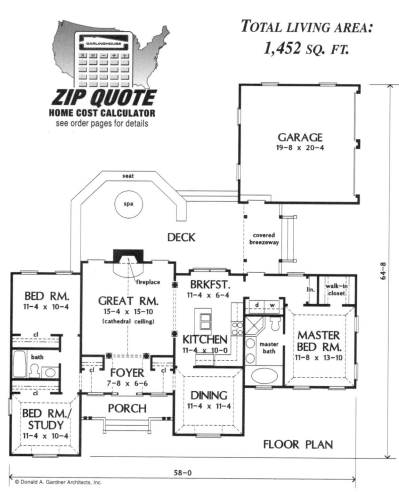

© Donald A. Gardner Architects, Inc.

To order your Blueprints, call 1-800-235-5700

An Estate of Epic Proportion

PRICE CODE: F

- ■ This plan features
  - — Four bedrooms
  - — Three full and one half baths
- ■ Front door opening into a grand Entry Way with a 20′ ceiling and a spiral staircase
- ■ Flanking the Entry Way on the right is the Living Room with cathedral ceiling and fireplace, and on the left is the bayed formal Dining Room
- ■ Walk down the Gallery to the Study with a full wall built-in bookcase
- ■ The enormous Master Bedroom has a walk in closet, sumptuous Bath and a bayed Sitting Area
- ■ Family Room has a wet bar, a fireplace, and a door which leads outside to the covered Verandah
- ■ An optional basement or crawl space foundation — please specify when ordering
- ■ A materials list is not available for this plan

FIRST FLOOR — 2,751 SQ. FT.
SECOND FLOOR — 1,185 SQ. FT.
BONUS — 343 SQ. FT.
GARAGE — 790 SQ. FT.

TOTAL LIVING AREA: 3,936 SQ. FT.

ZIP QUOTE
HOME COST CALCULATOR
see order pages for details

Open Spaces

PRICE CODE: A

- ■ This plan features:
  - — Three bedrooms
  - — Two full baths
- ■ A Family Room, Kitchen and Breakfast Area that all connects to form a great space
- ■ A central, double fireplace adding warmth and atmosphere to the Family Room, Kitchen and the Breakfast Area
- ■ An efficient Kitchen that is highlighted by a peninsula counter and doubles as a snack bar
- ■ A Master Suite that includes a walk-in closet, a double vanity, separate shower and tub bath
- ■ Two additional Bedrooms sharing a full hall bath
- ■ A wooden Deck that can be accessed from the Breakfast Area
- ■ An optional crawl space or slab foundation — please specify when ordering

MAIN FLOOR — 1,388 SQ. FT.
GARAGE — 400 SQ. FT.

TOTAL LIVING AREA: 1,388 SQ. FT.

ZIP QUOTE
HOME COST CALCULATOR
see order pages for details

MAIN FLOOR

Fireplace Center of Circular Living Area
PRICE CODE: B

- This plan features:
  — Three bedrooms
  — One full and one three-quarter baths
- A dramatically positioned fireplace as a focal point for the main area
- The Kitchen, Dining and Living Rooms form a circle that allows work areas to flow into living areas
- Sliding glass doors accessible to a Deck
- A convenient Laundry Room located off the Kitchen
- A double Garage providing excellent storage

MAIN AREA— 1,783 SQ. FT.
GARAGE — 576 SQ. FT.

TOTAL LIVING AREA:
1,783 SQ. FT.

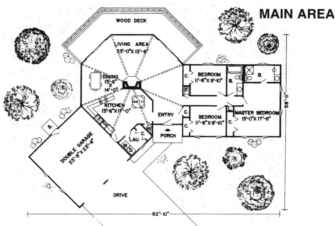

MAIN AREA

Coastal Delight
PRICE CODE: F

- This plan features:
  — Three bedrooms
  — Two full baths
- Living area above the Garage and Storage/Bonus areas offering a "piling" design for coastal, waterfront or low-lying terrain
- Double-door Entry into an open Foyer with landing staircase leads into the Great Room
- Three sets of double doors below a vaulted ceiling in the Great Room offer lots of air, light and easy access to both the Sun Deck and Veranda
- A Dining Room convenient to the Great Room and Kitchen with vaulted ceilings and decorative windows
- A glassed-in Nook adjacent to the efficient Kitchen with an island work center
- Two secondary Bedrooms, a full Bath and a Utility Room on the first floor
- A second floor Master Suite with a vaulted ceiling, double door to a private Deck, his and her closets and a plush Bath

FIRST FLOOR — 1,736 SQ. FT.
SECOND FLOOR — 640 SQ. FT.
CARPORT — 840 SQ. FT.
BONUS ROOM — 253 SQ. FT.

TOTAL LIVING AREA:
2,376 SQ. FT.

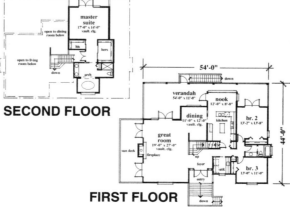

SECOND FLOOR

FIRST FLOOR

CARPORT

To order your Blueprints, call 1-800-235-5700

For The Young Family
PRICE CODE: D

■ This plan features:
— Three bedrooms
— Two full and one half baths
■ Built-in cabinets surrounding a beautiful fireplace add coziness for large family get-togethers
■ The Den has a unique window seat providing a retreat from the commotion of everyday life
■ A large island, centered in the Kitchen, supplies the perfect resting place for a quick snack or a convenient space to prepare special meals
■ No materials list is available for this plan

FIRST FLOOR — 1,339 SQ. FT.
SECOND FLOOR — 1,081 SQ. FT.

TOTAL LIVING AREA:
2,420 SQ. FT.

FIRST FLOOR

SECOND FLOOR

Impressive Manor
PRICE CODE: D

■ This plan features:
— Four bedrooms
— Two full and one half baths
■ The Foyer leads to the Dining Room and Parlor with windows overlooking the front yard
■ The Family Room has a fireplace and leads into the sunny Breakfast Bay
■ Upstairs find the Master Bedroom with a see-through fireplace and a Sitting Room
■ The Master Bath is spacious and includes a walk-in closet and a skylight
■ An optional basement or slab foundation — please specify when ordering
■ No materials list is available for this plan

FIRST FLOOR — 1,113 SQ. FT.
SECOND FLOOR — 1,148 SQ. FT.
BASEMENT — 1,113 SQ. FT.
GARAGE — 529 SQ. FT.

TOTAL LIVING AREA:
2,261 SQ. FT.

WIDTH 66'-0"
DEPTH 31'-0"

FIRST FLOOR PLAN

SECOND FLOOR PLAN

To order your Blueprints, call 1-800-235-5700

© 1997 Donald A. Gardner Architects, Inc.

Casual Country Charmer

Price Code: D

■ This plan features:

— Three bedrooms

— Two full baths

■ Columns and arches frame the front Porch

■ The open floor plan combines the Great Room, Kitchen and Dining Room

■ The Kitchen offers a convenient breakfast bar for meals on the run

■ The Master Suite features a private Bath oasis

■ Secondary Bedrooms share a full Bath with a dual vanity

MAIN FLOOR — 1,770 SQ. FT.
BONUS — 401 SQ. FT.
GARAGE — 630 SQ. FT.

TOTAL LIVING AREA:
1,770 SQ. FT.

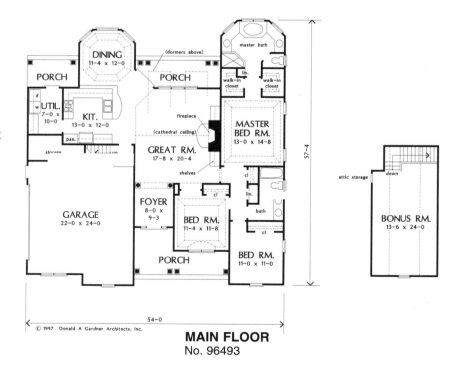

MAIN FLOOR
No. 96493

134

Convenient Floor Plan

PRICE CODE: B

■ This plan features:
— Three bedrooms
— Two full baths

■ Central Foyer leads to Den/Guest room with arched window below vaulted ceiling and Living Room accented by two-sided fireplace

■ Efficient, U-shaped Kitchen with peninsula counter/breakfast bar serving Dining Room and adjacent Utility/Pantry

■ Master Suite features large walk-in closet and private Bath with double vanity and whirlpool tub

■ Two additional Bedrooms with ample closet space share full Bath

MAIN FLOOR — 1,625 SQ. FT.
BASEMENT — 1,625 SQ. FT.
GARAGE — 455 SQ. FT.

TOTAL LIVING AREA : 1,625 SQ. FT.

ZIP QUOTE
HOME COST CALCULATOR
see order pages for details

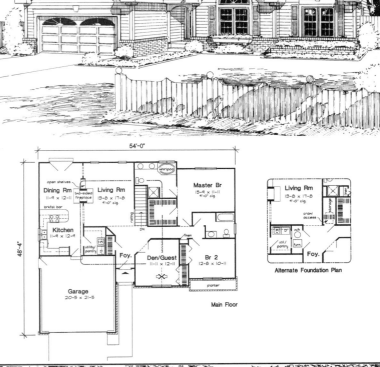

Compact and Comfortable

PRICE CODE: A

■ This plan features:
— Three bedrooms
— Two full baths

■ Arched window highlights front entrance, Foyer and staircase

■ Spacious Living Area with focal point fireplace and Deck access

■ Efficient, U-shaped Kitchen easily serves bright Dining Room and Deck

■ Private Master Bedroom with walk-in closet and double vanity Bath with a raised tub

■ Two additional Bedrooms with ample closets, share a full Bath

■ Lower level with Garage, Storage and future Playroom

MAIN FLOOR — 1,407 SQ. FT.
STAIRS — 40 SQ. FT.
BASEMENT — 732 SQ. FT.
GARAGE — 400 SQ. FT.
BONUS — 224 SQ. FT.

TOTAL LIVING AREA: 1,447 SQ. FT.

Country Classic
PRICE CODE: D

■ This plan features:
— Four bedrooms
— Two full and one half baths
■ All of the Bedrooms are located upstairs for privacy
■ A family Entry in the rear will cut down on tracked in dirt
■ A vaulted ceiling and fireplace complete the Family Room
■ Columns separate the Living and Dining Rooms
■ The L-shaped Kitchen includes an island with a cooktop
■ No materials list is available for this plan

FIRST FLOOR — 1,412 SQ. FT.
SECOND FLOOR — 1,003 SQ. FT.
BASEMENT — 992 SQ. FT.
GARAGE — 576 SQ. FT.

TOTAL LIVING AREA:
2,415 SQ. FT.

WIDTH 58'-0"
DEPTH 44'-0"

FIRST FLOOR

SECOND FLOOR

Three Bedroom Ranch
PRICE CODE: B

■ This plan features:
— Three bedrooms
— Two full baths
■ Formal Dining Room enhanced by a plant shelf and a side window
■ Wetbar located between the Kitchen and the Dining Room
■ Built-in Pantry, a double sink and a snack bar highlight the Kitchen
■ Breakfast Room containing a radius window and a French door to the rear yard
■ Large cozy fireplace framed by windows in the Great Room
■ Master Suite with a vaulted ceiling over the Sitting Area, a Master Bath and a walk-in closet
■ Two additional Bedrooms sharing the full Bath in the hall
■ An optional basement or crawl space foundation — please specify when ordering

MAIN FLOOR — 1,575 SQ. FT.
GARAGE — 459 SQ. FT.
BASEMENT — 1,658 SQ. FT.

TOTAL LIVING AREA:
1,575 SQ. FT.

WIDTH 50'-0"
DEPTH 52'-6"

MAIN FLOOR

© Frank Betz Associates, Inc.

To order your Blueprints, call 1-800-235-5700

Keystones, Arches and Gables

PRICE CODE: B

This plan features:
- Three bedrooms
- Two full and one half baths

▪ Tiled entry opens to Living Room with focal point fireplace

▪ U-shaped Kitchen with a built-in Pantry, eating bar and nearby Laundry/Garage entry

▪ Comfortable Dining Room with bay window and French doors to screen Porch expanding living area outdoors

▪ Corner Master Bedroom offers a great walk-in closet and private Bath

▪ Two additional Bedrooms with ample closets and double windows, share a full Bath

▪ No materials list is available for this plan

MAIN FLOOR — 1,642 SQ. FT.
BASEMENT — 1,642 SQ. FT.

TOTAL LIVING AREA:
1,642 SQ. FT.

MAIN FLOOR PLAN

Keystones and Arched Windows

PRICE CODE: B

▪ This plan features:
- Three bedrooms
- Two full baths

▪ A large arched window in the Dining Room offers eye-catching appeal

▪ A decorative column helps to define the Dining Room from the Great Room

▪ A fireplace and French door to the rear yard can be found in the Great Room

▪ An efficient Kitchen includes a serving bar, Pantry and pass through to the Great Room

▪ A vaulted ceiling over the Breakfast Room

▪ A plush Master Suite includes a private Bath and a walk-in closet

▪ Two additional Bedrooms share a full Bath in the hall

▪ An optional basement, slab or crawl space foundation — please specify when ordering

MAIN FLOOR — 1,670 SQ. FT.
GARAGE — 240 SQ. FT.

TOTAL LIVING AREA:
1,670 SQ. FT.

© Frank Betz Associates

MAIN FLOOR

To order your Blueprints, call 1-800-235-5700

© 1997 Donald A. Gardner Architects, Inc.

Stunning Southwestern Style
PRICE CODE: D

■ This plan features:
— Four bedrooms
— Two full and one half baths
■ Large circle top windows, stucco, and a tile roof add style to this home
■ The common space of the home is impressive with 12′ ceilings and columns
■ The Kitchen is partially enclosed by 8′ high walls
■ A screen Porch in the rear is perfect for entertaining guests
■ The Master Bedroom has a tray ceiling and a private Bath
■ A versatile room, the Study/Bedroom has a bay in the front of it
■ Two additional Bedrooms with ample closet space share a hall Bath
■ An optional slab or a crawl space foundation — please specify when ordering

MAIN FLOOR — 1,954 SQ. FT.

TOTAL LIVING AREA:
1,954 SQ. FT.

FLOOR PLAN

© 1997 Donald A Gardner Architects, inc.

Cozy Country Ranch
PRICE CODE: B

■ This plan features:
— Three bedrooms
— Two full baths
■ Front Porch shelters outdoor visiting and entrance into Living Room
■ Expansive Living Room highlighted by a boxed window and hearth fireplace between built-ins
■ Columns frame entrance to Dining Room with access to backyard
■ Efficient, U-shaped Kitchen with direct access to the screened Porch and the Dining Room
■ Master Bedroom wing enhanced by a large walk-in closet and a double vanity Bath with a whirlpool tub
■ Two additional Bedrooms with large closets share a double vanity Bath with Laundry Center

MAIN FLOOR — 1,576 SQ. FT.
BASEMENT — 1,454 SQ. FT.
GARAGE — 576 SQ. FT.

TOTAL LIVING AREA:
1,576 SQ. FT.

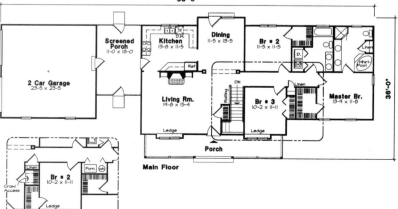

Main Floor

Alternate Crawl/Slab Plan

ZIP QUOTE
HOME COST CALCULATOR
see order pages for details

To order your Blueprints, call 1-800-235-5700

First Floor

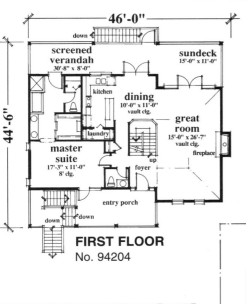

46'-0"

44'-6"

down

screened verandah
30'-8" x 8'-0"

kitchen

sundeck
15'-0" x 11'-0"

dining
10'-0" x 11'-0"
vault clg.

laundry

great room
15'-0" x 26'-7"
vault clg.

fireplace

up

master suite
17'-3" x 11'-0"
8' clg.

foyer

down   down

entry porch

FIRST FLOOR
No. 94204

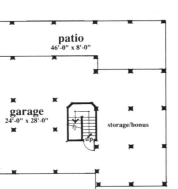

patio
46'-0" x 8'-0"

garage
24'-0" x 28'-0"

storage/bonus

up

GARAGE PLAN

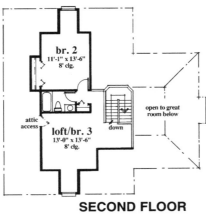

br. 2
11'-1" x 13'-6"
8' clg.

attic access

loft/br. 3
13'-0" x 13'-6"
8' clg.

open to great room below

down

SECOND FLOOR

Year Round Living
Price Code: B

■ This plan features:

— Three bedrooms

— Two full baths

■ An Entry Porch leads into the expansive Great Room with a hearth fireplace and a vaulted ceiling

■ An inviting Dining Area with a vaulted ceiling and and access to the screened Veranda and Sun Deck

■ An efficient Kitchen with a peninsula counter and adjacent Laundry

■ An airy Master Suite with a walk-in closet and outdoor access

■ Another Bedroom and a Bedroom/loft area on the second floor share a full Bath

■ No materials list is available with this plan

FIRST FLOOR — 1,189 SQ. FT.
SECOND FLOOR — 575 SQ. FT.
BONUS ROOM — 581 SQ. FT.
GARAGE — 658 SQ. FT

TOTAL LIVING AREA:
1,764 SQ. FT.

©1997 Donald A. Gardner Architects, Inc.

B. NATHAN

Style and Versatility

Price Code: E

■ This plan features:

— Four Bedrooms

— Three full baths

■ Traditional hip roof arched and picture windows, and a barrel vaulted entrance

■ Stunning Great Room with magnificent cathedral ceiling

■ Cozy fireplace with space saving built-ins shields the Great Room from Kitchen noise

■ Secluded Master Suite with twin walk-in closets and a stately tray ceiling in the Bedroom

■ Cathedral ceiling enhances both Bedrooms on the second floor

■ First floor Study/Bedroom providing ample flexibility

FIRST FLOOR — 1,687 SQ. FT.
SECOND FLOOR — 514 SQ. FT.
BONUS — 336 SQ. FT.
GARAGE — 489 SQ. FT.

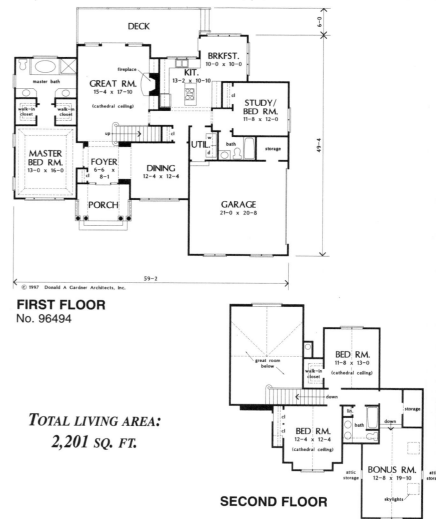

FIRST FLOOR
No. 96494

TOTAL LIVING AREA:
2,201 SQ. FT.

SECOND FLOOR

SECOND FLOOR

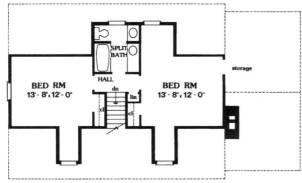

BED RM
13'-8"x12'-0"

BED RM
13'-8"x12'-0"

SPLIT BATH

HALL

storage

dn

lin

cl

cl

Adapt this Colonial to Your Lifestyle

Price Code: B

■ This plan features:
— Four bedrooms

— Two full baths

■ A Living Room with a beam ceiling and a fireplace

■ An eat-in Kitchen efficiently serving the formal Dining Room

■ A Master Bedroom with his and her closets

■ Two upstairs bedrooms sharing a split bath

FIRST FLOOR — 1,056 SQ. FT.
SECOND FLOOR — 531 SQ. FT.

TOTAL LIVING AREA:
1,587 SQ. FT.

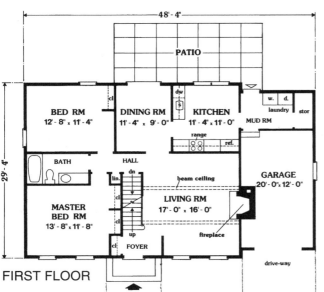

48'-4"

PATIO

BED RM
12'-8" x 11'-4"

DINING RM
11'-4" x 9'-0"

KITCHEN
11'-4" x 11'-0"

dw

range

ref.

w. d.

laundry

stor

MUD RM

cl

29'-4"

BATH

HALL

dn

lin

cl

cl

beam ceiling

MASTER BED RM
13'-8" x 11'-8"

LIVING RM
17'-0" x 16'-0"

fireplace

GARAGE
20'-0" x 12'-0"

up

cl

FOYER

drive-way

FIRST FLOOR

© 1994 Donald A. Gardner Architects, Inc.

Elegance And A Relaxed Lifestyle

Price Code: E

- ■ This plan features:
- — Four bedrooms
- — Three full baths

- ■ This family home has combined elegance with a relaxed lifestyle in an open plan full of surprises

- ■ Open two-level Foyer has a palladian window which visually ties in the formal Dining Area to the expansive Great Room

- ■ Windows all around, including bays in Master Suite and Breakfast Area provide natural light, while nine-foot ceilings create volume

- ■ Master Suite features a whirlpool tub, separate shower and his and her vanities

FIRST FLOOR — 1,841 SQ. FT.
SECOND FLOOR — 594 SQ. FT.
BONUS ROOM — 391 SQ. FT.
GARAGE & STORAGE — 584 SQ. FT.

SECOND FLOOR PLAN

TOTAL LIVING AREA:
2,435 SQ. FT.

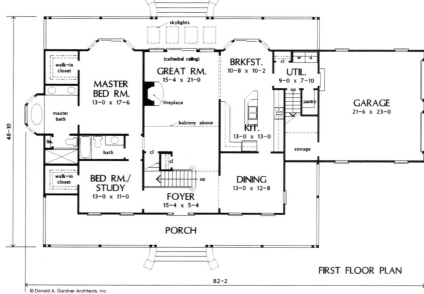

FIRST FLOOR PLAN

© Donald A. Gardner Architects, Inc.

To order your Blueprints, call 1-800-235-5700

English Tudor Styling

PRICE CODE: E

- This plan features:
— Four bedrooms
— Three full and one half baths
- This Tudor styled gem has a unique mix of exterior materials
- Inside the Entry either turn left to the Living Room or right into the Dining Room
- At the end of the Gallery is the Master Bedroom, which has dual walk in closets
- The Family Room has a sloped ceiling and a rear wall fireplace
- The Kitchen has a center island and opens to the Breakfast Area
- A skylight brightens the staircase to the second floor
- Upstairs find three large Bedrooms and two full Baths
- Also upstairs access the future Bonus Room that is located over the Garage
- No materials list is available for this plan

FIRST FLOOR — 2,082 SQ. FT.
SECOND FLOOR — 904 SQ. FT.
BONUS — 408 SQ. FT.
GARAGE — 605 SQ. FT.

TOTAL LIVING AREA: 2,986 SQ. FT.

FIRST FLOOR

SECOND FLOOR

ZIP QUOTE
HOME COST CALCULATOR
see order pages for details

Arches are Appealing

PRICE CODE: B

- This plan features:
— Three bedrooms
— Two full baths
- Welcoming front Porch enhanced by graceful columns and curved windows
- Parlor and Dining Room frame entry hall
- Expansive Great Room accented by a corner fireplace and outdoor access
- Open and convenient Kitchen with a work island, angled, peninsula counter/eating bar, and nearby Laundry and Garage entry
- Secluded Master Bedroom with a large walk-in closet and luxurious Bath with a dressing table
- Two additional Bedrooms with ample closets, share a double vanity Bath
- No materials list is available for this plan

MAIN FLOOR — 1,642 SQ. FT.
BASEMENT — 1,642 SQ. FT.
GARAGE — 430 SQ. FT.

TOTAL LIVING AREA: 1,642 SQ. FT.

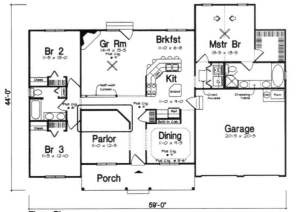

Floor Plan

Optional Basement Stairs

To order your Blueprints, call 1-800-235-5700

Energy Efficient Air-Lock Entry

PRICE CODE: B

- This plan features:
— Two bedrooms
— Two full baths
- The attractive covered Porch highlights the curb appeal of this charming home
- A cozy window seat and a vaulted ceiling enhance the private Den
- The sunken Great Room is accented by a fireplace that nestled between windows
- A screened Porch, accessed from the Dining Room, extends the living space to the outdoors
- The Master Bath features a garden tub, separate shower, his and her walk-in closets and a skylight
- No materials list is available for this plan

MAIN FLOOR — 1,771 SQ. FT.
BASEMENT — 1,194 SQ. FT.
GARAGE — 517 SQ. FT.

TOTAL LIVING AREA:
1,771 SQ. FT.

MAIN FLOOR

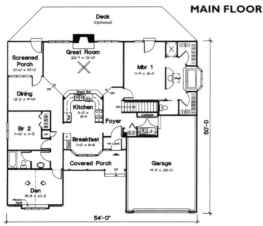

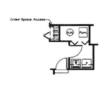

Victorian Inspired

PRICE CODE: B

- This plan features:
— Three bedrooms
— Two full baths
- A quaint exterior harkens back to time gone by
- A bay extends the space in the Dining Room
- The Kitchen is well planned and placed within the home
- A fireplace warms the open living space
- A screened Porch in the rear is perfect for pest free entertaining
- The Master Bedroom has a large walk-in closet
- No materials list is available for this plan

FIRST FLOOR — 949 SQ. FT.
SECOND FLOOR — 633 SQ. FT.
PORCH — 415 SQ. FT.

TOTAL LIVING AREA:
1,582 SQ.FT.

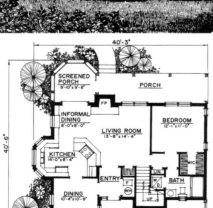

FIRST FLOOR PLAN

SECOND FLOOR PLAN

To order your Blueprints, call 1-800-235-5700

High Windows
PRICE CODE: C

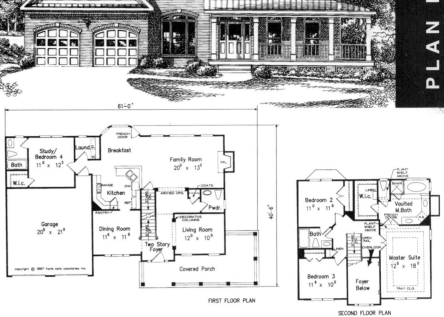

- This plan features:
  — Four bedrooms
  — Three full and one half baths
- The Dining Room enjoys the natural illumination from the large window to the left of the front door
- The Living Room has decorative columns defining the entrance into the room and over looks the Porch
- The second floor Master Suite is crowned in a tray ceiling and includes French doors to the lavish Master Bath
- An optional basement or crawl space foundation — please specify when ordering
- No materials list is available for this plan

FIRST FLOOR — 1,257 SQ. FT.
SECOND FLOOR — 871 SQ. FT.
BONUS ROOM — 444 SQ. FT.
BASEMENT — 1,275 SQ. FT.

TOTAL LIVING AREA: 2,128 SQ. FT.

SECOND FLOOR PLAN W/ OPT. BONUS ROOM

FIRST FLOOR PLAN

SECOND FLOOR PLAN

Elegantly Adorned
PRICE CODE: B

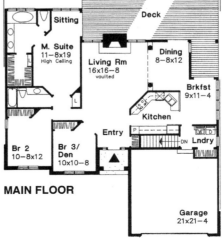

- This plan features:
  — Three bedrooms
  — Two full baths
- Only 1,633 square feet of living space, yet the designer never skimped on style and convenience.
- The Living Room has a dramatic appeal having a fireplace and a vaulted ceiling.
- Columns accent the entrance in to the formal Dining Room.
- A Laundry is conveniently located off the Kitchen.
- The Master Suite is designed with an intimate Sitting Area and a private Bath and walk-in closet.

MAIN FLOOR — 1,633 SQ. FT.
BASEMENT — 1,633 SQ. FT.
GARAGE — 450 SQ. FT.

TOTAL LIVING AREA: 1,633 SQ. FT.

WIDTH 52'-4"
DEPTH 57'-4"

MAIN FLOOR

Cozy Front Porch
PRICE CODE: B

■ This plan features:
— Three bedrooms
— Two full and one half bath
■ A Living Area enhanced by a large fireplace
■ A formal Dining Room that is open to the Living Area, giving a more spacious feel to the rooms
■ An efficient Kitchen that includes ample counter and cabinet space as well as double sinks and pass thru window to Living Area
■ A sunny Breakfast Area with vaulted ceiling and a door to the Sun Deck
■ A first floor Master Suite with separate tub & shower stall and walk-in closet
■ A first floor Powder Room with a hide-away laundry center
■ Two additional Bedrooms that share a full hall Bath

FIRST FLOOR — 1,045 SQ. FT.
SECOND FLOOR — 690 SQ. FT.
BASEMENT — 465 SQ. FT.
GARAGE — 580 SQ. FT.

TOTAL LIVING AREA:
1,735 SQ. FT.

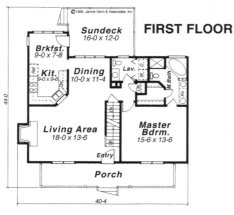

FIRST FLOOR

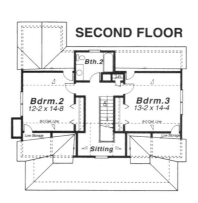

SECOND FLOOR

Gazebo Porch Creates Old-Fashioned Feel
PRICE CODE: A

■ This plan features:
— Three bedrooms
— Two full baths
■ An old-fashioned welcome is created by the covered Porch
■ The Breakfast Area overlooks the Porch and is separated from the Kitchen by an extended counter
■ The Dining Room and the Great Room are highlighted by a two-sided fireplace, enhancing the temperature as well as the atmosphere
■ The roomy Master Suite is enhanced by a whirlpool Bath with double vanity and a walk-in closet
■ Each of the two secondary Bedrooms feature a walk-in closet
■ No materials list is available for this plan

MAIN FLOOR — 1,452 SQ. FT.
GARAGE — 584 SQ. FT.

TOTAL LIVING AREA:
1,452 SQ. FT.

MAIN FLOOR

To order your Blueprints, call 1-800-235-5700

B. NATHAN.

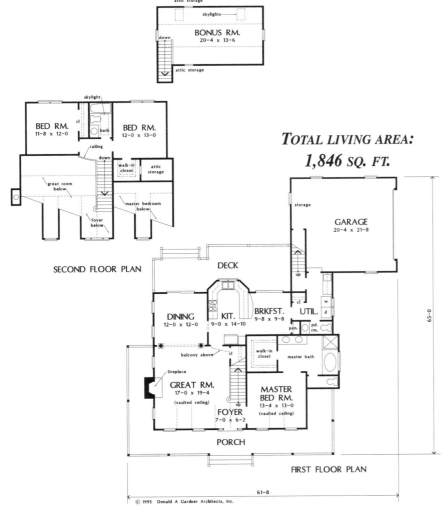

attic storage

skylights

BONUS RM.
20-4 x 13-6

down

attic storage

skylight

cl

bath

BED RM.
11-8 x 12-0

BED RM.
12-0 x 13-0

railing

down

walk-in closet

attic storage

great room below.

master bedroom below.

foyer below

SECOND FLOOR PLAN

TOTAL LIVING AREA:
1,846 SQ. FT.

storage

GARAGE
20-4 x 21-8

DECK

up

cl

w

d

DINING
12-0 x 12-0

KIT.
9-0 x 14-10

BRKFST.
9-8 x 9-8

UTIL.

pan.

pd. rm.

65-0

balcony above

cl

walk-in closet

master bath

fireplace

GREAT RM.
17-0 x 19-4
(vaulted ceiling)

up

FOYER
7-0 x 6-2

MASTER BED RM.
13-4 x 13-0
(vaulted ceiling)

PORCH

FIRST FLOOR PLAN

61-8

Farmhouse Charm

Price Code: D

■ This plan features:

— Three bedrooms

— Two full and one half baths

■ Nine foot ceilings and vaulted ceilings in Great Room and Master Bedroom add spaciousness

■ Dining Room accented by columns and accesses Deck for outdoor living

■ Efficient Kitchen features peninsula counter with serving bar for Breakfast Area

■ Master Bedroom Suite includes luxurious Bath with walk-in closet, garden tub, shower and double vanity

■ Two upstairs Bedrooms, one with walk-in closet, share full Bath with skylight

FIRST FLOOR — 1,380 SQ. FT.
SECOND FLOOR — 466 SQ. FT.
BONUS ROOM — 326 SQ. FT.
GARAGE — 523 SQ. FT.

© Frank Betz Associates, Inc.

Bathed in Natural Light
PRICE CODE: B

■ This plan features:
— Three bedrooms
— Two full and one half baths
■ A high arched window illuminates the Foyer and adds style to the exterior of the home
■ Vaulted ceilings in the formal Dining Room, Breakfast Room and Great Room create volume
■ The Master Suite is crowned with a decorative tray ceiling
■ The Master Bath has a double vanity, oval tub, separate shower and a walk-in closet
■ The Loft, with the option of becoming a fourth Bedroom, highlights the second floor
■ An optional basement or crawl space foundation — please specify when ordering

FIRST FLOOR — 1,133 SQ. FT.
SECOND FLOOR — 486 SQ. FT.
BASEMENT — 1,133 SQ. FT.
BONUS — 134 SQ. FT.
GARAGE — 406 SQ. FT.

TOTAL LIVING AREA: 1,619 SQ. FT.

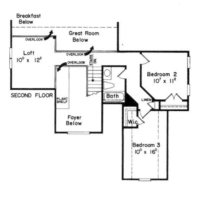

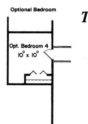

©1999 Donald A. Gardner, Inc.

Neat and Narrow
PRICE CODE: C

■ This plan features:
— Three bedrooms
— Two full baths
■ This plan is ideal for a narrow building lot
■ A lovely covered Porch entry leads to a Foyer with columns and arches
■ The Great Room houses a wall of built-in shelving with a large fireplace nestled in the center
■ Additional space on the upper level eases future expansion and storage issues

MAIN FLOOR — 1,481 SQ. FT.
GARAGE — 522 SQ. FT.
BONUS — 643 SQ. FT.

TOTAL LIVING AREA: 1,481 SQ. FT.

E. 1999 Donald A. Gardner, Inc. All rights reserved

To order your Blueprints, call 1-800-235-5700

Simply Cozy
PRICE CODE: A

- ■ This plan features:
- — Three bedrooms
- — Two full baths
- ■ Quaint front Porch sheltering Entry into the Living Area showcased by a massive fireplace and built-ins below a vaulted ceiling
- ■ Formal Dining Room accented by a bay of glass with Sun Deck access
- ■ Efficient, galley Kitchen with Breakfast Area, Laundry facilities and outdoor access
- ■ Secluded Master Bedroom offers a roomy walk-in closet and plush Bath with dual vanity and a garden window tub
- ■ Two additional Bedrooms with ample closets, share a full Bath with a skylight

MAIN FLOOR — 1,345 SQ. FT.
BASEMENT — 556 SQ. FT.
GARAGE — 724 SQ. FT.

TOTAL LIVING AREA:
1,345 SQ. FT.

ZIP QUOTE
HOME COST CALCULATOR
see order pages for details

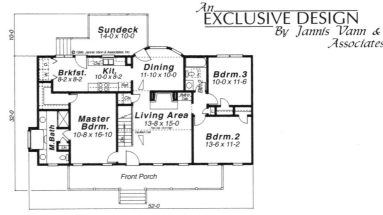

An
EXCLUSIVE DESIGN
By *Jannis Vann & Associates, Inc.*

Grand Design Highlighted by Turrets
PRICE CODE: F

- ■ This plan features:
- — Four bedrooms
- — Three full and one half baths
- ■ Triple arches at entry lead into Grand Foyer and Gallery with arched entries to all areas
- ■ Triple French doors catch the breeze and access to rear grounds in Living and Leisure Rooms
- ■ Spacious Kitchen with large walk-in Pantry, cooktop/work island and angled serving counter/snack-bar, glass Nook, Utility Room and Garage entry
- ■ Master Suite wing offers Veranda access, two closets and vanities, and a garden window tub
- ■ Three second floor Bedrooms with walk-in closets, balcony and full Bath access
- ■ No materials list is available for this plan

FIRST FLOOR — 3,546 SQ. FT.
SECOND FLOOR — 1,213 SQ. FT.
GARAGE — 822 SQ. FT.

TOTAL LIVING AREA:
4,759 SQ. FT.

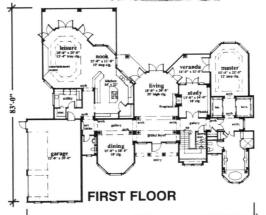

FIRST FLOOR

SECOND FLOOR

Split Bedroom Plan
PRICE CODE: A

■ This plan features:
— Three bedrooms
— Two full baths
■ A tray ceiling giving a decorative touch the Master Bedroom and a vaulted ceiling topping the five-piece Master Bath
■ A full bath located between the secondary Bedrooms
■ A corner fireplace and a vaulted ceiling highlighting the heart of the home, the Family Room
■ A wetbar, serving bar to the Family Room and a built-in Pantry adding to the convenience of the Kitchen
■ A formal Dining Room crowned in an elegant high ceiling
■ An optional basement, slab, or crawl space foundation — please specify when ordering

MAIN FLOOR — 1,429 SQ. FT.
BASEMENT — 1,472 SQ. FT.
GARAGE — 438 SQ. FT.

TOTAL LIVING AREA:
1,429 SQ. FT.

MAIN FLOOR

Bay Windows and a Terrific Front Porch
PRICE CODE: B

■ This plan features:
— Three bedrooms
— Two full baths
■ A country front porch
■ An expansive Living Area that includes a fireplace
■ A Master Suite with a private Master Bath and a walk-in closet, as well as a bay window view of the front yard
■ An efficient Kitchen that serves the sunny Breakfast Area and the Dining Room with equal ease
■ A built-in Pantry and a desk add to the conveniences in the Breakfast Area
■ Two additional Bedrooms that share the full hall Bath
■ A convenient main floor Laundry Room

MAIN FLOOR — 1,778 SQ. FT.
BASEMENT — 1,008 SQ. FT.
GARAGE — 728 SQ. FT.

TOTAL LIVING AREA:
1,778 SQ. FT.

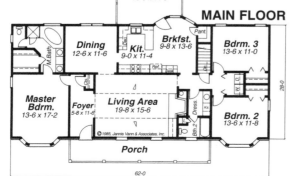

MAIN FLOOR

ZIP QUOTE
HOME COST CALCULATOR
see order pages for details

To order your Blueprints, call 1-800-235-5700

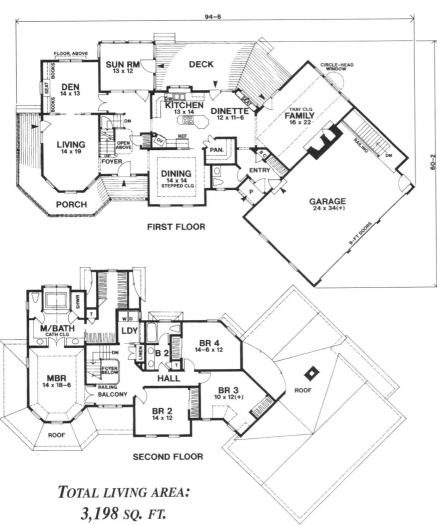

94–6

FLOOR, ABOVE

SUN RM
13 x 12

DECK

CIRCLE-HEAD WINDOW

DEN
14 x 13

BOOKS

SEAT

BOOKS

Dw
KITCHEN
13 x 14

DINETTE
12 x 11–6

TRAY CLG
FAMILY
16 x 22

DN

LIVING
14 x 19

OPEN
ABOVE

UP

DN

OV

REF

PAN.

RAILING

DN

FOYER

60–2

DINING
14 x 14
STEPPED CLG

ENTRY

P

B.C.

GARAGE
24 x 34(+)

PORCH

FIRST FLOOR

9-FT DOORS

SHWR

T

M/BATH
CATH CLG

T

W D

LDY

B 2

LINEN

T

BR 4
14–6 x 12

MBR
14 x 18–6

DN

FOYER
BELOW

HALL

ROOF

RAILING
BALCONY

BR 3
10 x 12(+)

BR 2
14 x 12

ROOF

ROOF

SECOND FLOOR

TOTAL LIVING AREA:
3,198 SQ. FT.

A Whisper of Victorian

Price Code: E

■ This plan features:

— Four bedrooms

— Two full and one half baths

■ A formal Living Room with wrap-around windows and access to the cozy Den

■ An elegant, formal Dining Room accented by a stepped ceiling

■ An efficient Kitchen equipped with a cooktop island/eating bar, a huge walk-in pantry and a Dinette with a window seat

■ An all-purpose glass-walled Sun Room

■ A fireplaced Family Room, with a tray ceiling topping a circle-head window

■ A Master Suite with a decorative ceiling and a Bath with a raised, atrium tub, and two vanities

■ Three additional bedrooms sharing a full bath with a double vanity

■ No materials list available

FIRST FLOOR — 1,743 SQ. FT.
SECOND FLOOR — 1,455 SQ. FT.

151

Cute Starter Home
PRICE CODE: B

- This plan features:
  - Three bedrooms
  - Two full baths
- Simple design with quality details provides charm inside and out
- Spacious Living/Dining Room allows comfortable gatherings with multiple windows and outdoor access
- Open Kitchen/Nook easily accesses Dining Area, Laundry closet and Garage
- Corner Master Bedroom boasts full view of rear yard, walk-in closet and private Bath
- Two additional Bedrooms with ample closets, share a full Bath
- No materials list is available for this plan

MAIN FLOOR — 1,557 SQ. FT.
BASEMENT — 1,557 SQ. FT.
GARAGE — 400 SQ. FT.

TOTAL LIVING AREA:
1,557 SQ. FT.

MAIN FLOOR PLAN

Country Character
PRICE CODE: D

- This plan features:
  - Three bedrooms
  - Two full and one half baths
- The wrap-around Porch adds style and living space
- Bays enhance the formal Living and Dining rooms
- A see-through fireplace warms the Living and Family Rooms
- The gallery upstairs is a quiet retreat
- The Master Bedroom has space saving built-in dressers
- No materials list is available for this plan

FIRST FLOOR — 1,308 SQ. FT.
SECOND FLOOR — 992 SQ. FT.
BASEMENT — 1,087 SQ. FT.
GARAGE — 455 SQ. FT.

TOTAL LIVING AREA:
2,300 SQ. FT.

FIRST FLOOR PLAN

SECOND FLOOR PLAN

To order your Blueprints, call 1-800-235-5700

© 1997 Donald A. Gardner Architects, Inc.

Victorian Charm

Price Code: D

■ This plan features:

— Four bedrooms

— Two full baths

■ This home combines Victorian charm with today's lifestyle needs

■ Ceilings vaulted in Great Room and ten feet height in Foyer, Dining Room, Kitchen/Breakfast bay and Bedroom/Study

■ Secluded Master Bedroom suite features tray ceiling, walk-in closet and private, skylit bath

■ Two additional bedrooms, located in separate wing, share a full bath

■ Front and rear Porches extend living area outdoors

MAIN FLOOR — 1,903 SQ. FT.
GARAGE & STORAGE — 531 SQ. FT.

TOTAL LIVING AREA:
1,903 SQ. FT.

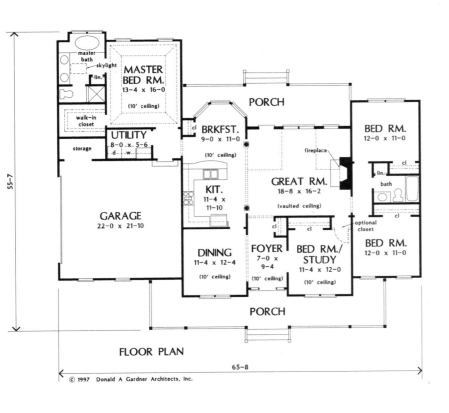

FLOOR PLAN

© 1997 Donald A Gardner Architects, Inc.

Country-Style Home

Price Code: D

■ This plan features:

— Four bedrooms

— Two full and two half baths

■ A typical farmhouse front porch sheltering the double door entrance

■ A sunken formal living room, enhanced by a focal point fireplace and a large windowed bay and a stepped ceiling

■ An elegant formal Dining Room angled to form an octagon

■ A large Kitchen with a central island

■ A fireplaced Family Room

■ Master Bedroom suite, with sitting bay, dressing area, three closets, and a deluxe bath

■ Three additional bedrooms sharing the full double vanity bath in the hall

■ Studio area above the garage includes a half-bath

FIRST FLOOR — 1,217 SQ. FT.
SECOND FLOOR — 1,249 SQ. FT.
BASEMENT — 1,217 SQ. FT.
GARAGE — 431 SQ. FT.

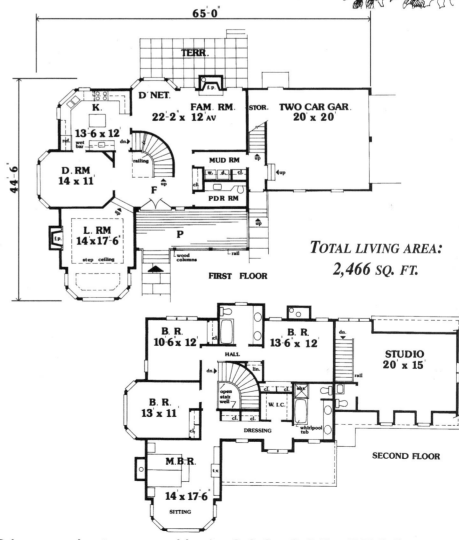

TOTAL LIVING AREA: 2,466 SQ. FT.

154

Rambling Farmhouse
PRICE CODE: E

This plan features:
- Three bedrooms
- Two full and one half baths
- Front and back dormers and wrapping Porches
- An unconventional rear staircase in the Great Room capped by an impressive second story balcony
- Master Suite privately situated downstairs with his-n-her walk-in closets, a linen closet, dual vanity and a separate tub and shower
- Dormer alcoves and walk-in closets in each second story Bedroom

FIRST FLOOR — 1,471 SQ. FT.
SECOND FLOOR — 577 SQ. FT.
BONUS — 368 SQ. FT.
GARAGE — 505 SQ. FT.

**TOTAL LIVING AREA:
2,048 SQ. FT.**

© Donald A. Gardner Architects, Inc.

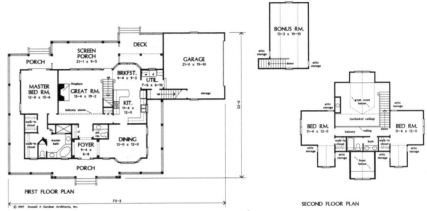

FIRST FLOOR PLAN

© 1997 Donald A Gardner Architects, Inc.

SECOND FLOOR PLAN

Champagne Style on a Soda-Pop Budget
PRICE CODE: A

This plan features:
- Three bedrooms
- One full and one three-quarter baths
- Multiple gables, circle-top windows, and a unique exterior setting this delightful Ranch apart in any neighborhood
- Living and Dining Rooms flowing together to create a very roomy feeling
- Sliding doors leading from the Dining Room to a covered Patio
- A Master Bedroom with a private Bath

MAIN FLOOR — 988 SQ. FT.
BASEMENT — 988 SQ. FT.
GARAGE — 280 SQ. FT
OPTIONAL 2-CAR GARAGE — 384 SQ. FT.

**TOTAL LIVING AREA:
988 SQ. FT.**

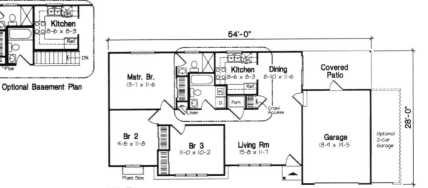

Optional Basement Plan

Main Floor

**ZIP QUOTE
HOME COST CALCULATOR**
see order pages for details

Impressive Elevation
PRICE CODE: E

■ This plan features:
— Three bedrooms
— Three full baths

■ Glass arch entrance into Foyer and Grand Room accented by fireplace between built-ins and multiple French doors leading to Veranda

■ Decorative windows highlight Study and formal Dining Room

■ Spacious Kitchen with walk-in Pantry and peninsula serving counter easily serves Nook, Veranda and Dining Room

■ Luxurious Master Suite with step ceiling, Sitting Area, his-n-hers closets and pampering Bath

■ Two additional Bedrooms, one with a private Deck, have bay windows and walk-in closets

FIRST FLOOR — 2,181 SQ. FT.
SECOND FLOOR — 710 SQ. FT.
GARAGE — 658 SQ. FT.

TOTAL LIVING AREA:
2,891 SQ. FT.

FIRST FLOOR

SECOND FLOOR

Always in Style
PRICE CODE: H

■ This plan features:
— Four bedrooms
— Four full and two half baths

■ Brick, gables and a traditional hip roof always seem to be in style

■ Inside find dramatic spaces that include the Dining room and the Great Room both with 14′ ceilings

■ The Study features a wall of built in bookshelves

■ The Kitchen has a center island with a cooktop

■ The Sun Room and the Breakfast Nook share a counter with the Kitchen

■ The Master Bedroom is opulent with dual Baths and closets

■ Storage space abounds with a walk-in Pantry, numerous closets, and storage space in the Garage

MAIN FLOOR — 4,523 SQ. FT.
GARAGE — 1,029 SQ. FT.

TOTAL LIVING AREA:
4,523 SQ. FT.

This plan is not to be built in Greenville County, SC

MAIN FLOOR

FIRST FLOOR
No. 91592

WIDTH 43'-0"
DEPTH 69'-0"

GARAGE
21/4 X 20/0

NOOK
10/6 X 13/0
(9' CLG.)

W D

REF.

10/6 X 13/0

DESK

FAMILY
15/0 X 16/4
(9' CLG.)

DINING
12/0 X 10/0
(9' CLG.)

UP

FOYER

LIVING
14/0 X 11/0 +/-
(9' CLG.)

DEN
14/0 X 10/0 +
(9' CLG.)

SECOND FLOOR

BR. 3
10/6 X 13/0

PLANT SHELF

FAMILY BELOW

LINEN

DN

BR. 2
12/4 X 11/0

VAULTED
MASTER
12/0 X 15/0 +

Cozy Accommodations
Price Code: E

■ This plan features:
— Three bedrooms
— Two full and one half baths

■ A quaint, wrapping porch sheltering the entrance

■ Foyer giving access to the combined Living and Dining rooms, and the secluded Den or Family Room

■ A terrific, two-sided fireplace accentuating the Den and Family Room

■ Second floor Master Suite with a vaulted ceiling

FIRST FLOOR — 1,371 SQ. FT.
SECOND FLOOR — 916 SQ. FT.

TOTAL LIVING AREA:
2,287 SQ. FT.

Rich Classic Lines

Price Code: D

■ This plan features:

— Four bedrooms

— Three full and one half baths

■ A two story Foyer flooded by light through a half-round transom

■ A vaulted ceiling in the Great Room that continues into the Master Suite

■ A corner fireplace in the Great Room with French doors to the Breakfast/Kitchen area

■ A center island in the Kitchen with a built-in desk and pantry

■ A tray ceiling and recessed hutch area in the formal Dining Room

■ A Master Suite with a walk-in closet, a whirlpool tub, and a double sink vanity

■ A materials list is not available with this plan

FIRST FLOOR — 1,496 SQ. FT.
SECOND FLOOR — 716 SQ. FT.
BASEMENT — 1,420 SQ. FT.
GARAGE — 460 SQ. FT.

TOTAL LIVING AREA:
2,212 SQ. FT.

SECOND FLOOR

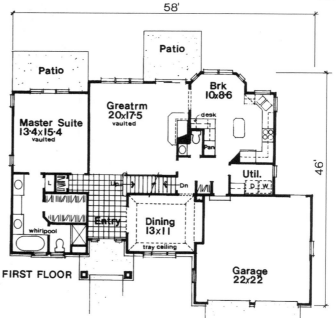

FIRST FLOOR

Charming Country Home
PRICE CODE: A

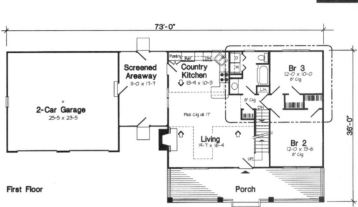

■ This plan features:
– Three bedrooms
– Two full baths
  A welcoming front Porch invites visiting and shelters entrance
  Cozy fireplace below a vaulted ceiling and dormer window in Living Room
■ Two first floor Bedrooms share a full Bath and Laundry
  Private second floor Master Suite offers a dormer window, walk-in closet and private Bath
■ No materials list is available for this plan

FIRST FLOOR — 1,018 SQ. FT.
SECOND FLOOR — 416 SQ. FT.
GARAGE — 624 SQ. FT.

TOTAL LIVING AREA:
1,434 SQ. FT.

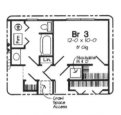

Alternate Foundation Plan

Second Floor

First Floor

Expansive Family Living Area
PRICE CODE: D

■ This plan features:
– Four bedrooms
– Two full baths and one half baths
■ A vaulted ceiling tops the Foyer, achieving a feeling of volume
■ The Living Room showcases a tray ceiling, and is enhanced by a boxed bay window
■ The Dining Room adjoins the Living Room and has direct access to the Kitchen
■ The Kitchen features a cooktop island and flows into the Dinette
■ The Family Room includes a fireplace framed by windows and adjoins the Dinette
■ Double doors add privacy to the Den
■ A tray ceiling tops the Master Bedroom which also includes a walk-in closet and a full Bath
■ The secondary Bedrooms are in close proximity to a full Bath
■ No materials list is available for this plan

FIRST FLOOR — 1,378 SQ. FT.
SECOND FLOOR — 1,084 SQ. FT.
BASEMENT — 1,378 SQ. FT.
GARAGE — 448 SQ. FT.

TOTAL LIVING AREA:
2,462 SQ. FT.

SECOND FLOOR

FIRST FLOOR
WIDTH= 61'-0"
DEPTH= 42'-0"

Traditional Ranch Plan

Price Code: D

■ This plan features:

— Three bedrooms

— Two full baths

■ Spacious Great Room adjacent to the open Kitchen /Breakfast Area

■ Secluded Master Bedroom highlighted by the Master Bath with a garden tub, separate shower, and his and her vanities

■ Bay window allows bountiful natural light into the Breakfast Area

■ Two additional Bedrooms sharing a full Bath

■ An optional basement or crawl space foundation — please specify when ordering

MAIN FLOOR — 2,218 SQ. FT.
BASEMENT — 1,658 SQ. FT.
GARAGE — 528 SQ. FT.

TOTAL LIVING AREA:
2,218 SQ. FT.

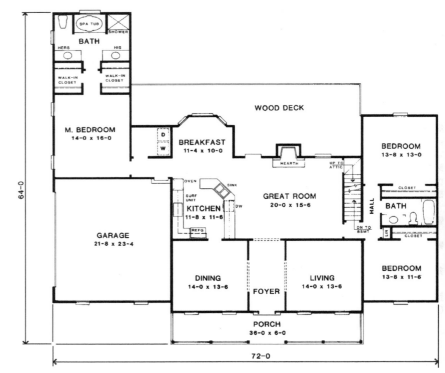

MAIN FLOOR

Expansive Living Room
PRICE CODE: A

PLAN NO. 98434

■ This plan features:
— Three bedrooms
— Two full baths

■ Vaulted ceiling crowns spacious Living Room highlighted by a fireplace

■ Built-in Pantry and direct access from the Garage adding to the conveniences of the Kitchen

■ Walk-in closet and a private five-piece Bath topped by a vaulted ceiling in the Master Bedroom Suite

■ Proximity to the full Bath in the hall from the secondary Bedrooms

■ An optional basement, slab or crawl space — please specify when ordering

MAIN FLOOR — 1,346 SQ. FT.
BASEMENT — 1,358 SQ. FT.
GARAGE — 385 SQ. FT.

TOTAL LIVING AREA:
1,346 SQ. FT.

© Frank Betz Associates, Inc.

MAIN FLOOR

A Comfortable Informal Design
PRICE CODE: C

PLAN NO. 94801

■ This plan features:
— Three bedrooms
— Two full baths

■ Warm, Country front Porch with wood details

■ Spacious Activity Room enhanced by a pre-fab fireplace

■ Open and efficient Kitchen/Dining Area highlighted by bay window, adjacent to Laundry and Garage Entry

■ Corner Master Bedroom offers a pampering Bath with a garden tub and double vanity topped by a vaulted ceiling

■ Two additional Bedrooms with ample closets, share a full Bath

■ An optional slab or crawl space foundation — please specify when ordering

MAIN FLOOR — 1,300 SQ. FT.
GARAGE — 576 SQ. FT.

TOTAL LIVING AREA:
1,300 SQ. FT.

MAIN FLOOR

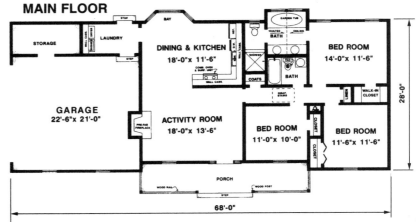

Stately Arched Entry
PRICE CODE: E

- This plan features:
  — Three bedrooms
  — Two full and one half baths
- The stately arched entry Porch is supported by columns
- The Dining Room has a tray ceiling and is defined by columns
- The Great Room has a fireplace and accessed the rear Porch/Deck
- The Kitchen is full of cabinet and counter space
- The Master Bedroom has a rear wall bay window and a tray ceiling
- The Master Bath features dual vanities and walk-in closets
- There are two secondary Bedrooms, one of which could be used as a Study
- A Bonus Room is located over the two-car Garage

MAIN FLOOR — 2,024 SQ. FT.
BONUS — 423 SQ. FT.
GARAGE — 623 SQ. FT.

TOTAL LIVING AREA:
2,024 SQ. FT.

Elegant Dining Room
PRICE CODE: D

- This plan features:
  — Four Bedrooms
  — Two full and one half baths
- Grand two-story Foyer with graceful staircase and access to Living and Dining rooms
- Double door entry into Dining Room with a boxed bay window, stepped ceiling and buffet recess
- Work island/snack bar, corner Pantry and a bright Dinette bay with Deck access highlight Kitchen
- Pocket doors lead into the expansive Family Room with cozy fireplace
- A tray ceiling, whirlpool tub with a separate shower, double vanity and a walk-in closet enhance the Master Suite
- No materials list is available for this plan

FIRST FLOOR — 1,194 SQ. FT.
SECOND FLOOR — 1,065 SQ. FT.
GARAGE — 672 SQ. FT.

TOTAL LIVING AREA:
2,259 SQ. FT.

To order your Blueprints, call 1-800-235-5700

SECOND FLOOR

TOTAL LIVING AREA:
4,106 SQ. FT.

Spectacular Stucco and Stone

Price Code: F

■ This plan features:

— Four bedrooms

— One full, two three-quarter and one half baths

■ Arches and columns accent formal spaces

■ Open Living Room with fireplace and multiple doors to rear grounds

■ Formal Dining Room has a bay window conveniently located

■ Angled Kitchen with walk-in Pantry and peninsula counter

■ Master wing offers a step ceiling, two walk-in closets and a lavish Bath

■ Two additional Bedrooms and a Guest Suite share second floor and Decks

FIRST FLOOR — 3,027 SQ. FT.
SECOND FLOOR — 1,079 SQ. FT.
BASEMENT — 3,027 SQ. FT.
GARAGE — 802 SQ. FT.

FIRST FLOOR
No. 94239

Spacious Feelings
PRICE CODE: B

- This plan features:
— Three bedrooms
— Two full baths
- Open layout with vaulted ceilings in Foyer, Great Room and Breakfast Area
- Kitchen with pass thru and Pantry, efficiently serves bright Breakfast Area, Great Room and formal Dining Room
- Luxurious Master Suite offers a tray ceiling, two walk-in closets and a double vanity Bath with vaulted ceiling
- Two secondary Bedrooms share a full Bath, and Laundry and closets
- No materials list is available for this plan

MAIN FLOOR — 1,363 SQ. FT.
BASEMENT — 715 SQ. FT.
GARAGE — 677 SQ. FT

TOTAL LIVING AREA:
1,363 SQ. FT.

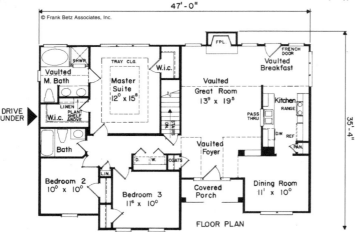

© Frank Betz Associates, Inc.

47'-0"

35'-4"

DRIVE UNDER

Vaulted M. Bath
W.i.c.
Master Suite 12⁰ x 15⁸
TRAY CLG.
W.i.c.
Bath
Bedroom 2 10⁰ x 10⁰
Bedroom 3 11⁶ x 10⁰
COATS
Covered Porch
Vaulted Foyer
FPL
Vaulted Great Room 13⁹ x 19⁵
PASS THRU
Kitchen
RANGE
D.W. REF
PAN.
FRENCH DOOR
Vaulted Breakfast
Dining Room 11' x 10'

FLOOR PLAN

Truly Western Approach to the Ranch House
PRICE CODE: C

- This plan features:
— Four bedrooms
— Three full baths
- Authentic Ranch styling with long Loggia, posts and braces, hand-split shake roof and cross-buck doors
- A Texas-sized hexagonal, sunken Living Room with two solid walls, one with a fireplace, and two 10' walls of sliding glass doors
- A Porch surrounding the Living Room on three sides
- A Master Suite with a private Master Bath
- An efficient well-equipped Kitchen flowing into the Family Room

MAIN FLOOR — 1,830 SQ. FT.
BASEMENT — 1,830 SQ. FT.
GARAGE — 540 SQ. FT.

TOTAL LIVING AREA:
1,830 SQ. FT.

86'-0"

65'-0"

pool
barbecue
DINING PORCH
LIVING PORCH
fireplace
sliding glass doors
sunken LIVING ROOM 21' x 20'
up two steps
BEDROOM 4 11' x 10'
BEDROOM 3 11' x 10'
vanity
master BEDROOM 1 (suite) 11' x 15'-10"
vanity
linen
Guest closet
down two steps
FOYER
dressing room
BATH
dish
DINING ROOM 10' x 11'-4"
china
FAMILY ROOM 12' x 9'-6"
BEDROOM 2 or study 10' x 9'-4"
BATH
STORAGE
BATH
LAUNDRY
KITCHEN 10' x 11'-6"
PORCH
TWO CAR GARAGE

MAIN FLOOR

To order your Blueprints, call 1-800-235-5700

© 1994 Donald A. Gardner Architects, Inc.

ZIP QUOTE
HOME COST CALCULATOR
see order pages for details

Perfect for Family Gatherings

Price Code: C

■ This plan features:

— Three bedrooms

— Two full baths

■ An open layout between the Great Room, Kitchen, and Breakfast Bay sharing a cathedral ceiling and a fireplace

■ Master Suite with a soaring cathedral ceiling, direct access to the Deck and a well-appointed Bath with a large walk-in closet

■ Additional Bedrooms sharing a full Bath in the hall

■ Centrally located Utility and Storage spaces

MAIN FLOOR — 1,346 SQ. FT.
GARAGE & STORAGE — 462 SQ. FT.

TOTAL LIVING AREA:
1,346 SQ. FT.

Floor Plan

MASTER BED RM.
14-8 x 13-0

DECK

master bath

walk-in closet

GREAT RM.
15-8 x 15-0

DINING
11-4 x 11-0

(cathedral ceiling)

fireplace

w   d

UTIL.

GARAGE
21-0 x 21-0

bath

lin.   sto.   cl

FOYER
6-8 x 5-8

KIT.
11-4 x 12-4

cl

BED RM.
10-0 x 10-4

cl

BED RM.
10-0 x 10-4

PORCH

44-2

65-0

© Donald A. Gardner Architects, Inc.

FLOOR PLAN

Grace with an Elegant Front Porch

PRICE CODE: B

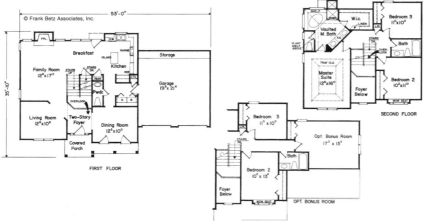

© Frank Betz Associates, Inc.

FIRST FLOOR

Opt. Bonus Room

OPT. BONUS ROOM

SECOND FLOOR

- This plan features:
  — Three bedrooms
  — Two full and one half baths
- The two-story Foyer accesses the Dining Room, Living Room and Family Room with ease
- The Kitchen opens to the Breakfast Area and in turn the Breakfast Area is open to the Family Room
- The Family Room is enhanced by a fireplace
- A work island adds counter space to the Kitchen
- The Master Suite with a private Bath is topped by a vaulted ceiling
- The front secondary Bedroom is highlighted by a window seat
- An optional basement, crawl space or slab — please specify when ordering
- No materials list is available for this plan

FIRST FLOOR — 926 SQ. FT.
SECOND FLOOR — 824 SQ. FT.
BONUS ROOM — 282 SQ. FT.
BASEMENT — 926 SQ. FT.
GARAGE — 440 SQ. FT.

TOTAL LIVING AREA:
1,750 SQ. FT.

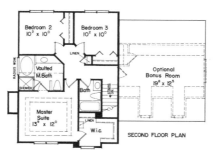

Covered Porch Shelters Entry

PRICE CODE: A

© Frank Betz Associates, Inc.

FIRST FLOOR PLAN

SECOND FLOOR PLAN

- This plan features:
  — Three bedrooms
  — Two full and one half baths
- There is a convenient pass-through from the Kitchen into the Family Room
- An easy flow into the Dining Room enhances the interaction of the living spaces on the first floor
- A fireplace highlights the spacious Family Room
- The Kitchen opens to the Breakfast Room which has a French door that accesses the rear yard
- Decorative ceiling treatment highlights the Master Bedroom while a vaulted ceiling tops the Master Bath
- Two additional Bedrooms share the use of the full Bath in the hall
- An optional basement or crawl space foundation — please specify when ordering

FIRST FLOOR — 719 SQ. FT.
SECOND FLOOR — 717 SQ. FT.
BASEMENT — 719 SQ. FT.
GARAGE — 480 SQ. FT.
BONUS — 290 SQ. FT.

TOTAL LIVING AREA:
1,436 SQ. FT.

Packed with Options

PRICE CODE: C

- This plan features:
  — Three bedrooms
  — Three full baths
- This home has a tiled entry and Gallery that connects the living space
- The Great Room has a rear wall fireplace that is set between windows
- Both Dining Areas are located steps away from the Kitchen
- The Study has a sloped ceiling and a front bay of windows
- The Master Bedroom has a private Bath and a galley-like walk-in closet
- Two secondary Bedrooms are on the opposite side of the home
- No materials list is available for this plan

MAIN FLOOR — 2,081 SQ. F.T
GARAGE — 422 SQ. F.T

TOTAL LIVING AREA:
2,081 SQ. FT.

ZIP QUOTE
HOME COST CALCULATOR
see order pages for details

MAIN FLOOR

Great Open Spaces

PRICE CODE: C

- This plan features:
  — Three bedrooms
  — Two full and one half baths
- The terrific covered front porch of this home leads into an impressive two story Foyer
- The expansive Family Room flows into the Breakfast Room and the Breakfast Room into the Kitchen for an easy open traffic pattern
- The formal areas, the Living Room and the Dining Room are located to the front of the home on either side of the Foyer
- The Master Suite includes a tray ceiling over the bedroom, a French door to the Master Bath, a vaulted ceiling over the Master Bath and walk-in closet
- An optional Bonus Room awaits future expansion
- An optional basement or crawl space foundation — please specify when ordering
- No materials list is available for this plan

FIRST FLOOR — 1,071 SQ. FT.
SECOND FLOOR — 924 SQ. FT.
BONUS ROOM — 280 SQ. FT.
BASEMENT — 1,071 SQ. FT.
GARAGE — 480 SQ. FT.

TOTAL LIVING AREA:
1,995 SQ. FT.

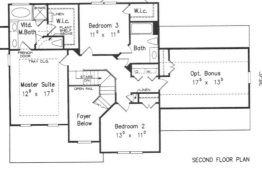

SECOND FLOOR PLAN

FIRST FLOOR PLAN

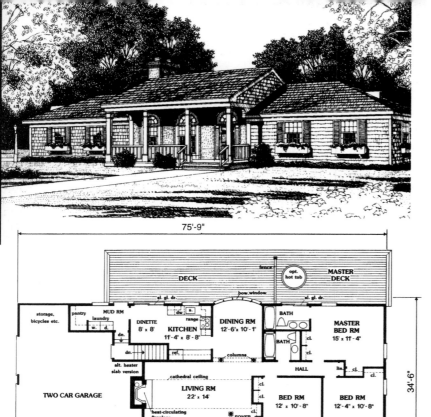

Formal Balance
PRICE CODE: A

- This plan features:
— Three bedrooms
— Two full baths
- A cathedral ceiling in the Living Room with a heat-circulating fireplace as the focal point
- A bow window in the Dining Room that adds elegance as well as natural light
- A well-equipped Kitchen that serves both the Dinette and the formal Dining Room efficiently
- A Master Bedroom with three closets and a private Master Bath with sliding glass doors to the Master Deck with a hot tub

MAIN FLOOR — 1,476 SQ. FT.
BASEMENT — 1,361 SQ. FT.
GARAGE — 548 SQ. FT.

TOTAL LIVING AREA:
1,476 SQ. FT.

MAIN FLOOR

Elegantly Styled
PRICE CODE: B

- This plan features:
— Three bedrooms
— Two full and one half baths
- Architectural details create eye-catching appeal to this home's facade
- The two-story Foyer is flanked by the formal Living and Dining Rooms
- A convenient Kitchen with angled snack bar has easy access to the Dining Room, Breakfast Area, backyard and the Laundry/Garage
- Open and comfortable, the Family Room is highlighted by a fireplace and windows
- The Master Suite is enhanced by a tray ceiling and a plush Bath with a vaulted ceiling
- Second floor offers an optional Bonus Room for future expansion
- An optional basement or crawl space foundation — please specify when ordering

FIRST FLOOR — 922 SQ. FT.
SECOND FLOOR — 778 SQ. FT.
BONUS ROOM — 369 SQ. FT.
GARAGE & STORAGE — 530 SQ. FT.

TOTAL LIVING AREA:
1,700 SQ. FT.

© Frank Betz Associates, Inc.

FIRST FLOOR PLAN

SECOND FLOOR PLAN

SECOND FLOOR W/ OPT. BONUS ROOM

To order your Blueprints, call 1-800-235-5700

Small and Stylish

PRICE CODE: B

This plan features:
- Three bedrooms
- Two full baths

The Kitchen includes a built-in Pantry and a peninsula counter/serving bar

■ The Great Room includes a fireplace and a French door to a covered Porch.

The Master Suite has a lavish Bath and a huge walk-in closet

No materials list is available for this plan

UPPER LEVEL — 1,509 SQ. FT.
LOWER LEVEL — 100 SQ. FT.
BASEMENT — 954 SQ. FT.
GARAGE — 484 SQ. FT.

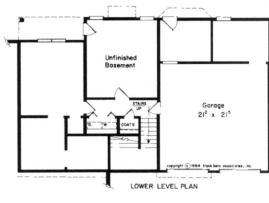

TOTAL LIVING AREA:
1,609 SQ. FT.

UPPER LEVEL PLAN

LOWER LEVEL PLAN

copyright (C) 1994 frank betz associates, inc.

Unique A-Frame

PRICE CODE: A

■ This plan features:
- Three bedrooms
- Two full baths

■ Exterior highlighted by fieldstone chimney, red cedar roof, vertical siding and a redwood Sun Deck

■ Open Living Room, Dining and Kitchen layout provides a spacious feeling

■ Efficient, U-shaped Kitchen with built-in Pantry and serving bar

■ Spacious first floor Bedroom convenient to full Bath and Laundry

■ Two second floor Bedrooms with ample closet space share a full Bath

FIRST FLOOR — 867 SQ. FT.
SECOND FLOOR — 442 SQ. FT.

TOTAL LIVING AREA:
1,309 SQ. FT.

FIRST FLOOR

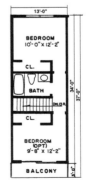

SECOND FLOOR

Columned Keystone
Arched Entry

Price Code: D

- This plan features:
- — Three bedrooms
- — Two full baths
- Keystone arches and arched transoms above the windows
- Formal Dining Room and Study flank the Foyer
- Fireplace in Great Room
- Efficient Kitchen with a peninsula counter and bayed Nook
- A step ceiling in the Master Suite and interesting Master Bath with a triangular area for the oval bath tub
- The secondary Bedrooms share a full Bath in the hall

MAIN FLOOR — 2,256 SQ. FT.
GARAGE — 514 SQ. FT.

TOTAL LIVING AREA:
2,256 SQ. FT.

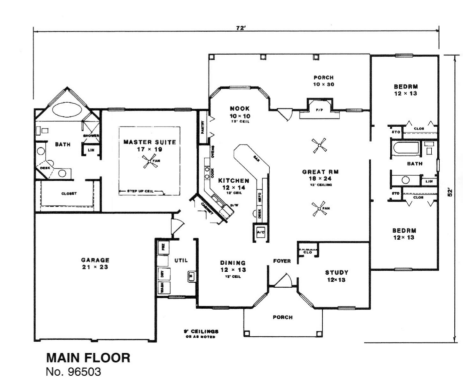

MAIN FLOOR
No. 96503

© 1996 Donald A Gardner Architects, Inc.

TOTAL LIVING AREA:
1,977 SQ. FT.

ZIP QUOTE
HOME COST CALCULATOR
see order pages for details

Unique and Desirable

Price Code: D

■ This plan features:
— Three bedrooms
— Two full baths

■ Private Master Bedroom has a walk-in closet and a skylight Bath

■ Two additional Bedrooms, one with a possible use as a Study, share a full Bath

■ From the Foyer pass through two columns into the Great Room with a cathedral ceiling and a fireplace

■ In the rear of the home is a skylight screen Porch and a Deck that features built in seats and a Spa

■ The Kitchen is conveniently located between the Dining Room and the skylight Breakfast Area

MAIN FLOOR — 1,977 SQ. FT.
BONUS ROOM — 430 SQ. FT
GARAGE & STORAGE — 610 SQ. FT.

Those Fabulous Details
PRICE CODE: D

- This plan features:
  — Four bedrooms
  — Two full and one half baths
- Unique style created by keystone, arched windows and entrance outside continue inside with arched openings
- Hub of home is vaulted Family Room with French door, arched window, cozy fireplace and pass thru to Kitchen
- Vaulted Breakfast Area expands efficient Kitchen for a busy household
- Spacious Master Suite boasts a Sitting Area with fireplace, tray ceiling, his and hers walk-in closets, and a vaulted Master Bath
- Three or four additional Bedrooms with large closets, share a full Bath
- Plan offers optional expansion to second floor Bonus Room and Bath
- An optional basement or crawl space foundation — please specify when ordering
- No materials list is available for this plan

MAIN FLOOR — 2,311 SQ. FT.
BONUS — 425 SQ. FT.
BASEMENT — 2,311 SQ. FT.
GARAGE — 500 SQ. FT.

TOTAL LIVING AREA:
2,311 SQ. FT.

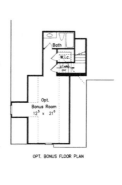

Photography supplied by The Meredith Corporation

Comfortable Cape
PRICE CODE: B

- This plan features:
  — Three bedrooms
  — Three full baths
- This home has plenty of space for outdoor entertaining
- The living room has a fireplace set between doors
- The Kitchen has plenty of counter space
- The Dining Room is brightened by a wall of windows
- No materials list is available for this plan

MAIN LEVEL — 936 SQ. FT.
UPPER LEVEL — 916 SQ. FT.
GARAGE — 576 SQ. FT.

TOTAL LIVING AREA:
1,852 SQ. FT.

WIDTH 70'-0"
DEPTH 68'-0"

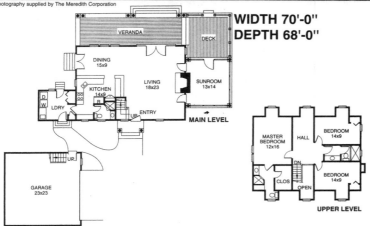

MAIN FLOOR

To order your Blueprints, call 1-800-235-5700

Outstanding Four Bedroom
PRICE CODE: C

■ This plan features:
— Four bedrooms
— Two full baths

■ Radius window highlighting the exterior and the formal Dining Room

■ High ceiling topping the Foyer for a grand first impression

■ Vaulted ceiling enhances the Great Room accented by a fireplace framed by windows to either side

■ Arched opening to the Kitchen from the Great Room

■ Breakfast Room topped by a vaulted ceiling and enhanced by elegant French door to the rear yard

■ Tray ceiling and a five-piece Bath gives luxurious presence to the Master Suite

■ Three additional Bedrooms share a full, double vanity Bath in the hall

■ An optional basement or crawl space foundation — please specify when ordering

MAIN FLOOR — 1,945 SQ. FT.

TOTAL LIVING AREA:
1,945 SQ. FT.

PLAN NO. 98435

© Frank Betz Associates

Classic Cottage
PRICE CODE: D

■ This plan features:
— Three bedrooms
— Two full and one half baths

■ An economic design for a narrow lot width

■ Twin dormers and a gabled Garage provide substantial curb appeal

■ Dramatic Great Room enhanced by two clerestory dormers and an overlooking Balcony

■ Crowned in an elegant tray ceiling, the first floor Master Suite has a private Bath and a walk-in closet

FIRST FLOOR — 1,336 SQ. FT.
SECOND FLOOR — 523 SQ. FT.
GARAGE & STORAGE — 492 SQ. FT.
BONUS ROOM — 225 SQ. FT.

TOTAL LIVING AREA:
1,859 SQ. FT.

PLAN NO. 98014

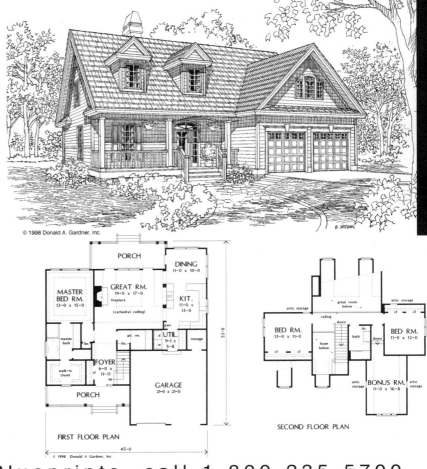

© 1998 Donald A. Gardner, Inc.

© 1995 Donald A Gardner Architects, Inc.

Tremendous Curb Appeal
PRICE CODE: C

■ This plan features:
— Three bedrooms
— Two full baths
■ Great Room topped by a cathedral ceiling and enhanced by a fireplace
■ Great Room, Dining Room and Kitchen open to each other for a feeling of spaciousness
■ Pantry, skylight and peninsula counter add to the comfort and efficiency of the Kitchen
■ Cathedral ceiling crowns the Master Suite and has these amenities; walk-in and linen closet, a luxurious private Bath
■ Swing Room, Bedroom or Study, topped by a cathedral ceiling
■ Skylight over full hall Bath naturally illuminates the room

MAIN FLOOR — 1,246 SQ. FT.
GARAGE — 420 SQ. FT.

TOTAL LIVING AREA:
1,246 SQ. FT.

FLOOR PLAN

© 1995 Donald A Gardner Architects, Inc.

© Frank Betz Associates, Inc.

Open Spaces
PRICE CODE: A

■ This plan features:
— Three bedrooms
— Two full baths
■ Open floor plan between the Family Room and the Dining Room
■ Vaulted ceilings adding volume and a fireplace in the Family Room
■ Three Bedrooms, the Master Suite with a five piece private Bath
■ Convenient laundry center located outside the Bedrooms
■ No materials list is available for this plan

MAIN FLOOR — 1,135 SQ. FT.

TOTAL LIVING AREA:
1,135 SQ. FT.

FLOOR PLAN

To order your Blueprints, call 1-800-235-5700

Isolated Master Suite
PRICE CODE: D

- This plan features:
— Three bedrooms
— Two full and one half baths
- A spacious, sunken Living Room with a cathedral ceiling
- An isolated Master Suite with a private Bath and walk-in closet
- Two additional Bedrooms with a unique Bath-and-a-half and ample Storage Space
- An efficient U-shaped Kitchen with a double sink, ample cabinets, counter space and a Breakfast Area
- A second floor Studio overlooking the Living Room
- An optional basement, slab or crawl space foundation — please specify when ordering

FIRST FLOOR — 2,213 SQ. FT.
SECOND FLOOR — 260 SQ. FT.
BASEMENT — 2,213 SQ. FT.
GARAGE — 422 SQ. FT.

TOTAL LIVING AREA:
2,473 SQ. FT.

WIDTH 91'-8"
DEPTH 45'-8"

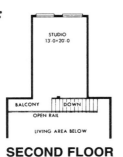

SECOND FLOOR

FIRST FLOOR

PLAN NO. 90420

Delightful Detailing
PRICE CODE: E

PLAN NO. 98426

- This plan features:
— Three bedrooms
— Two full and one half baths
- The vaulted ceiling extends from the Foyer into the Living Room
- The Dining Room is delineated by columns with a plant shelf above
- Family Room has a vaulted ceiling, and a fireplace with radius windows on either side
- The Kitchen equipped with an island serving bar, a desk, a wall oven, a Pantry and a Breakfast Bay
- The Master Suite is highlighted by a Sitting Room, a walk-in closet and a private Bath with a vaulted ceiling
- Two additional large Bedrooms share a Bath in the hall
- There is an optional Bonus Room located over the Garage
- An optional basement or a crawl space foundation — please specify when ordering

MAIN FLOOR — 2,622 SQ. FT.
BONUS ROOM — 478 SQ. FT.
BASEMENT — 2,622 SQ. FT.
GARAGE — 506 SQ. FT.

TOTAL LIVING AREA:
2,622 SQ. FT.

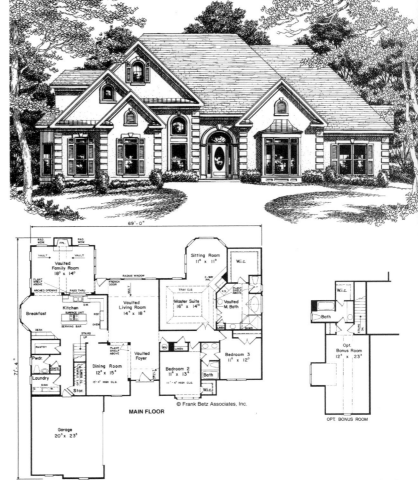

MAIN FLOOR

© Frank Betz Associates, Inc.

OPT. BONUS ROOM

© 1993 Donald A. Gardner Architects, Inc.

Economical Three Bedroom

Price Code: C

■ This plan features:

— Three bedrooms

— Two full baths

■ Dormers above the covered Porch casting light into the Foyer

■ Columns punctuating the entrance to the open Great Room/Dining Room Area with a shared cathedral ceiling and a bank of operable skylights

■ Kitchen with a breakfast counter, open to the Dining Area

■ Private Master Bedroom suite with a tray ceiling and luxurious Bath featuring a double vanity, separate shower, and skylights over the whirlpool tub

MAIN FLOOR — 1,322 SQ. FT.
GARAGE & STORAGE — 413 SQ. FT.

TOTAL LIVING AREA:
1,322 SQ. FT.

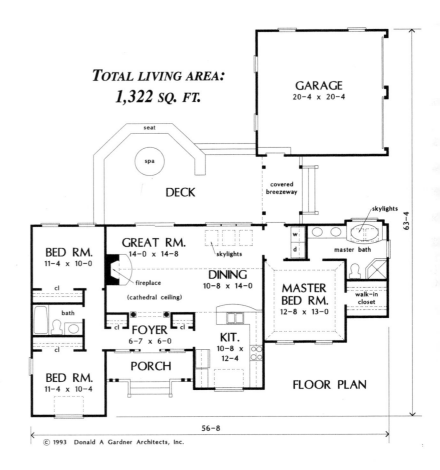

GARAGE
20-4 x 20-4

seat

spa

DECK

covered breezeway

skylights

63-4

BED RM.
11-4 x 10-0

cl

bath

cl

BED RM.
11-4 x 10-4

GREAT RM.
14-0 x 14-8

skylights

fireplace

(cathedral ceiling)

DINING
10-8 x 14-0

w
d

master bath

walk-in closet

MASTER BED RM.
12-8 x 13-0

cl   FOYER   cl
6-7 x 6-0

KIT.
10-8 x 12-4

PORCH

FLOOR PLAN

56-8

© 1993   Donald A Gardner Architects, Inc.

To order your Blueprints, call 1-800-235-5700

Vaulted Ceilings
PRICE CODE: D

■ This plan features:
— Four bedrooms
— Two full and one half baths
■ A vaulted ceiling crowns the Foyer and flows on into the Family Room
■ A fireplace adds a warm an cozy atmosphere to the entire home
■ Knee-walls with built-in shelves and a plant shelf above separate the Family Room form the Breakfast Room
■ An optional basement or crawl space foundation — please specify when ordering

FIRST FLOOR — 1,637 SQ. FT.
SECOND FLOOR — 671 SQ. FT.
BASEMENT — 1,637 SQ. FT.
GARAGE — 466 SQ. FT.

TOTAL LIVING AREA:
2,308 SQ. FT.

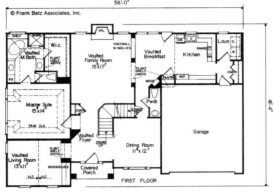

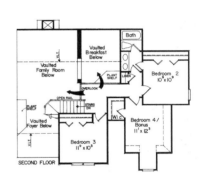

Massive Curb Appeal
PRICE CODE: C

■ This plan features:
— Four bedrooms
— Two full and one half baths
■ An arched two story entrances sets the luxurious stage of this fine home
■ The expansive Great Room boasts a large fireplace flanked by windows
■ The angled Kitchen has a large pass through to the Great Room
■ The first floor Master Suite includes sloped ceilings and a luxurious private Bath
■ No materials list is available for this plan

LOWER FLOOR — 1,472 SQ. FT.
UPPER FLOOR — 703 SQ. FT.
GARAGE — 540 SQ. FT.

TOTAL LIVING AREA:
2,175 SQ. FT.

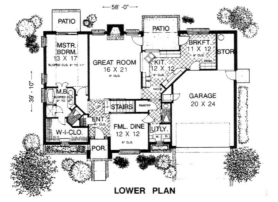

Charming Three Bedroom
PRICE CODE: A

- This plan features:
— Three bedrooms
— Two full baths
- Covered Porch leads into Foyer with plant shelves and Vaulted Family Room beyond
- Efficient Kitchen with Pantry, Laundry and pass-through opens to bright Breakfast Area
- Private Master Suite offers a vaulted ceiling, walk-in closet and vaulted Master Bath
- Two secondary Bedrooms, with spacious closets, share full Bath in the hall
- An optional basement or crawl space — please specify when ordering
- No materials list is available for this plan

MAIN FLOOR — 1,222 SQ. FT.
BASEMENT — 1,218 SQ. FT.
GARAGE — 410 SQ. FT.

TOTAL LIVING AREA:
1,222 SQ. FT.

OPTIONAL BASEMENT STAIR LOCATION

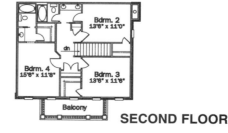

Italian Styled Exterior
PRICE CODE: E

- This plan features:
— Four bedrooms
— Three full and one half baths
- Ten-foot ceilings which add to the open feeling of the first floor design
- Interior columns and French doors add drama on entering the Foyer from the front Porch
- The large covered Porch at the rear extends the living area outdoors and also has an optional Kitchen for outdoor entertaining.
- No materials list is available for this plan.

FIRST FLOOR — 1,814 SQ. FT.
SECOND FLOOR — 884 SQ. FT.

TOTAL LIVING AREA:
2,698 SQ. FT.

FIRST FLOOR

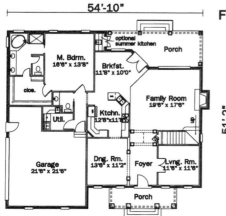

SECOND FLOOR

To order your Blueprints, call 1-800-235-5700

Country Exterior With Formal Interior

PRICE CODE: C

■ This plan features:
— Three bedrooms
— Two full and one half baths

■ Wrap-around Porch leads into central Foyer and formal Living and Dining rooms

■ Large Family Room with a cozy fireplace and Deck access

■ Convenient Kitchen opens to Breakfast Area with a bay window and built-in Pantry

■ Corner Master Bedroom with walk-in closet and appealing Bath

■ Two additional Bedrooms plus a Bonus Room share a full Bath and Laundry

■ An optional basement or crawl space foundation — please specify when ordering

FIRST FLOOR — 1,046 SQ. FT.
SECOND FLOOR — 1,022 SQ. FT.
BONUS — 232 SQ. FT.
BASEMENT — 1,046 SQ. FT.

TOTAL LIVING AREA:
2,068 SQ. FT.

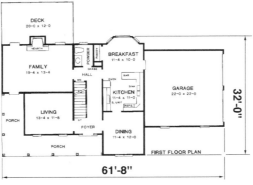

Decorative Ceilings Inside

PRICE CODE: A

■ This plan features:
— Three bedrooms
— Two full baths

■ The Family Room has a vaulted ceiling, a corner fireplace, and a French door to the rear yard

■ The Breakfast Nook is brightened by window on two of its walls

■ The galley Kitchen has a Pantry, and a serving bar into the Family Room

■ The Master Suite has a tray ceiling, a walk-in closet, and a private Bath

■ Two secondary Bedrooms have ample closet space, bright front wall windows, and one has a vaulted ceiling

■ This home has a two-car garage with Storage Space

■ No materials list is available for this plan

■ An optional basement, a slab or a crawl space foundation — please specify when ordering

MAIN FLOOR — 1,104 SQ. FT.
BASEMENT — 1,104 SQ. FT.
GARAGE — 400 SQ. FT.

TOTAL LIVING AREA:
1,104 SQ. FT.

MAIN FLOOR

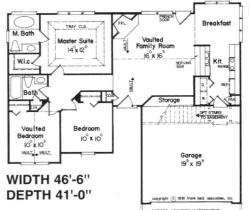

WIDTH 46'-6"
DEPTH 41'-0"

To order your Blueprints, call 1-800-235-5700

179

Private Master Suite
PRICE CODE: D

■ This plan features:
— Three bedrooms
— Two full and one half baths

■ Secluded Master Bedroom Suite tucked into the rear left corner of the home with a five-piece Bath and two walk in closets

■ Two additional Bedrooms at the opposite side of the home sharing the full Bath in the hall

■ Expansive Living Room highlighted by a corner fireplace and access to the rear Porch

■ Kitchen is located between the bright, bayed Nook and the formal Dining Room providing ease in serving

MAIN FLOOR — 2,069 SQ. FT.
GARAGE — 481 SQ. FT.

TOTAL LIVING AREA:
2,069 SQ. FT.

WIDTH 70'-0"
DEPTH 58'-0"

MAIN FLOOR

Sunken Family Room
PRICE CODE: D

■ This plan features:
— Four bedrooms
— Two full and one half baths

■ A grand two-story Foyer creates an impressive entry

■ The see-through fireplace n the Family Room is shared with the Keeping Room

■ A terrific informal living area is created by the open floor plan between the Kitchen, Breakfast Room and Keeping Room

■ The Master Suite has a tray ceiling above the Bedroom, an optional Sitting Room, a vaulted ceiling above the Master Bath and a walk-in closet

■ An optional basement or crawl space foundation — please specify when ordering

■ No materials list is available for this plan

FIRST FLOOR — 1,223 SQ. FT.
SECOND FLOOR — 1,163 SQ. FT.
BASEMENT — 1,223 SQ. FT.
GARAGE — 400 SQ. FT.
BONUS — 204 SQ. FT.

TOTAL LIVING AREA:
2,386 SQ. FT.

FIRST FLOOR PLAN

SECOND FLOOR PLAN

WIDTH 46'-0"
DEPTH 30'-0"

MAIN FLOOR

LOWER FLOOR

UPPER FLOOR

All Seasons

Price Code: E

- This plan features:
  — Three bedrooms
  — One full, one three-quarter and
    one half baths

- A wall of windows taking full
  advantage of the front view

- An open stairway to the upstairs Study
  and the Master Bedroom

- A Master Bedroom with a private
  master Bath and a walk-in wardrobe

- An efficient Kitchen including a breakfast bar that opens into the Dining Area

- A formal Living Room with a vaulted
  ceiling and a stone fireplace

MAIN FLOOR — 1,306 SQ. FT.
UPPER FLOOR — 598 SQ. FT.
LOWER FLOOR — 1,288 SQ. FT.

TOTAL LIVING AREA:
3,192 SQ. FT.

Luxurious One-Floor Living

Price Code: F

- This plan features:
- — Four bedrooms
- — Three full baths
- Decorative windows enhance the facade
- Formal Living Room accented by fireplace
- Formal Dining Room highlighted by decorative window
- Breakfast bar, work island, and an abundance of storage and counter space featured in Kitchen
- Bright alcove for informal Dining and Family rooms
- Spacious Master Bedroom has access to covered Patio, and huge a walk-in closet
- Three additional bedrooms have large closets
- No materials list is available for this plan

MAIN FLOOR — 3,254 SQ. FT.
GARAGE — 588 SQ. FT.

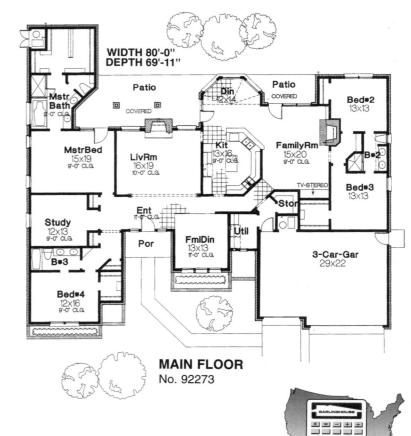

WIDTH 80'-0"
DEPTH 69'-11"

MAIN FLOOR
No. 92273

TOTAL LIVING AREA:
3,254 SQ. FT.

ZIP QUOTE
HOME COST CALCULATOR
see order pages for details

ZIP QUOTE
HOME COST CALCULATOR
see order pages for details

An Old-Fashioned Country Feeling

Price Code: C

■ This plan features:

— Three bedrooms

— Two full and one half baths

■ A large Living Room with a cozy fireplace opens to the Dining Room for easy entertaining

■ A formal Dining Room with a bay window and direct access to the Sun Deck

■ A U-shaped Kitchen, efficiently arranged with ample work space and a Pantry

■ A first floor Master Bedroom with an elegant bath complete with jacuzzi, two vanities and a walk-in closet

■ An optional basement, slab or crawl space foundation — please specify when ordering

FIRST FLOOR — 1,362 SQ. FT.
SECOND FLOOR — 729 SQ. FT.
BONUS ROOM — 384 SQ. FT.
GARAGE — 559 SQ. FT.

TOTAL LIVING AREA:
2,091 SQ. FT.

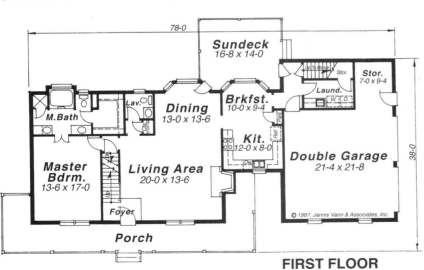

SECOND FLOOR

Study
11-2 x 11-0

Bdrm.2
13-6 x 13-4

Bdrm.3
12-0 x 13-4

Bth.2

Bonus Rm.
11-8 x 21-10

FIRST FLOOR

Sundeck
16-8 x 14-0

Dining
13-0 x 13-6

Brkfst.
10-0 x 9-4

Stor.
7-0 x 9-4

Laund.

M.Bath

Lav.

Kit.
12-0 x 8-0

Living Area
20-0 x 13-6

Double Garage
21-4 x 21-8

Master Bdrm.
13-6 x 17-0

Foyer

Porch

© 1987, Jannis Vann & Associates, Inc.

78-0

38-0

© 1993 Donald A Gardner Architects, Inc.

Traditional Beauty

Price Code: D

- This plan features:
  — Three bedrooms
  — Two full baths

- Traditional beauty with large arched windows, round columns, covered Porch and a brick veneer

- Clerestory dormers above covered Porch lighting the Foyer

- Cathedral ceiling enhancing the Great Room along with a cozy fireplace

- Island Kitchen with Breakfast Area accessing the large Deck with an optional spa

- Columns defining spaces

- Tray ceiling over the Master Bedroom, Dining Room and Bedroom/Study

- Dual vanity, separate shower, and whirlpool tub in the Master Bath

MAIN FLOOR — 1,576 SQ. FT.
GARAGE — 465 SQ. FT.

TOTAL LIVING AREA:
1,576 SQ. FT.

ZIP QUOTE
HOME COST CALCULATOR
see order pages for details

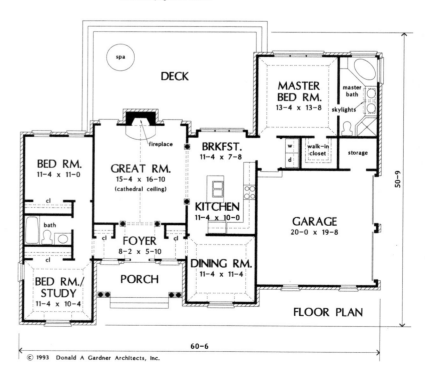

© 1993 Donald A Gardner Architects, Inc.

To order your Blueprints, call 1-800-235-5700

Varied Roof Heights Create Interesting Lines

PRICE CODE: B

This plan features:
- Three bedrooms
- Two full and one half baths
- A spacious Family Room with a heat-circulating fireplace, which is visible from the Foyer
- A large Kitchen with a cooktop island, opening into the Dinette bay
- A Master Suite with his-n-her closets and a private Master Bath
- Two additional Bedrooms which share a full hall Bath
- Formal Dining and Living Rooms, flowing into each other for easy entertaining

MAIN AREA — 1,613 SQ. FT.
BASEMENT — 1,060 SQ. FT.
GARAGE — 461 SQ. FT.

TOTAL LIVING AREA:
1,613 SQ. FT.

MAIN AREA

Windows Distinguish Design

PRICE CODE: F

This plan features:
- Five bedrooms
- Four full and one half baths
- Light shines into the Dining Room and the Living Room through their respective elegant windows
- A hall through the butler's Pantry leads the way into the Breakfast Nook
- The two-story Family Room has a fireplace with built in bookcases on either side
- The upstairs Master Suite has a Sitting Room and a French door that leads into the Master Bath
- There are three additional Bedrooms upstairs
- An optional basement or crawl space foundation — please specify when ordering

FIRST FLOOR — 1,786 SQ. FT.
SECOND FLOOR — 1,739 SQ. FT.
BASEMENT — 1,786 SQ. FT.
GARAGE — 704 SQ. FT.

TOTAL LIVING AREA:
3,525 SQ. FT.

© Frank Betz Associates

185

PLAN NO. 96506

Attractive Ceiling Treatments and Open Layout
PRICE CODE: B

- ■ This plan features:
- — Three bedrooms
- — Two full and one half baths
- ■ Great Room and Master Suite with step-up ceiling treatments
- ■ A cozy fireplace providing warm focal point in the Great Room
- ■ Open layout between Kitchen, Dining and Great Room lending a more spacious feeling
- ■ Five-piece, private Bath and walk-in closet pampering Master Suite
- ■ Two additional Bedrooms located at opposite end of home from the Master Suite
- ■ Master Suite sharing the full Bath in the hall

MAIN FLOOR — 1,654 SQ. FT.
GARAGE — 480 SQ. FT.

TOTAL LIVING AREA
1,654 SQ. FT.

WIDTH 68'-0"
DEPTH 46'-0"

MAIN FLOOR

PLAN NO. 97239

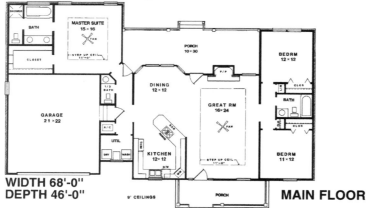

Impressive Presence
PRICE CODE: E

- ■ This plan features:
- — Four bedrooms
- — Three full and one half baths
- ■ The angled Garage combines with varied rooflines to create an impressive presence
- ■ The Living Room has a vaulted ceiling and a beautiful window
- ■ The Dining Room features a boxed bay window
- ■ Enter the Family Room through and arched opening from the Foyer
- ■ The Kitchen is open to the Nook and has a center island
- ■ The Master Suite is secluded behind the Garage on the first floor
- ■ Upstairs find three Bedrooms all with walk in closets
- ■ An optional Bonus Room is located over the Garage
- ■ No materials list is available for this plan
- ■ An optional basement and crawl space foundation — please specify when ordering

FIRST FLOOR — 1,904 SQ. FT.
SECOND FLOOR — 860 SQ. FT.
BONUS — 388 SQ. FT.
BASEMENT — 1,904 SQ. FT.
GARAGE — 575 SQ. FT.

TOTAL LIVING AREA:
2,764 SQ. FT.

FIRST FLOOR

SECOND FLOOR

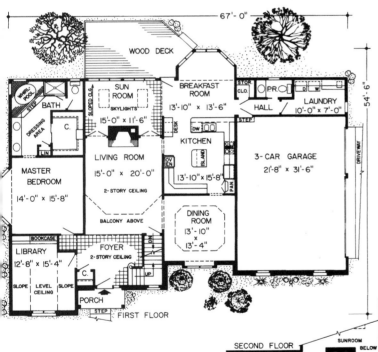

Traditional Energy Saver

Price Code: E

- This plan features:
- — Four bedrooms
- — Two full, one three-quarter and one half baths
- A heat storing floor in the Sun Room adjoining the Living Room and Breakfast Room
- A Living Room with French doors and a massive fireplace
- A balcony overlooking the soaring two-story Foyer and Living Room
- An island Kitchen centrally-located between the formal and informal Dining Rooms

FIRST FLOOR — 2,186 SQ. FT.
SECOND FLOOR — 983 SQ. FT.
BASEMENT — 2,186 SQ. FT.
GARAGE — 704 SQ. FT.

TOTAL LIVING AREA:
3,169 SQ. FT.

European Style

Price Code: F

■ This plan features:

— Four bedrooms

— Three full and one half baths

■ Central Foyer between spacious Living and Dining rooms with arched windows

■ Hub Kitchen with extended counter and nearby Utility/Garage entry, easily serves Breakfast Area and Dining Room

■ Spacious Den with a hearth fireplace between built-ins and sliding glass doors to Porch

■ Master Bedroom wing with decorative ceiling, plush Bath with two walk-in closets

■ An optional slab or crawl space foundation — please specify when ordering

MAIN AREA — 2,727 SQ. FT.
GARAGE — 569 SQ. FT.

TOTAL LIVING AREA:
2,727 SQ. FT.

WIDTH 70'-10"
DEPTH 64'-5"

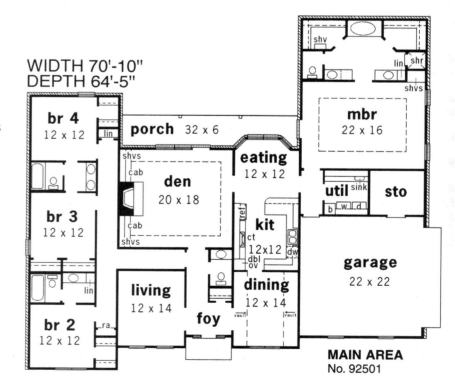

MAIN AREA
No. 92501

Moderate Ranch

PRICE CODE: C

■ This plan features:
— Three bedrooms
— Two full baths

■ A large Great Room with a vaulted ceiling and a stone fireplace with bookshelves on either side

■ A spacious Kitchen with ample cabinet space conveniently located next to the large Dining Room

■ A Master Suite having a large bath with a garden tub, double vanity and a walk-in closet

■ Two other large Bedrooms, each with a walk-in closet and access to the full Bath

■ An optional basement, slab or crawl space foundation — please specify when ordering

MAIN FLOOR — 1,811 SQ. FT.
BASEMENT — 1,811 SQ. FT.
GARAGE — 484 SQ. FT.

TOTAL LIVING AREA:
1,811 SQ. FT.

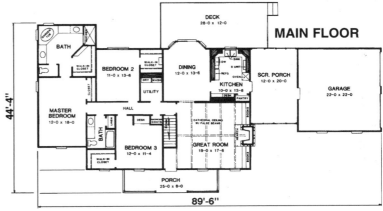

Cozy Yet Roomy

PRICE CODE: A

■ This plan features:
— Three bedrooms
— Two full and one half baths

■ A warm and cozy fireplace highlights the Great Room

■ The Dining Room and the Kitchen are adjoined, giving the living area a larger feel.

■ The Master Bedroom has a tray ceiling and a vaulted ceiling tops the Master Bath.

■ An optional basement, crawl space or a slab foundation — please specify when ordering

■ No materials list is available for this plan

FIRST FLOOR — 628 SQ. FT.
SECOND FLOOR — 660 SQ. FT.
BASEMENT — 628 SQ. FT.
GARAGE — 424 SQ. FT.

TOTAL LIVING AREA:
1,288 SQ. FT.

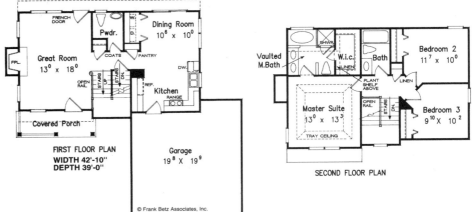

© Frank Betz Associates, Inc.

To order your Blueprints, call 1-800-235-5700

© 1998 Donald A. Gardner Architects, Inc.   B. NATHAN.

Porches Front and Rear

Price Code: D

- This plan features:
  — Three bedrooms
  — Two full and one half baths

- A covered front Porch wraps the front and side of the home while a screen Porch spans the rear

- The Foyer has a two-story ceiling and is separated from the Dining Room by columns

- The Kitchen has a well-planned work triangle for added convenience

- The Great Room and the Breakfast Nook both have a bay of windows that overlooks the rear Porch

- The Master Bedroom encompasses one whole side of the home

- Upstairs find two identical Bedrooms that share a full Bath

FIRST FLOOR — 1,271 SQ. FT.
SECOND FLOOR — 490 SQ. FT.
GARAGE — 543 SQ. FT.

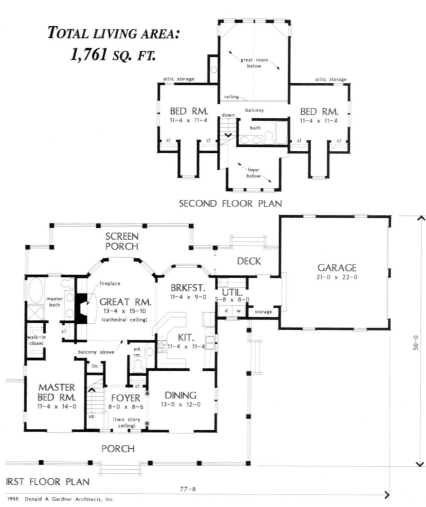

TOTAL LIVING AREA:
1,761 SQ. FT.

SECOND FLOOR PLAN

FIRST FLOOR PLAN

1998 Donald A Gardner Architects, Inc.

To order your Blueprints, call 1-800-235-5700

Easy Everyday Living and Entertaining

PRICE CODE: B

■ This plan features:
— Three bedrooms
— Two full baths
■ Front entrance accented by segmented arches, sidelight and transom windows
■ Open Living Room with focal point fireplace, wet bar and access to Patio
■ Dining area open to both the Living Room and the Kitchen
■ Efficient Kitchen with a cooktop island, walk-in Pantry and Utility area with a Garage entry
■ Large walk-in closet, double vanity Bath and access to Patio featured in the Master Bedroom Suite
■ Two additional Bedrooms share a double vanity Bath
■ No materials list is available for this plan

MAIN FLOOR — 1,664 SQ. FT.
BASEMENT — 1,600 SQ. FT.
GARAGE — 440 SQ. FT

TOTAL LIVING AREA: 1,664 SQ. FT.

Main Floor

ZIP QUOTE
HOME COST CALCULATOR
see order pages for details

Easy Living

PRICE CODE: A

■ This plan features:
— Three bedrooms
— Two full baths
■ The front Porch spans the width of the home
■ A fireplace warms the Family Room
■ The U-shaped Kitchen has an island in the center
■ All of the Bedrooms have ample closet space
■ The Carport has a connected Storage Space
■ No materials list is available for this plan

MAIN FLOOR — 1,333 SQ. FT.

TOTAL LIVING AREA: 1,333 SQ. FT

WIDTH 55'-6"
DEPTH 64'-3"

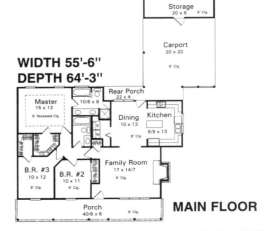

MAIN FLOOR

To order your Blueprints, call 1-800-235-5700

Two–Story Farmhouse

Price Code: D

- This plan features:
  — Three bedrooms
  — Two full and one half baths

- The wrap-around Porch gives a nostalgic appeal to this home

- The Great Room with fireplace is accessed directly from the Foyer

- The formal Dining Room has direct access to the efficient Kitchen

- An island, double sink, plenty of counter/cabinet space and a built-in Pantry complete the Kitchen

- The second floor Master Suite has a five-piece, private Bath

- An optional basement or crawl space foundation — please specify when ordering

MAIN FLOOR — 1,125 SQ. FT.
SECOND FLOOR — 1,138 SQ. FT.
BASEMENT — 1,125 SQ. FT.

TOTAL LIVING AREA:
2,263 SQ. FT.

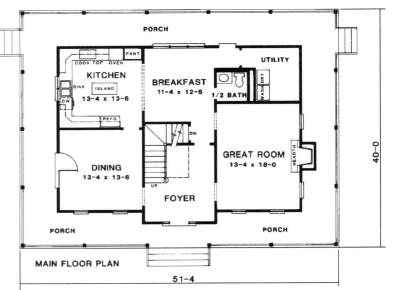

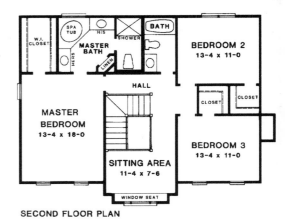

Striking Style

PRICE CODE: A

■ This plan features:
— Three bedrooms
— Two full baths

■ Windows and exterior detailing create a striking elevation

■ The Dining Room has a front window wall and arched openings

■ The secondary Bedrooms are in their own wing and share a Bath

■ The Great Room has a vaulted ceiling and a fireplace with a French door beside it

■ The Breakfast Bay is open to the galley Kitchen

■ The Master Suite features a tray ceiling, a walk-in closet and a private Bath

■ An optional basement or crawlspace foundation — please specify when ordering

MAIN FLOOR — 1,432 SQ. FT.
BASEMENT — 1,454 SQ. FT.
GARAGE — 440 SQ. FT.

TOTAL LIVING AREA:
1,432 SQ. FT.

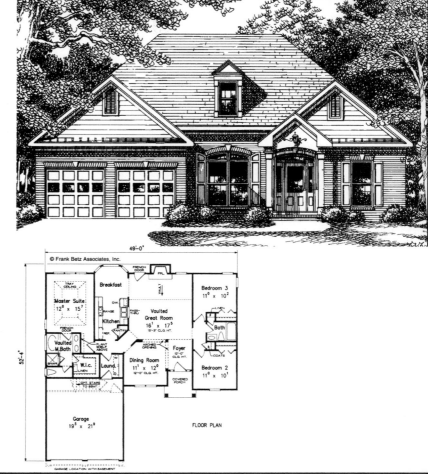

Year Round Leisure

PRICE CODE: A

■ This plan features:
— Three bedrooms
— Two full baths

■ A cathedral ceiling with exposed beams and a stone wall with heat-circulating fireplace in the Living Room

■ Three sliding glass doors leading from the Living Room to a large Deck

■ A built-in Dining Area that separates the Kitchen from the far end of the Living Room

■ A Master Suite with his and her closets and a private Bath

■ Two additional Bedrooms, one double sized, sharing a full hall Bath

MAIN FLOOR — 1,207 SQ. FT.

TOTAL LIVING AREA:
1,207 SQ. FT.

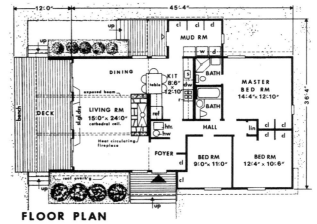

FLOOR PLAN

© 1997 Donald A Gardner Architects, Inc.

Dressed to Impress

Price Code: E

■ This plan features:

— Three bedrooms

— Two full and one half baths

■ A stone and stucco exterior plus a dramatic entry with square columns provide impressive curb appeal

■ The Great Room has a cathedral ceiling and adjoins the Breakfast Area

■ The Kitchen is enhanced by an angled counter with stove top, a Pantry and easy access to the formal Dining Room

■ A separate Utility Room with built-in cabinets and a counter top with a Laundry sink add efficiency

■ Double doors lead into the Master Suite with a box bay window, two walk-in closets and a lavish Bath

■ Two more Bedrooms are located upstairs along with a full Bath, a linen closet and a skylit Bonus Room

FIRST FLOOR — 1,572 SQ. FT.
SECOND FLOOR — 549 SQ. FT.
BONUS — 384 SQ. FT.
GARAGE & STORAGE — 540 SQ. FT.

FIRST FLOOR
No. 99824

© 1997 Donald A Gardner Architects, Inc.

TOTAL LIVING AREA:
2,121 SQ. FT.

SECOND FLOOR

To order your Blueprints, call 1-800-235-5700

Turret Study Creates Impact
PRICE CODE: F

■ This plan features:
— Three bedrooms
— Two full baths and one half bath
■ Entry doors opening into the formal Living Room focusing to the Lanai through sliding glass doors and a mitered glass corner
■ Double sided fireplace in the Living Room shared by the Master Suite
■ Wetbar easily serves the Living Room, Dining Room and Lanai
■ Island Kitchen easily serves all informal family areas
■ Octagon Nook with windows spanning to all views
■ Leisure Room with fireplace wall having built-ins along the back wall
■ Secondary Bedrooms share full Bath located between them
■ Spacious Master Suite including a fireplace, morning kitchen bar, and Lanai access

MAIN FLOOR — 3,477 SQ. FT.
GARAGE — 771 SQ. FT.

TOTAL LIVING AREA:
3,477 SQ. FT.

WIDTH 95'-0"
DEPTH 88'-8"

MAIN FLOOR

For The Busy Family
PRICE CODE: D

■ This plan features:
— Four Bedrooms
— Three full baths
■ Designed for a busy family that likes their privacy too
■ Porch shelters entry into Gallery, Formal Dining Area, and Living Room with cozy fireplace between book shelves and a wall of windows
■ Open and efficient Kitchen easily serves Breakfast Alcove, Patio and Dining Area
■ Corner Master Bedroom provides a huge walk-in closet and lavish Bath
■ Two Bedrooms , one with two closets and a window seat, share a full Bath, while fourth Bedroom has separate Bath
■ No materials list is available for this plan

MAIN FLOOR — 2,233 SQ. FT.
GARAGE — 635 SQ. FT.

TOTAL LIVING AREA:
2,233 SQ. FT.

WIDTH 63'-10"
DEPTH 56'-10"

MAIN FLOOR

Curb Appeal

Price Code: F

- This plan features:
- — Four bedrooms
- — Three full baths

- A private Master Bedroom with a raised ceiling and attached Bath with a spa tub

- A wing of three Bedrooms that share two full Baths on the right side of the home

- An efficient Kitchen is straddled by an Eating Nook and a Dining Room

- A cozy Den with a raised ceiling and a fireplace that is the focal point of the home

- A two-car Garage has a Storage Area

- An optional crawl space or slab foundation — please specify when ordering

MAIN FLOOR — 2,735 SQ. FT.
GARAGE — 561 SQ. FT.

TOTAL LIVING AREA:
2,735 SQ. FT.

WIDTH 68'-10"
DEPTH 67'-4"

MAIN FLOOR
No. 92550

Country Charmer

PRICE CODE: A

■ This plan features:
— Three bedrooms
— Two full baths
■ Quaint front Porch is perfect for sitting and relaxing
■ Great Room opening into Dining Area and Kitchen
■ Corner Deck in rear of home accessed from Kitchen and Master Suite
■ Master Suite with a private Bath, walk-in closet and built-in shelves
■ Two large secondary Bedrooms in the front of the home share a hall Bath
■ Two car Garage located in the rear of the home

MAIN FLOOR — 1,438 SQ. FT.
GARAGE — 486 SQ. FT.

TOTAL LIVING AREA:
1,438 SQ. FT.

MAIN FLOOR

Delightful Home

PRICE CODE: C

■ This plan features:
— Three bedrooms
— Two full baths
■ Grand Room with a fireplace, vaulted ceiling and double French doors to the rear Deck
■ Kitchen and Dining Room open to continue the overall feel of spaciousness
■ Kitchen has a large walk-in Pantry, island with a sink and dishwasher creating a perfect triangular workspace
■ Dining Room with doors to both Decks, has expanses of glass looking out to the rear yard
■ Master Bedroom features a double door entry, private bath
■ No material list is available for this plan

FIRST FLOOR — 1,342 SQ. FT.
SECOND FLOOR — 511 SQ. FT.

TOTAL LIVING AREA:
1,853 SQ. FT.

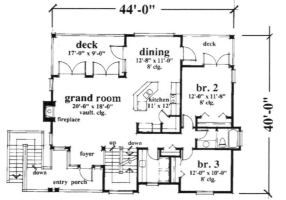

FIRST FLOOR

SECOND FLOOR

High Ceilings and Arched Windows

PRICE CODE: B

- This plan features:
— Three bedrooms
— Two full baths
- Natural illumination streaming into the Dining Room and Sitting area of the Master Suite through large arched windows
- Kitchen with convenient pass through to the Great Room and a serving bar for the Breakfast Room
- Great Room topped by a vaulted ceiling accented by a fireplace and a French door
- Decorative columns accenting the entrance of the Dining Room
- Tray ceiling over the Master Suite and a vaulted ceiling over the sitting room and the Master Bath
- An optional basement or crawl space foundation — please specify when ordering
- No materials list is available for this plan

MAIN FLOOR — 1,502 SQ. FT.
GARAGE — 448 SQ. FT.

***TOTAL LIVING AREA:
1,502 SQ. FT.***

© Frank Betz Associates

Cozy Yet Spacious

PRICE CODE: D

- This plan features:
— Four bedrooms
— Two full and one half baths
- The Living Room has an elegant arched opening from the Foyer and from the Dining Room
- The sunken Family Room has a fireplace and French doors to the rear yard
- The Breakfast Room is enhanced by decorative columns and a serving bar from the Kitchen adds to the room's convenience
- The Master Suite features a tray ceiling in the Bedroom, and a vaulted ceiling over the Master Bath
- An optional basement, crawl space or slab foundation — please specify when ordering
- No materials list is available for this plan

FIRST FLOOR — 1,186 SQ. FT.
SECOND FLOOR — 1,084 SQ. FT.
GARAGE — 440 SQ. FT.

***TOTAL LIVING AREA:
2,270 SQ. FT.***

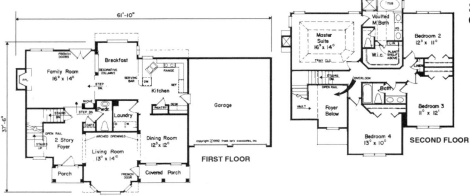

To order your Blueprints, call 1-800-235-5700

G. NATHAN.

© 1997 Donald A. Gardner Architects, Inc.

Illusion of Spaciousness

Price Code: C

- This plan features:
  — Three bedrooms
  — Two full baths
- Open living spaces and vaulted ceilings creating an illusion of spaciousness
- Cathedral ceilings maximize space in Great Room and Dining Room
- Kitchen features skylight and breakfast bar
- Well equipped Master Suite in rear for privacy
- Two additional Bedrooms in front share a full Bath

MAIN FLOOR — 1,246 SQ. FT.
GARAGE — 420 SQ. FT.

TOTAL LIVING AREA:
1,246 SQ. FT.

Floor Plan

DECK

SCREEN PORCH
10-0 x 12-0

KIT.
10-0 x 11-0

skylight

walk-in closet

MASTER BED RM.
14-0 x 11-8
(cathedral ceiling)

GARAGE
19-4 x 20-4

DINING
12-4 x 9-4

UTIL.
d   w

master bath

cl

cl   cl

(cathedral ceiling)

GREAT RM.
15-8 x 15-0
fireplace

BED RM.
13-4 x 10-0

PORCH

bath

BED RM./STUDY
11-0 x 11-4
(cathedral ceiling)

cl

10-0

48-0

60-0

FLOOR PLAN

© 1997 Donald A Gardner Architects, Inc.

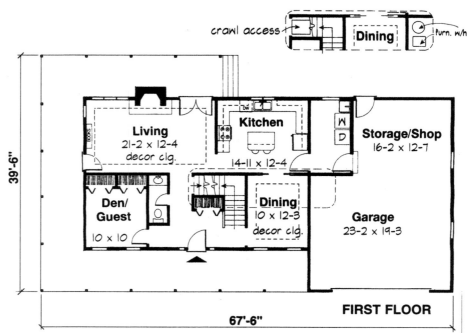

National Treasure

Price Code: C

■ This plan features:

— Three bedrooms

— Two full and one half baths

■ A wrap-around covered Porch

■ Decorative vaulted ceilings in the fireplaced Living Room

■ A large Kitchen with central island/breakfast bar

■ A sun-lit Sitting Area

FIRST FLOOR — 1,034 SQ. FT.
SECOND FLOOR — 944 SQ. FT.
BASEMENT — 984 SQ. FT.
GARAGE — 675 SQ. FT.

TOTAL LIVING AREA:
1,978 SQ. FT.

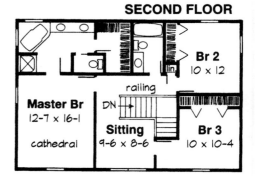

ZIP QUOTE
HOME COST CALCULATOR
see order pages for details

SECOND FLOOR

Master Br
12-7 x 16-1

cathedral

Br 2
10 x 12

railing

DN

Sitting
9-6 x 8-6

Br 3
10 x 10-4

crawl access

Dining

furn. w/h

FIRST FLOOR

39'-6"

Living
21-2 x 12-4
decor clg.

Kitchen
14-11 x 12-4

Storage/Shop
16-2 x 12-7

W
D

Den/
Guest
10 x 10

Dining
10 x 12-3
decor clg.

Garage
23-2 x 19-3

67'-6"

To order your Blueprints, call 1-800-235-5700

© 1993 Donald A. Gardner Architects, Inc.

PLAN NO. 96404

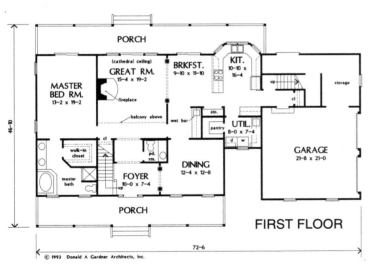

PORCH

(cathedral ceiling)
GREAT RM.
15–4 x 19–2

fireplace

BRKFST.
9–10 11–10

KIT.
10–10 x
16–4

up

storage

MASTER BED RM.
13–2 x 19–2

balcony above

wet bar

sto.

cl

46–10

walk-in closet

cl

pantry

UTIL.
8–0 x 7–4

d   w

GARAGE
21–8 x 21–0

master bath

pd. rm.

DINING
12–4 x 12–8

FOYER
10–0 x 7–4

up

PORCH

FIRST FLOOR

72–6

© 1993 Donald A Gardner Architects, Inc.

SECOND FLOOR

clerestory window with arched top

great room below

attic storage

attic storage

attic storage

down

attic storage

BED RM.
13–2 x 15–4

railing

balcony

BED RM.
12–4 x 15–4

down

bath

cl   cl

cl   cl

foyer below

BONUS RM.
13–0 x 33–2

clerestory with palladian window

Covered Porches Front and Back

Price Code: E

■ This plan features:

— Three bedrooms

— Two full and one half baths

■ Two-story Foyer with palladian, clerestory window and balcony overlooking Great Room

■ Great Room with cozy fireplace provides perfect gathering place

■ Columns visually separate Great Room from Breakfast Area and smart, U-shaped Kitchen

■ Privately located Master Bedroom accesses Porch and luxurious Master Bath with separate shower and double vanity

FIRST FLOOR — 1,632 SQ. FT.
SECOND FLOOR — 669 SQ. FT.
BONUS ROOM — 528 SQ. FT.
GARAGE & STORAGE — 707 SQ. FT.

TOTAL LIVING AREA:
2,301 SQ. FT.

Distinctive Design

Price Code: C

- This plan features:
- — Three bedrooms
- — Two full and one half baths
- Living Room is distinguished by a bay window and French doors leading to Family Room
- Built-in curio cabinet and hutch adds interest to formal Dining Room
- Well-appointed Kitchen with island cooktop, Breakfast Area, adjoining Laundry and Garage entry
- Family Room with focal point fireplace
- Spacious Master Bedroom Suite with vaulted ceiling and plush Dressing Area
- Secondary Bedrooms share a double vanity Bath

FIRST FLOOR — 1,093 SQ. FT.
SECOND FLOOR — 905 SQ. FT.
GARAGE — 527 SQ. FT.
BASEMENT — 1,093 SQ. FT.

TOTAL LIVING AREA:
1,998 SQ. FT.

SECOND FLOOR

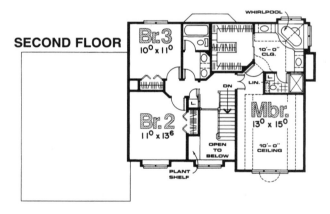

Br. 3
10⁰ x 11⁰

Br. 2
11⁰ x 13⁶

Mbr.
13⁰ x 15⁰

WHIRLPOOL

10'-0" CLG.

10'-0" CEILING

OPEN TO BELOW

PLANT SHELF

© design basics, inc.

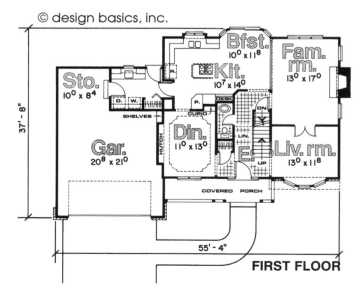

Sto.
10⁰ x 8⁴

Gar.
20⁸ x 21⁰

Bfst.
10⁰ x 11⁸

Kit.
10⁷ x 14⁰

Fam. rm.
13⁰ x 17⁰

Din.
11⁰ x 13⁰

Liv. rm.
13⁰ x 11⁸

SHELVES

CURIO

HUTCH

COVERED PORCH

37' - 8"

55' - 4"

FIRST FLOOR

Elegant Row House

PRICE CODE: C

This plan features:
- Three bedrooms
- Two full and one half baths
- Arched columns define the formal and casual spaces
- Wrap-around porticos on two levels provide views to the living areas
- Four sets of French doors let the outside in to the Great Room
- The Master Suite features a private Bath designed for two people
- Generous Bonus Space awaits your ideas for completion
- The Guest Bedroom leads to a gallery hallway with Deck access
- An optional slab or post foundation — please specify when ordering
- No materials list is available for this plan

MAIN FLOOR — 1,305 SQ. FT.
UPPER FLOOR — 1,215 SQ. FT.
LOWER FLOOR — 935 SQ. FT.
GARAGE — 480 SQ. FT.

TOTAL LIVING AREA:
2,520 SQ. FT.

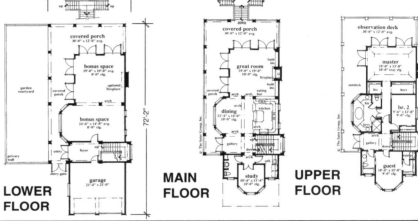

LOWER FLOOR

MAIN FLOOR

UPPER FLOOR

L-Shaped Front Porch

PRICE CODE: A

This plan features:
- Three bedrooms
- Two full baths
- Attractive wood siding and a large L-shaped covered Porch
- Front Entry leading to generous Living Room with a vaulted ceiling
- Large two-car Garage with access through Utility Room
- Roomy secondary Bedrooms share the full Bath in the hall
- Kitchen highlighted by a built-in Pantry and a garden window
- Vaulted ceiling adds volume to the Dining Room
- Master Suite in an isolated location enhanced by abundant closet space, separate vanity, and linen storage

MAIN FLOOR — 1,280 SQ. FT.

TOTAL LIVING AREA:
1,280 SQ. FT.

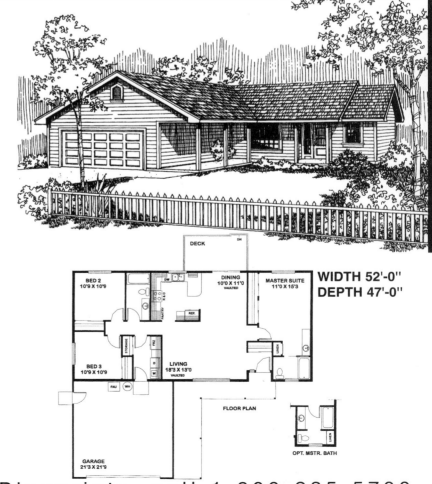

WIDTH 52'-0"
DEPTH 47'-0"

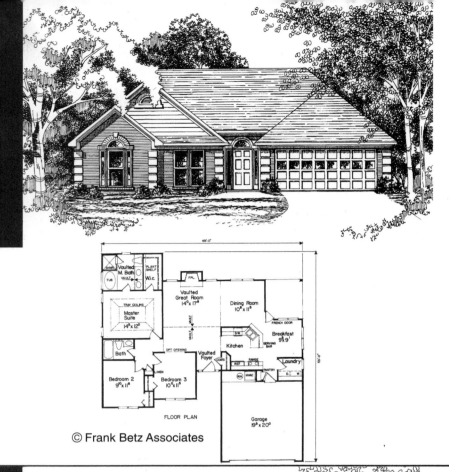

© Frank Betz Associates

One Floor Convenience
PRICE CODE: A

- This plan features:
  — Three bedrooms
  — Two full baths
- Vaulted Foyer blending with the vaulted Great Room giving a larger feeling to the home
- Formal Dining Room opening into the Great Room allowing for a terrific living area in which to entertain
- Kitchen including a serving bar and easy flow into the Breakfast Room
- Master Suite topped by a decorative tray ceiling and a vaulted ceiling in the Master Bath
- Two additional Bedrooms sharing the full Bath in the hall
- No materials list is available for this plan
- An optional crawl space or slab foundation — please specify when ordering

MAIN FLOOR — 1,359 SQ. FT.
GARAGE — 439 SQ. FT.

TOTAL LIVING AREA:
1,359 SQ. FT.

© 1997 Donald A Gardner Architects, Inc.

Luxuriant Living
PRICE CODE: F

- This plan features:
  — Four bedrooms
  — Three full and one half baths
- French doors, windows, and a high gabled Entry make a dramatic entrance to this home
- Formal Living Room features a box bay window and a fireplace
- Dining Room is illuminated by a bank of windows
- Large Family Room has a two-story ceiling, a fireplace and accessed the rear Patio
- Kitchen and Nook adjoin handy home Office that has a full Bath
- The Master Suite features a private Bath and a Sitting Area
- Upstairs find two Bedrooms each with a walk-in closet, a full Bath and a Bonus Room

FIRST FLOOR — 2,249 SQ. FT.
SECOND FLOOR — 620 SQ. FT.
BONUS — 308 SQ. FT.
GARAGE — 642 SQ. FT.

TOTAL LIVING AREA:
2,869 SQ. FT.

Clever Use of Interior Space
PRICE CODE: D

© 1994 Donald A. Gardner Architects, Inc.

This plan features:
- Three bedrooms
- Two full baths

Efficient interior with cathedral and tray ceilings create feeling of space

Great Room boosts cathedral ceiling above cozy fireplace, built-in shelves and columns

Octagon Dining Room and Breakfast Alcove bathed in light and easily access Porch

Open Kitchen features island counter sink and Pantry

Master Bedroom suite enhance by tray ceiling and plush Bath

MAIN FLOOR — 1,737 SQ. FT.
GARAGE & STORAGE — 517 SQ. FT.

TOTAL LIVING AREA:
1,737 SQ. FT.

© Donald A. Gardner Architects, Inc.

A Traditional Approach
PRICE CODE: C

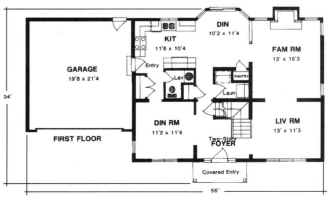

This plan features:
- Four bedrooms
- Two full and one half baths

A covered Entry leading to a two-story Foyer

A well-appointed Kitchen with direct access to the Garage

A bright and sunny Dinette for informal eating

An expansive Family Room highlighted by a large fireplace

A roomy Master Suite including a private Bath and a walk-in closet

Three additional Bedrooms sharing use of a full hall Bath

No materials list is available for this plan

FIRST FLOOR — 1,025 SQ. FT.
SECOND FLOOR — 988 SQ. FT.

TOTAL LIVING AREA:
2,013 SQ. FT.

To order your Blueprints, call 1-800-235-5700

One Floor Living

Price Code: A

- ■ This plan features:
- — Three bedrooms
- — Two full baths
- ■ A covered front Porch is supported by columns and accented by balusters
- ■ The Living Room features a cozy fireplace and a ceiling fan
- ■ The Kitchen is distinguished by an angled serving bar
- ■ The Dining Room is convenient to the Kitchen and accessed the rear Porch
- ■ Two secondary Bedrooms share a Bath in the hall
- ■ The Master Bedroom has a walk in closet and a private Bath
- ■ A two-car Garage with storage space is located in the rear of the home

MAIN FLOOR —1,247 SQ. FT.
GARAGE — 512 SQ. FT.

TOTAL LIVING AREA:
1,247 SQ. FT.

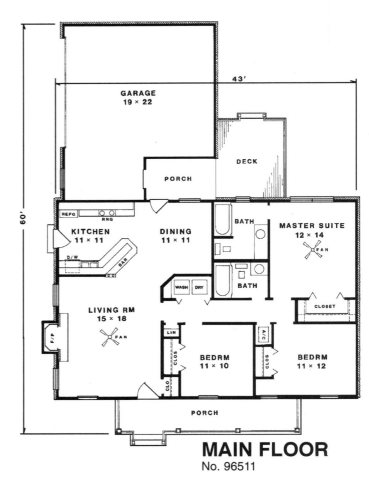

MAIN FLOOR
No. 96511

European Styling with a Georgian Flair

Price Code: D

WIDTH 72'-10"
DEPTH 54'-5"

bonus rm
12 x 15

mbr
15 x 14

shr

util 6 x 8
d W b

garage
24 x 22

ra

eating
8 x 10

por
4 x 7

br 4
11 x 12

kit
12x12
dw
rng
ref

den
17 x 16

lin

sto

dining
11 x 12

foy

br 2
11 x 11

br 3
11 x 12

11x9
porch

MAIN FLOOR
No. 92552

■ This plan features:

— Four bedrooms

— Two full baths

■ Arched windows, quoins and shutters create an eye-catching home

■ Formal Foyer accesses the Dining Room and Den

■ Kitchen flows into the informal Eating Area and is separated from the Den by an angled extended counter eating bar

■ Split Bedroom plan, Master Suite is privately place to the rear

■ Three additional Bedrooms share a full Bath in the hall

■ An optional crawl space or slab foundation — please specify when ordering

MAIN FLOOR — 1,873 SQ. FT.
BONUS — 145 SQ. FT.
GARAGE — 613 SQ. FT.

TOTAL LIVING AREA:
1,873 SQ. FT.

Luxurious Residence

Price Code: F

- ■ This plan features:
- — Three bedrooms
- — Three full and one half baths
- ■ High ceilings in the formal Living and Dining Areas
- ■ Gallery leads to the family gathering and secondary Bedroom Areas
- ■ Kitchen with cooking island opens to the round Nook and the Leisure Room
- ■ Spacious Master's wing includes a Study, Exercise Room, captivating Bath and pampering Suite
- ■ Outside there is an optional cooking area
- ■ No materials list is available for this plan

MAIN FLOOR — 4,565 SQ. FT.
GARAGE — 757 SQ. FT.

TOTAL LIVING AREA:
4,565 SQ. FT.

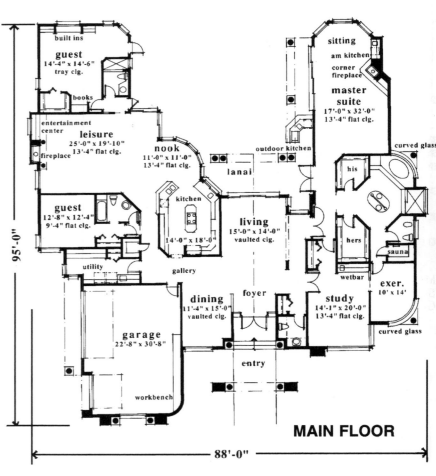

MAIN FLOOR

Impressive Entry

PRICE CODE: C

■ This plan features:
— Three bedrooms
— Two full and one half baths

■ High arched entry as a prelude to impressive floor plan

■ Living Room topped by a vaulted ceiling and enhanced by a gas fireplace

■ Dining Room topped by a vaulted ceiling adjoins the living room to create a large living space

■ Pocket doors opening to the Kitchen/Nook area from the Dining Room

■ A work island and a walk-in pantry add to the convenience and efficiency of the Kitchen

■ An attractive French door accesses the covered patio from Nook area

■ Family Room contains another gas fireplace

■ Master Suite includes a whirlpool bath and a separate shower

■ No materials list is available for this plan

FIRST FLOOR — 1,212 SQ. FT.
SECOND FLOOR — 922 SQ. FT.
BASEMENT — 1,199 SQ. FT.
GARAGE — 464 SQ. FT.

**TOTAL LIVING AREA:
2,134 SQ. FT.**

FIRST FLOOR

SECOND FLOOR

Style and Practicality

PRICE CODE: D

■ This plan features:
— Three bedrooms
— Two full baths

■ Slightly wrapping front and side porches

■ Plan easily fits on a narrow lot

■ A cathedral ceiling enhancing the Great Room with fireplace and built-ins

■ An optional Loft/Study above the Kitchen overlooking the Great Room,

■ Columns framing entry to the formal Dining Room top by a tray ceiling

■ Complete Master Suite with tray ceiling, bay window, side porch access, dual walk-in closets, and bath with garden tub and separate shower

MAIN FLOOR — 1,795 SQ. FT.
BONUS ROOM — 368 SQ. FT.
GARAGE — 520 SQ. FT.

**TOTAL LIVING AREA:
1,795 SQ. FT.**

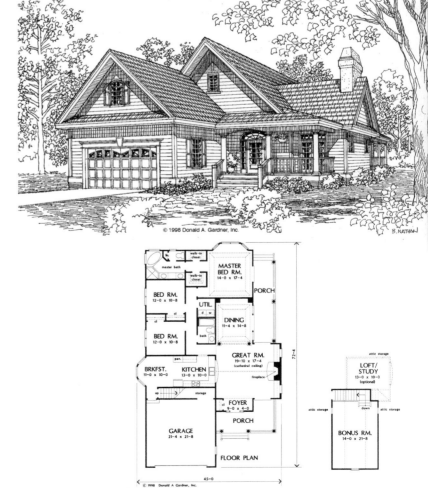

© 1998 Donald A. Gardner, Inc.

B. NATHAN

FLOOR PLAN

PLAN NO. 98445

Beautiful Stucco & Stone
PRICE CODE: C

■ This plan features:
— Three bedrooms
— Two full and one half baths

■ This home is accented by keystone arches and a turret styled roof

■ The two story Foyer includes a half bath

■ The vaulted Family Room is highlighted by a fireplace and French doors to the rear yard

■ The Dining Room adjoins the Family Room which has access to the covered porch and the Kitchen

■ The Master Bedroom is crowned by a tray ceiling, while Master Bath has a vaulted ceiling

■ Two additional bedrooms share a full double vanity bath

■ A Balcony overlooks the Family Room and Foyer below

■ This plan is available with a basement, slab or a crawl space foundation, please specify when ordering

FIRST FLOOR — 1,398 SQ. FT.
SECOND FLOOR — 515 SQ. FT.
BASEMENT — 1,398 SQ. FT.
GARAGE — 421 SQ. FT.

TOTAL LIVING AREA:
1,913 SQ. FT..

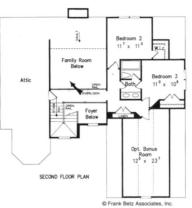

© Frank Betz Associates, Inc.

PLAN NO. 92557

Elegant Brick Exterior
PRICE CODE: B

■ This plan features:
— Three bedrooms
— Two full baths

■ Detailing and accenting columns highlighting the covered front Porch

■ Den is enhanced by a corner fireplace and adjoining with Dining Room

■ Efficient Kitchen well-appointed and with easy access to the utility/laundry room

■ Master Bedroom topped by a vaulted ceiling and pampered by a private bath and a walk-in closet

■ Two secondary bedrooms are located at the opposite end of home sharing a full bath located between the two rooms

■ An optional slab or crawl space foundation — please specify when ordering

MAIN FLOOR — 1,390 SQ. FT.
GARAGE — 590 SQ. FT.

TOTAL LIVING AREA:
1,390 SQ. FT.

MAIN FLOOR

Small Yet Stylish

PRICE CODE: A

■ This plan features:
— Three bedrooms
— Two full baths

■ The Living Room is topped by a ten foot ceiling and highlighted by a fireplace and a built-in entertainment center

■ A walk-in closet and a five-piece Bath further enhance the Master Suite

■ The Kitchen and the Dining Room are open to each other and topped by a cathedral ceiling

■ A walk-in pantry is located in the utility room and added storage

■ No materials list is available for this plan

MAIN FLOOR — 1,431 SQ. FT.
GARAGE — 410 SQ. FT.

TOTAL LIVING AREA:
1,431 SQ. FT.

Floor Plan

Window Boxes Add Romantic Charm

PRICE CODE: B

■ This plan features:
— Three bedrooms
— Two full and one half baths

■ A spacious Living Room and formal Dining Room combination that is perfect for entertaining

■ A Family Room with a large fireplace and an expansive glass wall that overlooks the Patio

■ An informal Dining bay, convenient to both the Kitchen and the Family Room

■ An efficient and well-equipped Kitchen with a peninsula counter dividing it from the Family Room

■ A Master Bedroom with his-n-her closets and a private Master Bath

MAIN AREA — 1590 SQ. FT.
BASEMENT — 900 SQ. FT.

TOTAL LIVING AREA:
1,590 SQ. FT.

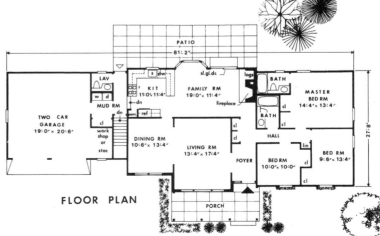

FLOOR PLAN

To order your Blueprints, call 1-800-235-5700

A Modern Slant On A Country Theme

Price Code: B

- This plan features:
- —Three bedrooms
- —Two full and one half baths

- Country styled front Porch highlighting exterior enhanced by dormer windows

- Modern open floor plan for a more spacious feeling

- Great Room accented by a quaint, corner fireplace and a ceiling fan

- Dining Room flowing from the Great Room for easy entertaining

- Kitchen graced by natural light from attractive bay window and a convenient snack bar for meals on the go

- Master Suite secluded in separate wing for total privacy

- Two additional Bedrooms sharing full Bath in the hall

MAIN FLOOR — 1,648 SQ. FT.
GARAGE — 479 SQ. FT.

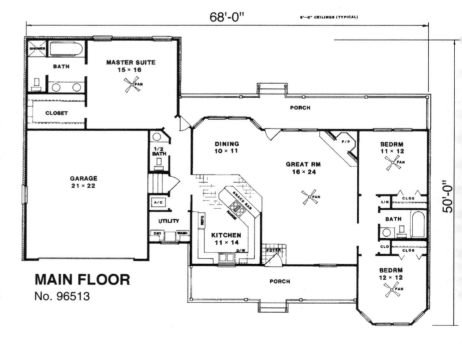

MAIN FLOOR
No. 96513

TOTAL LIVING AREA
1,648 SQ. FT.

To order your Blueprints, call 1-800-235-5700

European Styling
PRICE CODE: D

This plan features:

- Three bedrooms
- Two full and one half baths
- The large Foyer leads to the open Living and Dining rooms
- A large informal area includes the Kitchen, Gathering, and Breakfast rooms
- The Kitchen features an island bar, double sink, Pantry, desk, and a wall oven
- The home has two fireplaces, one in the Great Room the other in the Gathering Room
- Decorative ceiling can be found in the Dining Room, the Master Suite, and the Breakfast Nook
- The Master Suite features dual walk-in closets and a five-piece Bath
- An optional basement or a crawl space foundation — please specify when ordering

MAIN FLOOR — 2,290 SQ. FT.
BASEMENT — 2,290 SQ. FT.
BONUS — 304 SQ. FT.
GARAGE — 544 SQ. FT.

TOTAL LIVING AREA:
2,290 SQ. FT.

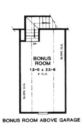

Essence of Style & Grace
PRICE CODE: E

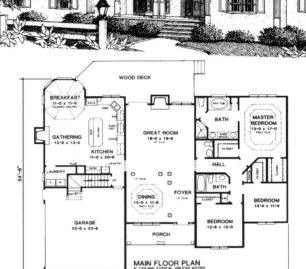

This plan features:

- Four bedrooms
- Three full and one half baths
- French doors introduce Study and columns define the Gallery and formal areas
- The expansive Family Room with an inviting fireplace and a cathedral ceiling opens to the Kitchen
- The Kitchen features a cooktop island, Butler's Pantry, Breakfast Area and Patio access
- The first floor Master Bedroom offers a private Patio, vaulted ceiling, twin vanities and a walk-in closet
- Three second floor Bedrooms each access a full Bath
- An optional basement or slab foundation — please specify when ordering
- No materials list is available for this plan

FIRST FLOOR — 2,036 SQ. FT.
SECOND FLOOR — 866 SQ. FT.
GARAGE — 720 SQ. FT.

TOTAL LIVING AREA:
2,902 SQ. FT.

WIDTH 65'-0"
DEPTH 53'-4"

To order your Blueprints, call 1-800-235-5700

213

Easy Street
PRICE CODE: C

- This plan features:
— Three bedrooms
— Two full and one half baths
- A two-story Foyer is a grand introduction to this home
- The Living Room and the Dining Room connect through an arched opening
- The Kitchen opens to the Breakfast Room and the Kitchen directly accesses the Dining Room
- The Family Room offers a vaulted ceiling, a fireplace with built-in bookcases and a plant shelf
- The Master Suite includes a tray ceiling and a French door into the Master Bathroom
- An optional basement or crawl space foundation — please specify when ordering

FIRST FLOOR — 1,073 SQ. FT.
SECOND FLOOR — 742 SQ. FT.
BONUS — 336 SQ. FT.
BASEMENT — 1,073 SQ. FT.
GARAGE — 495 SQ. FT.

TOTAL LIVING AREA:
1,815 SQ. FT.

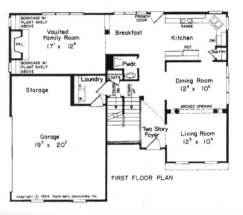

FIRST FLOOR PLAN

SECOND FLOOR PLAN

WIDTH 45'-0"
DEPTH 40'-0"

A Custom Look
PRICE CODE: E

- This plan features:
— Three bedrooms
— Three full and one half baths
- Wonderfully balanced exterior highlighted by triple arched glass in Entry Porch, leading into the Gallery Foyer
- Triple arches lead into Formal Living and Dining Room, Verandah and beyond
- Kitchen, Nook, and Leisure Room area easily flow together
- Owners' wing has a Master Suite with glass alcove to rear yard, a lavish Bath and a Study offering many uses
- Two additional Bedrooms with corner windows and over-sized closets access a full Bath
- No materials list is available for this plan

MAIN FLOOR — 2,978 SQ. FT
GARAGE — 702 SQ. FT.

TOTAL LIVING AREA:
2,978 SQ. FT.

MAIN FLOOR

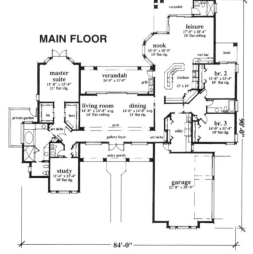

To order your Blueprints, call 1-800-235-5700

Exciting Ceilings And Open Spaces

PRICE CODE: C

■ This plan features:
— Three bedrooms
— Two full baths
■ Double gables and a covered Porch adding charm to the exterior
■ Common living areas in an open format topped by a cathedral ceiling
■ Front Bedroom, doubling as a Study, topped by a cathedral ceiling and accented by a picture window with circle-top
■ Master Bedroom crowned in a cathedral ceiling pampered by a lavish Bath

MAIN FLOOR — 1,298 SQ. FT.

TOTAL LIVING AREA:
1,298 SQ. FT.

Grand Front Window

PRICE CODE: B

■ This plan features:
— Three bedrooms
— Two full and one half baths
■ The high, arched front window gives this home curb appeal and natural illumination to the Living Room
■ The Living Room is topped by a cathedral ceiling and enhanced by a fireplace
■ The Master Suite has its own private corner of the home and includes a five-piece Bath and a walk-in closet
■ The secondary Bedrooms are on the second floor with a full Bath easily accessible
■ No materials list is available for this plan.

FIRST FLOOR — 1, 177 SQ. FT.
SECOND FLOOR — 406 SQ. FT.
GARAGE — 440 SQ. FT.

TOTAL LIVING AREA:
1,583 SQ. FT.

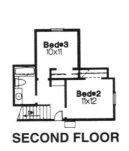

SECOND FLOOR

FIRST FLOOR

To order your Blueprints, call 1-800-235-5700

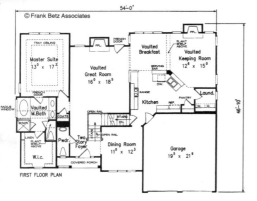

Details, Details, Details
PRICE CODE: C

- This plan features:
  — Three bedrooms
  — Two full and one half baths
- This elevation is highlighted by stucco, stone and detailing around the arched windows
- The two-story Foyer allows access to the Dining Room and the Great Room
- A vaulted ceiling and a fireplace can be found in the Great Room
- The Breakfast Room has a vaulted ceiling and flows into the Kitchen and the Keeping Room
- Two secondary Bedrooms, each with a walk-in closet, share a full hall Bath
- The Master Suite has a tray ceiling a huge walk-in closet and a compartmental Bath
- An optional basement or crawl space foundation — please specify when ordering

FIRST FLOOR — 1,628 SQ. FT.
SECOND FLOOR — 527 SQ. FT.
BONUS ROOM — 207 SQ. FT.
BASEMENT — 1,628 SQ. FT.
GARAGE — 440 SQ. FT.

TOTAL LIVING AREA: 2,155 SQ. FT.

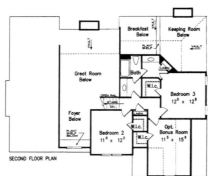

Stunning First Impression
PRICE CODE: D

- This plan features:
  — Four bedrooms
  — Two full and one half baths
- Dormer windows on the second floor, arched windows and entrance, brick quoin corners come together for a stunning first impression
- Large Living Room with a fireplace and an open formal Dining Area
- Family Room at the rear of home containing a bar
- Huge island Kitchen with a Breakfast area and plenty of work and storage space
- Luxurious Master Suite occupying an entire wing of the home and providing a quiet retreat
- Three additional Bedrooms on the second floor sharing a large Bath
- No materials list is available for this plan

FIRST FLOOR — 1,805 SQ. FT.
SECOND FLOOR — 659 SQ. FT.
BASEMENT — 1,800 SQ. FT.
GARAGE — 440 SQ. FT.

TOTAL LIVING AREA: 2,464 SQ. FT.

To order your Blueprints, call 1-800-235-5700

Fabulous Family Living
PRICE CODE: C

This plan features:
- Four bedrooms
- Two full and one half baths
- The covered Porch leads to an Entry with a cathedral ceiling
- The formal Dining Room adjoins the Great Room for an easy transition when entertaining
- A cathedral ceiling adds volume to the Master Suite
- An optional crawl space or slab foundation — please specify when ordering
- No materials list available for this plan

FIRST FLOOR — 1,359 SQ. FT.
SECOND FLOOR — 697 SQ. FT.
GARAGE — 440 SQ. FT.

TOTAL LIVING AREA: 2,056 SQ. FT.

Easy to Build
PRICE CODE: A

This plan features:
- Two bedrooms
- One bathroom
- Affordable ranch with all the amenities
- Covered entry leads into Foyer and Living and Dining Rooms
- Focal-point fireplace and bay window enhance the Living Room
- Country-style Kitchen opens to Dining Room, Nook, Utility Room and Garage
- Master Bedroom features an oversized closet and private access to full Bath with whirlpool tub
- Second Bedroom has an oversized closet and access to full bath

MAIN FLOOR — 1,313 SQ. FT.
GARAGE — 385 SQ. FT.

TOTAL LIVING AREA: 1,313 SQ. FT.

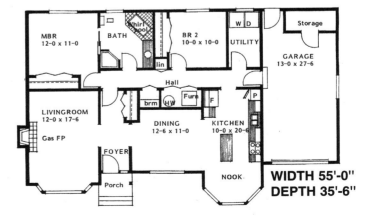

WIDTH 55'-0"
DEPTH 35'-6"

MAIN FLOOR

Brick Abounds
PRICE CODE: B

■ This plan features:
— Three bedrooms
— Two full baths
■ The covered front Porch opens into the entry that has a 10-foot ceiling and a coat closet
■ The large Living Room is distinguished by a fireplace and a front window wall
■ The Dining Room features a 10-foot ceiling and access to the rear covered Patio
■ The Kitchen is angled and has a Pantry, and a cooktop island
■ The Master Bedroom is located in the rear for privacy and boasts a triangular walk-in closet, plus a private Bath
■ Two more bedrooms each have large closets and share a hallway Bath
■ This home has a two-car Garage that is accessed through the Utility Room
■ No materials list is available for this plan

MAIN FLOOR — 1,528 SQ. FT.
GARAGE — 440 SQ. FT.

TOTAL LIVING AREA:
1,528 SQ. FT.

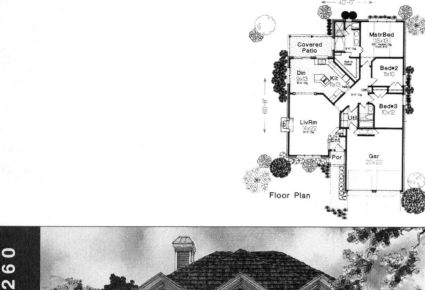

Floor Plan

Southampton Style Cottage
PRICE CODE: C

■ This plan features:
— Three bedrooms
— Two full baths
■ Stairs lead up to the covered Entry Porch and into the Foyer
■ An arched opening leads into the Grand Room, which has a fireplace
■ Five French doors in various rooms open out onto the rear Lanai
■ Access the Dining Room from the Kitchen through an arched opening
■ The Kitchen has a walk-in Pantry located next to the Nook
■ The secondary Bedrooms share a Bath in their own wing of the home
■ On the opposite side of the home are a Study and the Master Suite
■ The space on the ground level can be finished into a Recreation Room
■ No materials list is available for this plan

MAIN FLOOR — 2,068 SQ. FT.
BASEMENT — 1,402 SQ. FT.
GARAGE — 560 SQ. FT.

TOTAL LIVING AREA:
2,068 SQ. FT.

Covered Front and Rear Porches

Price Code: C

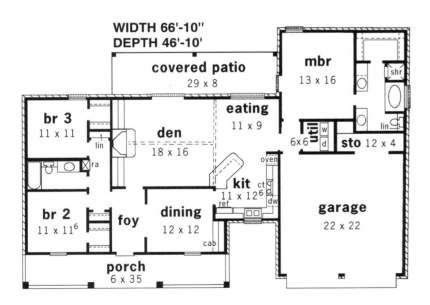

WIDTH 66'-10''
DEPTH 46'-10'

covered patio
29 x 8

mbr
13 x 16

shr

br 3
11 x 11

den
18 x 16

eating
11 x 9

lin

util
6x6   w
        d

sto 12 x 4

br 2
11 x 11⁶

foy

dining
12 x 12

oven

kit
11 x 12⁶

ct

ref

dw

cab

garage
22 x 22

porch
6 x 35

MAIN FLOOR
No. 92560

TOTAL LIVING AREA:
1,660 SQ. FT.

- This plan features:
—Three bedrooms
—Two full baths
- Traditional Country styling with front and rear covered Porches
- Peninsula counter/eating bar in Kitchen for meals on the go
- Informal Breakfast Area and formal Dining Room with built-in cabinet
- Vaulted ceiling and cozy fireplace highlighting Den
- Master Bedroom in private corner pampered by a five-piece bath
- Split Bedroom plan with additional bedrooms at the opposite of home sharing full Bath
- An optional slab or crawl space foundation — please specify when ordering

MAIN FLOOR — 1,660 SQ. FT.
GARAGE — 544 SQ. FT.

Stucco Captures Shade

Price Code: B

■ This plan features:

— Three bedrooms

— Two full baths

■ Sheltered Entry opens to airy Living/Dining Room with an inviting fireplace

■ Central Family Room with another fireplace opens to glass Nook with access to covered Patio

■ Open Kitchen easily serves nearby Dining Area, Nook and Patio beyond

■ French doors open to Master Suite with Patio access and a private Bath

■ Two additional Bedrooms with ample closets, share a full Bath and Laundry

MAIN FLOOR — 1,642 SQ. FT.

TOTAL LIVING AREA:
1,642 SQ. FT.

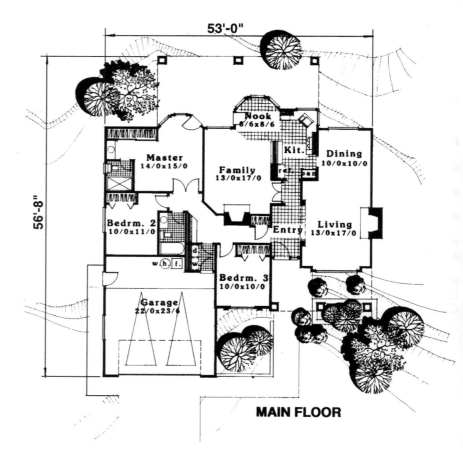

MAIN FLOOR

Distinctive Detailing
PRICE CODE: D

■ This plan features:
— Three bedrooms
— Two full and one half baths
■ Interior columns distinguishing the inviting two-story Foyer from the Dining Room
■ Spacious Great Room set off by two story windows and opening to the Kitchen and Breakfast Bay
■ Nine foot ceilings adding volume and drama to the first floor
■ Secluded Master Suite topped by a space amplifying tray ceiling and enhanced by a plush Bath
■ Two generous additional Bedrooms with ample closet and storage space
■ Skylit bonus room enjoying second floor access

FIRST FLOOR — 1,436 SQ. FT.
SECOND FLOOR — 536 SQ. FT.
GARAGE & STORAGE — 520 SQ. FT.
BONUS ROOM — 296 SQ. FT.

TOTAL LIVING AREA:
1,972 SQ. FT.

© 1995 Donald A. Gardner Architects, Inc.

SECOND FLOOR PLAN

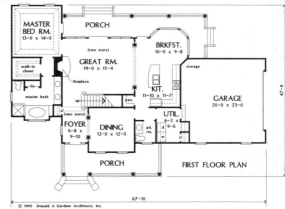

FIRST FLOOR PLAN

© 1995 Donald A Gardner Architects, Inc.

Split Bedroom
Floor Plan
PRICE CODE: A

■ This plan features:
— Three bedrooms
— Two full baths
■ A split Bedroom floor plan gives the Master Bedroom ultimate privacy
■ The Great Room is highlighted by a fireplace and a vaulted ten foot ceiling
■ A snack bar peninsula counter is one of the many conveniences of the Kitchen
■ The Patio is accessed from the Dining Room and expands dining to the outdoors
■ Two additional Bedrooms share the full Bath in the hall
■ An optional crawl space or a slab foundation — please specify when ordering this plan
■ No materials list is available for this plan

MAIN FLOOR — 1,234 SQ. FT.
GARAGE — 523 SQ. FT.

TOTAL LIVING AREA:
1,243 SQ. FT.

MAIN FLOOR

On A Grand Scale
PRICE CODE: E

- This plan features:
  — Four bedrooms
  — Four full baths
- The Dining Room's entrance is defined by columns and the Living Room is to the right of the Foyer
- The Family Room has a two-story ceiling and a cozy fireplace
- The Study is tucked into the right rear corner of the home
- The Kitchen includes a cook top island, a built-in Pantry and plenty of counter space
- The Master Suite is on the second floor and includes a tray ceiling over the Bedrooms and lavish Bath
- The sunny Sitting Room and two-walk-in closets completes the Suite
- An optional basement or a crawl space foundation — please specify when ordering
- No materials list is available for this plan

FIRST FLOOR — 1,595 SQ. FT.
SECOND FLOOR — 1,518 SQ. FT.
BASEMENT — 1,595 SQ. FT.
GARAGE — 475 SQ. FT.

TOTAL LIVING AREA:
3,113 SQ. FT.

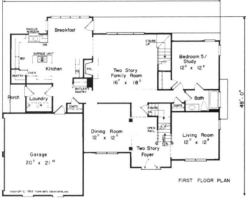

FIRST FLOOR PLAN

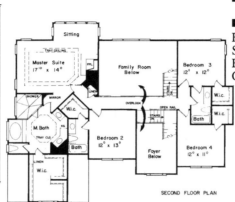

SECOND FLOOR PLAN

© 1996 Donald A Gardner Architects, Inc.

European Sophistication
PRICE CODE: D

- This plan features:
  — Three bedrooms
  — Two full baths
- Keystone arches, gables and stucco give the exterior European sophistication
- Large Great Room with fireplace, and U-shaped Kitchen and a large Utility Room nearby
- Octagonal tray ceiling dresses up the Dining Room
- Special ceiling treatments include a cathedral ceiling in the Great Room and tray ceilings in the Master and front Bedrooms
- Indulgent Master Bath with a separate toilet area, a garden tub, shower and twin vanities
- Bonus Room over the Garage adds flexibility

MAIN FLOOR — 1,699 SQ. FT.
BONUS — 386 SQ. FT.
GARAGE — 637 SQ. FT.

TOTAL LIVING AREA:
1,699 SQ. FT.

FLOOR PLAN

© 1996 Donald A Gardner Architects, Inc.

Old World Style

PRICE CODE: E

■ This plan features:
— Four bedrooms
— Three full and one half baths

■ The stone and brick veneer combines with eyebrow windows, a dormer window, and a bay window creating character for this elevation

■ Elegance is created by the curved staircase in the Gallery, and the columns and arched window in the Dining Room.

■ The angled Kitchen with brick accents and a large Pantry are open to the large informal Dining Area and the Family Room

■ An optional crawl space or slab foundation — please specify when ordering

■ No materials list is available for this plan

FIRST FLOOR — 2,263 SQ. FT.
SECOND FLOOR — 849 SQ. FT.
BONUS — 430 SQ. FT.
GARAGE — 630 SQ. FT.

TOTAL LIVING AREA:
3,112 SQ. FT.

Secluded Suite

PRICE CODE: C

■ This plan features:
— Three bedrooms
— Two full and one half baths

■ There are high ceilings in both the Great and Dining Rooms

■ Columns support a plant shelf at the entry to the Dining Room

■ The L-shaped Kitchen has an adjacent Snack Bar

■ The Master Bedroom is located for privacy on the first floor

■ A balcony and plant shelf overlook the first floor

■ The secondary Bedrooms upstairs share a Bath

■ No materials list is available for this plan

FIRST FLOOR — 973 SQ. FT.
SECOND FLOOR — 520 SQ. FT.
BASEMENT — 973 SQ. FT.
GARAGE — 462 SQ. FT.

TOTAL LIVING AREA:
1,493 SQ. FT.

Family-Sized Accommodations

Price Code: C

■ This plan features:

— Four bedrooms

— Two full and one half baths

■ A spacious feeling is created by a vaulted ceiling in Foyer

■ A fireplace is nestled by an alcove of windows in Family Room which invites cozy gatherings

■ An angled Kitchen with a work island and a pantry easily serves the Breakfast Area and the Dining Room

■ The Master Bedroom is accented by a tray ceiling, a lavish Bath and a walk-in closet

■ An optional basement or crawl space foundation — please specify when ordering this plan

FIRST FLOOR — 1,320 SQ. FT.
SECOND FLOOR — 554 SQ. FT.
BONUS ROOM — 155 SQ. FT.
GARAGE — 406 SQ. FT.

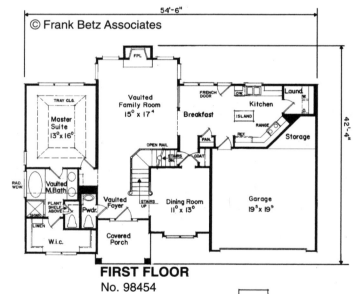

© Frank Betz Associates

54'-6"

42'-4"

FPL

Vaulted Family Room 15⁰ x 17⁴

Breakfast

FRENCH DOOR

DW

Kitchen

Laund.

W.

ISLAND

RANGE

TRAY CLG.

Master Suite 13⁰ x 16⁰

PAN.

REF.

Storage

RAD. WDW.

Vaulted M.Bath

OPEN RAIL

STAIRS DN.

COAT

PLANT SHELF ABOVE

Pwdr.

Vaulted Foyer

STAIRS UP

Dining Room 11⁰ x 13⁰

Garage 19⁵ x 19⁹

LINEN

SHOWER

W.i.c.

Covered Porch

FIRST FLOOR
No. 98454

TOTAL LIVING AREA:
1,874 SQ. FT.

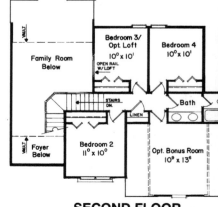

VAULT

Family Room Below

Bedroom 3/ Opt. Loft 10⁰ x 10¹

OPEN RAIL W/LOFT

Bedroom 4 10⁰ x 10¹

STAIRS DN.

Bath

VAULT

Foyer Below

LINEN

Bedroom 2 11⁰ x 10⁰

Opt. Bonus Room 10⁹ x 13⁶

SECOND FLOOR

To order your Blueprints, call 1-800-235-5700

Yesteryear Flavor

Price Code: D

■ This plan features:

— Three or four bedrooms

— Three full baths

■ Wrap-around Porch invites access into gracious Foyer with landing staircase

■ Formal Living Room/Guest Room

■ Family Room with a decorative ceiling, cozy fireplace, book shelves and Porch

■ Country-size Kitchen with island snackbar, built-in desk and nearby Dining Room, Laundry/Workshop and Garage access

■ Master Bedroom with a walk-in closet and plush Bath with a whirlpool tub

■ Two Bedrooms with walk-in closets, share a full Bath and Sitting Area

FIRST FLOOR — 1,236 SQ. FT.
SECOND FLOOR — 1,120 SQ. FT.

TOTAL LIVING AREA:
2,356 SQ. FT.

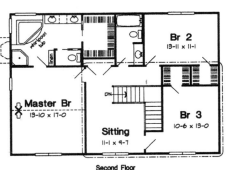

Master Br 13-10 x 17-0
Br 2 13-11 x 11-1
Sitting 11-1 x 9-7
Br 3 10-6 x 13-0

Second Floor

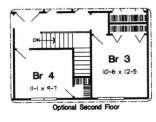

Br 4 11-1 x 9-7
Br 3 10-6 x 12-5

Optional Second Floor

Family Dining 8-10 x 14-1
Kit. 10-0 x 14-1

Optional Kitchen

Workshop 14-5 x 14-5

Crawl Space / Slab Option

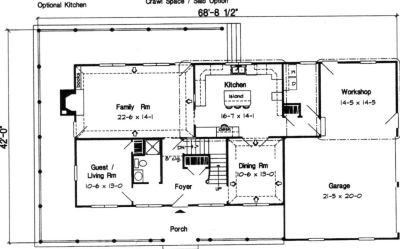

68'-8 1/2"

42'-0"

Family Rm 22-6 x 14-1
Kitchen Island 16-7 x 14-1
Workshop 14-5 x 14-5
Guest / Living Rm 10-6 x 13-0
Foyer
Dining Rm 10-6 x 13-0
Garage 21-5 x 20-0
Porch

First Floor

PLAN NO. 91091

Narrow Lot
PRICE CODE: A

■ This plan features:
— Three bedrooms
— Two full baths
■ This home will easily accommodate a narrow lot
■ A covered Porch and a trellis highlight the front
■ A vaulted ceiling and a wood stove complement the Living Room
■ The Kitchen flows into the Dining Room
■ The Garage is in the rear and has an optional door location
■ The secondary Bedrooms are on the second floor
■ The Master Bedroom is tucked in the rear of the home

FIRST FLOOR — 842 SQ. FT.
SECOND FLOOR — 408 SQ. FT.

TOTAL LIVING AREA:
1,250 SQ. FT.

FIRST FLOOR

SECOND FLOOR

PLAN NO. 97294

Convenience and Style
PRICE CODE: C

■ This plan features:
— Three bedrooms
— Two full baths
■ The Dining Room has decorative columns at its entrance in addition to a plant shelf above
■ The Family Room has a vaulted ceiling and a focal point fireplace
■ The Master Suite is topped by a tray ceiling in the sleeping area and a vaulted ceiling over the private Bath
■ There is a Private Suite at the other end of the house that includes a private Bath
■ An optional basement or a crawl space foundation — please specify when ordering
■ No materials list is available for this plan

MAIN FLOOR — 2,158 SQ. FT.
GARAGE — 485 SQ. FT.
BASEMENT — 2,190 SQ. FT.

TOTAL LIVING AREA:
2,158 SQ. FT.

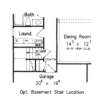

Cozy Three Bedroom
PRICE CODE: B

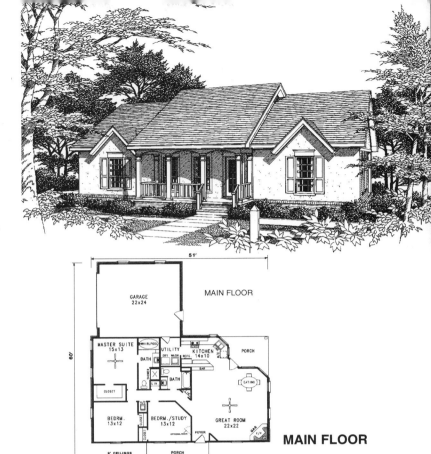

PLAN NO. 96522

■ This plan features:
— Three bedrooms
— Two full baths

■ The triple arched front Porch adds to the curb appeal of the home

■ The expansive Great Room is accented by a cozy gas fireplace

■ The efficient Kitchen includes an eating bar that separates it from the Great Room

■ The Master Bedroom is highlighted by a walk-in closet and a whirlpool Bath

■ Two secondary bedrooms share use of the full hall Bath

■ The rear Porch extends dining to the outdoors

■ An optional crawl space or slab foundation — please specify when ordering

MAIN FLOOR — 1,515 SQ. FT.
GARAGE — 528 SQ. FT.

TOTAL LIVING AREA:
1,515 SQ. FT.

MAIN FLOOR

Sophisticated
Southern Styling
PRICE CODE: E

PLAN NO. 92576

■ This plan features:
— Five bedrooms
— Three full and one half baths

■ Covered front and rear Porches expanding the living space to the outdoors

■ A Den with a large fireplace and built-in cabinets and shelves

■ A cooktop island, built-in desk, and eating bar complete the Kitchen

■ The Master Suite has two walk-in closets and a luxurious Bath

■ Four additional bedrooms, two on the first floor and two on the second floor, all have easy access to a full Bath

■ An optional slab or crawl space foundation — please specify when ordering

FIRST FLOOR — 2,256 SQ. FT.
SECOND FLOOR — 602 SQ. FT.
BONUS — 264 SQ. FT.
GARAGE — 484 SQ. FT.

TOTAL LIVING AREA:
2,858 SQ. FT.

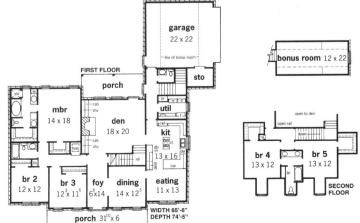

To order your Blueprints, call 1-800-235-5700

© 1994 Donald A. Gardner Architects, Inc.

Didn't Waste An Inch
PRICE CODE: D

■ This plan features:
— Three bedrooms
— Two full baths
■ Great Room with fireplace and built-in cabinets sharing a cathedral ceiling with angled Kitchen
■ Separate Dining Room allows for more formal entertaining
■ Master Bedroom topped by a cathedral ceiling, walk-in closet, and well-appointed Bath
■ Front and rear covered Porches encourage relaxation
■ Skylit Bonus Room makes a great Recreation Room or Office in the future

MAIN FLOOR — 1,575 SQ. FT.
BONUS — 276 SQ. FT.
GARAGE — 536 SQ. FT.

TOTAL LIVING AREA:
1,575 SQ. FT.

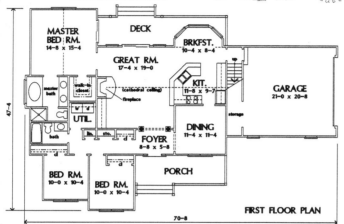

FIRST FLOOR PLAN

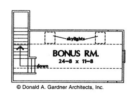

BONUS RM.
24-8 x 11-8

© Donald A. Gardner Architects, Inc.

Full Length Covered Porch
PRICE CODE: F

■ This plan features:
— Four bedrooms
— Three full and one half baths
■ Natural light floods the entrance Foyer through the dramatic palladium style window
■ A grand Family Room with a fireplace and a full length, covered entrance Porch
■ The first floor Master Suite features a large walk-in closet and a Bath with a separate bath tub and stall shower
■ Three additional Bedrooms, a Guest Room and two Bathrooms are on the second floor
■ No materials list is available for this plan

FIRST FLOOR — 2,538 SQ. FT.
SECOND FLOOR — 1,295 SQ. FT.
GARAGE — 900 SQ. FT.

TOTAL LIVING AREA:
3,833 SQ. FT.

MAIN FLOOR

To order your Blueprints, call 1-800-235-5700

© 1990 Donald A. Gardner Architects, Inc.

B. NATHAN

French Influenced One-Story

Price Code: E

DECK 25-2 × 10-0

seat

skylights

SUN RM. 16-0 × 7-6

wet bar

skylights

BRKFST. 8-6 × 10-10

MASTER BED RM. 13-4 × 17-8

master bath

walk-in closet

storage

pantry

BED RM. 11-4 × 11-8

cl

fireplace

GREAT RM. 18-0 × 16-2 (cathedral ceiling)

KIT. 12-0 × 10-0

cl

UTIL.

GARAGE 21-0 × 19-6

bath

lin

cl

FOYER 12-4 × 5-6

vaulted clerestory

storage

DINING 12-0 × 12-0

cl

BED RM. 12-0 × 12-0

PORCH 15-2 × 4-9

72-6

53-10

© Donald A. Gardner Architects, Inc.

FLOOR PLAN

TOTAL LIVING AREA: 2,045 SQ. FT.

pantry

cl

down

kitchen

garage

storage

ALTERNATE PLAN FOR BASEMENT

■ This plan features:

— Three bedrooms

— Two full baths

■ Elegant details including arched windows, round columns and brick veneer

■ Arched clerestory window in the Foyer introduces natural light to a large Great Room with cathedral ceiling and built-in cabinets

■ Skylit Sun Room with a wetbar opens onto a spacious Deck

■ Kitchen with cooking island has access to a large Pantry and Utility Room

■ Large Master Bedroom opening to the Deck and featuring a garden tub, separate shower and dual vanity

MAIN FLOOR — 2,045 SQ. FT.
GARAGE & STORAGE — 563 SQ. FT.

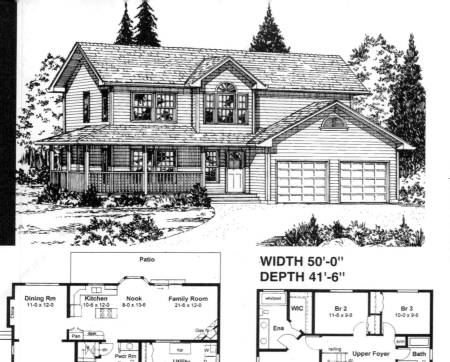

Fabulous Four
PRICE CODE: C

- This plan features:
  — Four bedrooms
  — Two full and one half baths
- A Verandah wraps the front and side of the home
- The formal Living Room opens to the Dining Room
- A space for your china is reserved in the Dining Room
- The Kitchen is open to the Nook and has a center island
- A gas fireplace is located in the Family Room
- Upstairs find four Bedrooms with ample closet space
- No materials list is available for this plan

FIRST FLOOR — 1,155 SQ. FT.
SECOND FLOOR — 1,027 SQ. FT.
BASEMENT — 1,136 SQ. FT.
GARAGE — 507 SQ. FT.

TOTAL LIVING AREA:
2,182 SQ. FT.

WIDTH 50'-0"
DEPTH 41'-6"

Brilliance in Brick and Fieldstone
PRICE CODE: B

- This plan features:
  — Three bedrooms
  — Two full baths
- Stately appearance of entrance and arched windows gives style to modest plan
- Hub of home is Great Room opening to Study/Formal Dining area, covered Patio and Dining/Kitchen
- An efficient Kitchen features a Pantry, serving ledge and bright Dining Area
- Master Bedroom wing offers access to covered Patio, a huge walk-in closet and a whirlpool Bath
- Two additional Bedrooms with large closets, share a full Bath, linen closet and Laundry utilities
- No materials list is available for this plan

MAIN FLOOR — 1,640 SQ. FT.
GARAGE — 408 SQ. FT.

TOTAL LIVING AREA:
1,640 SQ. FT.

To order your Blueprints, call 1-800-235-5700

Key West Island Style
PRICE CODE: E

■ This plan features:
— Three bedrooms
— Three full baths

■ Glass doors open the great room to a deck, while arch-top clerestory windows enhance the casual atmosphere with natural light

■ A corner fireplace and a wet bar create warmth and coziness in the Living and Dining rooms

■ The gourmet Kitchen has a center island/eating bar for easy meals, plus a window wrapped counter

■ A winding staircase leads to a luxurious upper-level MasterSuite that opens to a private balcony

FIRST FLOOR — 1,684 SQ. FT.
SECOND FLOOR — 1,195 SQ. FT.
LOWER FLOOR — 1,433 SQ. FT.

TOTAL LIVING AREA:
2,879 SQ. FT.

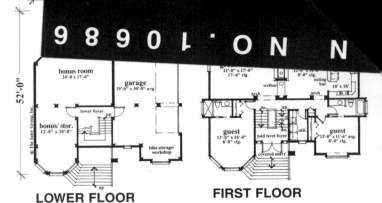

SECOND FLOOR

LOWER FLOOR

FIRST FLOOR

PLAN NO. 10686

Eye Catching Style
PRICE CODE: D

■ This plan features:
— Three bedrooms
— Two full and one half baths

■ Covered front Porch shelters from inclement weather and opens into tiled Entry hall

■ Dining Room has a cathedral ceiling and distinctive front windows

■ The Master Bedrooms has a bay at one end and includes a bath with a cathedral ceiling

■ Enter the Great Room through an arched soffit to view the rear wall fireplace

■ An L-shaped Kitchen with adjacent Nook also includes a curved snack bar

■ Two Bedrooms and a full Bath are located on the second floor

■ No materials list is available for this plan

FIRST FLOOR — 1,944 SQ. FT.
SECOND FLOOR — 495 SQ. FT.
BASEMENT — 1,944 SQ. FT.

TOTAL LIVING AREA:
2,439 SQ. FT.

PLAN NO. 99138

FIRST FLOOR

SECOND FLOOR

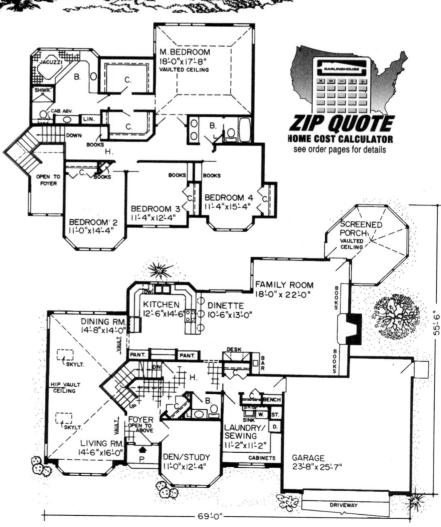

Every Luxurious Feature One Could Want

Price Code: F

■ This plan features:

— Four bedrooms

— Two full and one half baths

■ An open staircase leading to the bedrooms and dividing the space between the vaulted Living and Dining Rooms

■ A wide family area including the Kitchen, Dinette and Family Room complete with built-in bar, bookcases, and fireplace

■ A Master Bedroom with a vaulted ceiling, spacious closets and Jacuzzi

FIRST FLOOR — 1,786 SQ. FT.
SECOND FLOOR — 1,490 SQ. FT.
BASEMENT — 1,773 SQ. FT.
GARAGE — 579 SQ. FT.

**TOTAL LIVING AREA:
3,276 SQ. FT.**

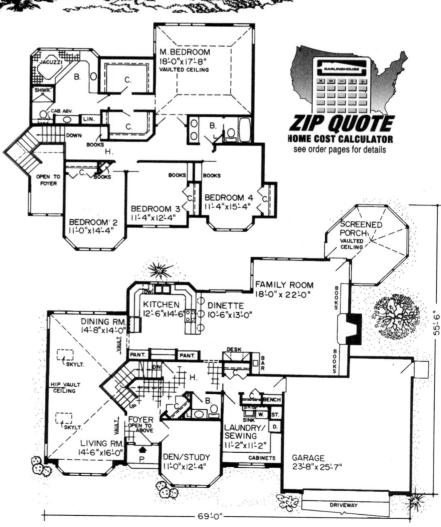

Executive Two-Story
PRICE CODE: C

This plan features:
- Three bedrooms
- Two full and one half baths
- Gracefully curving staircase dominating the Foyer and leading to the bedrooms
- Kitchen and Breakfast Nook separated from the Family Room by only a railing and a step down
- Built-in entertainment center and a warming fireplace highlighting the sunken Family Room
- Formal Living Room and Dining Room that adjoin and include a fireplace in the Living Room and a built-in china cabinet area in the Dining Room
- Lavish Master Suite boasts a sitting room and a deluxe five piece Bath
- Bonus Room to be finished for future needs
- No materials list is available for this plan

FIRST FLOOR — 1,258 SQ. FT.
SECOND FLOOR — 858 SQ. FT.
GARAGE — 441 SQ. FT.
BONUS — 263 SQ. FT.

TOTAL LIVING AREA:
2,116 SQ. FT.

FIRST FLOOR

SECOND FLOOR

Spacious Elegance
PRICE CODE: D

This plan features:
- Four bedrooms
- Three full baths
- Gables, a hip roof and keystone window accents
- The two-story Foyer with palladian window illuminates a lovely staircase and the Dining Room entry way
- The Family Room has a vaulted ceiling and an inviting fireplace
- Vaulted ceiling and a radius window highlight the Breakfast area and the efficient Kitchen
- The Master Bedroom Suite boasts a tray ceiling, luxurious Bath and a walk-in closet
- An optional basement or crawl space foundation — please specify when ordering

FIRST FLOOR — 1,761 SQ. FT.
SECOND FLOOR — 588 SQ. FT.
BONUS ROOM — 267 SQ. FT.
GARAGE — 435 SQ. FT.

TOTAL LIVING AREA:
2,349 SQ. FT.

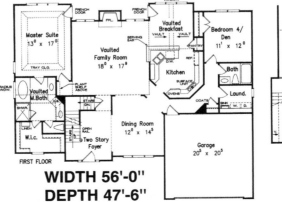

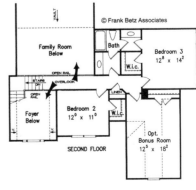

© Frank Betz Associates

WIDTH 56'-0"
DEPTH 47'-6"

© 1997 Donald A. Gardner Architects, Inc.

Private Master Suite
PRICE CODE: D

- This plan features:
  — Three bedrooms
  — Two full baths
- Working at the Kitchen island focuses your view to the Great Room with vaulted ceiling and a fireplace
- Clerestory dormers emanate light into the Great Room
- Both the Dining Room and Master Bedroom are enhanced by tray ceilings
- Skylights flood natural light into the Bonus space
- The private Master Suite has its own Bath and an expansive walk-in closet

MAIN FLOOR — 1,515 SQ. FT.
BONUS — 288 SQ. FT.
GARAGE — 476 SQ. FT.

TOTAL LIVING AREA:
1,515 SQ. FT.

© 1997 Donald A. Gardner Architects, Inc.

European Flair in Tune with Today
PRICE CODE: C

- This plan features:
  — Three bedrooms
  — Two full baths
- European flavor with decorative windows, gable roof lines and a stucco finish
- Formal Dining Room with floor to ceiling window treatment
- Expansive Activity Room with decorative ceiling, hearth fireplace and Deck access
- Open, efficient Kitchen with snack bar, Laundry, Breakfast area and Screened Porch beyond
- Private Master Bedroom suite with a decorative ceiling, large walk-in closet and luxurious Bath
- Two additional Bedrooms, one with a bay window share a full Bath

MAIN FLOOR — 1,855 SQ. FT.
GARAGE — 439 SQ. FT.

TOTAL LIVING AREA:
1,855 SQ. FT.

MAIN FLOOR

© 1991 Donald A. Gardner Architects, Inc.

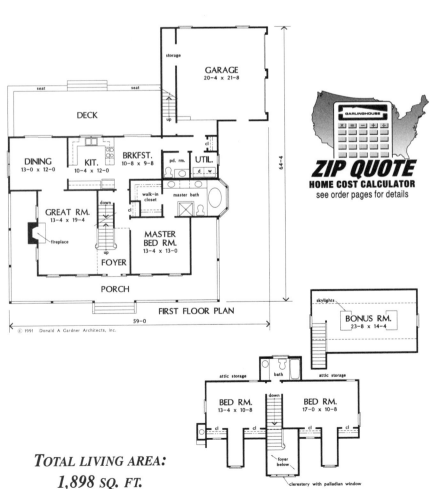

GARAGE 20-4 x 21-8

storage

seat ... seat

DECK

DINING 13-0 x 12-0

KIT. 10-4 x 12-0

BRKFST. 10-8 x 9-8

pd. rm.

UTIL. d w

cl

64-4

walk-in closet

master bath

GREAT RM. 13-4 x 19-4

fireplace

down

cl

MASTER BED RM. 13-4 x 13-0

FOYER

up

PORCH

FIRST FLOOR PLAN

59-0

© 1991 Donald A Gardner Architects, Inc.

skylights

BONUS RM. 23-8 x 14-4

attic storage

bath

attic storage

BED RM. 13-4 x 10-8

down

BED RM. 17-0 x 10-8

cl cl cl cl

foyer below

clerestory with palladian window

© 1991 Donald A Gardner Architects, Inc.

SECOND FLOOR PLAN

TOTAL LIVING AREA: 1,898 SQ. FT.

Country Farmhouse
Price Code: D

- This plan features:
  — Three bedrooms
  — Two full and one half baths

- Ready, set, grow with this lovely country home enhanced by wrap-around Porch and rear Deck

- Palladian window in clerestory dormer bathes two-story Foyer in natural light

- Private Master Bedroom suite offers everything: walk-in closet, whirlpool tub, shower, and double vanity

- Two upstairs Bedrooms with dormers and storage access, share a full Bath

- Keep growing with skylit bonus room over Garage and optional basement

FIRST FLOOR — 1,356 SQ. FT.
SECOND FLOOR — 542 SQ. FT.
BONUS ROOM — 393 SQ. FT.
GARAGE & STORAGE — 543 SQ. FT.

GARLINGHOUSE

ZIP QUOTE
HOME COST CALCULATOR
see order pages for details

© 1997 Donald A. Gardner Architects, Inc.

Perfect Home

Price Code: D

■ This plan features:

— Three bedrooms

— Two full and one half baths

■ Wraparound Porch and two-car Garage features unusual for narrow lot floor plan

■ Alcove of windows and columns add distinction to Dining Room

■ Cathedral ceiling above inviting fireplace accent spacious Great Room

■ Efficient Kitchen with peninsula counter accesses side Porch and Deck

■ Master suite on first floor and two additional Bedrooms and bonus room on second floor

First floor — 1,219 sq. ft.
Second floor — 450 sq. ft.
Bonus room — 406 sq. ft.
Garage — 473 sq. ft.

Total living area: 1,669 sq. ft.

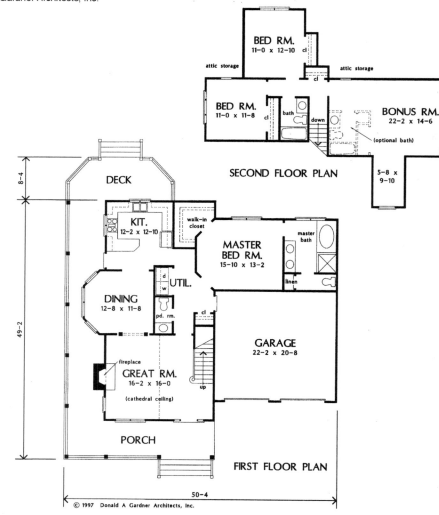

SECOND FLOOR PLAN

FIRST FLOOR PLAN

© 1997 Donald A Gardner Architects, Inc.

To order your Blueprints, call 1-800-235-5700

Surrounded with Sunshine

PRICE CODE: B

This plan features:
- Three bedrooms
- Two full baths

An Italianette style, featuring columns and tile originally designed to sit on the edge of a golf course

An open design with pananoramic vistas in every direction

Tile used from the Foyer, into the Kitchen and Nook, as well as in the Utility Room

A whirlpool tub in the elaborate and spacious Master Bedroom suite

A Great Room with a corner gas fireplace

A turreted Breakfast Nook and an efficient Kitchen with peninsula counter

Two family Bedrooms that share a full hall Bath

An optional basement or crawl space foundation — please specify when ordering

MAIN FLOOR— 1,731 SQ. FT.
GARAGE — 888 SQ. FT.
BASEMENT — 1,715 SQ. FT.

TOTAL LIVING AREA:
1,731 SQ. FT.

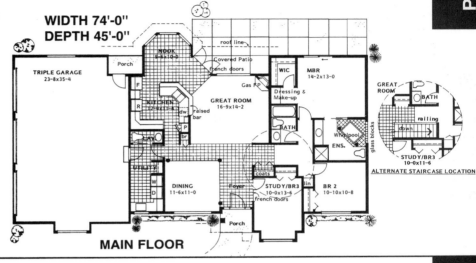

WIDTH 74'-0"
DEPTH 45'-0"

MAIN FLOOR

Grand Plan

PRICE CODE: F

This plan features:
- Five bedrooms
- Five full and two half baths

Separate Garages form a parking court alongside this regal home

A Guest Suite, complete with a full Bath and a large closet is located on the main level

The Master Suite is on the opposite side of the main level, where it is enhanced by a Sitting Bay and a luxurious Bath

Fireplaces warm the formal Living Room at the front of the home and the Family Room

No material list is available for this plan

LOWER LEVEL — 3,188 SQ. FT.
UPPER LEVEL — 1,426 SQ. FT.
GARAGE — 740 SQ. FT.

TOTAL LIVING AREA:
4,614 SQ. FT.

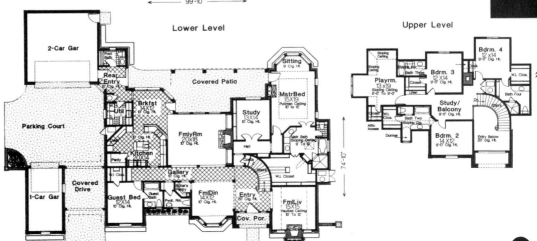

Lower Level

Upper Level

Updated Victorian
PRICE CODE: C

- This plan features:
— Three bedrooms
— Two full and one half baths
- A classic Victorian exterior design accented by a wonderful Turret Room and second floor covered Porch above a sweeping Veranda
- A spacious formal Living Room leading into a formal Dining Room for ease in entertaining
- An efficient, U-shaped Kitchen with loads of counter space and a peninsula snackbar, opens to an eating No[ok] and Family Room for informal gatherings and activitie[s]
- An elegant Master Suite with a unique, octagon Sitting Area, a private Porch, an oversized, walk-in closet and private Bath with a double vanity and a window tub
- Two additional Bedrooms with ample closets sharing a full hall Bath

FIRST FLOOR — 1,150 SQ. FT.
SECOND FLOOR — 949 SQ. FT.
GARAGE — 484 SQ. FT.

TOTAL LIVING AREA:
2,099 SQ. FT.

FIRST FLOOR

SECOND FLOOR

Expand Your Options
PRICE CODE: C

- This plan features:
— Three bedroom
— Two full and one half baths
- This plan has an optional lower level that includes two more Bedrooms
- Also on the lower level, find a Family Room with a fire[place] place and a bar
- On the main level, the Dining Room has a towering fro[nt] wall window
- The Great Room has a rear bow window
- The Kitchen is brightened by a window with a transom over the sink
- The Gathering Room shares a fireplace with the gazebo[-] shaped Breakfast Nook
- The Master Bedroom has a French door to the rear yard
- The large walk-in closet in the Master Bedroom contain[s] a built-in cedar chest

MAIN LEVEL — 1,887 SQ. FT.
LOWER LEVEL — 1,338 SQ. FT.
GARAGE — 738 SQ. FT.

TOTAL LIVING AREA:
3,225 SQ. FT.

MAIN LEVEL

LOWER LEVEL

To order your Blueprints, call 1-800-235-5700

Traditional Three Bedroom
PRICE CODE: C

This plan features:
- Three bedrooms
- Two full and one half baths

A vaulted Entry and Great Room provide this home with a wonderful first impression

The large three-stall Garage includes ample storage space for hobby materials and yard equipment

A covered Porch accessed from the Dining Room expands living space to the outdoors.

No materials list is available for this plan

FIRST FLOOR — 1,907 SQ. FT.
BASEMENT — 1,907 SQ. FT.
GARAGE — 678 SQ. FT.

TOTAL LIVING AREA : 1,907 SQ. FT.

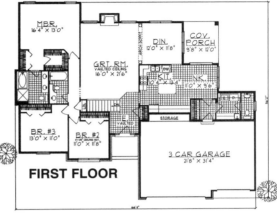

FIRST FLOOR

Symmetrical Southern Beauty
PRICE CODE: D

This plan features:
- Four bedrooms
- Three full and one half baths

Inviting front Porch shades arched windows in warm climate

Spacious Family Room with cozy fireplace and access to covered Porch and Patio

Open Dining Room accented by columns conveniently located

Peninsula counter/eating bar and adjoining Breakfast Area, Garage entry and Utility Room in efficient Kitchen

Corner Master Bedroom with large walk-in closet and double vanity bath

First floor Bedroom with a walk-in closet and private Bath

Two additional Bedrooms on second floor with walk-in closets, share a full Bath and Balcony

An optional slab or crawl space foundation — please specify when ordering

No materials list is available for this plan

FIRST FLOOR — 1,796 SQ. FT.
SECOND FLOOR — 610 SQ. FT.
GARAGE — 570 SQ. FT.

TOTAL LIVING AREA : 2,406 SQ. FT.

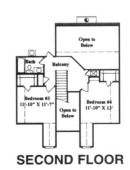

WIDTH 65'-8.5"
DEPTH 64'-8.5"

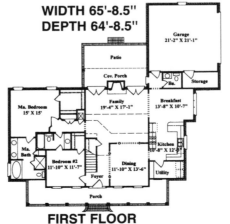

FIRST FLOOR

SECOND FLOOR

To order your Blueprints, call 1-800-235-5700

PLAN NO. 98456

High Ceilings Add Volume
PRICE CODE: B

- This plan features:
  — Three bedrooms
  — Two full baths
- A covered entry gives way to a 14-foot high ceiling in the Foyer
- An arched opening greets you in the Great Room that also has a vaulted ceiling and a fireplace
- The Dining Room is brightened by triple windows with transoms above
- The Kitchen is a gourmet's delight and is open to the Breakfast Nook
- The Master Suite is sweet with a tray ceiling, vaulted Sitting Area and private Bath
- Two Bedrooms on the opposite side of the home share Bath in the hall
- An optional basement, slab or crawl space foundation - please specify when ordering

MAIN FLOOR — 1,715 SQ. FT.
BASEMENT — 1,715 SQ. FT.
GARAGE — 450 SQ. FT.

TOTAL LIVING AREA:
1,715 SQ. FT.

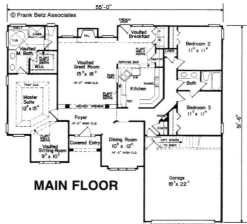

MAIN FLOOR

© Frank Betz Associates

PLAN NO. 97415

Enticing Design
PRICE CODE: B

- This plan features:
  — Three bedrooms
  — Two full baths
- The all brick facade offers the homeowner low exterior maintenance
- A three-sided fireplace which warms both the angled Great Room and the Hearth Room
- The Kitchen incorporates a peninsula snack bar that opens to the Great Room and the Hearth Room
- The private Master Suite has a nine-foot boxed ceiling, large walk-in closet, double vanity and a whirlpool tub
- An optional basement or slab foundation—please specify when ordering

MAIN FLOOR - 1,782 SQ. FT.
GARAGE - 466 SQ. FT

TOTAL LIVING AREA
1,782 SQ. FT.

MAIN FLOOR

© design basics inc.

240 To order your Blueprints, call 1-800-235-5700

© 1997 Donald A. Gardner Architects, Inc.

B. NATHAN

FIRST FLOOR

GARAGE
21-8 x 23-8

storage

PORCH

MASTER BED RM.
15-4 x 15-4

GREAT RM.
18-8 x 20-8
(vaulted ceiling)
fireplace

BRKFST.
15-8 x 10-6

UTIL.
14-2 x 6-8

storage

storage

KITCHEN
15-8 x 14-6

balcony above

sto.

up

up

walk-in closet

master bath

pd. rm.

DINING
13-8 x 12-8

FOYER
8-8 x 7-2

PORCH

82-0

64-2

© 1997 Donald A Gardner Architects, Inc.

SECOND FLOOR

BED RM.
12-4 x 13-0

great room below

BED RM.
12-8 x 13-0

BONUS RM.
14-2 x 23-8

railing

down

attic storage

attic storage

BED RM.
11-4 x 11-6

bath

bath

foyer below

attic storage

down

1997 Donald A Gardner Architects, Inc.

Perfect for Entertaining
Price Code: F

- ■ This plan features:
  - — Four bedrooms
  - — Three full and one half baths
- ■ With front dormers and a wrap-around Porch, the home offers formal entertaining and casual living
- ■ Dramatic Great Room boasts cathedral ceiling and fireplace nestled between built-in shelves
- ■ French doors expand living space to full length rear Porch
- ■ Center island and peninsula counter create an efficient Kitchen/Breakfast Area
- ■ First floor Master Bedroom Suite features walk-in closet and spacious Master Bath

FIRST FLOOR — 1,831 SQ. FT.
SECOND FLOOR — 941 SQ. FT.
BONUS ROOM — 539 SQ. FT.
GARAGE & STORAGE — 684 SQ. FT.

TOTAL LIVING AREA:
2,772 SQ. FT.

© 1995 Donald A. Gardner Architects, Inc.

Appealing Design

Price Code: D

■ This plan features:

— Three bedrooms

— Two full and one half baths

■ Comfortable farmhouse features an easy to build floor plan with all the extras

■ Active families will enjoy the Great Room which is open to the Kitchen and Breakfast Bay, as well as expanded living space provided by the full back Porch

■ For narrower lot restrictions, the Garage can be modified to open in front

■ Second floor Master Bedroom suite contains a walk-in closet and a private Bath with a garden tub and separate shower

■ Two more Bedrooms on the second floor, one with a walk-in closet, share a full Bath

FIRST FLOOR — 959 SQ. F.T

SECOND FLOOR — 833 SQ. FT.

BONUS ROOM — 344 SQ. FT.

GARAGE & STORAGE — 500 SQ. FT.

ZIP QUOTE

HOME COST CALCULATOR
see order pages for details

TOTAL LIVING AREA:
1,792 SQ. FT.

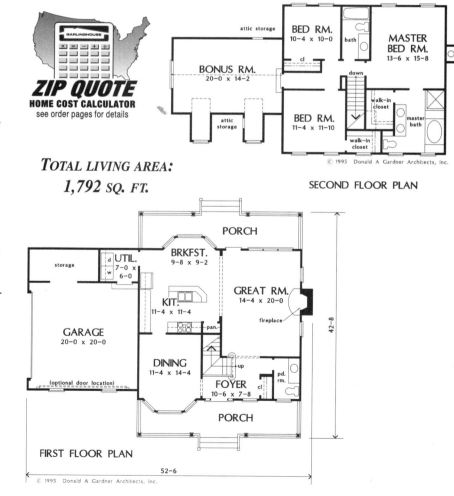

SECOND FLOOR PLAN

FIRST FLOOR PLAN

Cottage Influence

Price Code: D

- This plan features:
  — Three or four bedrooms
  — Three full and one half baths
- Expansive Great Room with focal point fireplace and access to covered Porch and Deck
- Cooktop island in Kitchen easily serves Breakfast bay and formal Dining Room
- Large Master Suite with access to Covered Porch, walk-in closet and double vanity Bath
- An optional crawl space or slab foundation available — please specify when ordering
- No materials list is available for this plan

FIRST FLOOR — 1,916 SQ. FT.
SECOND FLOOR — 617 SQ. FT.
GARAGE — 501 SQ. FT.

TOTAL LIVING AREA:
2,533 SQ. FT.

WIDTH 66'-0"
DEPTH 66'-0"

Garage
21'-4" x 23'-4"

Wd. Deck
33' x 8'

Cov. Porch
33' x 6'

Util.

Great Room
19'-4" x 18'

Ma. Suite
14' x 18'

Brkfst.
14' x 9'

Hall

Ma. Ba.

Kit.
12' x 12'

Dining
14'-10" x 11'-3"

Ba. 3

Stdy./Gst.Bdrm.
11'-4" x 11'-4"

Foyer

Porch
32' x 6'

FIRST FLOOR

Ba. 2

Dr.

Dr.

Bdrm. 2
11'-6" x 12'

open to below

Bdrm. 3
11'-6" x 12'

SECOND FLOOR

© design basics inc. 1990
G. MACDONALD

Enticing Elevation With Spacious Porch

Price Code: D

■ This plan features:

— Four bedrooms

— Two full and one half baths

■ The Parlor is enhanced by bright gazebo windows

■ A bright window wall and a cozy fireplace highlight the Gathering Room

■ The Kitchen has a work island and an angled Breakfast Area

■ There are gazebo windows in the third Bedroom and a walk-in closet in the fourth Bedroom.

■ No material list is available for this plan

FIRST FLOOR — 1,183 SQ. FT.
SECOND FLOOR — 1,209 SQ. FT.

TOTAL LIVING AREA:
2,392 SQ. FT.

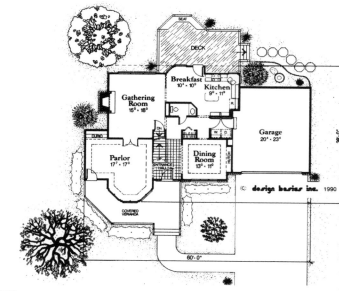

FIRST FLOOR

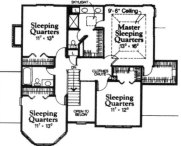

SECOND FLOOR

Captivating Views

PRICE CODE: B

This plan features:
- Three bedrooms
- One full and one three-quarter baths
- Appealing grade-level entry home is designed to capture a front view
- Combined formal Living and Dining rooms create a feeling of space
- A dream Kitchen with a peninsula counter, corner window and a Nook
- The Master Bedroom suite boasts a walk-in closet and a private Bath
- The lower level offers future expansion ideas
- No materials list is available for this plan

MAIN FLOOR — 1,388 SQ. FT.
LOWER FLOOR — 169 SQ. FT.
BASEMENT — 930 SQ. FT.
GARAGE — 453 SQ. FT.

TOTAL LIVING AREA: 1,557 SQ. FT.

MAIN FLOOR

LOWER FLOOR

Wonderful Windows

PRICE CODE: B

This plan features:
- Three bedrooms
- Two full baths
- Walls of windows let in plenty of sunshine
- A fireplace warms the Living Room
- The Dining Room is conveniently located near the Kitchen
- There is a convenient work triangle in the Kitchen
- The Master Bedroom has a private Deck
- The upstairs Loft is a great place for the kids to camp out
- Finish off the Basement as your needs require
- No materials list is available for this plan

FIRST FLOOR — 1,208 SQ. FT.
SECOND FLOOR — 547 SQ. FT.
BASEMENT — 1,208 SQ. FT.

TOTAL LIVING AREA: 1,755 SQ. FT.

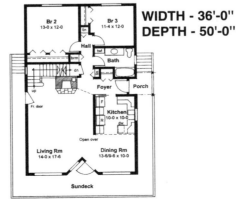

WIDTH - 36'-0"
DEPTH - 50'-0"

Main Floor Plan

Second Floor Plan

Hints of English Tudor
PRICE CODE: F

■ This plan features:
— Four bBedrooms
— Three full and one half baths

■ Built-in entertainment centers enhance the Living Room and the Master Suite

■ The Family Room has a fireplace and a door to one of the two covered rear Patios

■ A Recreation Room on the second floor keeps noisy play away from formal areas

■ The Kitchen, Breakfast Room and Family Room flow easily into each other forming a terrific informal living space

■ An optional basement or a slab foundation — please specify when ordering

■ No materials list is available for this plan

LOWER FLOOR — 2,755 SQ. FT.
UPPER FLOOR — 1,412 SQ. FT.

TOTAL LIVING AREA:
4,167 SQ. FT.

Lower Floor Plan

Upper Floor Plan

First Floor Master Suite
PRICE CODE: D

■ This plan features:
— Four bedrooms
— Three full and one half baths

■ Welcoming Country Porch adds to appeal and living space

■ Central Foyer provides ventilation and access to all areas of home

■ Spacious Living Room enhanced by fireplace and access to covered Porch

■ Efficient Kitchen with work island, built-in Pantry, Utility Room, Garage Entry and Breakfast Area

■ Spacious Master Bedroom Suite with a pampering, private Bath

■ Three second floor Bedrooms with walk-in closets, share two full Baths and a Game Room

■ An optional crawl space or slab foundation — please specify when ordering

■ No materials list is available for this plan

FIRST FLOOR — 1,492 SQ. FT.
SECOND FLOOR — 865 SQ. FT.
UNFINISHED GAME ROOM — 303 SQ. FT.
GARAGE — 574 SQ. FT.

TOTAL LIVING AREA:
2,357 SQ. FT.

WIDTH 66'-10"
DEPTH 49'-7"

SECOND FLOOR

FIRST FLOOR

FIRST FLOOR

Sun Rm
15-8 × 12-0

Mbr
15-4 × 14-0
11'-0" Vault

Bfst
15-0 × 12-0
12'-10" Vault

Br2
11-0 × 13-0

Bath

Grt Rm
20-0 × 19-0
12'-10" Clg. Ht.

Kit

Br3
11-0 × 13-0

Closet

Bath

WP

Din
11-4 × 12-0
13'-0" Clg. Ht.

Entry

Br4
11-0 × 13-0
10'-0" Vault

Gar
21-0 × 23-0

Porch

63-1½

58-4½

SECOND FLOOR

Opt Bath

Up   Attic

Down

Opt Closet

Br5
Or
Rec Rm
12-8 × 17-2
8' Vault

Family Matters
Price Code: E

■ This plan features:
— Five bedrooms
— Three full baths

■ A beautiful brick exterior is accentuated by double transoms over double windows

■ Big Bedrooms and an oversized Great Room, desirable for a large family

■ Volume ceilings in the Master Suite, Great Room, Dining Room, Kitchen, Breakfast Nook, and Bedroom Four

■ Three Bathrooms, including a plush Master Bath, with a double vanity

■ No materials list is available for this plan

FIRST FLOOR — 2,307 SQ. FT.
Second floor — 440 sq. ft.
Garage & Storage — 517 sq. ft.

TOTAL LIVING AREA:
2,747 SQ. FT.

Ranch of Distinction

PRICE CODE: C

- This plan features:
  — Three bedrooms
  — Two full and one half baths
- The recessed Entrance has an arched transom window over the door and a sidelight windows beside it
- Once inside the Living Room boasts a high ceiling and a warm fireplace
- The large Kitchen area includes the open Dining Area with a rear bay that accessed the backyard
- There is a large Utility Room, Garage Access, and a half Bath located off of the Kitchen
- The Master and third Bedrooms both have bay windows
- All of the Bedrooms have ample closet space and they are serviced by two full Baths
- This home has a three-car Garage
- No materials list is available for this plan

MAIN FLOOR — 1,906 SQ. FT.
BASEMENT — 1,906 SQ. FT.

TOTAL LIVING AREA:
1,906 SQ. FT.

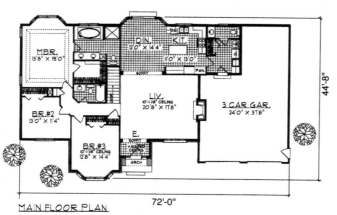

MAIN FLOOR PLAN   72'-0"

Details! Details!

PRICE CODE: D

- This plan features:
  — Three bedrooms
  — Two full and one half baths
- Decorative columns define the Dining Room entrance and a tray ceiling bringing elegance to the room
- The Living Room has a high ceiling and radius window at the far end
- The Kitchen includes a cooktop island/serving bar, a walk-in Pantry and ample work and storage space
- The Breakfast Room and the Family Room flow into the Kitchen for a feeling of spaciousness
- An optional basement or crawl space foundation — please specify when ordering
- No materials list is available for this plan

MAIN FLOOR — 2,491 SQ. FT.
BONUS ROOM — 588 SQ. FT.
BASEMENT — 2,491 SQ. FT.
GARAGE — 588 SQ. FT.

TOTAL LIVING AREA:
2,491 SQ. FT.

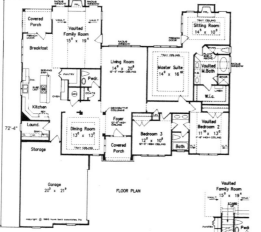

To order your Blueprints, call 1-800-235-5700

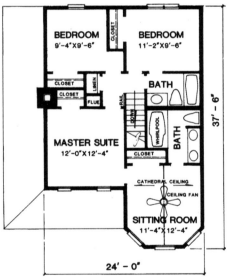

BEDROOM
9'-4"X9'-6"

BEDROOM
11'-2"X9'-6"

CLOSET

BATH

CLOSET

CLOSET

LINEN

FLUE

RAIL

MASTER SUITE
12'-0"X12'-4"

WHIRLPOOL

BATH

CLOSET

37' - 6"

CATHEDRAL CEILING

CEILING FAN

SITTING ROOM
11'-4"X12'-4"

24' - 0"

Compact Victorian Ideal for Narrow Lot

Price Code: B

■ This plan features:

— Three bedrooms

— Three full baths

■ A large, front Parlor with a raised hearth fireplace

■ A Dining Room with a sunny bay window

■ An efficient galley Kitchen serving the formal Dining Room and informal Breakfast Room

■ A beautiful Master Suite with two closets, an oversized tub and double vanity, plus a private sitting room with a bayed window and vaulted ceiling

■ An optional basement, slab or crawl space foundation — please specify when ordering

FIRST FLOOR — 954 SQ. FT.
SECOND FLOOR — 783 SQ. FT.

TOTAL LIVING AREA: *1,737 SQ. FT.*

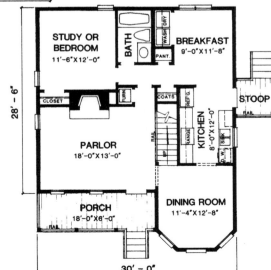

STUDY OR
BEDROOM
11'-6"X12'-0"

BATH

WASH

DRY

BREAKFAST
9'-0"X11'-8"

PANT.

CLOSET

FURN.

COATS

REF'G.

STOOP

RAIL

28' - 6"

RAIL

KITCHEN
8'-0"X12'-0"

RANGE

D.W.

SINK

UP

PARLOR
18'-0"X13'-0"

PORCH
18'-0"X6'-0"

DINING ROOM
11'-4"X12'-8"

RAIL

30' - 0"

© 1994 Donald A Gardner Architects, Inc.

Exciting Three Bedroom

Price Code: D

- This plan features:
- — Three bedrooms
- — Two full baths
- A Great Room enhanced by a fireplace, cathedral ceiling, and built-in bookshelves
- A Kitchen designed for efficiency with a food preparation island and a Pantry
- A Master Suite topped by a cathedral ceiling and pampered by a luxurious Bath and a walk-in closet
- Two additional Bedrooms, one with a cathedral ceiling and a walk-in closet, sharing a sky lit Bath
- A second floor bonus room, perfect for a Study or a Play Area

TOTAL LIVING AREA:
1,787 SQ. FT.

ZIP QUOTE
HOME COST CALCULATOR
see order pages for details

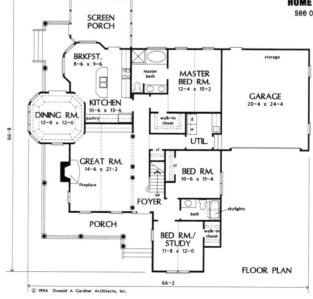

MAIN FLOOR — 1,787 SQ. FT.
GARAGE & storage — 521 SQ. FT.
BONUS ROOM — 326 SQ. FT.

Luxurious Styling

PRICE CODE: F

This plan features:

- Four bedrooms
- Three full and one half baths
- Elegance prevails in the master suite, which occupies a quiet corner of the main floor
- The Master Bedroom has a door to a covered rear Patio and shares a two sided fireplace with a Study
- The Living Room has a cathedral ceiling a fireplace, and a wetbar
- The Kitchen includes a pantry, a snack bar, and a work island
- An optional basement, slab or crawl space foundation — please specify when ordering
- No materials list is available for this plan

LOWER LEVEL — 2,860 SQ. FT.
UPPER LEVEL — 1,140 SQ. FT.

TOTAL LIVING AREA:
4,000 SQ. FT.

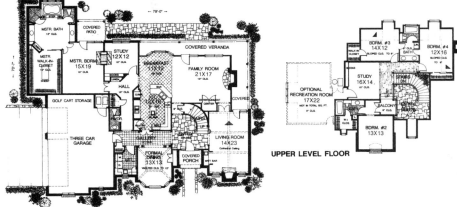

LOWER LEVEL FLOOR

UPPER LEVEL FLOOR

Double Gables
and Exciting Entry

PRICE CODE: D

This plan features:

- Four bedrooms
- Two full and one half baths
- Impressive exterior features double gables and arched window
- Spacious Foyer separates the formal Dining Room and Living Room
- Roomy Kitchen and Breakfast Bay are adjacent to the large Family Room which has a fireplace and accesses the rear Deck
- Spacious Master Bedroom features private Bath with dual vanity, shower stall and whirlpool tub
- Three additional Bedroom share a full hall Bath
- No materials list is available for this plan

FIRST FLOOR — 1,207 SQ. FT.
SECOND FLOOR — 1,181 SQ. FT.
BASEMENT — 1,207 SQ. FT.

TOTAL LIVING AREA:
2,388 SQ. FT.

FIRST FLOOR

SECOND FLOOR

ZIP QUOTE
HOME COST CALCULATOR
see order pages for details

Splendid Space
PRICE CODE: C

■ This plan features:
— Three bedrooms
— Two full baths
■ A split Bedroom plan allows for privacy
■ Arched entries lead into the Living and Dining Rooms
■ A Sunroom is located in the rear
■ The Nook has a built-in desk
■ Plant ledges are a nice touch
■ No materials list is available for this plan

MAIN FLOOR — 1,983 SQ. FT.
GARAGE — 492 SQ. FT.

TOTAL LIVING AREA:
1,983 SQ. FT.

MAIN FLOOR

Easy Maintenance
PRICE CODE: A

■ This plan features:
— Two bedroom
— Two full baths
■ Abundant glass and a wrap-around Deck to enjoy the outdoors
■ A tiled entrance into a large Great Room with a field-stone fireplace and dining area below a sloped ceiling
■ A compact tiled Kitchen opens to a Great Room and is adjacent to the Utility Area
■ Two Bedrooms, one with a private Bath, offer ample closet space
■ No materials list is available for this plan

MAIN FLOOR — 786 SQ. FT.

TOTAL LIVING AREA:
786 SQ. FT.

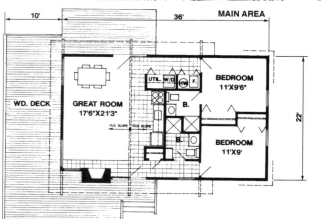

To order your Blueprints, call 1-800-235-5700

Columns Accentuate with Flair

PRICE CODE: D

This plan features:
- Four bedrooms
- Two full baths
- Four columns accentuate the front Porch
- The Foyer leads to the Living Room or the Dining Room
- The Kitchen includes a peninsula counter, plenty of storage space and an easy flow into the Breakfast Room
- The Master Bedroom is topped by a decorative ceiling treatment and has a compartmental Bath with a whirlpool tub
- Two additional Bedrooms with walk-in closets share a double vanity Bath in the hall
- No materials list is available for this plan

MAIN FLOOR — 2,400 SQ. FT.
GARAGE — 534 SQ. FT.

TOTAL LIVING AREA: 2,400 SQ. FT.

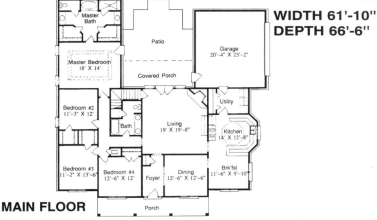

WIDTH 61'-10"
DEPTH 66'-6"

MAIN FLOOR

Room for a Large Family

PRICE CODE: C

This plan features:
- Four bedrooms
- Two full and one half baths
- Front Porch leads into a two-story Foyer with an open L-shaped staircase
- Gracious Living Room archway leads into the formal Dining Room
- Relax by the fire in the Family Room
- The L-shaped Kitchen opens into the Nook and has a built-in planning desk
- The Master Bedroom is located on the second floor and has a private Bath
- Three more Bedrooms and a full Bath serve the rest of the family
- No materials list is available for this plan

FIRST FLOOR — 1,000 SQ. FT.
SECOND FLOOR — 960 SQ. FT.
BASEMENT — 1,000 SQ. FT.

TOTAL LIVING AREA: 1,960 SQ. FT.

MAIN FLOOR PLAN

SECOND FLOOR PLAN

Modern Luxury

Price Code: E

- This plan features:
  — Four bedrooms
  — Three full and one half baths

- A feeling of spaciousness is created by the two-story Foyer and volume ceilings

- Arched openings and decorative windows enhance the Dining and Living rooms

- The efficient Kitchen has a work island, a Pantry and a Breakfast Area open to the Family Room

- The plush Master Suite features a tray ceiling above and an alcove of windows

- Three secondary Bedrooms on the second floor have walk-in closets

- An optional basement or crawl space foundaion — please specify when ordering

FIRST FLOOR — 1,883 SQ. FT.
SECOND FLOOR — 803 SQ. FT.
BASEMENT — 1,883 SQ. FT.
GARAGE — 495 SQ. FT.

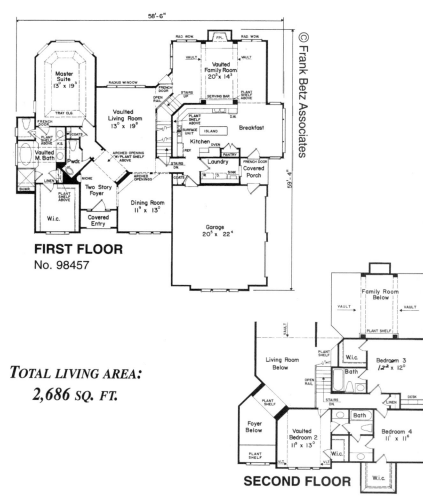

FIRST FLOOR
No. 98457

© Frank Betz Associates

TOTAL LIVING AREA:
2,686 SQ. FT.

SECOND FLOOR

To order your Blueprints, call 1-800-235-5700

Narrow Lot

PRICE CODE: B

This plan features:
- Three bedrooms
- Two full and one half baths
- At almost 38 feet wide this home is suited to a narrow lot
- The Dining Room has a tray ceiling above it
- The Living Rroom has a corner fireplace
- The Galley Kitchen is adjacent to the Nook
- The Master Suite has a large walk-in closet
- Additional Bedrooms and Bonus Space are upstairs
- No materials list is available for this plan

FIRST FLOOR — 1,188 SQ. FT.
SECOND FLOOR — 513 SQ. FT.
GARAGE — 411 SQ. FT.

TOTAL LIVING AREA: 1,701 SQ. FT.

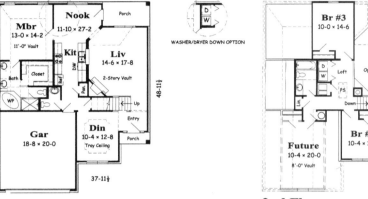

1st Floor

2nd Floor

Cottage Appeal

PRICE CODE: F

This plan features:
- Four bedrooms
- Three full and one half baths
- A curving staircase accents the formal Entry with gracious elegance
- Enhanced by a fireplace and a bay window, the Living Room is a welcoming spot
- The Great Room has a fireplace and access to the rear Patio
- Each Bedroom has private access to a full Bath
- Three car Garage offers additional Storage Space and an easy Entry into the home
- An optional basement or slab foundation — please specify when ordering
- No material list is available for this plan

FIRST FLOOR — 2,337 SQ. FT.
SECOND FLOOR — 882 SQ. FT.

TOTAL LIVING AREA: 3,219 SQ. FT.

WIDTH 70'-0"
DEPTH 63'-2"

SECOND FLOOR

FIRST FLOOR

Grand Country Porch

Price Code: E

- This plan features:
  - — Four bedrooms
  - — Three full baths
- Large front Porch provides shade and Southern hospitality
- Spacious Living Room with access to Covered Porch and Patio, and a cozy fireplace between built-in shelves
- Country Kitchen with a cooktop island, bright Breakfast bay, Utility Room, Garage entry
- Corner Master Bedroom with a walk-in closet and private bath
- First floor Bedroom with private access to a full bath
- Two additional second floor bedrooms with dormers, walk-in closets and vanities, share a full bath
- An optional crawl space or slab foundation — please specify when ordering
- No materials list is available for this plan

FIRST FLOOR — 1,916 SQ. FT.
SECOND FLOOR — 749 SQ. FT.
GARAGE — 479 SQ. FT.

TOTAL LIVING AREA:
2,665 SQ. FT.

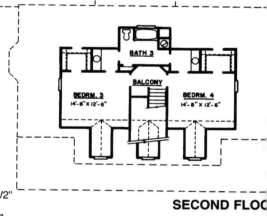

SECOND FLOOR

FIRST FLOOR

WIDTH 62'-0"
DEPTH 63'-8 1/2"

To order your Blueprints, call 1-800-235-5700

Made To Order

Price Code: B

■ This plan features:

— Three bedrooms

— Two full baths

■ The Master Suite has a vaulted ceiling, private access to the backyard, and columns lining the entrance to the Bath

■ There is a corner fireplace and a vaulted ceiling in the Living Room

■ The Dining Room is topped by an eleven-foot ceiling and has easy access to the Kitchen

■ The entry from the Garage is into the Laundry Room creating a Mudroom effect

■ No material list is available for this plan

MAIN FLOOR — 1,561 SQ. FT.
GARAGE & STORAGE — 445 SQ. FT.

TOTAL LIVING AREA:
1,561 SQ. FT.

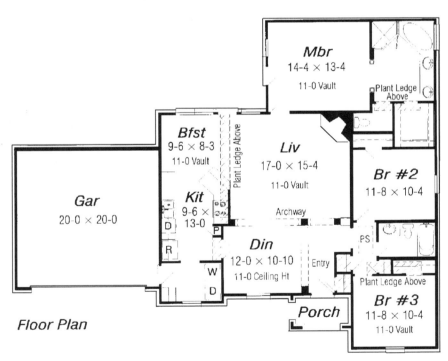

Mbr
14-4 × 13-4
11-0 Vault

Plant Ledge Above

Bfst
9-6 × 8-3
11-0 Vault

Plant Ledge Above

Liv
17-0 × 15-4
11-0 Vault

Br #2
11-8 × 10-4

Gar
20-0 × 20-0

Kit
9-6 × 13-0

Archway

Din
12-0 × 10-10
11-0 Ceiling Ht

Entry

Br #3
11-8 × 10-4
11-0 Vault

Plant Ledge Above

Porch

Floor Plan

WIDTH 60'-8"
DEPTH 49'-4"

Multiple Porches Provide Added Interest

PRICE CODE: E

- ■ This plan features:
  - — Four bedrooms
  - — Three full and one half baths
- ■ Two-story central Foyer flanked by Living and Dining rooms
- ■ Spacious Great Room with large fireplace between french doors to Porch and Deck
- ■ Country-size Kitchen with cooktop work island, walk-in Pantry and Breakfast Area with Porch access
- ■ Pampering Master Bedroom offers a decorative ceiling, Sitting Area, Porch and Deck access, a huge walk-in closet and lavish Bath
- ■ Three second floor Bedrooms with walk-in closets, have private access to a full Bath
- ■ An optional crawl space or slab foundation — please specify when ordering
- ■ No materials list is available for this plan

FIRST FLOOR — 2,033 SQ. FT.
SECOND FLOOR — 1,116 SQ. FT.

TOTAL LIVING AREA:
3,149 SQ. FT.

WIDTH 66'-0"
DEPTH 56'-0"

SECOND FLOOR

FIRST FLOOR

Modern Comfort

PRICE CODE: E

- ■ This plan features:
  - — Three bedrooms
  - — Two full and one half baths
- ■ This home is a Traditional Ranch with Country trimmings
- ■ Highly windowed Great Room is illuminated by natural light creating an airy atmosphere
- ■ Split-bedroom layout for a private Master Suite
- ■ There is a see-through fireplace from the Master Bedroom to the Master Bath
- ■ Formal Dining and a casual Nook, you can entertain for any occasion
- ■ No materials list available for this plan

MAIN FLOOR — 2,730 SQ. FT.
BASEMENT — 2,730 SQ. FT.
GARAGE — 707 SQ. FT.

TOTAL LIVING AREA:
2,730 SQ. FT.

MAIN FLOOR PLAN

To order your Blueprints, call 1-800-235-5700

Home Sweet Home
PRICE CODE: A

PLAN NO. 24723

■ This plan features:
— Three bedrooms
— Two full baths

■ Single level format allows for step-saving convenience

■ Large Living Room, highlighted by a fireplace and built-in entertainment center, adjoins the Dining Room

■ Skylights, a ceiling fan and room defining columns accent the Dining Room

■ A serving bar to the Dining Room, and ample counter and cabinet space in the Kitchen

■ Decorative ceiling treatment over the Master Bedroom and a private Master Bath

■ Two secondary Bedrooms with easy access to the full Bath in the hall

■ No materials list is available for this plan

MAIN FLOOR — 1,112 SQ. FT.
GARAGE — 563 SQ. FT.

TOTAL LIVING AREA:
1,112 SQ. FT.

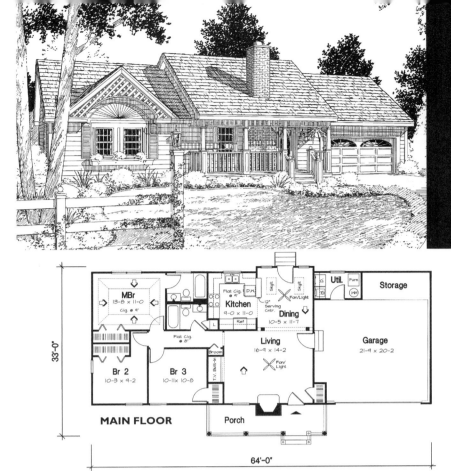

Welcoming Exterior
PRICE CODE: F

PLAN NO. 96403

■ This plan features:
— Four bedrooms
— Two full and one half baths

■ Columns between the Foyer and Living Room/Study hint at all the extras in this four Bedroom Country estate with a warm, welcoming exterior

■ Transom windows over French doors open up the Living Room/Study to the front Porch, while a generous Family Room accesses the covered back Porch

■ Deluxe Master Suite is topped by a tray ceiling and includes a Bath with a sunny garden tub bay and ample closet space

FIRST FLOOR — 1,483 SQ. FT.
SECOND FLOOR — 1,349 SQ. FT.
GARAGE — 738 SQ. FT.
BONUS — 486 SQ. FT.

TOTAL LIVING AREA:
2,832 SQ. FT.

SECOND FLOOR PLAN

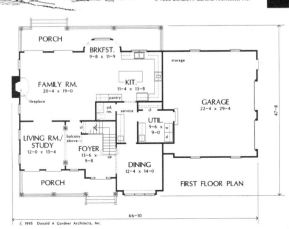

© 1995 Donald A. Gardner Architects, Inc.

FIRST FLOOR PLAN

To order your Blueprints, call 1-800-235-5700

Stupendous Plan
PRICE CODE: A

■ This plan features:
— Four bedrooms
— Two full baths
■ The spacious Living Room has an optional fireplace and a vaulted ceiling
■ The L-shaped Kitchen and Nook have a great bay window naturally illuminating the room and giving a view of the rear yard
■ The Master Bedroom is split from the others and has a vaulted ceiling, walk-in closet and private Master Bath
■ No materials list is available for this plan

MAIN FLOOR — 1,370 SQ. FT.
PORCH — 78 SQ. FT.

TOTAL LIVING AREA:
1,370 SQ. FT.

MAIN FLOOR

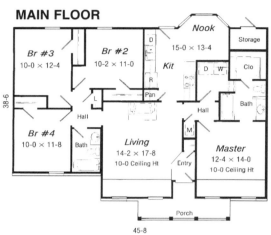

European Flavor
PRICE CODE: E

■ This plan features:
— Three bedrooms
— Two full and one half baths
■ The exterior is stucco with ornate iron railings
■ The Family Room is enhanced by a fireplace and is open to the Dining Room
■ There are pocket doors separating the Study from the Family Room
■ The Kitchen includes a cooktop island with a snack bar, and is open to the Breakfast Area
■ The Master Bedroom Suite is lavishly appointed and includes two walk-in closets.
■ No materials list is available for this plan

FIRST FLOOR — 2,005 SQ. FT.
SECOND FLOOR — 639 SQ. FT.
GARAGE — 443 SQ. FT.

TOTAL LIVING AREA:
2,644 SQ. FT.

WIDTH 61'-0"
DEPTH 54'-6"

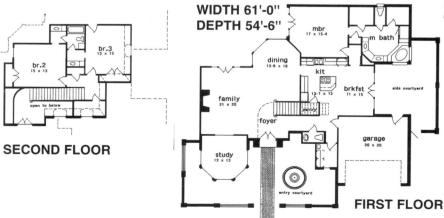

SECOND FLOOR

FIRST FLOOR

To order your Blueprints, call 1-800-235-5700

© 1993 Donald A. Gardner Architects, Inc.

B. NATHAN

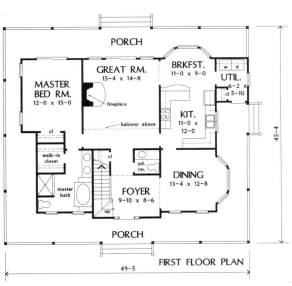

PORCH

MASTER BED RM.
12–0 x 15–0

fireplace

balcony above

cl

walk-in closet

master bath

cl

FOYER
9–10 x 8–6

up

GREAT RM.
15–4 x 14–8

BRKFST.
11–0 x 9–0

UTIL.
6–2 x cl 5–10

w d

KIT.
11–0 x 12–0

pd. rm.

DINING
13–4 x 12–8

PORCH

45–4

49–5

FIRST FLOOR PLAN

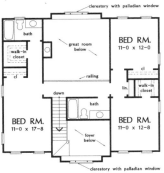

clerestory with palladian window

bath

walk-in closet

cl

great room below

railing

BED RM.
11–0 x 12–0

cl

lin.

walk-in closet

BED RM.
11–0 x 17–8

down

bath

foyer below

BED RM.
11–0 x 12–8

clerestory with palladian window

SECOND FLOOR PLAN

Whimsical Two-story Farmhouse

Price Code: E

■ This plan features:
— Four bedrooms
— Three full and one half baths

■ Double gable with palladian, clerestory window and wrap-around Porch provide country appeal

■ First floor enjoys nine foot ceilings throughout

■ Palladian windows flood two-story Foyer and Great Room with natural light

■ Both Master Bedroom and Great Room access covered, rear Porch

■ One upstairs Bedroom offers private Bath and walk-in closet

FIRST FLOOR — 1,346 SQ. FT.
SECOND FLOOR — 836 SQ. FT.

TOTAL LIVING AREA:
2,182 SQ. FT.

Open Rail Staircase
PRICE CODE: E

■ This plan features:
— Five bedrooms
— Three full baths
■ A cover Porch and two-story Foyer greet you
■ The Dining Room has a Room expanding bay window
■ A fireplace warms the vaulted Family Room
■ A Guestroom or Study is tucked in the rear
■ The second floor contains the balance of the sleeping quarters
■ An optional basement or crawl space foundation — please specify when ordering
■ No materials list is available for this plan

FIRST FLOOR — 1,438 SQ. FT.
SECOND FLOOR — 1,395 SQ. FT.
BASEMENT — 1,438 SQ. FT.
GARAGE — 498 SQ. FT.

TOTAL LIVING AREA:
2,833 SQ. FT.

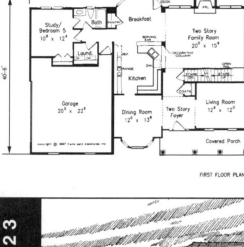

FIRST FLOOR PLAN

SECOND FLOOR PLAN

Keystone Arches and Decorative Windows
PRICE CODE: B

■ This plan features:
— Three bedrooms
— Two full baths
■ Brick and stucco enhance the dramatic front elevation and volume entrance
■ Inviting Entry leads into expansive Great Room with hearth fireplace framed by transom window
■ Bay window Dining Room topped by decorative ceiling convenient to the Great Room and the Kitchen/Breakfast Area
■ Corner Master Suite enjoys a tray ceiling, roomy walk-in closet and a plush Bath with a double vanity and whirlpool window tub
■ Two additional Bedrooms with large closets, share a full Bath

MAIN FLOOR — 1,666 SQ. FT.
BASEMENT — 1,666 SQ. FT.
GARAGE — 496 SQ. FT.

TOTAL LIVING AREA:
1,666 SQ. FT.

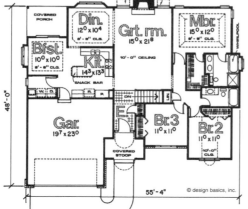

MAIN FLOOR

© design basics, inc.

Roomy, Yet Practical Home

PRICE CODE: E

■ This plan features:
— Three bedrooms
— Two full and one half baths

■ A smart exterior conceals an economical use of interior space

■ The two-story Foyer leads to the Great Room with a fireplace, a wall of windows and access to the back Porch

■ Columns divide the Great Room from the Breakfast Room which is open to an angled Kitchen with pantry

■ A handy Utility Room leads to a two-car Garage with ample storage space

■ A split-bedroom plan places the Master Suite with two walk-in closets on the second floor

FIRST FLOOR — 1,489 SQ. FT.
SECOND FLOOR — 534 SQ. FT.
GARAGE & STORAGE — 568 SQ. FT.
BONUS — 393 SQ. FT.

TOTAL LIVING AREA:
2,023 SQ. FT.

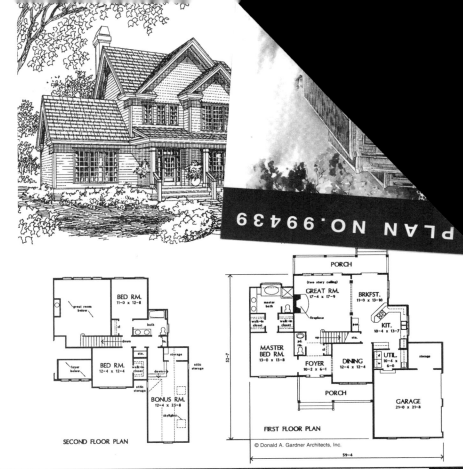

PLAN NO. 99439

SECOND FLOOR PLAN

FIRST FLOOR PLAN

© Donald A. Gardner Architects, Inc.

Central Courtyard Features Pool

PRICE CODE: C

■ This plan features:
— Three bedrooms
— One full and one three-quarter baths

■ A central Courtyard complete with a pool

■ A secluded Master Bedroom accented by a skylight, a spacious walk-in closet, and a private Bath

■ A convenient Kitchen easily serving the Patio for comfortable outdoor entertaining

■ A detached two-car Garage

MAIN FLOOR — 2,194 SQ. FT.
GARAGE — 576 SQ. FT.

TOTAL LIVING AREA:
2,194 SQ. FT.

PLAN NO. 10507

ZIP QUOTE
HOME COST CALCULATOR
see order pages for details

MAIN FLOOR

Touch of French Styling
PRICE CODE: F

- This plan features:
  — Four bedrooms
  — Three and a half baths
- A grand stair case dominating the Foyer and providing an elegant impression
- A fireplace and an abundance of windows accent the Great Room
- The first floor Master Suite includes a whirlpool Bath and a large walk-in closet
- Three secondary Bedrooms, two Baths and a Game Room make the second floor a private retreat
- No material list available for this plan

FIRST FLOOR — 2,274 SQ. FT.
SECOND FLOOR — 1,476 SQ. FT.
GARAGE — 744 SQ. FT.

TOTAL LIVING AREA:
3,750 SQ. FT.

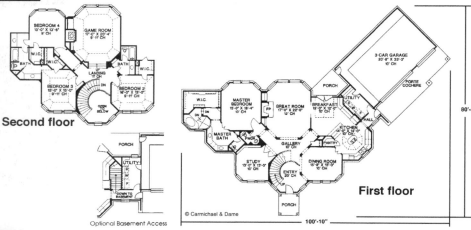

Second floor

First floor

© Carmichael & Dame

Optional Basement Access

100'-10"

80'-5"

Family Room at the Heart of the Home
PRICE CODE: D

- This plan features:
  — Four bedrooms
  — Three full baths
- The Living Room and Dining Room are to the right and left of the Foyer
- The Dining Room with French doors opens to the Kitchen
- An extended counter maximizes the work space in the Kitchen
- The Breakfast Room includes access to the Utility Room and to the secondary Bedroom wing
- The Master Bedroom is equipped with a double vanity bath, two walk-in closets and a linear closet
- A cozy fireplace and a decorative ceiling highlight the Family Room
- Secondary Bedrooms have easy access to two full Baths
- No materials list is available for this plan

MAIN FLOOR — 2,558 SQ. FT.
GARAGE — 549 SQ. FT.

TOTAL LIVING AREA:
2,558 SQ. FT.

WIDTH 63'-6"
DEPTH 71'-6"

MAIN FLOOR

To order your Blueprints, call 1-800-235-5700

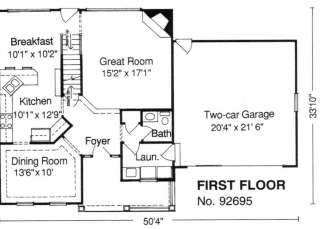

Breakfast
10'1" x 10'2"

Great Room
15'2" x 17'1"

stairs up

Kitchen
10'1" x 12'9"

Two-car Garage
20'4" x 21' 6"

Foyer

Bath

Laun.

Dining Room
13'6" x 10'

FIRST FLOOR
No. 92695

33'10"

50'4"

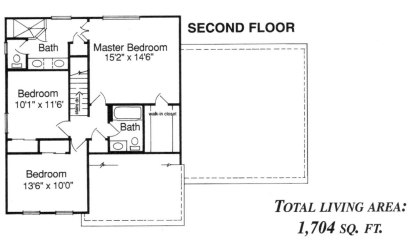

SECOND FLOOR

Bath

Master Bedroom
15'2" x 14'6"

Bedroom
10'1" x 11'6"

stairs dn

walk-in closet

Bath

Bedroom
13'6" x 10'0"

TOTAL LIVING AREA:
1,704 SQ. FT.

Enchanting Elevation

Price Code: B

■ This plan features:

— Three bedrooms

— One full, one three quarter , and one half baths

■ The covered front Porch provides a warm welcome

■ The large Foyer showcases interesting angled entries to the rooms beyond

■ The Dining Room has a tray ceiling and is directly connected to the Kitchen

■ The Great Room has a corner fireplace

■ The Kitchen features a serving bar

■ The Breakfast Nook has to the rear yard and stairs to the second floor

■ Upstairs, find three Bedrooms, all with ample closet space and two Baths

■ No materials list is available for this plan

FIRST FLOOR — 906 SQ. FT.
SECOND FLOOR — 798 SQ. FT.
BASEMENT — 906 SQ. FT.
GARAGE — 437 SQ. FT.

Contemporary Design
PRICE CODE: A

■ This plan features:
— Three bedrooms
— One full and one half baths
■ A solar design with southern glass doors, windows, and an air-lock entry
■ R-26 insulation used for floors and sloping ceilings
■ A deck rimming the front of the home
■ A Dining Room separated from the Living Room by a half wall
■ An efficient Kitchen with an eating bar

FIRST FLOOR — 911 SQ. FT.
SECOND FLOOR — 576 SQ. FT.
BASEMENT — 911 SQ. FT.

TOTAL LIVING AREA:
1,487 SQ. FT.

FIRST FLOOR

SECOND FLOOR

ZIP QUOTE
HOME COST CALCULATOR
see order pages for details

Those Special Touches
PRICE CODE: B

■ This plan features:
— Three bedrooms
— Two full and one half baths
■ The two-story Foyer adds volume to the entry area
■ The Dining Room and Family Room are crowned in vaulted ceilings
■ The Master Suite has a tray ceiling and a five-piece Master Bath
■ An optional Bonus Room over the Garage is available for future expansion
■ No materials list is available for this plan

FIRST FLOOR — 1,067 SQ. FT.
SECOND FLOOR — 464 SQ. FT.
BONUS ROOM — 207 SQ. FT.
BASEMENT — 1,067 SQ. FT.
GARAGE — 398 SQ. FT.

TOTAL LIVING AREA
1,531 SQ. FT.

FIRST FLOOR PLAN

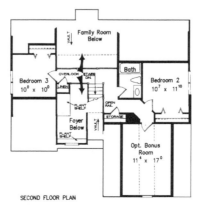

SECOND FLOOR PLAN

To order your Blueprints, call 1-800-235-5700

Down Home Goodness

PRICE CODE: B

■ This plan features:
- Three bedrooms
- Two full baths

This home has a split-bedroom floor plan allow more privacy for the Master Suite

The Master Suite includes a full-size Bath with separate shower

The Dining Room is crowned in a tray ceiling and has an add shape to enhance its formal aspect

There is a large Living Room that adds a more open feel to the house as a half wall is between it and the Breakfast Area

No materials list is available for this plan

MAIN FLOOR — 1,589 SQ. FT.
GARAGE & STORAGE — 481 SQ. FT.

TOTAL LIVING AREA:
1,589 SQ. FT.

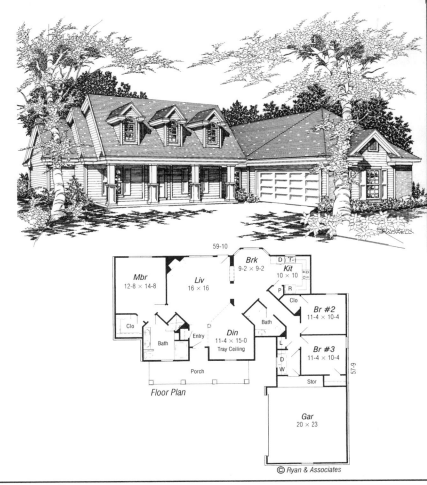

Floor Plan

© Ryan & Associates

Built to Please

PRICE CODE: C

■ This plan features:
— Three bedrooms
— Two full and one half baths

■ The Living Room has a vaulted ceiling and a corner fireplace

■ There is both an informal Nook and a formal Dining Room located to either side of the Kitchen for ease in serving

■ The optional bay windows will add character and light with a touch of class

■ A balcony overlooks the Entry and the Living Room below

■ There is a Bonus Room over the Garage for room to grow

■ No materials list is available for this plan

FIRST FLOOR — 1,405 SQ. FT.
SECOND FLOOR — 554 SQ. FT.
GARAGE & STORAGE — 457 SQ. FT.

TOTAL LIVING AREA:
1,959 SQ. FT.

1st Floor Plan

© Ryan & Associates

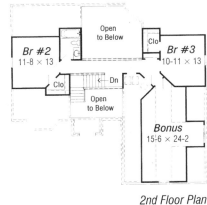

2nd Floor Plan

MAIN FLOOR

© design basics, inc.

One Level Beauty
PRICE CODE: D

■ This plan features:
— Three bedrooms
— Two full and one half baths
■ From the tiled entry one can view the terrific Great Room
■ Highlights of the Great Room include a built-in wetbar and a three-sided fireplace that is shared with the Hearth Room
■ The Hearth Room, which is open to the Kitchen and the Breakfast Room has a built-in entertainment center
■ A sloped gazebo-style ceiling and a built-in hutch accent the Breakfast Room
■ The Master Bedroom is impressive with a luxurious Bath and a walk-in closet
■ Secondary Bedrooms have private access to a full Bath

MAIN FLOOR — 2,355 SQ. FT.
GARAGE — 673 SQ. FT.

TOTAL LIVING AREA:
2,355 SQ. FT.

High Impact Two-Story
PRICE CODE: F

■ This plan features:
— Four bedrooms
— Three full and one half baths
■ A high impact two-story, double door transom Entry
■ A two-story Family Room with a wall consisting of a fireplace and windows
■ A spacious Master Suite with unique curved glass block behind the tub in the Master Bath and a semi-circular window wall with see-through fireplace in Sitting Area
■ A gourmet Kitchen and Breakfast Area opening to a Lanai
■ A Guest Suite with private Deck and walk-in closet

FIRST FLOOR — 3,158 SQ. FT.
SECOND FLOOR — 1,374 SQ. FT.

TOTAL LIVING AREA:
4,532 SQ. FT.

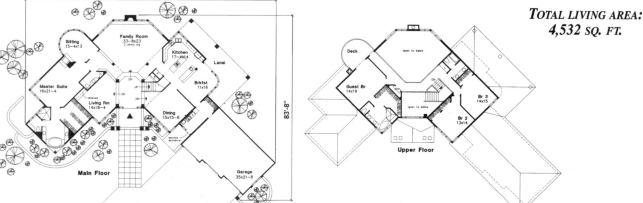

To order your Blueprints, call 1-800-235-5700

Notable Master Suite

PRICE CODE: E

This plan features:
- Three bedrooms
- Two full and one half baths
- The open entry and Great Room gives the feeling of roominess and grandeur
- A large Kitchen with an island and an adjacent Nook provides ample space for creating both casual and formal meals
- Master Suite with his and her walk-in closets, double sinks, a private shower and a corner whirlpool Bath
- Loft at the top of the stairs could be converted into a Sitting Area or Study
- No materials list is available for this plan

FIRST FLOOR — 2,018 SQ. FT.
SECOND FLOOR — 655 SQ. FT.
BASEMENT — 2,018 SQ. FT.

Toatl living area:
2,673 SQ. FT.

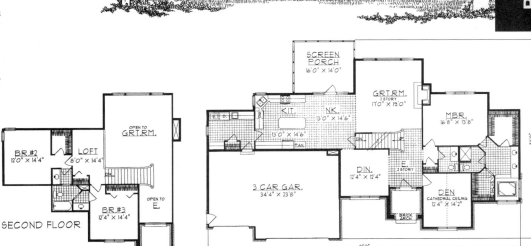

SECOND FLOOR

MAIN FLOOR

Superb Southern Styling

PRICE CODE: E

This plan features:
- Four bedrooms
- Three full baths
- Terrific front Porch and dormers create a homey Southern style
- A corner fireplace enhancing the Family Room
- A cooktop island and a peninsula counter adding to the efficiency of the Kitchen
- Convenient peninsula counter separates the Kitchen from the Breakfast Room
- Lavish Master Suite includes a whirlpool tub and a walk-in closet
- Secondary Bedrooms located in close proximity to a full Bath
- An optional crawl space or slab foundation — please specify when ordering
- No materials list is available for this plan

FIRST FLOOR — 2,135 SQ. FT.
SECOND FLOOR — 538 SQ. FT.
BONUS — 225 SQ. FT.
GARAGE — 436 SQ. FT.

Total living area:
2,673 SQ. FT.

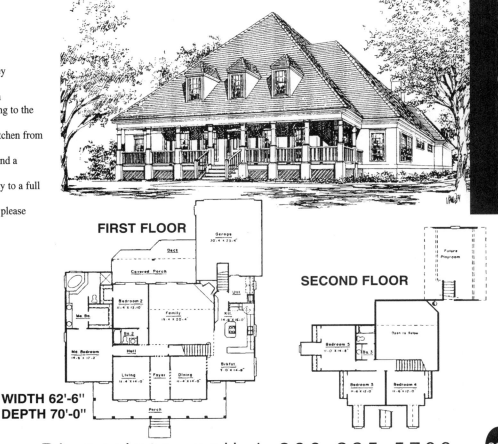

FIRST FLOOR

SECOND FLOOR

WIDTH 62'-6"
DEPTH 70'-0"

To order your Blueprints, call 1-800-235-5700

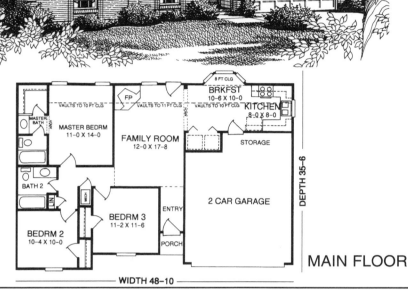

Quoin Accents
Distinguish this Plan
PRICE CODE: A

- This plan features:
  — Three bedrooms
  — Two full baths
- A traditional brick elevation with quoin accents
- A large Family Room with a corner fireplace and direct access to the outside
- An arched opening leading to the Breakfast Area
- A bay window illuminating the Breakfast Area with natural light
- An efficiently designed, U-shaped Kitchen with ample cabinet and counter space
- A Master Suite with a private master bath
- Two additional bedrooms that share a full hall bath
- No material list is available for this plan

MAIN FLOOR — 1,142 SQ. FT.
GARAGE — 428 SQ. FT.

TOTAL LIVING AREA: 1,142 SQ. FT.

MAIN FLOOR

WIDTH 48–10

European Flair
PRICE CODE: B

- This plan features:
  — Three bedrooms
  — Two full baths
- Large fireplace serving as an attractive focal point for the vaulted Family Room
- Decorative column defining the elegant Dining Room
- Kitchen including a serving bar for the Family Room and a Breakfast area
- Master Suite topped by a tray ceiling over the bedroom and a vaulted ceiling over the five piece Master Bath
- Optional bonus room for future expansion
- Specify a basement or crawl space foundation
- No material list is available for this plan

MAIN FLOOR — 1,544 SQ. FT.
BONUS ROOM — 284 SQ. FT.
GARAGE — 440 SQ. FT.

TOTAL LIVING AREA: 1,544 SQ. FT.

WIDTH 54'-0"
DEPTH 47'-6"

OPT. BASEMENT STAIR LOCATION

OPTIONAL BONUS ROOM

© Frank Betz Associates, Inc.

To order your Blueprints, call 1-800-235-5700

This plan cannot be built within a 25 mile radius of Cedar Rapids, IA.

OPEN TO
FAMILY RM.

BEDROOM #2
9'-0" x 9'-0"

DN

DN

BEDROOM #4
13'-0" x 13'-0"

OPEN TO
FOYER

BEDROOM #3
12'-0" x 12'-0"

SECOND FLOOR

ZIP QUOTE
HOME COST CALCULATOR
see order pages for details

TOTAL LIVING AREA:
3,397 SQ. FT.

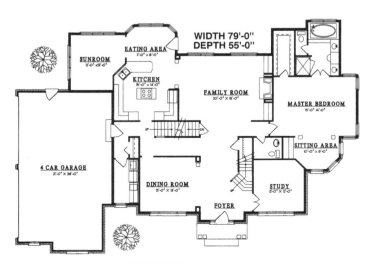

WIDTH 79'-0"
DEPTH 55'-0"

SUNROOM
12'-0" x 13'-0"

EATING AREA
11'-0" x 8'-0"

KITCHEN
16'-0" x 14'-0"

FAMILY ROOM
20'-0" x 19'-0"

MASTER BEDROOM
18'-0" x 14'-0"

4 CAR GARAGE
21'-0" x 36'-0"

SITTING AREA
10'-0" x 9'-0"

DINING ROOM
13'-0" x 13'-0"

STUDY
12'-0" x 12'-0"

FOYER

MAIN FLOOR

Contemporary Plan With An Old-Fashioned Look

Price Code: F

■ This plan features:

— Four bedrooms

— Three full and one half baths

■ Gracious entry with arched window, sidelights and two-story Foyer

■ Formal Dining Room and quiet Study have decorative windows

■ Convenient Kitchen with cooktop island, opens to Eating Area

■ Expansive Family Room accented by cozy fireplace

■ Secluded Master Bedroom offers a bright Sitting Area

MAIN FLOOR — 2,385 SQ. FT.
SECOND FLOOR — 1,012 SQ. FT.
GARAGE — 846 SQ. FT.
BASEMENT — 2,385 SQ. FT.

To order your Blueprints, call 1-800-235-5700

Special Sitting Room

Price Code: D

- This plan features:
  — Three bedrooms
  — Two full and one half baths
- Dual walk-in closets are featured in the Master Suite
- A walk-in Pantry and double ovens add convenience to the Kitchen
- A radius window and fireplace add warmth to the Keeping Room
- An optional basement or crawl space foundation — please specify when ordering
- No materials list is available for this plan

FIRST FLOOR — 1,972 SQ. FT.
SECOND FLOOR — 579 SQ. FT.
BONUS — 256 SQ. FT.
BASEMENT — 1,972 SQ. FT.
GARAGE — 505 SQ. FT.

TOTAL LIVING AREA:
2,551 SQ. FT.

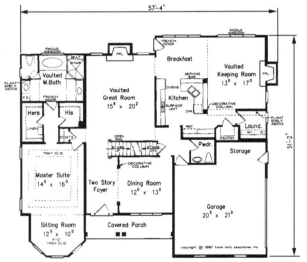

FIRST FLOOR PLAN

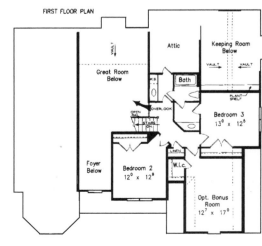

SECOND FLOOR PLAN

To order your Blueprints, call 1-800-235-5700

© 1991 Donald A. Gardner Architects, Inc.

FIRST FLOOR

48-4

© 1991 Donald A Gardner Architects, Inc.

SECOND FLOOR

Deck Includes Spa

Price Code: D

■ This plan features:
— Three bedrooms
— Two full and one half baths

■ An exterior Porch giving the home a traditional flavor

■ Great Room highlighted by a fireplace and a balcony above as well as a pass-through into the Kitchen

■ Kitchen Eating Area with sky lights and bow windows overlooking the Deck with a Spa

■ Two additional Bedrooms with a full Bath on the second floor

■ Master Suite on the first floor and naturally illuminated by two skylights

FIRST FLOOR — 1,325 SQ. FT.
SECOND FLOOR — 453 SQ. FT.

TOTAL LIVING AREA:
1,778 SQ. FT.

Windows Add Warmth

Price Code: B

■ This plan features:

— Three bedrooms

— Two full baths

■ A Master Suite with huge his and her walk-in closets and private Bath

■ A second and third Bedroom with ample closet space

■ A Kitchen equipped with an island counter, and flowing easily into the Dining and Family Rooms

■ A Laundry Room conveniently located near all three Bedrooms

■ An optional Garage

MAIN AREA— 1,672 SQ. FT.
GARAGE — 566 SQ. FT.

TOTAL LIVING AREA:
1,672 SQ. FT.

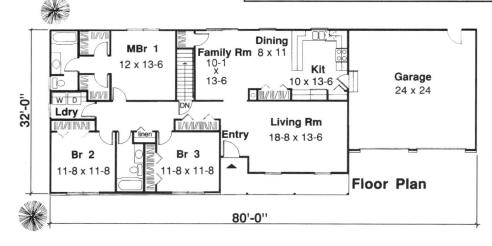

MBr 1 12 x 13-6
Family Rm 10-1 x 13-6
Dining 8 x 11
Kit 10 x 13-6
Garage 24 x 24
Ldry
W D
linen
DN
Br 2 11-8 x 11-8
Br 3 11-8 x 11-8
Entry
Living Rm 18-8 x 13-6
32'-0"
80'-0"
Floor Plan

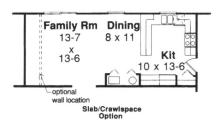

Family Rm 13-7 x 13-6
Dining 8 x 11
Kit 10 x 13-6
optional wall location
Slab/Crawlspace Option

ZIP QUOTE
HOME COST CALCULATOR
see order pages for details

To order your Blueprints, call 1-800-235-5700

Window Box Adds Warmth to Exterior

PRICE CODE: C

- This plan features:
— Four bedrooms
— Two full and one half baths
- The luxurious Master Suite includes a tray ceiling and a built-in plant shelf
- The Master Bath has a vaulted ceiling, and a large walk-in closet with a second built-in plant shelf
- The stairway includes an open rail and leads to a balcony overlook
- An optional basement or crawl space foundation — please specify when ordering
- No materials list is available for this plan

FIRST FLOOR — 1,209 SQ. FT.
SECOND FLOOR — 931 SQ. FT.
BONUS — 175 SQ. FT.
BASEMENT — 1,216 SQ. FT.
GARAGE — 410 SQ. FT.

TOTAL LIVING AREA: 2,140 SQ. FT.

FIRST FLOOR PLAN

SECOND FLOOR PLAN

Porches Expands Living Space

PRICE CODE: C

- This plan features:
— Three bedrooms
— Two full and one half baths
- Porches on the front and the rear of this home expand the living space to the outdoors
- The rear porch is accessed directly from the Great Room
- The spacious Great Room is enhanced by a twelve foot ceiling and a fireplace
- The well-appointed Kitchen has an extended counter/eating bar and easy access to the Dining Room
- Secondary bedrooms have a full Bath located between the rooms
- The Master Suite is enhanced by his and hers walk-in closets, a whirlpool tub and a separate shower
- There is a Bonus Room for the future expansion

MAIN FLOOR — 2,089 SQ. FT.
BONUS ROOM — 497 SQ. FT.
GARAGE — 541 SQ. FT.

TOTAL LIVING AREA: 2,089 SQ. FT.

MAIN FLOOR

To order your Blueprints, call 1-800-235-5700

275

Stone and Siding
PRICE CODE: E

■ This plan features:
— Four bedrooms
— Three full and one half baths

■ Attractive styling using a combination of stone and siding and a covered Porch add to the curb appeal

■ Former Foyer giving access to the bedroom wing, Library or Activity Room

■ Activity Room showcasing a focal point fireplace and including direct access to the rear Deck and the Breakfast Room

■ Breakfast Room is topped by a vaulted ceiling and flows into the Kitchen

■ A snack bar/peninsula counter highlights the Kitchen which also includes a built-in Pantry.

■ A secluded guest Bedroom suite is located off the Kitchen Area

■ Master Suite topped by a tray ceiling and pampered by five-piece Bath

MAIN FLOOR — 2,690 SQ. FT.
BASEMENT — 2,690 SQ. FT.
GARAGE — 660 SQ. FT.

TOTAL LIVING AREA:
2,690 SQ. FT.

MAIN AREA

WIDTH 87'-6"
DEPTH 56'-10"

Economical Vacation Home
Provides Viewing Deck
PRICE CODE: A

■ This plan features:
— Three bedrooms
— Two full baths

■ A large rectangular Living Room with a fireplace at one end and plenty of room for separate activities at the other end

■ A galley-style Kitchen with adjoining Dining Area

■ A second-floor Master Bedroom with a Children's Dormitory across the hall

■ A second-floor Deck outside the Master Bedroom

FIRST FLOOR — 784 SQ. FT.
SECOND FLOOR — 504 SQ. FT.

TOTAL LIVING AREA:
1,288 SQ. FT.

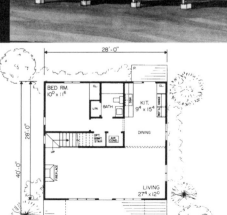

FIRST FLOOR

SECOND FLOOR

To order your Blueprints, call 1-800-235-5700

SECOND FLOOR

- WHIRLPOOL TUB
- M. BATH
- WALL BELOW
- B.R. 4 — 9'-6" X 11'-6"
- BATH 2
- B.R. 3 — 10'-6" X 11'-0"
- W.I.C.
- BALCONY
- LIN.
- ROOF
- M.B.R. — 14'-0" X 15'-0"
- FOYER BELOW
- SLANT SHELF
- B.R. 2 — 12'-0" X 11'-6"
- TWL.

FIRST FLOOR

- FLR. ABV.
- GAS FIREPLACE
- DINETTE — 9'-0" X 13'-6"
- KITCHEN — 18'-0" X 13'-6"
- LS
- SHELF
- PDR.
- LND.
- L TUB
- FAMILY RM. — 16'-0" X 13'-6"
- WORK ISLAND
- FLR. ABV.
- ENTRY
- PNT.
- REFR.
- BC
- STEP
- LIVING RM. — 14'-0" X 12'-6"
- UP
- FOYER — HIGH CLG.
- FLR. ABV.
- DINING RM. — 12'-0" X 12'-6"
- GARAGE — 22'-0" X 26'-0"
- PORCH
- WIDTH= 59'-4"
- DEPTH= 37'-4"
- 16 FT. GAR. DOOR

Speaking of Colonials

Price Code: C

- ■ This plan features:
- — Four bedrooms
- — Two full and one half baths
- ■ Entry Porch leads into central Foyer between formal Living and Dining Rooms
- ■ Comfortable Family Room with a corner fireplace and back yard view
- ■ Hub Kitchen with a work island, Pantry, Dinette Area with outdoor access, and nearby Laundry and Garage entry
- ■ Corner Master Bedroom offers a walk-in closet and a double vanity Bath with a whirlpool tub
- ■ No materials list is available for this plan

FIRST FLOOR — 1,110 SQ. FT.
SECOND FLOOR — 992 SQ. FT.
BASEMENT — 1,110 SQ. FT.
GARAGE — 530 SQ. FT.

TOTAL LIVING AREA:
2,102 SQ. FT.

One Great Choice
PRICE CODE: C

- This plan features:
  — Three bedrooms
  — Two full baths
- The Great Room has a fireplace and built-in shelves with a ledge above for display
- The back Porch integrates outdoor activities with the comfort of being close to the indoors
- Informal and formal eating space efficiently flanks the Kitchen
- Garage enters into the Kitchen for ease in unloading packages
- No materials list is available for this plan

MAIN FLOOR — 1,862 SQ. FT.
GARAGE & STORAGE — 481 SQ. FT.

TOTAL LIVING AREA:
1,862 SQ. FT.

Mbr
13-6 × 15-0
10'-9" Clg Ht

Porch

Din
12-2 × 11-10
10'-9" Clg Ht

Great Rm
16-6 × 19-0
10'-9" Clg Ht

Mba

Kit
10-6 × 12-3

Closet

Ba

Entry

Nook
10-6 × 9-9
10'-9" Clg Ht

Pan

W D Util

Br #2
11-0 × 11-6

Porch

Stor

Garage
20-0 × 21-0

Br #3
14-8 × 10-0
Vaulted

Floor Plan   50-4½   © Ryan & Associates

56-11½

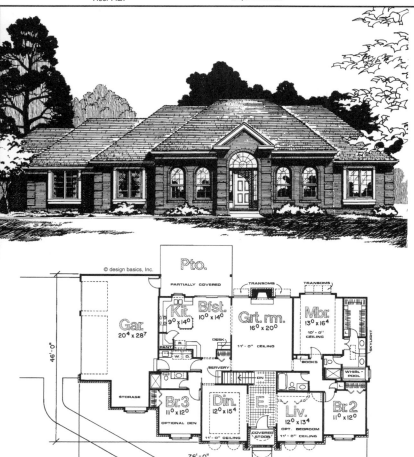

Appealing Brick Elevation
PRICE CODE: C

- This plan features:
  — Three bedrooms
  — Two full and one three-quarter bath
- Formal Living and Dining Room flanking the Entry
- Impressive Great Room topped by an eleven-foot ceiling and enhanced by picture awing windows framing the raised hearth fireplace
- Attractive Kitchen/Dinette Area includes an island, Desk, wrapping counters, a walk-in Pantry and access to the covered Patio
- Pampering Master Suite with a skylight Dressing Area, a walk-in closet, double vanity, a whirlpool tub and a decorative plant shelf

MAIN FLOOR — 2,172 SQ. FT.
GARAGE — 680 SQ. FT.

TOTAL LIVING AREA:
2,172 SQ. FT.

© design basics, Inc.

Pto.
PARTIALLY COVERED

Gar.
20⁴ × 28⁷

Kit.
9⁰ × 14⁰

Bfst.
10⁰ × 14⁰

Grt. rm.
16⁰ × 20⁰
11' - 0" CEILING

Mbr.
13⁰ × 16⁴
10' - 0" CEILING

STORAGE

Br.3
11⁰ × 12⁰
OPTIONAL DEN

Din.
12⁰ × 15⁴

Liv.
12⁰ × 13⁴
OPT. BEDROOM

Br.2
11⁰ × 12⁰

WHIRL-POOL

46'-0"

76'-0"

MAIN FLOOR

B. LeBold

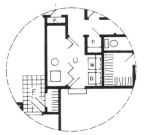

MAIN FLOOR

BEDROOM 3
11'-6"
X
11'-8"

DINING
11'-0"
X
11'-6"

KITCHEN

BRKFST.

DESK

MAST. BEDROOM
14'-0"
X
15'-4"

10'-6" X 11'-6"

LIVING ROOM
21'-4"
X
13'-6"
(12' CEIL.)

BEDROOM 2
11'-6"
X
11'-8"

DESK

GARAGE
21'-4"
X
21'-8"

52'-0"

60'-0"

ZIP QUOTE
HOME COST CALCULATOR
see order pages for details

Exclusive Master Suite

Price Code: C

■ This plan features:

— Three bedrooms

— Two full and one half baths

■ Front Porch entry into Foyer and open Living and Dining Room

■ Huge fireplace and double window highlight Living Room

■ Convenient Kitchen with cooktop island/snackbar, pantry, and bright Breakfast Area with backyard access

■ Corner Master Bedroom offers a decorative ceiling, walk-in closets and a double vanity Bath

■ Two additional Bedrooms with ample closets and private access to a full Bath

MAIN FLOOR — 1,831 SQ. FT.
GARAGE — 484 SQ. FT.

TOTAL LIVING AREA:
1,831 SQ. FT.

To order your Blueprints, call 1-800-235-5700

Photography supplied by The Meredith Corporation

New England Cottage

Price Code: C

- The plan features:
— Three bedrooms
— Three full baths
- A Porch and a screened Porch add options for outdoors entertaining
- A fireplace warms the Living Room
- The U-shaped Kitchen is open to the Dining Room
- A full Bath is located next to the Den/Bedroom
- The Master Bedroom has a private Bath

MAIN LEVEL — 1,109 SQ. FT.
UPPER LEVEL — 772 SQ. FT.

TOTAL LIVING AREA: 1,881 SQ. FT.

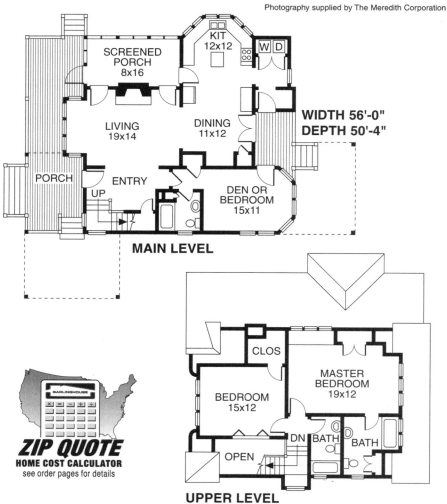

ZIP QUOTE
HOME COST CALCULATOR
see order pages for details

Captivating Sun-Catcher
PRICE CODE: A

This plan features:
- Two bedrooms
- Two full baths
- A glass-walled Breakfast Room adjoining the vaulted-ceiling Kitchen
- A fireplaced, vaulted ceiling Living Room that flows from the Dining Room
- A greenhouse window over the tub in the luxurious Master Bath
- Two walk-in closets and glass sliders in the Master Bedroom

MAIN AREA — 1,421 SQ. FT.
GARAGE — 400 SQ. FT.

TOTAL LIVING AREA:
1,421 SQ. FT.

PLAN NO. 99303

MAIN FLOOR

Exterior Shows
Attention to Detail
PRICE CODE: D

This plan features:
- Three bedrooms
- Two full baths
- Privately located Master Suite is complimented by a luxurious Bath with two walk-in closets
- Two additional Bedrooms have ample closet space and share a full Bath
- The Activity Room has a sloped ceiling, large fireplace and is accented with columns
- Access to Sun Deck from the Dining Room
- The island Kitchen and Breakfast Area have access to Garage for ease when bringing in groceries

MAIN FLOOR — 2,165 SQ. FT.
GARAGE — 484 SQ. FT.

TOTAL LIVING AREA:
2,165 SQ. FT.

PLAN NO. 94811

MAIN FLOOR

Central Staircase
PRICE CODE: E

■ This plan features:
— Five bedrooms
— Four full and one half baths
■ The Family Room is open to the Kitchen Area
■ The Dining Room has a bay window
■ A formal Living Room is included
■ The Laundry is conveniently placed on the second floor
■ A huge walk-in closet is a part of the Master Bedroom
■ An optional basement or crawl space foundation — please specify when ordering
■ No materials list is available for this plan

FIRST FLOOR — 1,575 SQ. FT.
SECOND FLOOR — 1,480 SQ. FT.
BASEMENT — 1,575 SQ. FT.
GARAGE — 492 SQ. FT.

TOTAL LIVING AREA:
3,055 SQ. FT.

FIRST FLOOR

65'-4"

Two Story Family Room 20² x 14¹⁰
Breakfast
FRENCH DOOR
Kitchen
Bedroom 5/ Study 12⁰ x 12⁰
41'-0"
Garage 20⁶ x 23²
Pwdr.
COATS
Dining Room 13³ x 15¹⁰
Two Story Foyer
Living Room 13³ x 12⁶
Bath
Covered Porch

SECOND FLOOR

RADIUS WINDOW
Family Room Below
Bedroom 3 12⁰ x 11¹⁰
Bath
W.I.C.
Master Suite 18⁸ x 14⁸
TRAY CEILING
Bedroom 4 12⁷ x 14⁸
Laund.
Bath
LINEN
Vaulted M.Bath
FRENCH DOORS
Bedroom 2 11⁰ x 12⁸
Foyer Below
W.I.C.
W.I.C.
SEAT

Open Plan is
Full of Air & Light
PRICE CODE: B

■ This plan features:
— Three bedrooms
— Two full and one half baths
■ Foyer open to the Family Room and highlighted by a fireplace
■ Dining Room with a sliding glass door to rear yard adjoins Family Room
■ Kitchen and Nook in an efficient open layout
■ Second floor Master Suite topped by tray ceiling over the Bedroom and a vaulted ceiling over the lavish Bath
■ Two additional Bedrooms sharing a full Bath in the hall
■ An optional basement or crawl space foundation — please specify when ordering
■ No materials list is available for this plan

FIRST FLOOR — 767 SQ. FT.
SECOND FLOOR — 738 SQ. FT.
BONUS ROOM — 240 SQ. FT.
BASEMENT — 767 SQ. FT.
GARAGE — 480 SQ. FT.

TOTAL LIVING AREA:
1,505 SQ. FT.

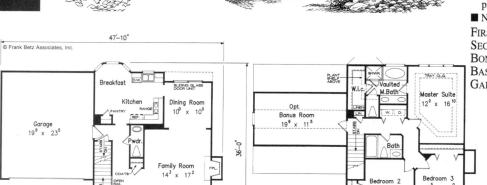

© Frank Betz Associates, Inc.

47'-10"

Breakfast
Kitchen
SLIDING GLASS DOOR UNIT
Dining Room 10⁰ x 10⁰
PANTRY
Garage 19⁹ x 23⁵
Pwdr.
COATS
Family Room 14³ x 17²
FPL.
Foyer
Covered Porch
FIRST FLOOR PLAN

36'-0"
W.I.C.
Vaulted M.Bath
Master Suite 12⁰ x 16¹⁰
TRAY CLG.
Opt. Bonus Room 19⁹ x 11⁵
LINEN
Bath
Bedroom 2 12⁰ x 10⁰
Bedroom 3 10⁵ x 10⁰
SECOND FLOOR PLAN

To order your Blueprints, call 1-800-235-5700

© 1994 Donald A. Gardner Architects, Inc.

P. NATHAN

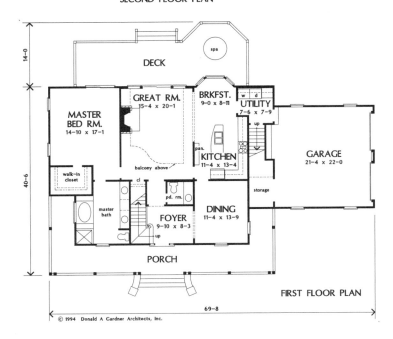

SECOND FLOOR PLAN

FIRST FLOOR PLAN

Four-Bedroom Country Classic

Price Code: E

■ This plan features:

— Four bedrooms

— Two full and one half baths

■ Foyer open to the Dining Room creating a hall with a balcony over the vaulted Great Room

■ Great Room opens to the Deck and to the island Kitchen with convenient Pantry

■ Nine-foot ceilings on the first floor expand volume

■ Master Suite pampered by a whirlpool tub, double vanity, separate shower, and access to the Deck

■ Bonus Room to be finished now or later

FIRST FLOOR — 1,499 SQ. FT.
SECOND FLOOR — 665 SQ. FT.
GARAGE & STORAGE — 567 SQ. FT.
BONUS ROOM — 332 SQ. FT.

TOTAL LIVING AREA:
2,164 SQ. FT.

Practical Living Spaces
PRICE CODE: A

- This plan features:
— Three bedrooms
— Two full and one half baths
- The Living Room has a vaulted ceiling and a fireplace
- The Kitchen has a large snack bar for busy times and meals on the go
- The U-shaped Kitchen offers an easy access to all the appliances
- The Master Suite has to window seats, a large walk-in closet and a private Bath
- No materials list is available for this plan

FIRST FLOOR — 625 SQ. FT.
SECOND FLOOR — 848 SQ. FT.
GARAGE & STORAGE — 409 SQ. FT.

TOTAL LIVING AREA:
1,473 SQ. FT.

© Ryan & Associates

Kit 9-6 × 10-6
Din 7-10 × 10-6
Gar 18-4 × 20-0
Mec
Liv 14-2 × 15-8 Vaulted
1st Floor Plan
37-4¾
37-7½
Porch

Clo
Bath
Br2 10-0 × 11-8
Mbr 18-8 × 14-5
Dn
Br3 12-2 × 11-0
Open
2nd Floor Plan

Impressive Two-Sided Fireplace
PRICE CODE: B

- This plan features:
— Three bedrooms
— Two full baths
- Foyer directs traffic flow into the Great Room enhanced by an impressive two-sided fireplace
- Formal Dining Area is open to the Great Room offering a view of the fireplace
- French doors off entry access Kitchen with a large pantry, a planning desk and a snack bar
- Dinette accesses a large comfortable screen Porch
- Laundry Room is strategically located off the Kitchen providing direct access from the Garage
- French doors provide access to the Master Suite topped by an elegant, decorative ceiling and highlighted by a pampering Bath

MAIN FLOOR — 1,580 SQ. FT.
GARAGE — 456 SQ. FT.

TOTAL LIVING AREA:
1,580 SQ. FT.

Mbr 13⁰ × 13⁰
Grt. rm. 14⁴ × 20¹⁰
Din. 10⁴ × 11⁰
Bfst. 10⁰ × 14³
Kit. 9⁴ × 13⁰
Br.3 10⁰ × 11⁰
Br.2 10⁴ × 11⁰
Gar. 19³ × 22⁴
Den 10⁴ × 13⁴
OPTIONAL DEN
© Design Basics, Inc.
MAIN FLOOR
60'-0"
48'-0"

To order your Blueprints, call 1-800-235-5700

© 1992 Donald A. Gardner Architects, Inc.

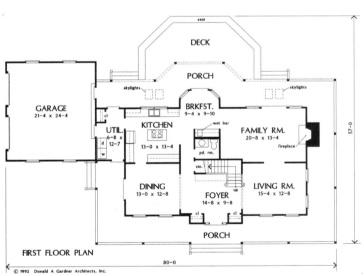

DECK

PORCH

skylights   skylights

BRKFST.
9-4 x 9-10

KITCHEN
13-0 x 13-4

FAMILY RM.
20-8 x 13-4

wet bar

pd. rm.

fireplace

GARAGE
21-4 x 24-4

UTIL.
6-8 x
12-7

cl

sto.

DINING
13-0 x 12-8

FOYER
14-8 x 9-8

LIVING RM.
15-4 x 12-8

up

cl   cl

PORCH

FIRST FLOOR PLAN

© 1992 Donald A Gardner Architects, Inc.

57-0

80-0

walk-in
closet

lin.

master bath

bath

skylight

BED RM.
11-8 x 11-8

cl

MASTER
BED RM.
13-0 x 19-0

down

cl

BED RM.
15-4 x 12-0

cl

BED RM.
12-4 x 10-0

SECOND FLOOR PLAN

Grand Four Bedroom Farmhouse

Price Code: F

■ This plan features:

— Four bedrooms

— Two full and one half baths

■ Double gables, wrap-around Porch and custom window details add appeal to farmhouse

■ Formal Living and Dining rooms connected by Foyer in front, while casual living areas expand rear

■ Efficient Kitchen with island cooktop and easy access to all eating areas

■ Fireplace, wetbar and rear Porch and Deck provide great entertainment space

■ Spacious Master Bedroom features walk-in closet and pampering Bath

FIRST FLOOR — 1,357 SQ. FT.
SECOND FLOOR — 1,204 SQ. FT.
GARAGE & STORAGE — 546 SQ. FT.

TOTAL LIVING AREA:
2,561 SQ. FT.

PLAN NO. 97629

Multiple Gables
PRICE CODE: E

- This plan features:
  — Five bedrooms
  — Four full baths
- Multiple gables highlight the exterior
- The Dining Room and living room flank the Foyer
- A den or guest Bedroom is on the first floor
- The Family Room has a rear wall fireplace
- A tray ceiling is above the Master Suite
- No materials list is available for this plan

FIRST FLOOR — 1,409 SQ. FT.
SECOND FLOOR — 1,300 SQ. FT.
BASEMENT — 1,409 SQ. FT.
GARAGE — 528 SQ. FT.

TOTAL LIVING AREA:
2,709 SQ. FT.

PLAN NO. 32122

With Cottage Ambiance
PRICE CODE: A

- This plan features:
  — Two bedrooms
  — One full bath
- Covered Entry mimicks twin gables of activity and sleeping areas of home
- High ceilings and gable windows keep interior light and airy
- Spacious Living Area with window alcove opens to Screen Porch, and Kitchen with washer/dryer and Pantry
- Two Bedrooms share a full Bath and easy access to courtyard and Deck beyond

MAIN FLOOR — 1,112 SQ. FT.
BASEMENT — 484 SQ. FT.

TOTAL LIVING AREA:
1,112 SQ. FT.

Photography Supplied by The Meredith Corporation

WIDTH 47'-0"
DEPTH 45'-6"

MAIN FLOOR

ZIP QUOTE
HOME COST CALCULATOR
see order pages for details

To order your Blueprints, call 1-800-235-5700

Quaint Front Porch and Lovely Details

PRICE CODE: C

This plan features:
- Four bedrooms
- Two full and one half baths
- A Covered Porch and Victorian touches create unique elevation
- A one and a half story entry hall leads into formal Dining Room
- A volume ceiling above abundant windows and a see-through fireplace highlight the Great Room
- Kitchen/Breakfast area shares the fireplace and has a snack bar, desk, walk-in pantry and abundant counter space
- Laundry area provides access to Garage and side yard
- Secluded Master Suite crowned by a vaulted ceiling and a luxurious Bath
- Three additional Bedrooms on the second floor share a full Bath

FIRST FLOOR — 1,421 SQ. FT.
SECOND FLOOR — 578 SQ. FT.
BASEMENT — 1,421 SQ. FT.
GARAGE — 480 SQ. FT.

TOTAL LIVING AREA:
1,999 SQ. FT.

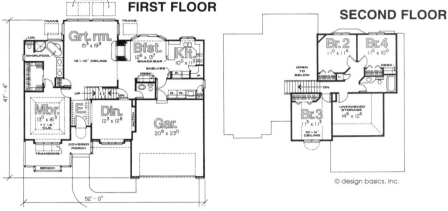

FIRST FLOOR

SECOND FLOOR

© design basics, inc.

Timeless Two-Story

PRICE CODE: B

This plan features:
- Three bedrooms
- Two full and one half baths
- This plan has functionality with out sacrificing style
- The Dining Room runs the width of the home with a corner fireplace for added coziness
- The Kitchen/Dining area is arranged for convenience and efficiency
- The Bedrooms are all located on the second floor
- No materials list is available for this plan

FIRST FLOOR — 786 SQ. FT.
SECOND FLOOR — 723 SQ. FT.
BASEMENT — 786 SQ. FT.
GARAGE — 406 SQ. FT.

TOTAL LIVING AREA:
1,509 SQ. FT.

SECOND FLOOR PLAN

MAIN FLOOR PLAN

To order your Blueprints, call 1-800-235-5700

PLAN NO. 96440

© 1993 Donald A. Gardner Architects, Inc.

For Four or More
PRICE CODE: D

■ This plan features:
— Three bedrooms
— Two full baths
■ Covered porches front and back with an open interior capped by a cathedral ceiling
■ Cathedral ceiling timing the Great Room, Kitchen/Dining and loft/study into an impressive living space
■ Kitchen equipped with an island cooktop and counter opening to both the Great Room and the Dining Room
■ A cathedral ceiling topping the front Bedroom/Study,
■ A large bay cozies up the rear Bedroom
■ Luxurious Master Suite located upstairs for extra privacy

FIRST FLOOR—1,146 SQ. FT.
SECOND FLOOR—567 SQ. FT.

TOTAL LIVING AREA:
1,713 SQ. FT.

FIRST FLOOR PLAN
© Donald A. Gardner Architects, Inc.

SECOND FLOOR PLAN

PLAN NO. 98211

Executive Features
PRICE CODE: E

■ This plan features:
— Four bedrooms
— Three full and one half baths
■ High volume ceilings
■ An extended staircase highlights the Foyer as columns define the Dining Room and the Grand Room
■ A massive glass exterior rear wall and high ceiling in the Master Bedroom
■ His and her walk-in closets and a lavish five-piece Bath highlight the Master Bedroom
■ The island Kitchen, Keeping Room and Breakfast Room create an open living space
■ A fireplace accents both the Keeping Room and the two story Grand Room
■ Three additional Bedrooms with private Bathroom access and ample closet space
■ An optional basement or crawl space foundation — please specify when ordering
■ No materials list is available for this plan

FIRST FLOOR — 2,035 SQ. FT.
SECOND FLOOR — 1,028 SQ. FT.
BASEMENT — 2,035 SQ. FT.
GARAGE — 530 SQ. FT.

TOTAL LIVING AREA:
3,063 SQ. FT.

WIDTH 56'-0"
DEPTH 62'-6"

FIRST FLOOR PLAN

SECOND FLOOR PLAN

Four Bedroom Charmer

Price Code: C

■ This plan features:

— Four bedrooms

— Two full baths

■ A vaulted ceiling in the naturally lighted Entry

■ A Living Room with a masonry fireplace, large windowed bay and vaulted ceiling

■ A large Family Room with a wood stove alcove

■ An island cooktop, built-in Pantry and a telephone desk in the efficient Kitchen

■ Two additional Bedrooms sharing a full Bath

■ A Study with a window seat and built-in bookshelves

MAIN FLOOR — 2,185 SQ. FT.

TOTAL LIVING AREA:
2,185 SQ. FT.

Floor Plan Labels

DECK

BREAKFAST

SERVING BAR

DW

DBL SINK

KITCHEN
10'-0" X 13'-0"

JENN-AIRE RANGE

PANTRY   DESK

VAULTED
FAMILY RM.
19'-4" X 18'-8"

MSTR. BDRM.
16'-0" X 13'-4"

GLASS BLOCKS

5/0 WHIRLPOOL
GARDEN TUB

WALK-IN
WARDROBE

M.
BATH

48" x 36"
SHOWER

DBL. VANITORY

LINEN

COFFERED CLG'T
DINING RM.
11'-0" X 11'-6"

CHINA

WOODSTOVE ALCOVE

8' HIGH WALL

2'10 x 2'10
SKYLIGHT

VANITORY
BATH

5/0 TUB
SHOWER

WARDROBE

BDRM. #3
11'-2" X 10'-0"

LINEN

OPTIONAL
DOOR POSITION

VAULTED
STUDY/BDRM. #4
10'-6" X 11'-8"

LAUNDRY

DRYER   WASHER

STAIR WAY

BDRM. #2
11'-2" X 11'-0"

VLT'D.
ENTRY

2'10 x 4'0
SKYLIGHT

WARDROBE

W/H   EFF-GAS
FURN.

VAULTED
LIVING RM.
13'-0" X 18'-0"

FIREPLACE

BOOKS   WNDW. SEAT   BOOKS

GARAGE
27'-4" X 20'-0" / 24'-0"

WIDTH — 58'-0"
DEPTH — 60'-0"

MAIN FLOOR

Rustic Styling

Price Code: B

■ This plan features:

— Two bedrooms

— Two full baths

■ A large Sun Deck wraps around this rustic home

■ The Living Room and Dining Room are combined

■ The Living Room has a gas fireplace and sliders to the Deck

■ The large Kitchen features an angled counter

■ There is a Bedroom, Bath and a Utility Room on the first floor

■ Upstairs the Master Bedroom has two closets and a private Deck

■ Relax in the whirlpool tub in the Master Bath

■ An optional basement or crawl space foundation — please specify when ordering

First floor — 1,064 sq. ft.
Second floor — 613 sq. ft.

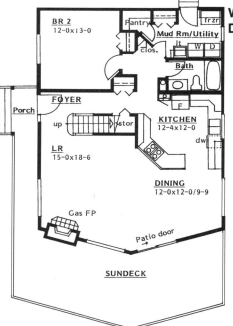

WIDTH 28'-0"
DEPTH 40'-0"

BR 2
12-0x13-0

Pantry

frzr

Mud Rm/Utility

clos.

W D

Bath

FOYER

Porch

up

stor

F

KITCHEN
12-4x12-0

dw

LR
15-0x18-6

DINING
12-0x12-0/9-9

Gas FP

Patio door

SUNDECK

FIRST FLOOR
No. 99914

Total Living Area:
1,677 sq. ft.

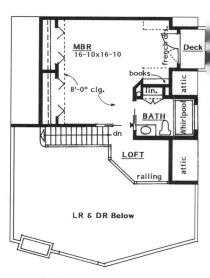

MBR
16-10x16-10

Deck

french drs.

books

attic

8'-0" clg.

lin.

BATH

Whirlpool

dn

LOFT

railing

attic

LR & DR Below

SECOND FLOOR

Perfect Compact Ranch

Price Code: B

■ This plan features:
— Two bedrooms
— Two full baths

■ A large, sunken Great Room, centralized with a cozy fireplace

■ A Master Bedroom with an unforgettable Bathroom including a skylight

■ A huge three-car Garage, including a work area for the family carpenter

■ A Kitchen, including a Breakfast Nook for family gatherings

MAIN FLOOR — 1,738 SQ. FT.
BASEMENT — 1,083 SQ. FT.
GARAGE — 796 SQ. FT.

TOTAL LIVING AREA:
1,738 SQ. FT.

Floor plan labels:

66'-0"

Optional Deck

Master Br
11-6 x 16-0

Great Rm
22-5 x 15-0

Screened Porch
9-9 x 9-9

Whirlpool

Skylight

Brkfst Bar

Dining Rm
15-0 x 9-6

52'-0"

Kitchen
11-4 x 9-0

DN

DN

Ref

Foyer

Cabinets

Railing

Br
9-0 x 11-0

Pantry

Breakfast
11-0 x 8-0

Air-Lock

Desk

Garage
32-0 x 28-0

Porch

Main Floor

Den
15-0 x 10-0
8'-6" Clg.

Crawl / Slab Option:

Furn.

WH

Crawl Space Access

Crawl / Slab Option

GARLINGHOUSE

ZIP QUOTE
HOME COST CALCULATOR
see order pages for details

© 1995 Donald A. Gardner Architects, Inc.

Designed for Today's Family

Price Code: E

■ This plan features:

— Three bedrooms

— Two full and one half baths

■ Volume and nine foot ceilings add elegance to a comfortable, open floor plan

■ Secluded Bedrooms designed for pleasant retreats at the end of the day

■ Airy Foyer topped by a vaulted dormer sends natural light streaming in

■ Formal Dining Room delineated from the Foyer by columns topped with a tray ceiling

■ Extra flexibility in the front Bedroom as it could double as a Study

■ Tray ceiling, skylights and a garden tub, in the Bath highlight the Master Suite

MAIN FLOOR — 2,192 SQ. FT.
GARAGE & STORAGE — 582 SQ. FT.
BONUS — 390 SQ. FT.

TOTAL LIVING AREA:
2,192 SQ. FT.

ZIP QUOTE
HOME COST CALCULATOR
see order pages for details

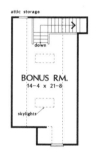

attic storage

down

BONUS RM.
14-4 x 21-8

skylights

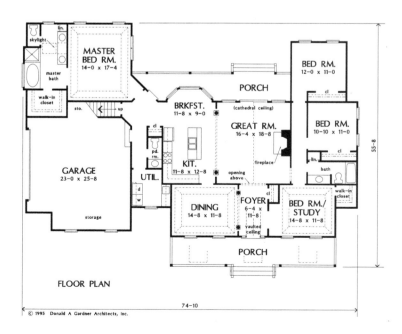

FLOOR PLAN

© 1995 Donald A Gardner Architects, Inc.

292

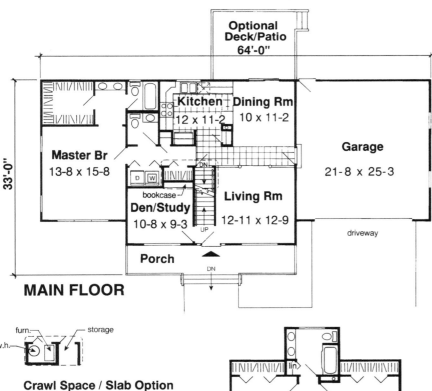

Optional Deck/Patio 64'-0"

33'-0"

Kitchen 12 x 11-2

Dining Rm 10 x 11-2

Garage 21-8 x 25-3

Master Br 13-8 x 15-8

bookcase

D | W

Den/Study 10-8 x 9-3

DN

UP

Living Rm 12-11 x 12-9

driveway

Porch

DN

MAIN FLOOR

furn.   storage

w.h.

Crawl Space / Slab Option

Br 2 10-8 x 13-7

DN

Br 3 12-11 x 13-7

slope   slope

UPPER FLOOR

Roomy Three Bedroom Cape

Price Code: B

■ This plan features:
— Three bedrooms
— Two full and one half baths

■ Large front Porch with Country appeal

■ Den includes picture window and built-in bookcase

■ Dining Room flows into Living Room for easy entertaining

■ L-shaped Kitchen has a double sink and ample counter space

■ Main floor Master Bedroom has bright front windows and a private Bath

■ Upstairs there are two secondary Bedrooms and a full Bath

MAIN FLOOR — 1,120 SQ. FT.
UPPER FLOOR — 592 SQ. FT.
GARAGE — 528 SQ. FT.

TOTAL LIVING AREA:
1,712 SQ. FT.

© Frank Betz Associates

57'-0"

56'-4"

Covered Porch

Vaulted Sitting Area

Breakfast
TRAY CLG.

Master Suite
17⁰ x 13⁰
TRAY CLG.

Kitchen
RANGE
D.W.
REF.
PANTRY

Vaulted Family Room
15⁵ x 20⁷
14'-0" HIGH CEILING

Bedroom 2
12⁶ x 10⁴

Bath

Vaulted M.Bath
W.I.c.
LINEN
Laund.

Vaulted M.Bath
W.I.c.
LINEN
Laund.

Foyer
14'-0" HIGH

DECORATIVE COLUMNS

PLANT SHELF ABOVE

Dining Room
12⁵ x 12⁷
14'-0" HIGH CEILING

Bedroom 3
10⁸ x 12⁰

Covered Entry

Garage
22⁵ x 20²

FLOOR PLAN

Garage
22⁵ x 20²

OPT. BASEMENT STAIR LOCATION

GARAGE LOCATION W/ BASEMENT

European Flavor
PRICE CODE: B

- This plan features:
  — Three bedrooms
  — Two full baths
- A covered Entry reveals a Foyer inside with a 14-foot ceiling
- The Family Room has a vaulted ceiling, a fireplace, and a French door to the rear yard
- The Breakfast Area has a tray ceiling and a bay of windows that overlooks the backyard
- The Kitchen has every imaginable convenience including a walk-in Pantry
- The Dining Room is delineated by columns and has a plant shelf above it
- The privately located Master Suite has a tray ceiling, a walk-in closet and a private Bath
- Two other Bedrooms share a full Bath on the opposite side of the home
- An optional basement or crawl space foundation — please specify when ordering
- No materials list available for this plan

MAIN FLOOR — 1,779 SQ. FT.
BASEMENT — 1,818 SQ. FT.
GARAGE — 499 SQ. FT.

TOTAL LIVING AREA:
1,779 SQ. FT.

optional DECK

DINING
10'-8" X 11'-4"

LIVING ROOM
14'-8" X 21'-0"
SLOPED CLG.

KITCHEN
10'-8" X 10'-8"

DW

Slab/Crawlspace Option

MBR 1
13'-4" X 13'-8"

BR 2
13'-10" X 11'-4"

DEN/ BR 3
10'-4" X 11'-10"

FOYER

GARAGE
20'-4" X 21'-4"

48'-0"

56'-0"

MAIN AREA

Master Retreat Welcomes You Home
PRICE CODE: A

- This plan features:
  — Three bedrooms
  — Two full baths
- Foyer opens into an huge Living Room with a fireplace below a sloped ceiling and Deck access
- Efficient Kitchen with a Pantry, serving counter, Dining area, laundry closet and Garage entry
- Corner Master Bedroom offers a walk-in closet and pampering Bath with a raised tub
- Two more Bedrooms, one with a Den option, share a full Bath

MAIN FLOOR — 1,486 SQ. FT.
GARAGE — 462 SQ. FT.

TOTAL LIVING AREA:
1,486 SQ. FT.

ZIP QUOTE
HOME COST CALCULATOR
see order pages for details

© 1995 Donald A Gardner Architects, Inc.

ZIP QUOTE
HOME COST CALCULATOR
see order pages for details

Cathedral Ceiling

Price Code: C

■ This plan features:

— Three bedrooms

— Two full baths

■ Cathedral ceiling expanding the Great Room, Dining Room and Kitchen

■ A versatile Bedroom or Study topped by a cathedral ceiling accented by double circle-top windows

■ Master Suite complete with a cathedral ceiling, including a Bath with a garden tub, linen closet and a walk-in closet

MAIN FLOOR — 1,417 SQ. FT.
GARAGE — 441 SQ. FT.

TOTAL LIVING AREA:
1,417 SQ. FT.

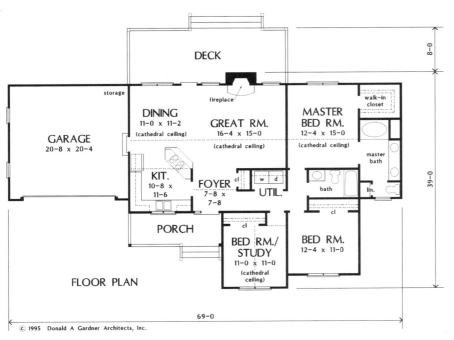

FLOOR PLAN

© 1995 Donald A Gardner Architects, Inc.

© 1997 Donald A Gardner Architects, Inc.

Columns Punctuate the Interior Space

Price Code: E

■ This plan features:

— Three bedrooms

— Two full and one half baths

■ A two-story Great Room and two-story Foyer, both with dormer windows, welcome natural light into this graceful country classic with a wrap-around Porch

■ Large Kitchen, featuring a center cooking island with counter and large Breakfast Area, opens to the Great Room for easy entertaining

■ Columns punctuate the interior spaces and a separate Dining Room provides a formal touch to the plan

■ Master Bedroom suite, privately situated on the first floor, has a double vanity, garden tub, and separate shower

FIRST FLOOR — 1,618 SQ. FT.
SECOND FLOOR — 570 SQ. FT.
BONUS ROOM — 495 SQ. FT.
GARAGE & STORAGE — 649 SQ. FT.

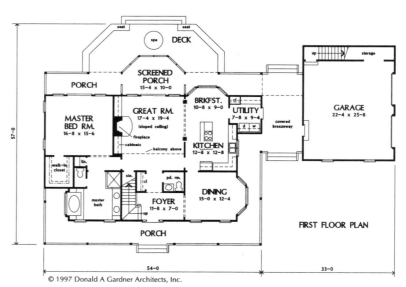

First Floor Plan labels: seat, seat, DECK, spa, SCREENED PORCH 15-4 x 10-0, PORCH, BRKFST. 10-8 x 9-0, UTILITY 7-8 x 9-4, covered breezeway, GARAGE 22-4 x 25-8, up, storage, GREAT RM. 17-4 x 19-4 (sloped ceiling), MASTER BED RM. 16-8 x 15-6, fireplace, cabinets, balcony above, KITCHEN 12-8 x 12-8, walk-in closet, lin., master bath, sto., cl., pd. rm., DINING 15-0 x 12-4, FOYER 11-8 x 7-0, up, PORCH, 54-0, 33-0, 57-0, FIRST FLOOR PLAN

© 1997 Donald A Gardner Architects, Inc.

ZIP QUOTE
HOME COST CALCULATOR
see order pages for details

Second Floor Plan labels: clerestory with palladian window, attic storage, great room below, attic storage, BED RM. 12-8 x 12-0, railing, balcony, BED RM. 12-8 x 12-0, down, bath, foyer below, clerestory with palladian window, SECOND FLOOR PLAN, BONUS RM. 15-4 x 29-4, down

TOTAL LIVING AREA:
2,188 SQ. FT.

To order your Blueprints, call 1-800-235-5700

Foyer Isolates Bedroom Wing
PRICE CODE: B

This plan features:
Three bedrooms
Two full baths
A Living Room complete with a window wall, flanking a massive fireplace
A Dining Room with recessed ceilings and a pass-through for convenience
A Master Suite tucked behind the two-car Garage for maximum noise protection
A spacious Kitchen with built-ins and access to the two-car Garage

AIN AREA — 1,568 SQ. FT.
ASEMENT — 1,568 SQ. FT.
ARAGE — 484 SQ. FT.

TOTAL LIVING AREA:
1,568 SQ. FT.

ZIP QUOTE
HOME COST CALCULATOR
see order pages for details

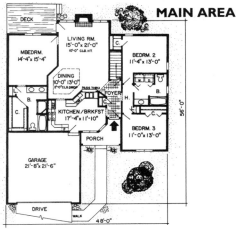

WIDTH 48'-0'
DEPTH 56'-0'

MAIN AREA

One Story Country Home
PRICE CODE: A

This plan features:
- Three bedrooms
- Two full baths
A Living Room with an imposing, high ceiling that slopes down to a normal height of eight feet, focusing on the decorative heat-circulating fireplace at the rear wall
An efficient Kitchen that adjoins the Dining Room that views the front Porch
A Dinette Area for informal eating in the Kitchen that can comfortably seat six people
A Master Suite arranged with a large dressing area that has a walk-in closet plus two linear closets and space for a vanity
Two family Bedrooms that share a full hall Bath

MAIN AREA — 1,367 SQ. FT.
BASEMENT — 1,267 SQ. FT.
GARAGE — 431 SQ. FT.

TOTAL LIVING AREA:
1,367 SQ. FT.

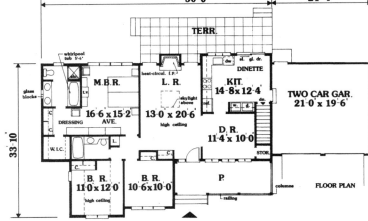

To order your Blueprints, call 1-800-235-5700

© 1995 Donald A. Gardner Architects, Inc.

Casually Elegant

Price Code: D

■ This plan features:

— Three bedrooms

— Two full baths

■ Arched windows, dormers and charming front and back Porches with columns creating Country flavoring

■ Central Great Room topped by a cathedral ceiling, a fireplace and a clerestory window

■ Breakfast Bay for casual dining is open to the Kitchen

■ Columns accenting the entryway into the formal Dining Room

■ Cathedral ceiling crowning the Master Bedroom

■ Master Bath with skylights, whirlpool tub, shower, and a double vanity

■ Two additional Bedrooms sharing a Bath located between the rooms

MAIN FLOOR — 1,561 SQ. FT.
GARAGE & STORAGE — 346 SQ. FT.

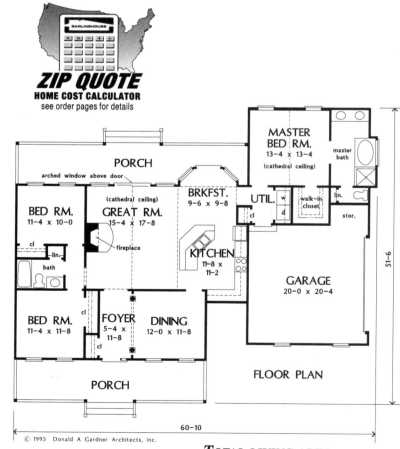

ZIP QUOTE
HOME COST CALCULATOR
see order pages for details

© 1995 Donald A Gardner Architects, Inc.

TOTAL LIVING AREA:
1,561 SQ. FT.

To order your Blueprints, call 1-800-235-5700

Fieldstone Facade and Arched Windows

PRICE CODE: C

- This plan features:
  — Three bedrooms
  — Two full and one half baths
- Inviting covered Porch shelters entrance
- Expansive Great Room enhanced by warm fireplace and three transom windows
- Breakfast Area adjoins Great Room giving a feeling of more space
- An efficient Kitchen with counter snack bar and nearby Laundry and Garage entry
- A first floor Master Bedroom Suite with an arched window below a sloped ceiling and a double vanity Bath
- A Bonus Area for future expansion on the second floor

FIRST FLOOR — 1,405 SQ. FT.
SECOND FLOOR — 453 SQ. FT.
BONUS ROOM — 300 SQ. FT.
BASEMENT — 1,405 SQ. FT.
GARAGE — 490 SQ. FT.

TOTAL LIVING AREA: 1,858 SQ. FT.

ZIP QUOTE
HOME COST CALCULATOR
see order pages for details

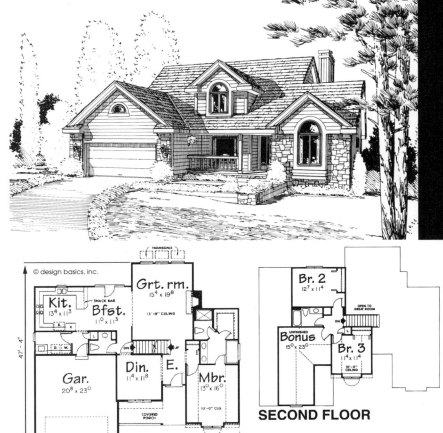

FIRST FLOOR

SECOND FLOOR

Celebrate the Outdoors

PRICE CODE: E

- This plan features:
  — Three bedrooms
  — Two full and one half baths
- This Country classic celebrates the outdoors with a wrap-around Porch, Sun Room, and spacious rear Deck
- A palladian window in front, a grand arched window in the rear plus skylights in the Sun Room in let the sunlight
- A second floor balcony overlooks the generous Great Room which has a cathedral ceiling and clerestory window
- The large Country Kitchen with a pass-through to the Great Room has a center island for easy food preparation
- The private Master Suite has access to the Sun Room through a luxurious Master Bath

FIRST FLOOR — 1,651 SQ. FT.
SECOND FLOOR — 567 SQ. FT.

TOTAL LIVING AREA: 2,218 SQ. FT.

© 1990 Donald A. Gardner Architects, Inc.

FIRST FLOOR PLAN

SECOND FLOOR PLAN

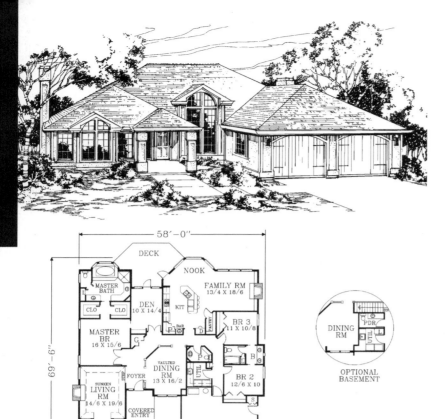

Accent on Privacy
PRICE CODE: D

- This plan features:
— Three bedrooms
— Two full and one half bath
- Stucco exterior and arched windows create a feeling of grandeur
- Sunken Living Room has a fireplace and elegant decorative ceiling
- Sweeping views of the backyard and direct access to the rear deck from the Family Room, Kitchen and Breakfast Nook
- Gourmet Kitchen with two Pantries, full height shelving, and a large island snack bar
- Master Bedroom enjoys its privacy on the opposite side of the home from the other Bedrooms
- Fabulous Master Bath with recessed tub and corner shower
- Continental Bath connecting the two secondary Bedrooms
- An optional basement, slab or crawl space foundation — please specify when ordering

MAIN FLOOR — 2,591 SQ. FT.
BASEMENT — 2,591 SQ. FT.

TOTAL LIVING AREA:
2,591 SQ. FT.

MAIN FLOOR

Kitchen Island Includes a Serving Bar
PRICE CODE: D

- This plan features:
— Four bedrooms
— Two full and one half baths
- This home includes two floor plans for the second floor; one incorporates a Bonus Room for expanding needs
- The Bedrooms are all found upstairs, helping your children to sleep undisturbed
- An optional basement or crawlspace foundation — please specify when ordering
- No materials list is available for this plan

FIRST FLOOR — 1,032 SQ. FT.
SECOND FLOOR — 988 SQ. FT.
GARAGE — 500 SQ. FT.

TOTAL LIVING AREA:
2,020 SQ. FT.

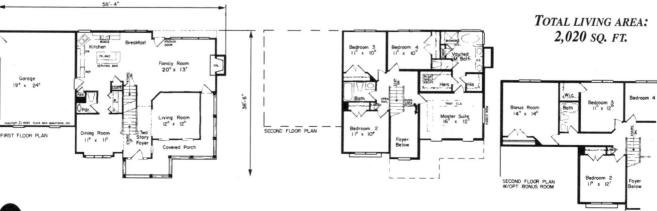

To order your Blueprints, call 1-800-235-5700

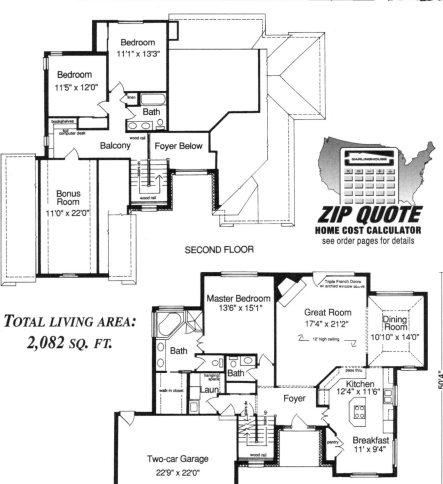

Bedroom
11'1" x 13'3"

Bedroom
11'5" x 12'0"

bookshelves
computer desk

linen

Bath

Balcony   Foyer Below

wood rail

Bonus
Room
11'0" x 22'0"

wood rail

SECOND FLOOR

ZIP QUOTE
HOME COST CALCULATOR
see order pages for details

GARLINGHOUSE

TOTAL LIVING AREA:
2,082 SQ. FT.

Master Bedroom
13'6" x 15'1"

Triple French Doors
w/ arched window above

Great Room
17'4" x 21'2"

Dining
Room
10'10" x 14'0"

12' high ceiling

Bath

hanging
space

Bath

pass thru

walk-in closet

Laun

Kitchen
12'4" x 11'6"

Foyer

pantry

stairs up

50'4"

Two-car Garage
22'9" x 22'0"

wood rail

Breakfast
11' x 9'4"

FIRST FLOOR

60'

An Elegant and Stylish Manner

Price Code: C

■ This plan features:

— Three bedrooms

— Two full and one half baths

■ Brick trim, sidelights and a transom window at the front door

■ A high ceiling through the Foyer and Great Room

■ A cozy fireplace and a built-in entertainment center in the Great Room

■ Kitchen serving the formal Dining Room and the Breakfast Area

■ A whirlpool tub, shower stall, his-n-her vanities and a spacious walk-in closet in the Master Suite

■ Study Loft overlooking the Great Room

■ No materials list is available for this plan

FIRST FLOOR — 1,524 SQ. FT.
SECOND FLOOR — 558 SQ. FT.
BONUS — 267 SQ. FT.
BASEMENT — 1,460 SQ. FT.

Delightful Doll House
PRICE CODE: A

- This plan features:
  — Three bedrooms
  — Two full baths
- A sloped ceiling in the Living Room which also has a focal point fireplace
- An efficient Kitchen with a peninsula counter and a built-in Pantry
- A decorative ceiling and sliding glass doors to the Deck in the Dining Room
- A Master Suite with a decorative ceiling, ample closet space and a private full Bath
- Two additional Bedrooms that share a full hall Bath

MAIN FLOOR — 1,307 SQ. FT.
BASEMENT — 1,298 SQ. FT.
GARAGE — 462 SQ. FT.

TOTAL LIVING AREA:
1,307 SQ. FT.

MAIN AREA

Rear Elevation

Slab/Crawl Space Option

ZIP QUOTE
HOME COST CALCULATOR
see order pages for details

© design basics inc.

Beautiful See-Through Fireplace
PRICE CODE: D

- This plan features:
  — Four bedrooms
  — Two full and one half baths
- Large repeating windows to the rear of the Great Room illuminate naturally
- The Great Room and the cozy Hearth Room share a beautiful see-through fireplace
- The bayed Breakfast Area is a bright and cheery way to start your day
- The gourmet Kitchen includes a Pantry, work island, ample corner space and a corner sink
- Secluded Master Suite has a skylight in the Dressing Area and a large walk-in closet
- The secondary Bedrooms share a generous, compartmented Bathroom

FIRST FLOOR — 1,733 SQ. FT.
SECOND FLOOR — 672 SQ. FT.
BASEMENT — 1,733 SQ. FT.
GARAGE — 613 SQ. FT.

TOTAL LIVING AREA:
2,405 SQ. FT.

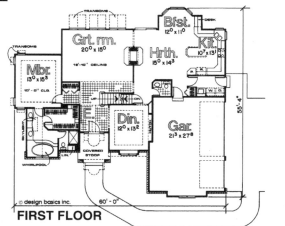

© design basics inc.

FIRST FLOOR

SECOND FLOOR

To order your Blueprints, call 1-800-235-5700

© 1995 Donald A Gardner Architects, Inc.

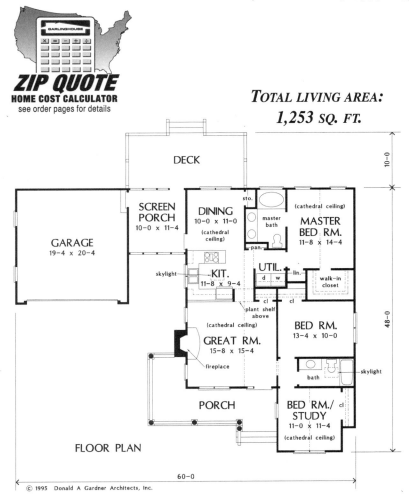

ZIP QUOTE
HOME COST CALCULATOR
see order pages for details

TOTAL LIVING AREA:
1,253 SQ. FT.

DECK

10-0

SCREEN PORCH
10-0 x 11-4

DINING
10-0 x 11-0
(cathedral ceiling)

sto.

master bath

(cathedral ceiling)

MASTER BED RM.
11-8 x 14-4

GARAGE
19-4 x 20-4

skylight

KIT.
11-8 x 9-4

pan.

UTIL.
d w

lin.

walk-in closet

plant shelf above

(cathedral ceiling)

cl   cl

48-0

BED RM.
13-4 x 10-0

GREAT RM.
15-8 x 15-4

fireplace

bath

skylight

PORCH

BED RM./ STUDY
11-0 x 11-4

cl

(cathedral ceiling)

FLOOR PLAN

60-0

© 1995 Donald A Gardner Architects, Inc.

Amenities Normally Found In Larger Homes

Price Code: C

■ This plan features:
— Three bedrooms
— Two full baths

■ A continuous cathedral ceiling in the Great Room, Kitchen, and Dining Room giving a spacious feel to this efficient plan

■ Skylighted Kitchen with a seven foot high wall by the Great Room and a popular plant shelf

■ Master Suite opens up with a cathedral ceiling and contains walk-in and linen closets and a private Bath with garden tub and dual vanity

■ Cathedral ceiling as the crowning touch to the front Bedrooms/Study

MAIN FLOOR — 1,253 SQ. FT.
GARAGE & STORAGE — 420 SQ. FT.

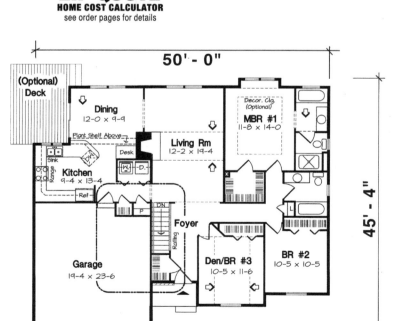

Easy Living

Price Code: A

- This plan features:
  — Three bedrooms
  — Two full baths
- A dramatic sloped ceiling and a massive fireplace in the Living Room
- A Dining Room crowned by a sloping ceiling and a plant shelf also has sliding doors to the Deck
- A U-shaped Kitchen with abundant cabinets, a window over the sink and a walk-in Pantry
- A Master Suite with a private full Bath, decorative ceiling and walk-in closet
- Two additional Bedrooms that share a full Bath

MAIN FLOOR — 1,456 SQ. FT.
BASEMENT — 1,448 SQ. FT.
GARAGE — 452 SQ. FT.

TOTAL LIVING AREA:
1,456 SQ. FT.

ZIP QUOTE
HOME COST CALCULATOR
see order pages for details

MAIN FLOOR

50' - 0"

45' - 4"

(Optional) Deck

Dining
12-0 x 9-9

Plant Shelf Above

Sink
Range
Kitchen
9-4 x 13-4
Ref

Desk
D.

Living Rm
12-2 x 19-4

Decor. Clg.
(Optional)
MBR #1
11-8 x 14-0

DN
P
Foyer
Railing
DN

Garage
19-4 x 23-6

Den/BR #3
10-5 x 11-6

BR #2
10-5 x 10-5

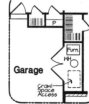

Garage
Furn.
WH
P
Crawl Space Access

SLAB/CRAWL SPACE OPTION

To order your Blueprints, call 1-800-235-5700

An Air of Refinement

PRICE CODE: E

■ This plan features:
- Four bedrooms
- Three full baths

■ Hip roof, brick veneer and arched windows catch attention

■ Foyer, flanked by Dining Room and Bedroom/Study, opens to Great Room with cozy fireplace and wall of windows

■ Cathedral ceilings and arched windows bathe Dining Room and Breakfast Area in natural light

■ Private Master Suite has cathedral ceiling and sumptuous Bath with whirlpool tub, shower and dual vanity

■ Two more Bedrooms and Bonus Room share third full Bath

FIRST FLOOR — 1,694 SQ. FT.
SECOND FLOOR — 436 SQ. FT.
BONUS ROOM — 345 SQ. FT.
GARAGE & STORAGE — 567 SQ. FT.

TOTAL LIVING AREA: 2,130 SQ. FT.

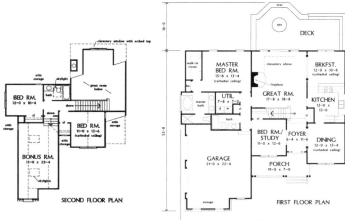

© 1993 Donald A. Gardner Architects, Inc.

Friendly Front Porch

PRICE CODE: C

■ This plan features:
- Three bedrooms
- One full and one half baths

■ Country, homey feeling with wrap-around Porch

■ Adjoining Living Room and Dining Room creates spacious feeling

■ Efficient Kitchen easily serves Dining Area with extended counter and a built-in Pantry

■ Spacious Family Room with optional fireplace and access to Laundry/Garage entry

■ Large Master Bedroom with a walk-in closet and access to a full Bath, offers a private Bath option

■ Two additional Bedrooms with ample closets and full Bath access

■ No materials list is available for this plan

FIRST FLOOR — 900 SQ. FT.
SECOND FLOOR — 676 SQ. FT.
BASEMENT — 900 SQ. FT.
GARAGE — 448 SQ. FT.

TOTAL LIVING AREA: 1,576 SQ. FT.

WIDTH 58'-0"
DEPTH 34'-0"

To order your Blueprints, call 1-800-235-5700

Classic Ranch
PRICE CODE: B

■ This plan features:
— Three bedrooms
— Two full baths
■ A fabulous Great Room with a step ceiling and a cozy fireplace
■ An elegant arched soffit connects the Great Room to the Dining Room
■ The Kitchen has wrap-around counters, a center island and a Nook
■ The Master Bedroom is completed with a walk-in closet and a private Bath
■ Two additional Bedrooms with ample closet space share a full Bath
■ No materials list is available for this plan

MAIN FLOOR — 1,794 SQ. FT.
BASEMENT — 1,794 SQ. FT.

TOTAL LIVING AREA:
1,794 SQ. FT.

MAIN FLOOR PLAN

Plan for the Future
PRICE CODE: A

■ This plan features:
— Three bedrooms
— Two full baths
■ Entry leads up to Living Area accented by a vaulted ceiling and arched window
■ Compact, efficient Kitchen with serving counter/snack-bar, serves Dining Area and Deck beyond
■ Comfortable Master Bedroom with a walk-in closet and double vanity Bath with a window tub
■ Two additional Bedrooms with large closets, share a full Bath
■ Entry leads down to Laundry, Garage and future Playroom

MAIN FLOOR — 1,269 SQ. FT.
FINISHED STAIRCASE — 56 SQ. FT.
BASEMENT — 382 SQ. FT.
GARAGE — 598 SQ. FT.

TOTAL LIVING AREA:
1,325 SQ. FT.

FIRST FLOOR

SECOND FLOOR

ZIP QUOTE
HOME COST CALCULATOR
see order pages for details

To order your Blueprints, call 1-800-235-5700

Family Living Made Easy

PRICE CODE: B

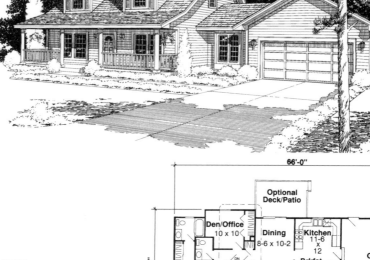

This plan features:
- Three bedrooms
- Two full and one half baths
- A welcoming Country Porch sheltering the entrance
- A large Living Room that flows into the Dining Room creating a great area for entertaining
- An efficient U-shaped Kitchen that includes an informal Breakfast area and a Laundry Center
- A convenient entrance from the Garage into the Kitchen
- A private Master Suite with a full Bath and two closets
- A Den/Office with ample closet space, enabling it to double as a Guest Room
- Two additional Bedrooms on the second floor that share a full hall Bath
- An optional Deck/Patio that will increase your living space in the warmer weather

FIRST FLOOR — 1,081 SQ. FT.

SECOND FLOOR — 528 SQ. FT.

TOTAL LIVING AREA:
1,609 SQ. FT.

Second Floor

Crawl Space / Slab Option

First Floor

Secluded Vacation Retreat

PRICE CODE: C

This plan features:
- Two bedrooms
- Three full baths
- A high vaulted ceiling in the Living Area with a large masonry fireplace and circular stairway
- A wall of windows along the full cathedral height of the Living Area
- A Kitchen with ample storage and counter space including a sink and a chopping block island
- Private full Baths for each of the bedrooms with 10-foot closets
- A Loft with windowed doors opening to a Deck

MAIN FLOOR — 1,448 SQ. FT.

LOFT — 389 SQ. FT.

CARPORT — 312 SQ. FT.

TOTAL LIVING AREA:
1,837 SQ. FT.

LOFT

MAIN FLOOR

To order your Blueprints, call 1-800-235-5700

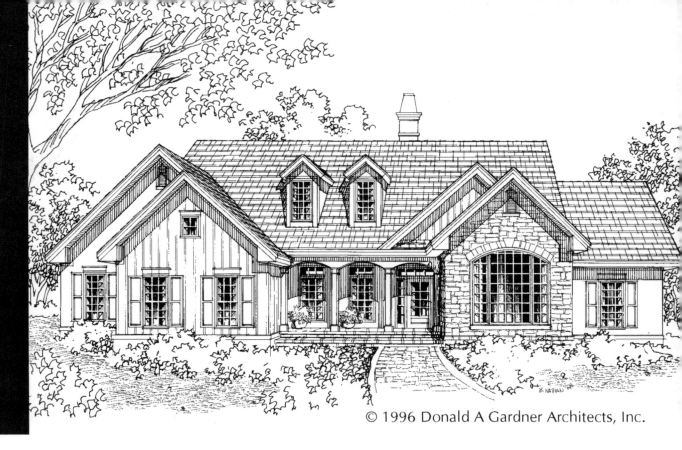

© 1996 Donald A Gardner Architects, Inc.

Great As A Mountain Retreat

Price Code: D

ZIP QUOTE
HOME COST CALCULATOR
see order pages for details

■ This plan features:

— Three bedrooms

— Two full baths

■ Board and batten siding, stone, and stucco combine to give this popular plan a casual feel

■ User friendly Kitchen with huge pantry for ample storage and island counter

■ Casual family meals in sunny Breakfast bay; formal gatherings in the columned Dining area

■ Master Suite is topped by a deep tray ceiling, has a large walk-in closet, an extravagant private bath and direct access to back porch

MAIN FLOOR — 1,912 SQ. FT.
GARAGE — 580 SQ. FT.
BONUS — 398 SQ. FT.

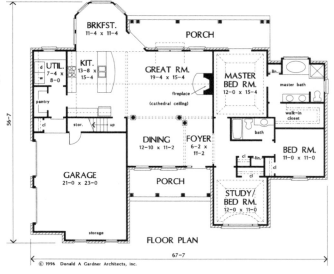

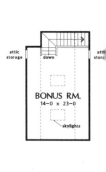

TOTAL LIVING AREA:
1,912 SQ. FT.

To order your Blueprints, call 1-800-235-5700

© 1992 Donald A Gardner Architects, Inc.

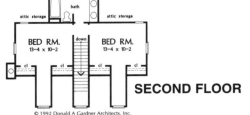

ZIP QUOTE
HOME COST CALCULATOR
see order pages for details

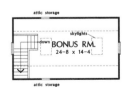

FIRST FLOOR

© 1992 Donald A Gardner Architects, Inc.

SECOND FLOOR

© 1992 Donald A Gardner Architects, Inc.

TOTAL LIVING AREA:
1,663 SQ. FT.

Classic Farmhouse
Price Code: C

■ This plan features:

— Three bedrooms

— Two full and one half baths

■ Covered Porch gives a classic country farmhouse look, and includes multiple dormers, a great layout for entertaining, and a bonus room

■ Clerestory dormer window bathes the two-story Foyer in natural light

■ Large Great Room with fireplace opens to the Dining/Breakfast /Kitchen space, which leads to a spacious Deck with optional Spa and seating for easy indoor/outdoor entertaining

■ First floor Master Suite offers privacy and luxury with a separate shower, whirlpool tub, and a double vanity

FIRST FLOOR — 1,145 SQ. FT.
SECOND FLOOR — 518 SQ. FT.
BONUS ROOM — 380 SQ. FT.
GARAGE & STORAGE — 509 SQ. FT.

Three Car Garage
PRICE CODE: F

■ This plan features:
— Five bedrooms
— Four full and one half baths
■ The Living and Dining Rooms are located off the Foyer
■ Columns separate the Family Room from the Kitchen
■ A Study/Bedroom is tucked away on the first floor
■ The Laundry Room is located upstairs
■ The Master Suite is warmed by a fireplace in its Sitting Room
■ An optional basement or crawl space foundation — please specify when ordering
■ No materials list is available for this plan

MAIN FLOOR — 1,577 SQ. FT.
UPPER FLOOR — 1,689 SQ. FT.
BASEMENT — 1,577 SQ. FT.
GARAGE — 694 SQ. FT.

TOTAL LIVING AREA:
3,266 SQ. FT.

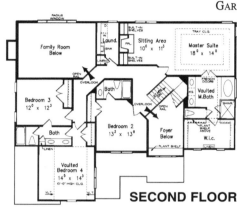

FIRST FLOOR

SECOND FLOOR

Economy at It's Best
PRICE CODE: B

■ This plan features:
— Three bedrooms
— Three full baths
■ Attractive Porch adds to the curb appeal of this economical to build home
■ A vaulted ceiling topping the Entry, Living and Dining Rooms
■ A lovely bay window, adding sophistication to the Living Room, which includes direct access to a side Deck
■ A Master Suite with a walk-in closet, and a private compartment Bath with an oversized shower
■ Two additional Bedrooms share a full hall Bath topped by a skylight
■ A vaulted ceiling topping the Dining Area which flows from the efficient island Kitchen
■ A walk-in Pantry adds to the storage space of the cooktop island Kitchen, which is equipped with a double sink with a window above
■ Garage offers direct entrance to the house

MAIN FLOOR — 1,717 SQ. FT.
GARAGE — 782 SQ. FT.

TOTAL LIVING AREA:
1,717 SQ. FT.

WIDTH 80'-0"
DEPTH 42'-0"

MAIN FLOOR

Enchanting Entry

PRICE CODE: C

■ This plan features:
— Three bedrooms
— Two full and one half baths

■ Split Entry leads down to Family Room, Utility Room, Den, half bath and two-car Garage

■ Up a half-flight of stairs leads to the large Living Room highlighted by a double window

■ Dining Room convenient to Living Room and Kitchen

■ Efficient Kitchen with rear yard access and room for eating

■ Corner Master Bedroom offers an over-sized closet and private Bath

■ Two additional Bedrooms with double windows, share a full Bath

UPPER FLOOR — 1,331 SQ. FT.
LOWER FLOOR — 663 SQ. FT.
GARAGE — 584 SQ. FT.

TOTAL LIVING AREA:
1,994 SQ. FT.

ZIP QUOTE
HOME COST CALCULATOR
see order pages for details

Plan floor plans:

MBr 1
14-6 X 13-6

Kitchen
12 X 13-6

Dining Rm
12 X 13-6

Br 2
11-1 X 13-6

Br 3
10-4 X 10-1

Living Rm
16 X 13-6

Entry

DN UP

UPPER FLOOR

28'-0"

48'-0"

Garage
20 X 24-8

Utility

W D

Den
11-6 X 12-8

wndw. well

UP

Family Rm
15-4 X 11

LOWER FLOOR

For the Growing Family

PRICE CODE: C

■ This plan features:
— Three bedrooms
— Three full baths

■ Formal areas are located to either side of the impressive two-story Foyer

■ An open rail staircase adorning the Living Room while the Dining Room features easy access to the Kitchen

■ Kitchen equipped with a corner double sink and a wrap-around snack bar is open to the Family Room and Breakfast Area

■ Fireplace in the Family Room giving warmth and atmosphere to living space

■ Secondary Bedroom or Study privately located in the left rear corner of the home with direct access to a full Bath

■ Master Suite decorated by a tray ceiling in the Bedroom and a vaulted ceiling in the Master Bath

■ An optional basement or crawl space foundation — please specify when ordering

■ No materials list is available for this plan

FIRST FLOOR — 1,103 SQ. FT.
SECOND FLOOR — 759 SQ. FT.
BASEMENT — 1,103 SQ. FT.
GARAGE — 420 SQ. FT.

TOTAL LIVING AREA:
1,862 SQ. FT.

50'-4"

Bedroom 4/ Study
10^0 x 11^7

Bath

PANTRY

FRENCH DOOR

Breakfast

Family Room
17^2 x 13^2

FPL

35'-0"

RANGE
Kitchen
DW.
REF.

COATS

STAIRS DN.

STAIRS UP

OPEN RAIL

Garage
19^8 x 20^4

Dining Room
10^0 x 11^0

Two Story Foyer

Living Room
10^6 x 10^0

Covered Porch

FIRST FLOOR

© Frank Betz Associates

SHWR

Vaulted M.Bath

TRAY CLG.

Master Suite
17^2 x 13^2

PLANT SHELF ABOVE

W.i.c.

W.i.c.

Bath

STAIRS DN.

LINEN

W.i.c.

Bedroom 2
10^0 x 10^2

OPEN RAIL

Foyer Below

PLANT SHELF

Bedroom 3
10^2 x 10^0

SECOND FLOOR

Easy Living Ranch
PRICE CODE: B

■ This plan features:
— Three bedrooms
— Two full baths
■ Distinct exterior features, including vinyl siding, a series of gables, an arched window in the Dining Room and a protected front door with sidelights
■ Dining Room with a 14-foot ceiling
■ Directly behind the Dining Room is the Kitchen with a serving bar
■ Breakfast Area with easy access to the Great Room
■ Master Bedroom crowned in a tray ceiling
■ Master Bath including a large walk-in closet and separate shower and garden tub
■ No materials list is available for this plan

MAIN FLOOR — 1,590 SQ. FT.
BASEMENT — 1,590 SQ. FT.
GARAGE — 560 SQ. FT.

TOTAL LIVING AREA:
1,590 SQ. FT.

MAIN FLOOR

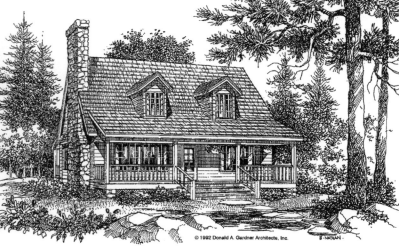

© 1992 Donald A. Gardner Architects, Inc.

Rustic Three Bedroom
PRICE CODE: D

■ This plan features:
— Three bedrooms
— Two full baths
■ Spacious covered Porches on the front of the home and on the rear of the home
■ Openness in the Great Room to the Kitchen/Dining area provides a spacious feeling of a much larger home
■ Cooktop island Kitchen includes L-shaped counter for ample work space
■ Master Suite, with a generous walk-in closet and pampering Master Bath
■ Two second floor Bedrooms, one overlooking the Great Room for added drama

FIRST FLOOR — 1,039 SQ. FT.
SECOND FLOOR — 583 SQ. FT.

TOTAL LIVING AREA:
1,622 SQ. FT.

© Donald A. Gardner Architects, Inc. FIRST FLOOR

SECOND FLOOR PLAN

© design basics, inc.

Gar.
19⁸ x 23⁴

30'-0"

56'-0"

FIRST FLOOR
No. 94944

Bfst.
10⁰ x 13⁰

Kit.
9⁰ x 13⁶

COVERED PORCH

SERVERY

W. D.

R. P.

DN

UP

Grt. rm.
14⁰ x 19⁴

Din.
14⁰ x 10⁰

TRANSOM

STOOP

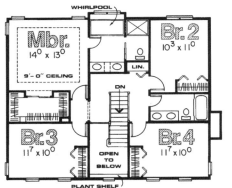

ZIP QUOTE
HOME COST CALCULATOR
see order pages for details

WHIRLPOOL

Mbr.
14⁰ x 13⁰

9'-0" CEILING

Br. 2
10³ x 11⁰

LIN.

DN

Br. 3
11⁷ x 10⁰

OPEN TO BELOW

Br. 4
11⁷ x 10⁰

PLANT SHELF

SECOND FLOOR

Spectacular Sophistication

Price Code: C

■ This plan features:

— Four bedrooms

— Two full and one half baths

■ Open Foyer with circular window and a plant shelf leads into the Dining Room

■ Great Room with an inviting fireplace and windows front and back

■ Open Kitchen has a work island and accesses the Breakfast Area

■ Master Bedroom features a nine-foot boxed ceiling, a walk-in closet and whirlpool Bath

■ Three additional Bedrooms share a full Bath with a double vanity

FIRST FLOOR — 941 SQ. FT.
SECOND FLOOR — 992 SQ. FT.
BASEMENT — 941 SQ. FT.
GARAGE — 480 SQ. FT.

TOTAL LIVING AREA:
1,933 SQ. FT.

Porch Adorns Elegant Bay
PRICE CODE: C

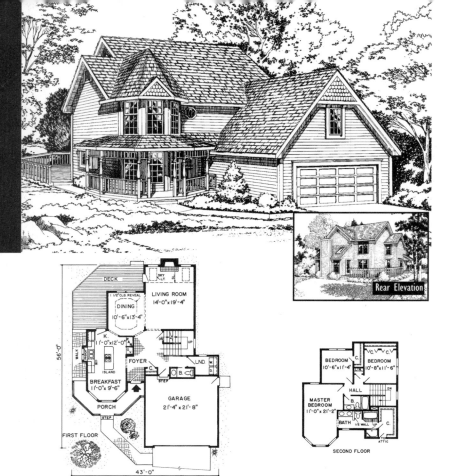

- This plan features:
— Three bedrooms
— Two full and one half baths
- A Master Suite with a romantic bay window and full Bath
- Bedrooms with huge closets and use of the full hall Bat
- A roomy island Kitchen with a modern, efficient layout
- A Formal Dining Room with a recessed decorative ceiling
- Sloping skylit ceilings illuminating the fireplaced Livin Room
- A rear Deck accessible from both the Kitchen and the Living Room

FIRST FLOOR — 1,027 SQ. FT.
SECOND FLOOR — 974 SQ. FT.
GARAGE — 476 SQ. FT.
BASEMENT — 978 SQ. FT.

TOTAL LIVING AREA:
2,001 SQ. FT.

Rear Elevation

Beckoning Country Porch
PRICE CODE: B

- This plan features:
— Three bedrooms
— Two full and one half baths
- Country styled exterior with dormer windows above friendly front Porch
- Vaulted ceiling and central fireplace accent the spacious Great Room
- L-shaped Kitchen/Dining Room with work island and atrium door to back yard
- First floor Master Suite with vaulted ceiling, walk-in closet, private bath and optional private Deck with hot tub
- Two additional Bedrooms on the second floor with easy access to full Bath

FIRST FLOOR — 1,061 SQ. FT.
SECOND FLOOR — 499 SQ. FT.
BASEMENT — 1,061 SQ. FT.

TOTAL LIVING AREA:
1,560 SQ. FT.

Rear Elevation

ZIP QUOTE
HOME COST CALCULATOR
see order pages for details

second floor

br 3
13⁶ x 12

br 4
12 x 12

open to foyer

DN

lin

WIDTH 57'-10"
DEPTH 56'-10"

first floor

porch
33 x 10

eating
14 x 10

util
8 x 10

den
19 x 20

mbr
14 x 16

sto
6 x 8

kit
14 x 12

ct
dw
oven
ref

garage
22 x 22

dining
12 x 14

foy

UP

br 2
12 x 14

porch
4 x 21

shr
shvs
lin
lin
ra

French Flavor

Price Code: E

■ This plan features:

— Four bedrooms

— Three full baths

■ Porch entry into open Foyer with a lovely, landing staircase

■ Elegant columns define Dining and Den area for gracious entertaining

■ Efficient, U-shaped Kitchen with a serving counter, Eating Bay, and nearby Utility Area and Garage

■ Decorative ceiling tops Master Bedroom offering a huge walk-in closet and plush Bath

■ Three additional Bedrooms with walk-in closets, access full Baths

■ An optional crawl space or slab foundation — please specify when ordering

FIRST FLOOR — 1,911 SQ. FT.
SECOND FLOOR — 579 SQ. FT.
GARAGE — 560 SQ. FT.

TOTAL LIVING AREA:
2,490 SQ. FT.

Classic Exterior with Modern Interior

Price Code: C

■ This plan features:

— Three or four bedrooms

— Two full and one half baths

■ Front Porch leads into an open Foyer and Great Room

■ An efficient Kitchen with a cooktop island, walk-in Pantry, a bright Dining Area and nearby Screened Porch, Laundry and Garage entry

■ Deluxe Master Bedroom wing with a decorative ceiling, large walk-in closet and plush Bath

■ Two or three Bedrooms on the second floor share a double vanity Bath

■ No materials list is available for this plan

FIRST FLOOR — 1,348 SQ. FT.
SECOND FLOOR — 528 SQ. FT.
BASEMENT — 1,300 SQ. FT.
BONUS — 195 SQ. FT.

TOTAL LIVING AREA:
1,876 SQ. FT.

WIDTH 56'- 2"
DEPTH 48'- 0"

Screened-in Porch

Master Bedroom 14'1" x 15'1"

Great Room 16'8" x 15'4"

Dining Area 10'1" x 14'1"

Bath

slope ceiling

slope ceiling

Laun.

Dressing

Foyer

walk-in closet

Kitchen 13'2" x 11'8"

pantry

Two-car Garage 20' x 27'5"

Porch

FIRST FLOOR

Bedroom 10'5" x 12'

Foyer Below

Bedroom 11'6" x 11'5"

wood rail

stairs dn

Hall

Bath

computer desk

SECOND FLOOR

Bonus Bedroom 10' x 18'2"

skylight

To order your Blueprints, call 1-800-235-5700

Triple Arched Porch

PRICE CODE: B

PLAN NO. 98474

- This plan features:
- — Four bedrooms
- — Three full baths
- A triple arched front Porch, segmented arched window keystones and shutters accent the exterior
- An impressive two-story Foyer adjoins the elegant Dining Room
- The Family Room, Breakfast Room and Kitchen have an open layout
- The Study/Bedroom Four is topped by a vaulted ceiling and is located close to a full Bath
- The Master Suite is topped by a tray ceiling while there is a vaulted ceiling over the Bath
- An optional Bonus Room offers expansion for future needs
- An optional basement or crawl space foundation — please specify when ordering
- No materials list is available for this plan

FIRST FLOOR — 972 SQ. FT.
SECOND FLOOR — 772 SQ. FT.
BONUS ROOM — 358 SQ. FT.
BASEMENT — 972 SQ. FT.
GARAGE — 520 SQ. FT.

TOTAL LIVING AREA: 1,744 SQ. FT.

SECOND FLOOR

FIRST FLOOR

OPT. BONUS ROOM

© Frank Betz Associates

Rewards of Success

PRICE CODE: D

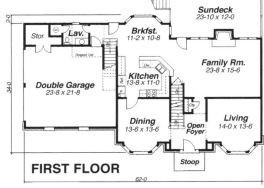

PLAN NO. 93254

- This plan features:
- — Three bedrooms
- — Three full and one half baths
- Formal areas, the Living Room and Dining Room, located in the front of the house, each enhanced by a bay window
- An expansive Family Room, including a fireplace flanked by windows, at the rear of the house
- An open layout between the Family Room, Breakfast Bay and the Kitchen
- A lavish Master Suite crowned by a decorative ceiling and pampered by a private Master Bath
- Two additional Bedrooms, one has use of a full hall Bath the other has a private Bath
- An optional basement, crawl space or slab foundation — please specify when ordering
- No materials list is available for this plan

FIRST FLOOR — 1,282 SQ. FT.
SECOND FLOOR — 1,227 SQ. FT.
BONUS ROOM — 314 SQ. FT.
GARAGE — 528 SQ. FT.
BASEMENT — 1,154 SQ. FT.

TOTAL LIVING AREA: 2,509 SQ. FT.

SECOND FLOOR

FIRST FLOOR

To order your Blueprints, call 1-800-235-5700

©1994 Donald A. Gardner Architects, Inc.

Country Covered Porches
PRICE CODE: D

■ This plan features:
— Three bedrooms
— Two full and one half baths
■ A smart, user Friendly Kitchen and a generous Great Room share a cathedral ceiling
■ Both the front Bedroom and the Master Bedroom enjoy cathedral ceilings
■ The Master Suite is privately tucked away with a luxurious Bath, walk-in closet and access to the Porch
■ The spacious Utility Room offers convenience with built-in cabinets
■ The Bonus Room is available for future expansion

MAIN FLOOR — 1,807 SQ. FT.
GARAGE — 669 SQ. FT.
BONUS ROOM — 419 SQ. FT.

TOTAL LIVING AREA:
1,807 SQ. FT.

FIRST FLOOR PLAN

© Donald A. Gardner Architects, Inc.

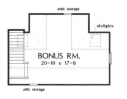

BONUS RM.
20-10 x 17-8

Vaulted Family Room
PRICE CODE: B

■ This plan features:
— Three bedrooms
— Two full and one half baths
■ A fireplace and vaulted ceiling highlight the Family Room
■ The Dining Room and Nook are set between the Kitchen
■ Upstairs the Master Suite has a tray ceiling
■ Two additional Bedrooms share a full Bath
■ A covered front Porch adds character
■ An optional basement or crawl space foundation — please specify when ordering
■ No materials list is available for this plan

FIRST FLOOR — 760 SQ. FT.
SECOND FLOOR — 854 SQ. FT.
BASEMENT — 760 SQ. FT.
GARAGE — 399 SQ. FT.

TOTAL LIVING AREA:
1,614 SQ. FT.

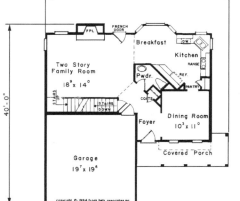

FIRST FLOOR PLAN

SECOND FLOOR PLAN

To order your Blueprints, call 1-800-235-5700

TOTAL LIVING AREA:
1,448 SQ. FT.

FIRST FLOOR
No. 96528

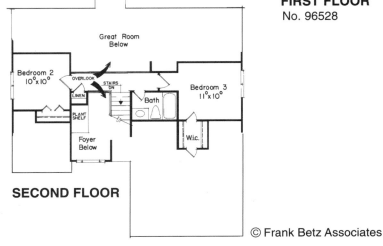

SECOND FLOOR

© Frank Betz Associates

Stylish Smaller Home
Price Code: A

■ This plan features:

— Three bedrooms

— Two full and one half baths

■ Two-story Foyer leads into the Family Room with a vaulted ceiling

■ A cozy atmosphere created by a fireplace in the Family Room

■ Breakfast Room adjoins the Family Room and the Kitchen

■ An extended counter adds to the work area of the Kitchen

■ A tray ceiling and a private master Bath in the Master Suite

■ Two additional Bedroom with ample closet space sharing the full Bath in the hall

■ An optional basement, crawl space or slab foundation — please specify when ordering

■ No materials list is available for this plan

FIRST FLOOR — 1,049 SQ. FT.
SECOND FLOOR — 399 SQ. FT.
BASEMENT — 1,051 SQ. FT.
GARAGE — 400 SQ. FT.

© 1996 Donald A. Gardner Architects, Inc.

Home Builders on a Budget

Price Code: C

ZIP QUOTE
HOME COST CALCULATOR
see order pages for details

■ This plan features:

— Three bedrooms

— Two full baths

■ Down-sized country plan for home builder on a budget

■ Columns punctuate open, one-level floor plan and connect Foyer with clerestory window dormers

■ Front Porch and large, rear Deck extend living space outdoors

■ Tray ceilings decorate Master Bedroom, Dining Room and Bedroom/Study

■ Private Master Bath features garden tub, double vanity, separate shower and skylights

MAIN FLOOR — 1,498 SQ. FT.
GARAGE & STORAGE — 427 SQ. FT.

TOTAL LIVING AREA:
1,498 SQ. FT

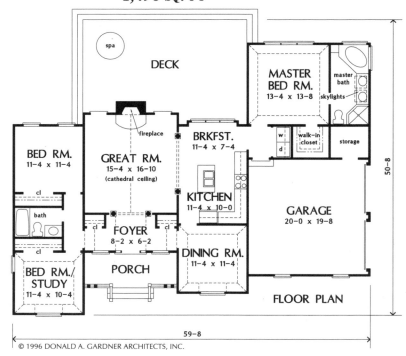

FLOOR PLAN

© 1996 DONALD A. GARDNER ARCHITECTS, INC.

To order your Blueprints, call 1-800-235-5700

© 1994 Donald A. Gardner Architects, Inc.

Exciting Ceilings Add Appeal

Price Code: C

■ This plan features:
— Three bedrooms
— Two full baths

■ Open design enhanced by cathedral and tray ceilings above arched windows

■ Foyer with columns defining Great Room with central fireplace and Deck access

■ Cooktop island in Kitchen provides cooks with convenience and company

■ Ultimate Master Bedroom Suite offers walk-in closet, tray ceiling, and whirlpool bath

■ Front Bedroom/Study offers multiple uses with tray ceiling and arched window

MAIN FLOOR — 1,475 SQ. FT.
GARAGE & STORAGE — 478 SQ. FT.

TOTAL LIVING AREA: 1,475 SQ. FT.

FLOOR PLAN

DECK

spa

GARAGE
20-4 x 22-5

storage

fireplace
(cathedral ceiling)

KIT.
10-4 x 13-6

UTIL.

w
d

walk-in
closet

GREAT RM.
15-4 x 16-0

BED RM.
11-4 x 10-0

cl

lin.

bath

cl

cl

MASTER
BED RM.
13-4 x 14-4

master
bath

FOYER
15-4 x 3-8

DINING
10-4 x 12-0

BED RM./
STUDY
11-4 x 10-4

PORCH

54-7

59-6

© Donald A. Gardner Architects, Inc.

Spacious Family Living

Price Code: D

- ■ This plan features:
- — Four bedrooms
- — Two full and one half baths
- ■ Front Porch welcomes friends and family home
- ■ Entry opens to spacious Living Room with a tiered ceiling and Dining Room beyond
- ■ Hub Kitchen easily serves the Dining Room, the Breakfast bay and the Family Room
- ■ Corner Master Bedroom has access to a private Bath
- ■ Three additional Bedrooms share a double vanity Bath

FIRST FLOOR — 1,269 SQ. FT.
SECOND FLOOR — 1,034 SQ. FT.
BASEMENT — 1,269 SQ. FT.
GARAGE — 485 SQ. FT.

TOTAL LIVING AREA :
2,303 SQ. FT.

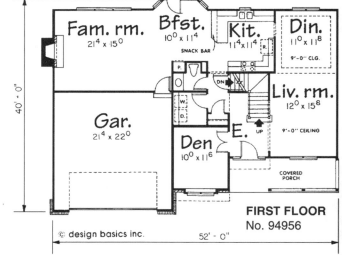

Fam. rm. 21⁴ x 15⁰
Bfst. 10⁰ x 11⁴
Kit. 11⁴ x 11⁴
Din. 11⁰ x 11⁸   9'-0'' CLG.
SNACK BAR
Gar. 21⁴ x 22⁰
Liv. rm. 12⁰ x 15⁸   9'-0'' CEILING
Den 10⁰ x 11⁶
E.
COVERED PORCH
40' - 0"
52' - 0"
© design basics inc.

FIRST FLOOR
No. 94956

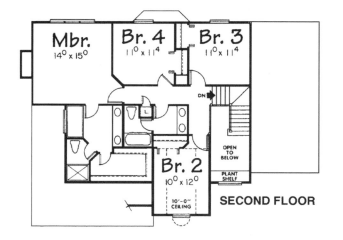

Mbr. 14⁰ x 15⁰
Br. 4 11⁰ x 11⁴
Br. 3 11⁰ x 11⁴
Br. 2 10⁰ x 12⁰   10'-0'' CEILING
OPEN TO BELOW
PLANT SHELF
DN

SECOND FLOOR

ZIP QUOTE
HOME COST CALCULATOR
see order pages for details

Family Get-Away
PRICE CODE: B

■ This plan features:
— Three bedrooms
— Two full and one half baths
■ A wrap-around Porch for views and visiting provides access into the Great Room and Dining Area
■ A spacious Great Room with a two-story ceiling and dormer window above a massive fireplace
■ A combination Dining/Kitchen with an island work area and breakfast bar opening to a Great Room and adjacent to the Laundry/Storage and half Bath area
■ A private two-story Master Bedroom with a dormer window, walk-in closet, double vanity Bath and optional Deck with hot tub
■ Two additional Bedrooms on the second floor sharing a full Bath

First floor — 1,061 sq. ft.
Second floor — 499 sq. ft.
Basement — 1,061 sq. ft.

Total Living Area:
1,560 sq. ft.

PLAN NO. 34602

SECOND FLOOR

Br 2
10-10 x 12-6

Br 3
11-6 x 12-6

1/2 wall
open to great room below
DN
master bedroom below

Alternate Foundation Plan

Optional Deck w/ Hot Tub
furn
privacy fence
crawl space access
stair
Master Br

FIRST FLOOR

44'-0"
34'-0"

Dining
9-3 x 12-7

Kitchen
8-7 x 12-7

storage

Optional Deck w/ Hot Tub
privacy fence

breakfast bar
flat clg @ 9'

line of floor above

Master Br
12-0 x 14-6

Great Room
14-7 x 14-10

flat clg @ 15'-7"

Porch

Balcony Overlooks
Living Room Below
PRICE CODE: A

■ This plan features:
— Three bedrooms
— Two full and one half baths
■ A vaulted ceiling Living Room with a balcony above and a fireplace
■ An efficient, well-equipped Kitchen with stovetop island and easy flow of traffic into the Dining Room
■ A deck accessible from the Living Room
■ A luxurious Master Suite with a bay window seat, walk-in closet, Dressing Area, and a private shower
■ Two additional Bedrooms that share a full hall Bath

Main floor — 674 sq. ft.
Upper floor — 677 sq. ft.
Basement — 674 sq. ft.

PLAN NO. 90356

Total Living Area:
1,351 sq. ft.

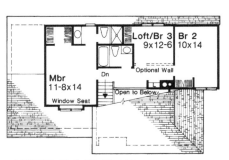

Loft/Br 3
9x12-6

Br 2
10x14

Mbr
11-8x14

Dn
Optional Wall

Window Seat
Open to Below

UPPER FLOOR PLAN

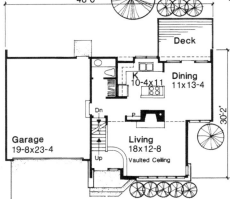

48'-0"
30'-2"

Deck

K
10-4x11

Dining
11x13-4

Dn
P

Garage
19-8x23-4

Living
18x12-8
Vaulted Ceiling

Up

MAIN FLOOR PLAN

© Frank Betz Associates

Refinement with Brilliancy
PRICE CODE: E

■ This plan features:
— Four bedrooms
— Three full baths

■ Two-story foyer dominated by an open rail staircase

■ Two story Family Room enhanced by a fireplace

■ Walk-in pantry and ample counter space highlighting the Breakfast room

■ Secluded Study easily becoming an additional bedroom with a private bath

■ Second floor Master Suite with tray ceiling, bayed sitting area and a vaulted ceiling over the private bath

■ An optional basement, slab or crawl space foundation — please specify when ordering

■ No material list is available for this plan

FIRST FLOOR — 1,548 SQ. FT.
SECOND FLOOR — 1,164 SQ. FT.
BONUS — 198 SQ. FT.
BASEMENT — 1,548 SQ. FT.
GARAGE — 542 SQ. FT.

TOTAL LIVING AREA:
2,712 SQ. FT.

FIRST FLOOR PLAN
54'-6"
52'-0"

Breakfast
FRENCH DOOR
FP.
Bedroom 4/ Study 12'0 x 12'2
PANTRY
MICRO OVEN COMBO
DW.
SURFACE UNIT
Bath
Kitchen
Two Story Family Room 20'0 x 15'0
LINEN
REF.
Laund.
D W
LINEN
COATS
BUTLER'S PANTRY
STAIRS DN.
OPEN RAIL
Garage 20'0 x 25'0
Dining Room 13'0 x 13'0
Two Story Foyer
Vaulted Living Room 11'8 x 13'3
VLT.

SECOND FLOOR PLAN
PLANT SHELF ABOVE
Sitting Area
RADIUS WINDOW
RADIUS WINDOW
W.I.C.
Vaulted M.Bath
TRAY CLG.
Master Suite 16'8 x 21'8
Family Room Below
SHWR.
LINEN
W.I.C.
Bedroom 2 12'0 x 12'0
W.I.C.
OVERLOOK
STAIRS DN.
Bath
W.I.C.
W.I.C.
Bedroom 3 13'0 x 12'0
Foyer Below
Opt. Bonus 12'5 x 12'3

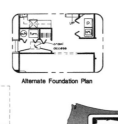

Country Porch
Topped by Dormer
PRICE CODE: A

■ This plan features:
— Three bedrooms
— Two full baths

■ Front Porch offers outdoor living and leads into tiled entry and spacious Living Room with focal point fireplace

■ Side entrance leads into Utility Room and central Foyer with a landing staircase

■ Country-size Kitchen with cooktop island, bright Breakfast Area and access to Deck

■ Second floor Master Bedroom offers lovely dormer window, vaulted ceiling, walk-in closet and double vanity Bath

■ Two additional Bedrooms with ample closets, share a full Bath

FIRST FLOOR — 1,035 SQ. FT.
SECOND FLOOR — 435 SQ. FT.
BASEMENT — 1,018 SQ. FT.

TOTAL LIVING AREA:
1,470 SQ. FT.

FIRST FLOOR
35'-0"
42'-0"

Deck
Brkfst 4'-0 x 6'-0
flat clg.
Kit. 11'-6 x 4'-9
Foyer flat clg.
Utility
Br #2 12'-2 x 4'-11
UP
Living Rm 18'-11 x 12'-11
Br #3 12'-2 x 4'-9
Porch

SECOND FLOOR
open to below
DN
Master Br 14'-5 x 12'-11

Alternate Foundation Plan
crawl access

ZIP QUOTE
GARLINGHOUSE
HOME COST CALCULATOR
see order pages for details

To order your Blueprints, call 1-800-235-5700

Charming Bow Window

Price Code: A

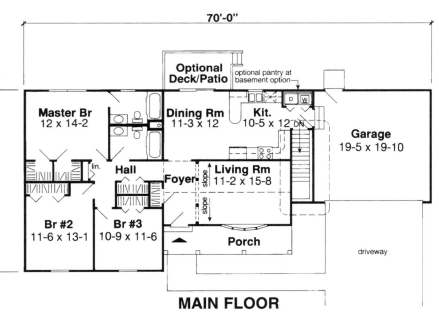

Optional Deck/Patio

optional pantry at basement option

Master Br
12 x 14-2

Dining Rm
11-3 x 12

Kit.
10-5 x 12 DN

Garage
19-5 x 19-10

lin.

Hall

Foyer

slope

Living Rm
11-2 x 15-8

slope

D W

Br #2
11-6 x 13-1

Br #3
10-9 x 11-6

Porch

driveway

70'-0"

MAIN FLOOR

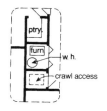

ptry.

furn

w. h.

crawl access

Crawl Space / Slab Option

■ This plan features:

— Three bedrooms

— Two full baths

■ An inviting Porch leads into Foyer and Living Room with a bow window and sloping ceiling

■ Open Kitchen provides easy access to Dining Room, Deck/Patio, Laundry and Garage

■ Private Master Bedroom offers two walk-in closets and a full Bath

■ Two additional Bedrooms with large closets, share a full Bath in the hall

MAIN FLOOR — 1,373 SQ. FT.
GARAGE — 400 SQ. FT.

TOTAL LIVING AREA:
1,373 SQ. FT.

© 1993 Donald A. Gardner Architects, Inc.

B. NATHAN

Quaint and Cozy

Price Code: D

■ This plan features:

— Three bedrooms

— Two full and one half baths

■ Spacious floor plan with large Great Room crowned by cathedral ceiling

■ Central Kitchen with angled counter opens to the Breakfast Area and Great Room for easy entertaining

■ Privately located Master Bedroom has a cathedral ceiling and nearby access to the Deck with an optional Spa

■ Operable skylights over the tub accent the luxurious Master Bath

■ Bonus room over the Garage makes expanding easy

MAIN FLOOR — 1,864 SQ. FT.
GARAGE — 614 SQ. FT.
BONUS — 420 SQ. FT.

TOTAL LIVING AREA:
1,864 SQ. FT.

ZIP QUOTE
HOME COST CALCULATOR
see order pages for details

© 1993 Donald A Gardner Architects, Inc.

To order your Blueprints, call 1-800-235-5700

© 1997 Donald A Gardner Architects, Inc.

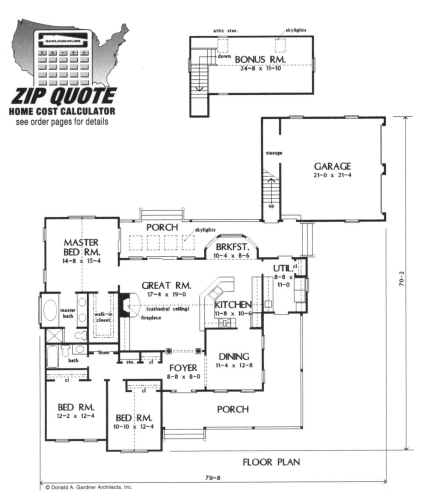

ZIP QUOTE
HOME COST CALCULATOR
see order pages for details

attic stor.   skylights
BONUS RM.
24-8 x 11-10
down

storage
GARAGE
21-0 x 21-4
up

PORCH   skylights

BRKFST.
10-4 x 8-6

UTIL. cl.
8-8 x 11-0

70-2

MASTER BED RM.
14-8 x 15-4

GREAT RM.
17-4 x 19-0
(cathedral ceiling)
fireplace

master bath

walk-in closet

KITCHEN
11-8 x 10-6

linen   sto.   cl

DINING
11-4 x 12-8

bath

cl

FOYER
8-8 x 8-0

BED RM.
12-2 x 12-4

BED RM.
10-10 x 12-4

cl

PORCH

FLOOR PLAN

70-8

© Donald A. Gardner Architects, Inc.

Country-Style Home With Corner Porch

Price Code: D

■ This plan features:

— Three bedrooms

— Two full baths

■ Dining Room has four floor to ceiling windows that overlook front Porch

■ Great Room topped by a cathedral ceiling, enhanced by a fireplace, and sliding doors to the back Porch

■ Utility Room located near Kitchen and Breakfast Nook

■ Master Bedroom has a walk-in closet and private Bath

■ Two additional Bedrooms with ample closet space share a full Bath

■ A skylight Bonus Room over the two-car Garage

MAIN FLOOR — 1,815 SQ. FT.
GARAGE — 522 SQ. FT.
BONUS — 336 SQ. FT.

TOTAL LIVING AREA:
1,815 SQ. FT.

© 1996 Donald A. Gardner Architects, Inc.

Compact Plan

Price Code: C

■ This plan features:

— Three bedrooms

— Two full baths

■ A Great Room topped by a cathedral ceiling, combining with the openness of the adjoining Dining Room and Kitchen, to create a spacious living area

■ A bay window enlarging the Dining Room and a palladian window allowing ample light into the Great Room

■ An efficient U-shaped Kitchen leading directly to the garage, convenient for unloading groceries

■ A Master Suite highlighted by ample closet space and a private a skylit Bath enhanced by a dual vanity and a separate tub and shower

MAIN FLOOR — 1,372 SQ. FT.
GARAGE & STORAGE — 537 SQ. FT.

TOTAL LIVING AREA:
1,372 SQ. FT.

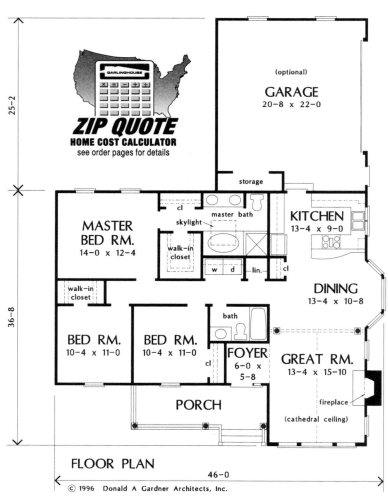

ZIP QUOTE
HOME COST CALCULATOR
see order pages for details

GARAGE (optional)
20-8 x 22-0

storage

MASTER BED RM.
14-0 x 12-4

cl

master bath

skylight

walk-in closet

KITCHEN
13-4 x 9-0

w d lin.

cl

walk-in closet

DINING
13-4 x 10-8

BED RM.
10-4 x 11-0

BED RM.
10-4 x 11-0

bath

cl

FOYER
6-0 x 5-8

GREAT RM.
13-4 x 15-10

fireplace

(cathedral ceiling)

PORCH

25-2

36-8

46-0

FLOOR PLAN

© 1996 Donald A Gardner Architects, Inc.

To order your Blueprints, call 1-800-235-5700

Inviting Front Porch
PRICE CODE: B

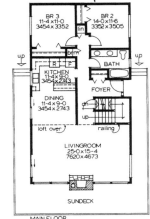

PLAN NO. 93298

This plan features:
- Three bedrooms
- Two full and one half baths
- Detailed gables and inviting front Porch create a warm welcoming facade
- Open Foyer features an angled staircase, a half Bath and a coat closet
- The expansive, informal living area at the rear of the home features a fireplace and opens onto the Sun Deck
- The efficient Kitchen has easy access to both the formal and informal Dining Areas
- Master Bedroom includes a walk-in closet and compartmented private Bath
- Two secondary Bedrooms share a Bath with a double vanity
- An optional basement, crawl space or slab foundation — please specify when ordering
- No materials list is available for this plan

FIRST FLOOR — 797 SQ. FT.
SECOND FLOOR — 886 SQ. FT.
BASEMENT — 797 SQ. FT.
GARAGE — 414 SQ. FT.

TOTAL LIVING AREA:
1,683 SQ. FT.

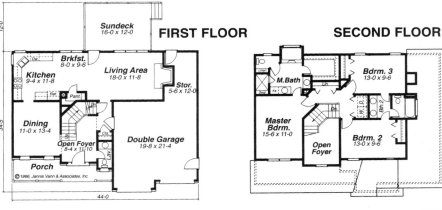

FIRST FLOOR **SECOND FLOOR**

A–Frame for Year-Round Living
PRICE CODE: B

PLAN NO. 90930

This plan features:
- Three bedrooms
- One full and one three-quarter baths
- A vaulted ceiling in the Living Room with a massive fireplace
- A wrap-around Sun Deck that gives you a lot of outdoor living space
- A luxurious Master Suite complete with a walk-in closet, full Bath and private Deck
- Two additional Bedrooms that share a full hall Bath

MAIN FLOOR — 1,238 SQ. FT.
LOFT — 464 SQ. FT.
BASEMENT — 1,175 SQ. FT.

TOTAL LIVING AREA:
1,702 SQ. FT.

WIDTH 34'-0"
DEPTH 56'-0"

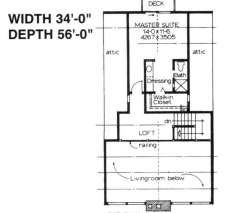

Open Space Living
PRICE CODE: B

■ This plan features:
— Three bedrooms
— Two full and one half baths
■ A wrap-around Deck providing outdoor living space, ideal for a sloping lot
■ Two and a half-story glass wall and two separate atrium doors providing natural light for the Living/Dining Room area
■ An efficient galley Kitchen with easy access to the Dining Area
■ A Master Bedroom with a half Bath and ample closet space
■ Another Bedroom on the first floor adjoins a full hall Bath
■ A second floor Bedroom/Studio, with a private Deck, adjacent to a full hall bath and a Loft area

FIRST FLOOR — 1,086 SQ. FT.
SECOND FLOOR — 466 SQ. FT.
BASEMENT — 1,080 SQ. FT.

TOTAL LIVING AREA: 1,552 SQ. FT.

FIRST FLOOR

SECOND FLOOR

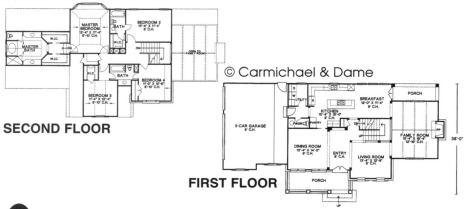

A Livable Home
PRICE CODE: E

■ This plan features:
— Four bedrooms
— Two full, one three-quarter and one half baths
■ The Master Bedroom is complete with a tray ceiling, two walk-in closets, and a large Bath
■ Three additional Bedrooms upstairs, all have ample closet space and share two full Baths
■ The Dining and Living rooms both have decorative windows that let in plenty of light
■ The Family Room has a beamed ceiling and a fireplace
■ This home has a three-car Garage with plenty of storage space

FIRST FLOOR — 1,400 SQ. FT.
SECOND FLOOR — 1,315 SQ. FT.
BASEMENT — 1,400 SQ. FT.
GARAGE — 631 SQ. FT.

TOTAL LIVING AREA: 2,715 SQ. FT.

© Carmichael & Dame

SECOND FLOOR

FIRST FLOOR

ZIP QUOTE
HOME COST CALCULATOR
see order pages for details

© 1990 Donald A. Gardner Architects, Inc.

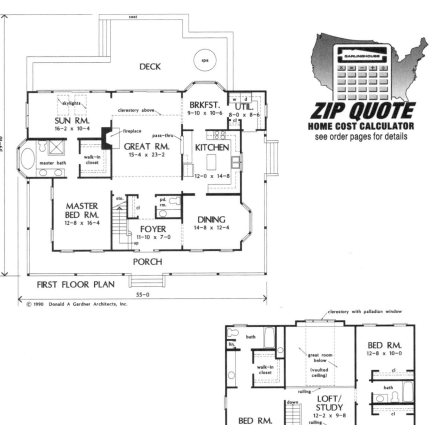

DECK

spa

seat

SUN RM.
16-2 x 10-4

skylights

clerestory above

fireplace

BRKFST.
9-10 x 10-6

w   d

UTIL.
8-0 x 8-6

cl

pass-thru

GREAT RM.
15-4 x 23-2

walk-in
closet

KITCHEN

12-0 x 14-8

master bath

MASTER
BED RM.
12-8 x 16-4

sto.

cl

pd.
rm.

DINING
14-8 x 12-4

FOYER
11-10 x 7-0
up

PORCH

FIRST FLOOR PLAN

55-0

© 1990 Donald A Gardner Architects, Inc.

ZIP QUOTE
HOME COST CALCULATOR
see order pages for details

Stately Elegance
Price Code: F

■ This plan features:
— Four bedrooms

— Three full and one half baths

■ Impressive double gable roof with front and rear palladian windows and wrap-around Porch

■ Vaulted ceilings in two-story Foyer and Great Room accommodates Loft/Study Area

■ Spacious, first floor Master Bedroom suite offers walk-in closet and luxurious Bath

■ Living space expanded outdoors by wrap-around Porch and large Deck

■ Upstairs, one of three Bedrooms could be a second master suite

FIRST FLOOR — 1,734 SQ. FT.
SECOND FLOOR — 958 SQ. FT.

TOTAL LIVING AREA: 2,692 SQ. FT.

clerestory with palladian window

bath

lin.

walk-in
closet

great room
below

(vaulted
ceiling)

BED RM.
12-8 x 10-0

cl

railing

bath

cl

BED RM.
12-8 x 16-4

down

LOFT/
STUDY
12-2 x 9-8

railing

(vaulted
ceiling)
foyer
below

BED RM.
12-8 x 10-0

clerestory with palladian window

SECOND FLOOR PLAN

To order your Blueprints, call 1-800-235-5700

Stately Exterior with an Open Interior

Price Code: E

■ This plan features:

— Four bedrooms

— Two full and one half baths

■ Open entry accented by a lovely landing staircase and access to quiet Study and formal Dining Room

■ Central Family Room with an inviting fireplace and a cathedral ceiling extending into Kitchen

■ Spacious Kitchen offers a work island/snackbar, built-in Pantry, glass Breakfast Area and nearby Porch, Utilities and Garage entry

■ Secluded Master Bedroom enhanced by a large walk-in closet and lavish Bath

■ No materials list is available for this plan

FIRST FLOOR — 1,906 SQ. FT.
SECOND FLOOR — 749 SQ. FT.
BASEMENT — 1,906 SQ. FT.
GARAGE — 682 SQ. FT.

ZIP QUOTE
HOME COST CALCULATOR
see order pages for details

TOTAL LIVING AREA:
2,655 SQ. FT.

© Carmichael & Dame

© Frank Betz Associates

FIRST FLOOR
No. 97210

SECOND FLOOR

Notable Exterior
Price Code: E

- ■ This plan features:
  - — Four bedrooms
  - — Three full baths
- ■ Two-story Foyer adds a feeling of volume
- ■ Family Room topped by vaulted ceiling and accented by a fireplace
- ■ Formal Living Room with an eleven-foot ceiling
- ■ Private Master Suite with a five-piece Bath and a large walk-in closet
- ■ Rear Bedroom/Study located close a full Bath
- ■ No materials list is available for this plan
- ■ An optional basement, slab or crawl space foundation — please specify when ordering

FIRST FLOOR — 2,003 SQ. FT.
SECOND FLOOR — 598 SQ. FT.
BONUS — 321 SQ. FT.
BASEMENT — 2,003 SQ. FT.
GARAGE — 546 SQ. FT.

TOTAL LIVING AREA:
2,601 SQ. FT.

Spectacular Views
PRICE CODE: E

■ This plan features:
— Four Bedrooms
— Two full and one three-quarter baths
■ Creates an indoor/outdoor relationship with terrific deck and large glass expanses
■ Family Room and Living Room enjoy highly glassed walls taking in the vistas
■ Living Room enhanced by a cathedral ceiling and a warm fireplace
■ Dining Room and Kitchen are in an open layout and highlighted by a center cooktop island/snack bar in the Kitchen and large window in the Dining Room
■ Master Bedroom enhanced by floor to ceiling windowed area allowing natural light to filter in
■ Two additional downstairs Bedrooms, a three quartered Bath and a Family Room complete the lower level

FIRST FLOOR — 1,707 SQ. FT.
BASEMENT FLOOR — 901 SQ. FT.

TOTAL LIVING AREA: 2,608 SQ. FT.

First Floor — 61'-0", 34'-6"
Util. 13-6 x 7-2
Br #2 14 x 9-6
M.Bath
Dining 11-6 x 15
CATH. CLG.
Living 18 x 20
Kit.
M. Br 12-6 x 14-6
Entry
Deck / Deck

Basement Floor
Shop 18 x 9
Br #3 11-6 x 10-6
Garage 23-6 x 25
STOR.
Family 18 x 20
Br #4 11 x 11-2
DECK LINE ABOVE

©1995 Donald A. Gardner Architects, Inc.

Country Charm and Modern Convenience
PRICE CODE: E

■ This plan features:
— Three bedrooms
— Two full and one half baths
■ Great Room topped by a cathedral ceiling and a cozy fireplace with built-ins
■ Centrally located Kitchen with a nearby Pantry serving the informal Breakfast Area and the formal Dining Area
■ Elegantly appointed Master Suite with a walk-in closet and a Bath with a whirlpool tub, shower and dual vanity
■ Sitting Room with a bay window off the Master Suite
■ Balcony overlooking Great Room below
■ Two secondary Bedrooms sharing a full Bath

FIRST FLOOR — 1,778 SQ. FT.
SECOND FLOOR — 592 SQ. FT.
GARAGE & STORAGE — 622 SQ. FT.
BONUS ROOM — 404 SQ. FT.

TOTAL LIVING AREA: 2,370 SQ. FT.

FIRST FLOOR PLAN — 81-0, 44-2, 9-8
DECK
SITTING 17-8 x 8-10
GREAT RM. 15-4 x 21-2 (cathedral ceiling) fireplace / balcony above
BRKFST. 10-8 x 9-10
UTILITY 8-8 x 7-10
w d
walk-in closet
KIT. 12-8 x 13-8
pan.
GARAGE 22-0 x 21-10
storage
master bath
MASTER BED RM. 12-8 x 16-4
FOYER 11-10 x 7-2
DINING RM. 12-8 x 12-8
PORCH

SECOND FLOOR PLAN
great room below
attic storage
railing
attic storage
BED RM. 12-8 x 13-0
BED RM. 12-8 x 13-0
down
bath
foyer below

skylights
BONUS RM. 22-0 x 13-0
down

© 1995 Donald A Gardner Architects, Inc.

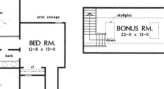

To order your Blueprints, call 1-800-235-5700

Attention to Details
PRICE CODE: B

This plan features:
- Three bedrooms
- Two full and one half baths
- Foyer, Family Room, and Dining Room have 15'8" ceilings
- Breakfast Room and the Master Bath have vaulted ceilings
- Master Suite topped by a tray ceiling
- Arched openings to the Dining Room from the Family Room and Foyer
- Split Bedroom floor plan, affording additional privacy to the Master Suite
- Master Suite enhanced by a five-piece master Bath and a walk-in closet
- An optional basement or crawl space foundation — please specify when ordering
- No materials list is available for this plan

MAIN FLOOR — 1,575 SQ. FT
BASEMENT — 1,612 SQ. FT.
GARAGE — 456 SQ. FT.

TOTAL LIVING AREA:
1,575 SQ. FT.

© Frank Betz Associates

Beautiful Arched Window
PRICE CODE: C

This plan features:
- Three bedrooms
- Two full baths
- Ten-foot ceilings topping the Entry and the Great Room
- A see-through fireplace is shared between the Great Room and the Hearth Room
- Built-in entertainment center and a bayed window highlighting the Hearth Room
- Breakfast Room and Hearth Room in an open layout separated by only a snack bar in the Kitchen
- Built-in Pantry and corner sinks enhancing efficiency in the Kitchen
- Split Bedroom plan assuring homeowner's privacy in the Master Suite which includes a decorative ceiling, private Bath and a large walk-in closet
- Two additional Bedrooms at the opposite side of the home share a full, skylit Bath in the hall

MAIN FLOOR — 1,911 SQ. FT.
GARAGE — 481 SQ. FT.

TOTAL LIVING AREA:
1,911 SQ. FT.

© design basics, inc.

MAIN FLOOR

MAIN FLOOR PLAN

A Very Distinctive Ranch
PRICE CODE: C

■ This plan features:
— Three bedrooms
— Two full and one half baths
■ This hip roofed ranch has an exterior mixing brick and siding
■ The recessed entrance has sidelights which work to create a formal entry
■ The formal Dining Room has a butler's Pantry for added convenience
■ The Great Room features a vaulted ceiling and a fireplace for added atmosphere
■ The large open Kitchen has ample cupboard space and spacious Breakfast Area
■ The Master Suite includes a walk-in closet, private Bath and an elegant bay window
■ A Laundry Room is on the main floor between the three car Garage and the Kitchen
■ No materials list is available for this plan

MAIN FLOOR — 1,947 SQ. FT.
BASEMENT — 1,947 SQ. FT.

TOTAL LIVING AREA:
1,947 SQ. FT.

© 1994 Donald A. Gardner Architects, Inc.

FIRST FLOOR PLAN
© Donald A. Gardner Architects, Inc.

SECOND FLOOR PLAN

Focal-Point Family Room
PRICE CODE: E

■ This plan features:
— Three bedrooms
— Two full and one half baths
■ A balcony overlooks the Family Room, which has a fireplace and Patio access
■ The Dining Room and Living Room/Study are showcased in the front of the home
■ A patio expands living space to the outdoors
■ A bayed Sitting Area accents the Master Suite

FIRST FLOOR — 1,715 SQ. FT.
SECOND FLOOR — 620 SQ. FT.
BONUS — 265 SQ. FT.
GARAGE — 555 SQ. FT.

TOTAL LIVING AREA:
2,335 SQ. FT.

To order your Blueprints, call 1-800-235-5700

Life's Simple Pleasures

PRICE CODE: E

This plan features:
- Three bedrooms
- Two full and one half baths
- Living Room/Study with an optional fireplace
- Large Dining Room is convenient to the Kitchen
- Kitchen is well equipped with a cooktop island
- Sunny Breakfast Room with a window wall also access the Patio
- Family Room has a beamed ceiling and a fireplace
- Located upstairs are three large Bedrooms and two full Baths

FIRST FLOOR — 1,428 SQ. FT.
SECOND FLOOR — 1,067 SQ. FT.
BONUS — 342 SQ. FT.
GARAGE — 584 SQ. FT.

TOTAL LIVING AREA: 2,495 SQ. FT.

© 1996 Donald A Gardner Architects, Inc.

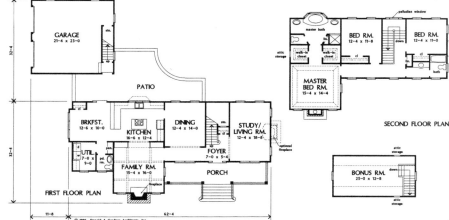

Brick Magnificence

PRICE CODE: E

This plan features:
- Four bedrooms
- Three full baths
- Large windows and attractive brick detailing using segmented arches give fantastic curb appeal
- Convenient Ranch layout allows for step-saving one floor ease
- A fireplace in the Living Room adds a warm ambience
- The Family Room sports a second fireplace and built-in shelving
- Two additional Bedrooms include private access to a full double vanity Bath
- No materials list is available for this plan

MAIN FLOOR — 2,858 SQ. FT.
GARAGE — 768 SQ. FT.

TOTAL LIVING AREA: 2,858 SQ. FT.

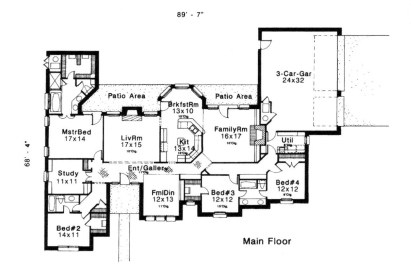

Perfect for a Woodland Setting

PRICE CODE: A

- This plan features:
  — Two bedrooms
  — One full bath
- A Living Room and Dining Room/Kitchen located to th[e] front of the house
- A sloped ceiling adding to the cozy feeling of the home
- A built-in entertainment center in the Living Room adding convenience
- An L-shaped Kitchen that includes a double sink and Dining area
- A full hall Bath easily accessible from either Bedroom
- A Loft and Balcony that overlooks the Living Room an[d] the Dining area
- Storage on either side of the Loft

FIRST FLOOR — 763 SQ. FT.
SECOND FLOOR — 264 SQ. FT.

TOTAL LIVING AREA:
1,027 SQ. FT.

First Floor

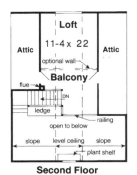

Second Floor

European Richness

PRICE CODE: F

- This plan features:
  — Four bedrooms
  — Three full and one half baths
- The exterior of this home is graced by dual box bay win[dows] dows and curved stairs
- A grand Foyer leading to the Gallery greets your guests
- The Dining Room and the Library each take advantage of light from their front windows
- The immense Master Suite includes a huge walk-in closet and Bath
- Informal gathering can be held in the warm Hearth Room or the Breakfast nook
- A rear terrace is perfect for entertaining in warm weath[er]
- A three-car Garage completes this luxurious home
- No materials list is available for this plan

FIRST FLOOR — 3,392 SQ. FT.
SECOND FLOOR — 1,197 SQ. FT.
BASEMENT — 3,392 SQ. FT.

TOTAL LIVING AREA:
4,589 SQ. FT.

WIDTH 87'-0"
DEPTH 82'-0'

To order your Blueprints, call 1-800-235-5700

Victorian Accents the Exterior

PRICE CODE: D

© 1991 Donald A. Gardner Architects, Inc.

■ This plan features:
– Three bedrooms
– Two full baths

The covered wrap around Porch connects to the rear Deck

■ The Foyer opens into the octagonal Great Room that is warmed by a fireplace

■ The Dining Room has a tray ceiling and convenient access to the Kitchen

■ The galley Kitchen opens into the Breakfast Bay

■ The Master Bedroom has a Bay Area in the rear, a walk-in closet, and a fully appointed Bath

■ Two more Bedrooms complete this plan as does another full Bath

MAIN FLOOR — 1,865 SQ. FT.
GARAGE — 505 SQ. FT.

TOTAL LIVING AREA:
1,865 SQ. FT.

MAIN FLOOR

© 1991 Donald A. Gardner Architects, Inc.

Flexible Spaces

PRICE CODE: D

©1994 Donald A. Gardner Architects, Inc.

■ This plan features:
– Three bedrooms
– Two full and one half baths

■ The large common area combines the Great Room and the Dining Room under a vaulted ceiling that is punctuated with skylights

■ The Kitchen/Breakfast Bay includes a peninsula counter/snack bar

■ From the Great Room extend entertaining outdoors to the covered back Porch

■ The Master Suite has a generous Bath and ample closet space

■ The front Bedroom/Study doubles as a Guest Room

■ On the second floor the Loft/Study makes a terrific Office or Play Room

FIRST FLOOR — 1,234 SQ. FT.
SECOND FLOOR — 609 SQ. FT.
GARAGE — 496 SQ. FT.

TOTAL LIVING AREA:
1,843 SQ. FT.

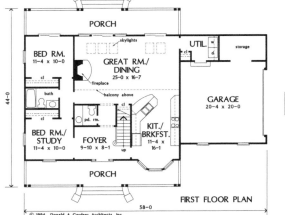

FIRST FLOOR PLAN

SECOND FLOOR PLAN

© 1994 Donald A Gardner Architects, Inc.

Bricks and Arches
Detail this Ranch

Price Code: D

■ This plan features:

— Two bedrooms

— Two full and one half baths

■ A Master Bedroom with a vaulted ceiling, luxurious bath, complimented by a skylit walk-in closet

■ A second Bedroom shares a full Bath with the Den/optional Bedroom, which has built-in curio cabinets

■ Columns and arched windows define the elegant Dining Room

■ A Great Room shares a see-through fireplace with the Hearth Room, which also has a built-in entertainment center

■ A gazebo-shaped Nook opening into the Kitchen with a center island, snack bar and desk

MAIN FLOOR — 2,512 SQ. FT.
GARAGE — 783 SQ. FT.

TOTAL LIVING AREA:
2,512 SQ. FT.

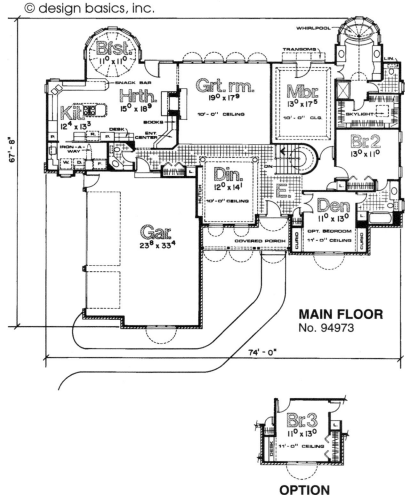

© design basics, inc.

MAIN FLOOR
No. 94973

74' - 0"

OPTION

Br. 3
11⁰ x 13⁰
11'-0" CEILING

To order your Blueprints, call 1-800-235-5700

Luxurious Appointments
PRICE CODE: F

This plan features:
– Five bedrooms
– Four full and one half baths

■ Formal areas located conveniently to promote elegant entertaining and family interaction

■ Arched openings from the Foyer into the formal Dining Room and the Living Room

■ Decorative columns highlighting the entrance to the Breakfast Room

■ Two-Story ceiling topping the Family Room, highlighted by a fireplace

■ Efficiency emphasized in the island Kitchen with a walk-in Pantry and abundant counter space

■ Master Suite with lavish Bath topped by a vaulted ceiling

■ An optional basement or crawl space foundation — please specify when ordering

■ No material list is available for this plan

FIRST FLOOR — 1,527 SQ. FT.
SECOND FLOOR — 1,495 SQ. FT.
BASEMENT — 1,527 SQ. FT.
GARAGE — 440 SQ. FT.

TOTAL LIVING AREA:
3,022 SQ. FT.

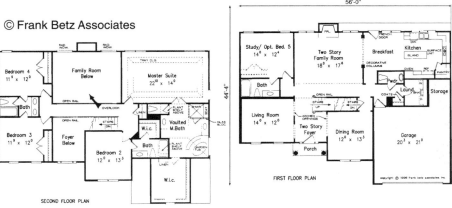

© Frank Betz Associates

Compact and Convenient Colonial
PRICE CODE: A

■ This plan features:
– Three bedrooms
– Two full and one half baths

■ Traditional Entry with landing staircase, closet and powder room

■ Living Room with focal point fireplace opens to formal Dining Room for ease in entertaining

■ Efficient, L-shaped Kitchen with built-in Pantry, eating Nook and Garage entry

■ Corner Master Bedroom with private Bath and attic access

■ Two additional Bedrooms with ample closets share a double vanity Bath

FIRST FLOOR — 624 SQ. FT.
SECOND FLOOR — 624 SQ. FT.
GARAGE — 510 SQ. FT.

TOTAL LIVING AREA:
1,248 SQ. FT.

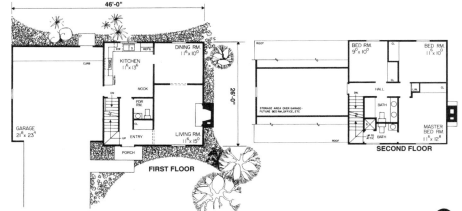

To order your Blueprints, call 1-800-235-5700

Luxurious Masterpiece
PRICE CODE: F

- This plan features:
— Four bedrooms
— Three full and one half baths
- An elegant and distinguished exterior
- An expansive formal Living Room with a fourteen-foot ceiling and a raised hearth fireplace
- Informal Family Room offers another fireplace, wetbar, cathedral ceiling and access to the covered Patio
- A hub Kitchen with a cooktop island, peninsula counter/snackbar, and a bright Breakfast Area
- French doors lead into a quiet Study offering many uses
- Private Master Bedroom enhanced by a pullman ceiling, lavish his and her Baths, and a garden window tub in one of them
- Three additional Bedrooms with walk-in closets and private access to a full Bath
- No materials list is available for this plan

MAIN FLOOR — 3,818 SQ. FT.
GARAGE — 816 SQ. FT.

TOTAL LIVING AREA:
3,818 SQ. FT.

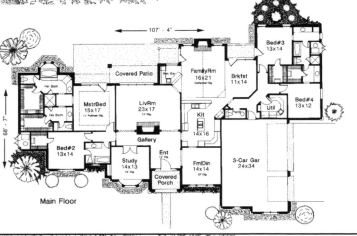

Main Floor

© 1992 Donald A. Gardner Architects, Inc.

Country on the Outside,
Contemporary on the Inside
PRICE CODE: D

- This plan features:
— Three bedrooms
— Two full baths
- Wrap-around Porch and rear Deck expanding living outdoors
- Columns dramatically open and lead the Foyer into a generous Great Room
- Great Room open to the Kitchen/Breakfast area for a feeling of more space
- Natural light from the dormer windows flow into Foyer and Dining Room
- Master Suite is privately located at the rear pampered by a private Bath and a walk-in closet
- Two front Bedrooms share the full hall Bath

MAIN FLOOR — 1,590 SQ. FT.
GARAGE & STORAGE — 506 SQ. FT.

TOTAL LIVING AREA:
1,590 SQ. FT.

© 1992 Donald A. Gardner Architects, Inc.

To order your Blueprints, call 1-800-235-5700

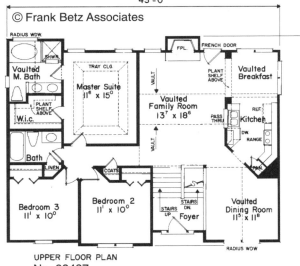

© Frank Betz Associates

43'-0"

RADIUS WDW.

Vaulted M. Bath

TRAY CLG.

Master Suite
11⁶ x 15⁰

Vaulted Family Room
13⁷ x 18⁶

FPL.

FRENCH DOOR

Vaulted Breakfast

PLANT SHELF ABOVE

Kitchen

PASS THRU

REF.

DW.

RANGE

PAN.

PLANT SHELF ABOVE

W.i.c.

Bath

LINEN

COATS

Bedroom 3
11' x 10⁰

Bedroom 2
11' x 10⁰

STAIRS UP

STAIRS DN.

Foyer

Vaulted Dining Room
11⁵' x 11⁸

33'-6"

RADIUS WDW

UPPER FLOOR PLAN
No. 98487

TOTAL LIVING AREA:
1,401 SQ. FT.

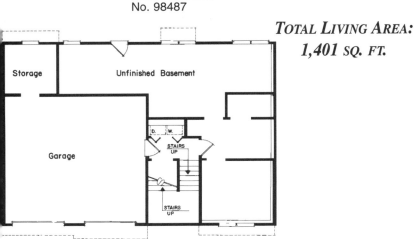

Storage

Unfinished Basement

Garage

D. W.

STAIRS UP

STAIRS UP

LOWER LEVEL PLAN

Voluminous Vaulted Ceilings

Price Code: A

■ This plan features:

— Three bedrooms

— Two full baths

■ The Dining Room, Family Room and Breakfast Nook have vaulted ceilings

■ The Family Room has a rear wall fireplace with a French door to one side

■ There is a plant shelf above the entrance to the Nook

■ With an angle at one end a new twist is placed on this galley style Kitchen

■ The Master Suite has a tray ceiling as well as a private Bath

■ Two identical Bedrooms are located next to each other and share a Bath in the hall

■ On the lower level find the garage and plenty of unfinished space

■ No materials list is available for this plan

UPPER FLOOR — 1,349 SQ. FT.
FINISHED STAIRCASE — 52 SQ. FT.
BASEMENT — 871 SQ. FT.
GARAGE — 478 SQ. FT.

To order your Blueprints, call 1-800-235-5700

Southern Hospitality
PRICE CODE: C

■ This plan features:
— Three bedrooms
— Two full baths
■ Welcoming covered Veranda catches breezes
■ Easy-care, tiled Entry leads into Great Room with field-stone fireplace and atrium door to another covered Veranda topped by a cathedral ceiling
■ A bright Kitchen/Dining Room includes a stovetop island/ snackbar, built-in Pantry and desk and access to covered Veranda
■ Vaulted ceiling crowns Master Bedroom that offers a plush Bath and huge walk-in closet
■ Two additional Bedrooms with ample closets share a double vanity Bath

MAIN FLOOR — 1,830 SQ. FT.
GARAGE — 759 SQ. FT.

TOTAL LIVING AREA:
1,830 SQ. FT.

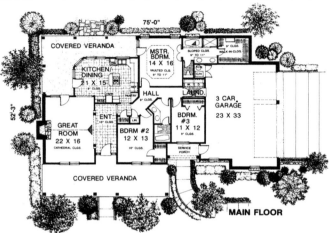

MAIN FLOOR

ZIP QUOTE
HOME COST CALCULATOR
see order pages for details

Simple Yet Practical
PRICE CODE: A

■ This plan features:
— One bedroom
— One full bath
■ Simple yet practical cabin designed for weekend retreats
■ A large Bedroom downstairs and a Loft upstairs provide plenty of sleeping room
■ Interesting sloped ceiling in the first floor living space
■ Efficient U-shaped Kitchen opens into Dining Area
■ Spacious front Deck

FIRST FLOOR — 763 SQ. FT.
SECOND FLOOR — 240 SQ. FT.

TOTAL LIVING AREA:
1,003 SQ. FT.

First Floor

Second Floor

Slab/ Crawl Space Option

U-Shaped Staircase
PRICE CODE: C

This plan features:
- Four bedrooms
- Two full and one half baths
- The Laundry room is conveniently located on the second floor, no traveling up and down the stairs with loaded laundry baskets
- A Butler's Pantry connects that Kitchen and the Dining Room will be helpful when entertaining
- No materials list is for this plan

FIRST FLOOR - 1,070 SQ. FT.
SECOND FLOOR - 1,050 SQ. FT.

TOTAL LIVING AREA:
2,120 SQ. FT.

SECOND FLOOR

FIRST FLOOR

Extra Special Luxuries
PRICE CODE: F

This plan features:
- Three bedrooms
- Two full and one half baths
- The Foyer leads to the formal Dining Room on the left
- The large Great Room includes a cathedral ceiling, a fireplace, built-ins and access to an airy Sun Room
- The Kitchen has a center work island and accent columns at the entrance to the Great Room
- Indulgent Master Suite with a skylit, plush Bath and a walk-in closet
- Two additional Bedrooms share the full Bath in the hall

MAIN FLOOR — 2,602 SQ. FT.
GARAGE — 715 SQ. FT.
BONUS — 399 SQ. FT.

TOTAL LIVING AREA:
2,602 SQ. FT.

© 1997 Donald A Gardner Architects, Inc.

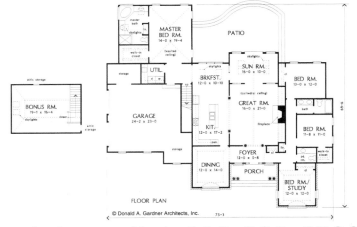

FLOOR PLAN

© Donald A. Gardner Architects, Inc.

© 1993 Donald A. Gardner Architects, Inc.

Windows Abound
PRICE CODE: E

- ■ This plan features:
- — Four bedrooms
- — Three full baths
- ■ Distinctive windows brighten this home
- ■ The Master Suite includes a walk-in closet, a quadruple window, and a Bath with a garden tub and double vanity
- ■ The grand Great Room topped by a cathedral ceiling and accented by a fireplace is a terrific place for family gatherings
- ■ The open floor plan between the Kitchen, Breakfast Area and the Great Room create the illusion of more space
- ■ Two additional Bedrooms are located on the second floor, each with a walk-in closet
- ■ A Bonus Room stands ready for future expansion

FIRST FLOOR — 1,839 SQ. FT.
SECOND FLOOR — 527 SQ. FT.
BONUS — 344 SQ. FT.
GARAGE — 517 SQ. FT.

TOTAL LIVING AREA:
2,366 SQ. FT.

FIRST FLOOR PLAN

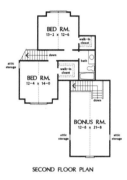

SECOND FLOOR PLAN

© 1993 Donald A. Gardner Architects, Inc.

Multiple Gables
PRICE CODE: D

- ■ This plan features:
- — Three bedrooms
- — Three full and one half baths
- ■ Impressive Foyer offers dramatic view past the Dining Room and open stairs through the Great Room to the rear yard
- ■ Exquisite columns, 13-ft ceiling heights and detailed ceiling treatments decorating the Dining Room and Great Room
- ■ Gourmet Kitchen with island and snack bar combines with the spacious Breakfast Room and the Hearth Room to create a warm atmosphere
- ■ The Master Suite has a fireplace complemented by a deluxe Dressing Room with whirlpool tub, shower and dual vanity
- ■ No materials list is available for this plan

MAIN FLOOR — 3,570 SQ. FT.
BASEMENT — 1,203 SQ. FT.
BONUS — 2,367 SQ. FT.

TOTAL LIVING AREA:
3,570 SQ. FT.

WIDTH 84'-6"
DEPTH 69'-4"

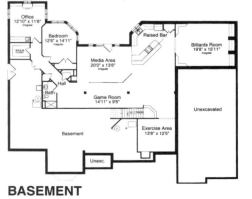

BASEMENT

MAIN FLOOR

To order your Blueprints, call 1-800-235-5700

Ten Foot Entry
PRICE CODE: B

This plan features:
- Three bedrooms
- Two full baths

Large volume Great Room highlighted by a fireplace flanked by windows

See-through wetbar enhancing the Breakfast Area and the Dining Room

Decorative ceiling treatment giving elegance to the Dining Room

Fully equipped Kitchen with a planning desk and a Pantry

Roomy Master Bedroom has a volume ceiling and special amenities; a skylighted dressing Bath area, plant shelf, a large walk-in closet, a double vanity and a whirlpool tub

Secondary Bedrooms with ample closets sharing a convenient hall Bath

MAIN FLOOR — 1,604 SQ. FT.

GARAGE — 466 SQ. FT.

TOTAL LIVING AREA
1,604 SQ. FT.

© design basics, inc.

MAIN FLOOR

Welcoming Front Porch
PRICE CODE: D

This plan features:
- Three bedrooms
- Two full and one half baths

The covered front Porch provides a warm welcome

The Great Room has a fireplace with built in cabinets to one side

Enter the nook through and arched soffit, the Kitchen is just beyond

Access the screen Porch from the nook

The Master Bedroom has a tray ceiling, a walk in closet, and a private Bath

Located upstairs for privacy are the secondary Bedrooms

This home has a three car Garage

There is no materials list available for this plan

FIRST FLOOR — 1,835 SQ. FT.

SECOND FLOOR — 573 SQ. FT.

BASEMENT — 1,835 SQ. FT.

TOTAL LIVING AREA:
2,408 SQ. FT.

FIRST FLOOR   **SECOND FLOOR**

Country Charm and Convenience
PRICE CODE: D

■ This plan features:
— Three bedrooms
— Two full baths
■ The open design pulls the Great Room, Kitchen and Breakfast Bay into one common area
■ Cathedral ceilings in the Great Room, Master Bedroom and a secondary Bedroom
■ The rear Deck expands the living and entertaining space
■ The Dining Room provides a quiet place for relaxed family dinners
■ Two additional Bedrooms share a full Bath

MAIN FLOOR — 1,512 SQ. FT.
GARAGE & STORAGE — 455 SQ. FT.

TOTAL LIVING AREA: 1,512 SQ. FT.

Stunning Family Plan
PRICE CODE: C

■ This plan features:
— Four bedrooms
— Two full and one half baths
■ Windows, brick, and columns combine to create an eye-catching elevation
■ A pair of columns greets you as you enter the Living Room
■ The formal Dining Room is located just steps away from the Kitchen
■ Set on a unique angle the Family Room has a rear wall fireplace
■ The open Kitchen has a center island, which makes for easy meal prep
■ Set away from the active areas the Master Bedroom is a quiet retreat
■ Three additional Bedrooms are located in their own wing of the home
■ A Patio in the rear and a two-car Garage complete this home plan
■ No materials list is available for this plan

MAIN FLOOR — 2,194 SQ. FT.
GARAGE — 462 SQ. FT.

TOTAL LIVING AREA : 2,194 SQ. FT.

To order your Blueprints, call 1-800-235-5700

SECOND FLOOR

Sit. 11 x 7

Mbr. 18⁸ x 15⁴ 9'-6" CEILING

DRESSING
SKYLIGHT
W/P
DRESSER
LINEN
CLOTHES CHUTE
LIN.

Br. 13⁰ x 12⁰

DN

OPEN TO BELOW

Br. 12⁴ x 13⁰ 12'-0" CEILING

Br. 11⁰ x 14⁰

TRANS.

© design basics, inc.

ZIP QUOTE
GARLINGHOUSE
HOME COST CALCULATOR
see order pages for details

FIRST FLOOR

Bfst. 11 x 13⁴

SNACK BAR
DESK
Kit. 22⁰ x 15⁰
SALAD SINK
WET BAR

Fam. rm. 21⁶ x 15⁰

TRANS.
11'-0" CEILING
Dn. 12⁰ x 13⁶

UP
R.
P.
DN
LAUNDRY
W.
F.

Gar. 22⁴ x 31⁴

ARCHED CEILING
Liv. rm. 15⁴ x 12'10"

UP

Libr. 13⁴ x 11⁷

BOOKS

COVERED STOOP

55'-4"

62'-0"

Glorious Gables

Price Code: F

■ This plan features:

— Four bedrooms

— Two full, one three-quarter and one half baths

■ Arched ceiling topping decorative windows

■ Hub Kitchen with angled, work island/snackbar

■ Comfortable Family Room with hearth fireplace framed by decorative windows

■ Private Master Bedroom Suite offers a Sitting Area, two walk-in closets, and luxurious Bath

■ Three additional Bedrooms with ample closets and private access to a full Bath

FIRST FLOOR — 1,709 SQ. FT.
SECOND FLOOR — 1,597 SQ. FT.
GARAGE — 721 SQ. FT.
BASEMENT — 1,709 SQ. FT.

TOTAL LIVING AREA:
3,306 SQ. FT.

Terrific Open Layout
PRICE CODE: C

■ This plan features:
— Four Bedrooms
— Two full and one half bath
■ An impressive entrance leads to an Entry hall that has access to a Powder Room and both the formal and informal areas
■ Generous corner Kitchen is open to the bayed Nook bringing in an abundance of natural sunlight
■ Family Room including a focal point fireplace enjoyed from the Nook and Kitchen
■ Large Master Suite with a luxurious Bath and a walk-in closet
■ Three additional Bedrooms with a full Bath located in proximity

FIRST FLOOR — 1,041 SQ. FT.
SECOND FLOOR — 954 SQ. FT.

TOTAL LIVING AREA:
1,995 SQ. FT.

First floor

Second floor

Bonus Space
PRICE CODE: E

■ This plan features:
— Four bedrooms
— Two full and one half baths
■ A Country covered porch enhances the front elevation
■ The Kitchen, Nook and Family Room adjoin into a large living space
■ The Living Room and Dining Room adjoin with columns accenting the entry between the rooms
■ The Bonus Area over the Garage offers expansion in the future
■ No materials list is available for this plan

FIRST FLOOR — 1,618 SQ. FT.
SECOND FLOOR — 1,380 SQ. FT.
BONUS ROOM — 590 SQ. FT.

TOTAL LIVING AREA:
2,998 SQ. FT.

FIRST FLOOR

SECOND FLOOR

Unique V-Shaped Home
PRICE CODE: F

This plan features:
- Two bedrooms
- Three full baths

Bookshelves, interspersed with windows, line the long hallway that provides access to the owner's wing

Four skylights brighten the already sunny Eating Nook in the huge country Kitchen

A walk-in Pantry, range-top work island, built-in barbecue and a sink add to the amenities of the Kitchen

A wide window bay and an entire wall of windows along its length illuminate the Living Room

Master Suite with his and her closets, and adjacent dressing area plus a luxurious private Bath

A Guest Suite with a private Sitting Area and full Bath

No materials list is available for this plan

MAIN FLOOR — 3,417 SQ. FT.
GARAGE — 795 SQ. FT.

TOTAL LIVING AREA:
3,417 SQ. FT.

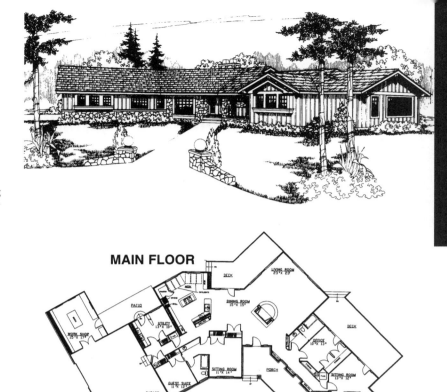

MAIN FLOOR

WIDTH 128'-6"
DEPTH 79'-6"

Country Classic
PRICE CODE: D

This plan features:
- Three bedrooms
- Two full and one half baths

Casually elegant exterior with dormers, gables and a charming front Porch

U-shaped Kitchen easily serves both adjacent Eating Areas

Nine-foot ceilings amplify the first floor

Master Suite highlighted by a vaulted ceiling and dormer

Garden tub with a double window are focus of the Master Bath

Two Bedrooms with walk-in closets sharing a hall Bath, while back stairs lead to a spacious Bonus Room

FIRST FLOOR — 1,313 SQ. FT.
SECOND FLOOR — 525 SQ. FT.
BONUS ROOM — 367 SQ. FT.
GARAGE — 513 SQ. FT.

TOTAL LIVING AREA:
1,838 SQ. FT.

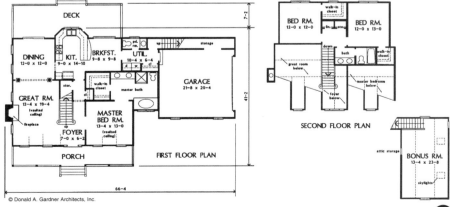

©1995 Donald A. Gardner Architects, Inc.

FIRST FLOOR PLAN

SECOND FLOOR PLAN

BONUS RM.

© Donald A. Gardner Architects, Inc.

PLAN NO. 99721

PLAN NO. 96461

To order your Blueprints, call 1-800-235-5700

Timeless Beauty

Price Code: E

■ This plan features:

— Four bedrooms

— Two full, two three-quarter and one half bath

■ Two-story entry hall accesses formal Dining and Living room

■ Spacious Great Room with cathedral ceiling, fireplace between floor to ceiling windows

■ Ideal Kitchen with built-in desk and Pantry

■ Master Bedroom wing offers a decorative ceiling, and luxurious Dressing/Bath Area

■ Three second floor Bedrooms with roomy closets and private Baths

FIRST FLOOR — 2,063 SQ. FT.
SECOND FLOOR — 894 SQ. FT.
GARAGE — 666 SQ. FT.
BASEMENT — 2,063 SQ. FT.

TOTAL LIVING AREA:
2,957 SQ. FT.

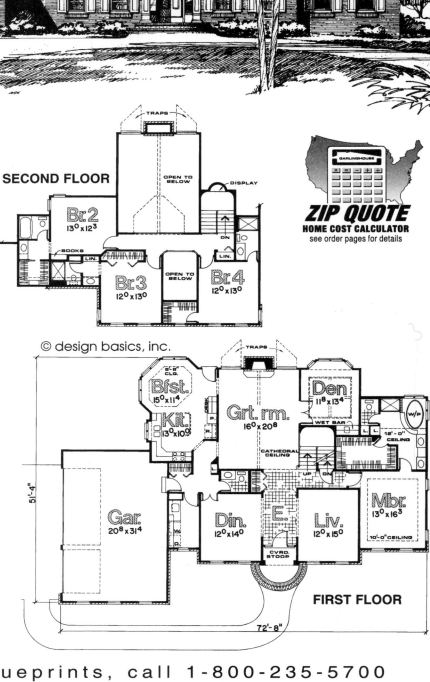

SECOND FLOOR

ZIP QUOTE
HOME COST CALCULATOR
see order pages for details

© design basics, inc.

FIRST FLOOR

Cozy and Restful

PRICE CODE: A

■ This plan features:
- Three bedrooms
- One full and one half baths
□ A decorative ceiling in the Master Bedroom with private access to the full hall sky-lit Bath
□ A convenient laundry center near the Bedrooms
□ An efficient Kitchen with ample counter and cabinet space and a double sink under a window
□ A Dining/Living Room combination that makes for easy entertaining
■ A Family Room with a cozy fireplace and convenient half bath

UPPER LEVEL — 1,139 SQ. FT.
LOWER LEVEL — 288 SQ. FT.
GARAGE — 598 SQ. FT.

TOTAL LIVING AREA:
1,427 SQ. FT.

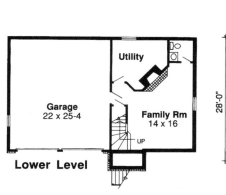

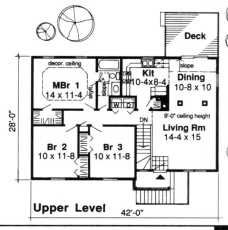

Dramatic Windows and Gables

PRICE CODE: D

© 1991 Donald A. Gardner Architects, Inc.

■ This plan features:
- Three bedrooms
- Two full and one half baths
■ The barrel vaulted entrance is flanked by columns
■ Interior columns add elegance while visually dividing the Foyer from the Dining Room and the Great Room from the Kitchen
■ The Great Room is enlarged by its cathedral ceiling and a bank of windows
■ An angled center island and breakfast counter in the Kitchen
■ The first floor Master Suite has his and her closets plus a garden tub with skylight above

FIRST FLOOR — 1,416 SQ. FT.
SECOND FLOOR — 445 SQ. FT.
BONUS — 284 SQ. FT.
GARAGE — 485 SQ. FT.

TOTAL LIVING AREA:
1,861 SQ. FT.

Style and Convenience
PRICE CODE: B

- This plan features:
  — Three bedrooms
  — Two full baths
- A sheltered Porch leads into an easy-care tile Entry
- Spacious Living Room offers a cozy fireplace, triple window and access to Patio
- An efficient Kitchen with a skylight, work island, Dining Area, walk-in Pantry and Utility/Garage entry
- Secluded Master Bedroom highlighted by a vaulted ceiling, access to Patio and a lavish Bath
- Two additional Bedrooms, one with a cathedral ceiling, share a full Bath
- No materials list is available for this plan

MAIN FLOOR — 1,653 SQ. FT.
GARAGE — 420 SQ. FT.

TOTAL LIVING AREA:
1,653 SQ. FT.

Main Floor

Splendor and Hospitality
PRICE CODE: E

- This plan features:
  — Four bedrooms
  — Three full and one half baths
- A Great Room has a fireplace and an eighteen-foot ceiling height
- The Kitchen, Breakfast Area and Hearth Room arrangement creates an enjoyable family gathering place
- The first floor Master Bedroom Suite has a deluxe Bath is topped with a raised ceiling treatment
- An open stairway decorated with a rich wood rail leads to the second floor balcony
- No materials list is available for this plan

FIRST FLOOR — 2,045 SQ. FT.
SECOND FLOOR — 919 SQ. FT.

TOTAL LIVING AREA:
2,964 SQ. FT.

To order your Blueprints, call 1-800-235-5700

© Frank Betz Associates

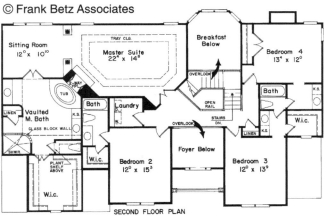

Sitting Room
12⁰ x 10¹⁰

Master Suite
22⁶ x 14⁸

TRAY CLG.

Breakfast
Below

Bedroom 4
13⁴ x 12⁰

OVERLOOK

2-WAY FPL

LINEN

Vaulted
M. Bath

TUB

Bath

Laundry

Bath

K.S.

GLASS BLOCK WALL

K.S.

OPEN RAIL

STAIRS DN.

W.

LINEN

K.S.

W.i.c.

SHWR.

PLANT SHELF ABOVE

W.i.c.

Bedroom 2
12⁰ x 15³

OVERLOOK

Foyer Below

Bedroom 3
12⁰ x 13⁹

W.i.c.

SECOND FLOOR PLAN

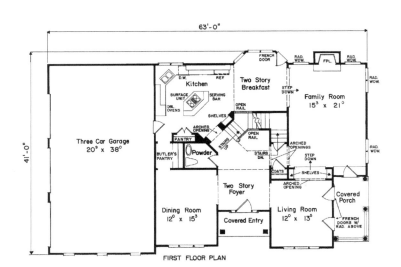

63'-0"

41'-0"

Three Car Garage
20⁹ x 38⁰

FRENCH DOOR

D.W.

REF

Kitchen

SURFACE UNIT

DBL OVENS

SERVING BAR

Two Story
Breakfast

SHELVES

OPEN RAIL

RAD. WDW.

FPL

RAD. WDW.

Family Room
15³ x 21⁰

RAD. WDW.

ARCHED OPENING

PANTRY

STAIRS UP

Powder

BUTLER'S PANTRY

OPEN RAIL

STAIRS DN.

ARCHED OPENINGS

STEP DOWN

RAD. WDW.

COATS

SHELVES

Dining Room
12⁰ x 15³

Two Story
Foyer

Covered Entry

Living Room
12⁰ x 13⁵

ARCHED OPENING

Covered Porch

FRENCH DOORS W/ RAD. ABOVE

FIRST FLOOR PLAN

Exquisite Detail

Price Code: F

■ This plan features:

— Four bedrooms

— Three full and one half baths

■ Two-story Foyer

■ Formal Living Room with access to Covered Porch

■ Radius windows and arches enhance Family Room

■ Kitchen with Pantry and cooktop/serving bar

■ Master Bedroom offers a tray ceiling and a cozy Sitting Room

■ An optional basement or crawl space foundation — please specify when ordering

FIRST FLOOR — 1,418 SQ. FT.
SECOND FLOOR — 1,844 SQ. FT.
BASEMENT — 1,418 SQ. FT.
GARAGE — 840 SQ. FT.

TOTAL LIVING AREA:
3,262 SQ. FT.

©1996 Donald A. Gardner Architects, Inc.

Offering an Inviting Welcome

Price Code: D

■ This plan features:

— Three bedrooms

— Two full and one half baths

■ A cathedral ceiling highlights the Great Room which also includes defining columns and a cozy fireplace

■ The octagonal Dining Room has a tray ceiling and easy access to the Porch for summer dining outdoors

■ The Kitchen is equipped with a Pantry and a work island

■ The Master Suite has a roomy walk-in closet and Bath

■ Upstairs, two Bedrooms share a full Bath

FIRST FLOOR — 1,512 SQ. FT.
SECOND FLOOR — 477 SQ. FT.
BONUS ROOM — 347 SQ. FT.
GARAGE & STORAGE — 636 SQ. FT.

TOTAL LIVING AREA:
1,989 SQ. FT.

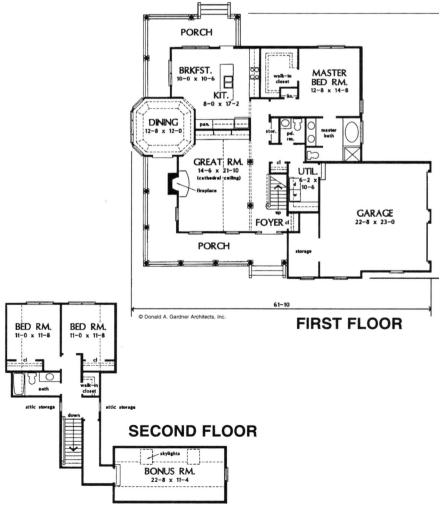

Outdoor Living Options

PRICE CODE: D

This plan features:
- Three bedrooms
- Two full baths
- Living areas that are open and casual

Great Room crowned by a cathedral ceiling which continues out to the screened Porch

Kitchen opens to a sunny breakfast bay and is adjacent to the formal Dining Room

Master Suite topped by a tray ceiling and enhanced by an indulgent Bath with a roomy walk-in closet

Two additional Bedrooms sharing a full Bath

Main floor — 1,609 sq. ft.

Garage & storage — 500 sq. ft.

TOTAL LIVING AREA:
1,609 SQ. FT.

© 1997 Donald A. Gardner Architects, Inc.

FLOOR PLAN

© 1997 Donald A Gardner Architects, Inc.

Home on a Hill

PRICE CODE: A

This plan features:
- Two bedrooms
- Two full baths
- Sweeping panels of glass and a wood stove, creating atmosphere for the Great Room

An open plan that draws the Kitchen into the warmth of the Great Room's wood stove

A sleeping Loft that has a full Bath all to itself

Main floor — 988 sq. ft.

Upper floor — 366 sq. ft.

Basement — 742 sq. ft.

Garage — 283 sq. ft.

TOTAL LIVING AREA:
1,354 SQ. FT.

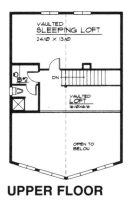

UPPER FLOOR

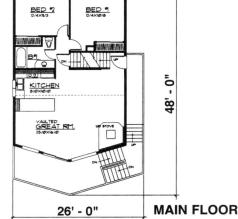

MAIN FLOOR

To order your Blueprints, call 1-800-235-5700

Open Living Plan
PRICE CODE: B

- This plan features:
  - Three bedrooms
  - Two full and one half baths
- Kitchen, Breakfast Bay, and Family Room blend into a spacious open living area
- Convenient Laundry Center is tucked into the rear of the Kitchen
- Luxurious Master Suite is topped by a tray ceiling while a vaulted ceiling is in the Bath
- Two roomy secondary Bedrooms share the full Bath in the hall
- An optional basement, crawl space or slab foundation — please specify when ordering

FIRST FLOOR — 828 SQ. FT.
SECOND FLOOR — 772 SQ. FT.
BASEMENT — 828 SQ. FT.
GARAGE — 473 SQ. FT.

TOTAL LIVING AREA:
1,600 SQ. FT

© Frank Betz Associates

FIRST FLOOR

SECOND FLOOR

One Floor Comfort
PRICE CODE: B

- This plan features:
  - Three bedrooms
  - Two full baths
- Arched windows, keystones, and shutters highlight the exterior
- The Great Room and the Breakfast Nook feature vaulted ceilings
- There is direct access from the Dining Room to the Kitchen
- The Kitchen has a space saving Pantry and plenty of counter space
- Both secondary Bedrooms have spectacular front wall windows
- The Master Suite is enormous and features a glass walled Sitting Area
- A walk-in closet, a dual vanity and a whirlpool tub highlights the Master Bath
- This home has a convenient drive under Garage
- No materials list is available for this plan

MAIN FLOOR — 1,743 SQ. FT.
BASEMENT — 998 SQ. FT.
GARAGE — 763 SQ. FT.

TOTAL LIVING AREA:
1,743 SQ. FT.

MAIN FLOOR

© Frank Betz Associates

To order your Blueprints, call 1-800-235-5700

© Frank Betz Associates

Stately Stone and Stucco

Price Code: F

■ This plan features:

— Four bedrooms

— Three full and one half baths

■ Two story Foyer with angled staircase

■ Expansive two story Great Room enhanced by a fireplace

■ Convenient Kitchen with a cooktop island

■ Open Keeping Room accented by a wall of windows and backyard access

■ Master Suite wing offers a tray ceiling, a plush Bath and roomy walk-in closet

■ An optional basement, slab or crawl space foundation — please specify when ordering

FIRST FLOOR — 2,130 SQ. FT.
SECOND FLOOR — 897 SQ. FT.
BASEMENT — 2,130 SQ. FT.
GARAGE — 494 SQ. FT.

TOTAL LIVING AREA:
3,027 SQ. FT.

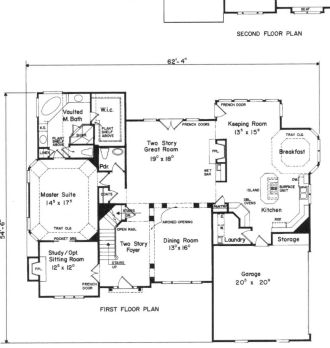

SECOND FLOOR PLAN

FIRST FLOOR PLAN

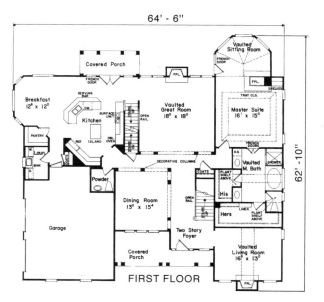

© Frank Betz Associates

Luxurious Yet Cozy

Price Code: F

■ This plan features:

— Four bedrooms

— Three full and one half baths

■ Covered Porch leads into two-story Foyer and Living Room

■ Decorative columns define Dining Room and Great Room

■ Open and convenient Kitchen with a work island

■ Corner Master Suite includes a cozy fireplace

■ Three second floor Bedrooms with walk-in closets

■ An optional basement, slab or crawl space foundation — please specify when ordering

FIRST FLOOR — 2,467 SQ. FT.
SECOND FLOOR — 928 SQ. FT.
BONUS — 296 SQ. FT.
BASEMENT — 2,467 SQ. FT.
GARAGE — 566 SQ. FT.

TOTAL LIVING AREA:
3,395 SQ. FT.

Open Floor Plan
PRICE CODE: C

This plan features:

Four bedrooms

Two full and one half baths

The Living Area on the first floor is open

Open space combined with columns and a vaulted ceiling in the Living Room adds plenty of architectural interest

A Den on the second floor is cozy and private, a quiet place to relax

FIRST FLOOR — 1,072 SQ. FT.

SECOND FLOOR — 1,108 SQ. FT.

TOTAL LIVING AREA:
2,180 SQ. FT.

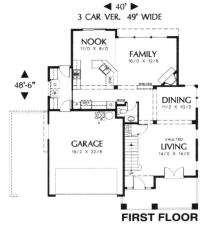

◄ 40' ►
3 CAR VER. 49' WIDE

48'-6"

NOOK 11/0 X 8/0

FAMILY 16/0 X 12/8

DINING 11/2 X 10/0

GARAGE 19/2 X 22/8

VAULTED LIVING 14/0 X 14/0

FIRST FLOOR

MASTER 12/0 X 14/8

BR. 2 11/4 X 10/0

DEN 10/10 X 9/8

3 CAR VER. 20/4 X 10/0

BR. 3 11/4 X 10/0

OPEN TO BELOW

BR. 4 10/8 X 10/8

SECOND FLOOR

Spectacular Curving Stairway
PRICE CODE: E

© design basics, inc.

This plan features:

- Four bedrooms

- Two full, one three-quarter and one half baths

Spacious formal Entry with arched transom, is enhanced by curved staircase

Great Room is inviting with a cozy fireplace, a wetbar and triple arched windows

Open Kitchen, Breakfast and Hearth area combine efficiency and comfort for all

Master Bedroom retreat offers a private back door, a double walk-in closet and a whirlpool Bath

Generous closets and Baths enhance the three second floor Bedrooms

FIRST FLOOR — 2,252 SQ. FT.

SECOND FLOOR — 920 SQ. FT.

BASEMENT — 2,252 SQ. FT.

GARAGE — 646 SQ. FT.

TOTAL LIVING AREA:
3,172 SQ. FT.

ZIP QUOTE
HOME COST CALCULATOR
see order pages for details

Br3 13⁵ x12⁰

Br4 13⁰ x12⁰

Br2 12⁰ x14⁸

OPEN TO BELOW

SECOND FLOOR

Mbr. 16⁴ x15⁰

Grt. rm. 18⁴ x18⁴

Hrth. 13³ x16⁰

Bfst. 13⁹ x11⁰

Kit. 13⁹ x11⁰

Din. 13⁰ x16⁴

Den 12⁰ x14⁴

Gar. 20⁸ x30⁴

57'-4"

73'-4"

FIRST FLOOR

To order your Blueprints, call 1-800-235-5700

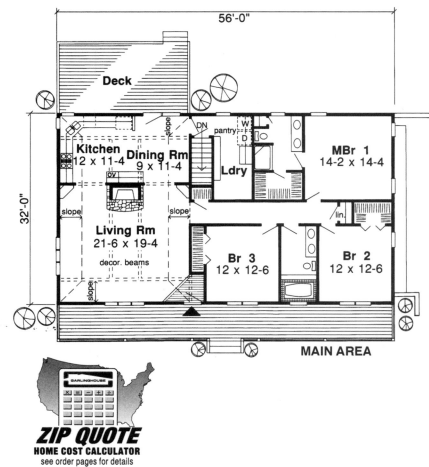

Dramatic Ranch

Price Code: B

- This plan features:
— Three bedrooms
— Two full baths

- A large Living Room with a stone fireplace and a decorative beamed ceiling

- A Kitchen/Dining Room arrangement which makes the rooms seem more spacious

- A Laundry with a large Pantry located close to the Bedrooms and the Kitchen

- A Master Bedroom with a walk-in closet and a private master Bath

- Two additional Bedrooms, one with a walk-in closet, that share the full hall Bath

MAIN AREA — 1,792 SQ. FT.
BASEMENT — 818 SQ. FT.
GARAGE — 857 SQ. FT.

TOTAL LIVING AREA:
1,792 SQ. FT.

ZIP QUOTE
HOME COST CALCULATOR
see order pages for details

56'-0"

32'-0"

Deck

Kitchen
12 x 11-4

Dining Rm
9 x 11-4

DN
pantry
W
D
Ldry

MBr 1
14-2 x 14-4

Living Rm
21-6 x 19-4
decor. beams

Br 3
12 x 12-6

Br 2
12 x 12-6

lin.

MAIN AREA

To order your Blueprints, call 1-800-235-5700

FAM. RM.
VAULTED CLG.
18-0 X 16-0

DINETTE
12-0 X 10-6

WOOD DECK

M. BATH

13" COUNTER EXTENSION

KITCHEN
12-0 X 12-6

LND.

PDR.

M.B.R.
TRAY CLG.
14-0 X 16-6

FOYER

DINING RM.
11-6 X 13-0

GARAGE
24-6 X 26-0

PORCH

RAILING

FIRST FLOOR
WIDTH= 63'-0"
DEPTH= 47'-0"

(2) 9 FT. GAR. DOORS

FAM. RM. BELOW

B.R. 3
12-0 X 12-0

RAILING

BALCONY

BATH 2

STORAGE

FOYER BELOW

SLOPED CLG.

B.R. 2
12-0 X 11-0

ROOF

ROOF

SECOND FLOOR
No. 93349

Conventional and Classic Comfort

Price Code: C

■ This plan features:

— Three bedrooms

— Two full and one half baths

■ Cozy Porch accesses two-story Foyer with decorative window

■ Formal Dining Room accented by a recessed window adjoins Kitchen

■ Spacious Family Room crowned by a vaulted ceiling over a hearth fireplace

■ Efficient Kitchen with an extended counter/eating bar and access to Deck

■ First floor Master Bedroom with walk-in closet and Master Bath with double vanity

■ No materials list is available for this plan

FIRST FLOOR — 1,454 SQ. FT.
SECOND FLOOR — 507 SQ. FT.
BASEMENT — 1,454 SQ. FT.
GARAGE — 624 SQ. FT.

TOTAL LIVING AREA:
1,961 SQ. FT.

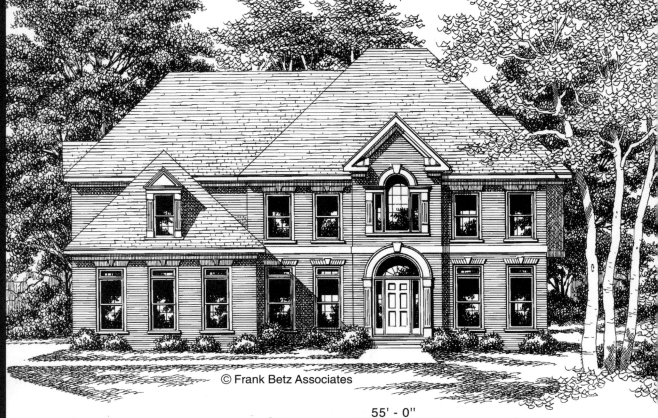

© Frank Betz Associates

Regal Residence

Price Code: F

- This plan features:
  — Five bedrooms
  — Four full baths
- Keystone, arched windows accent entrance into two-story Foyer
- Spacious Family Room is enhanced by a fireplace
- Kitchen with a cooktop island/serving bar and a walk-in Pantry
- First floor Guest Room/Study adjoins a full Bath
- Master Suite offers a tray ceiling and a vaulted Bath with a radius window
- Three additional Bedrooms have walk-in closets
- An optional basement or crawl space foundation — please specify when ordering

FIRST FLOOR — 1,488 SQ. FT.
SECOND FLOOR — 1,551 SQ. FT.
BASEMENT — 1,488 SQ. FT.
GARAGE — 667 SQ. FT.

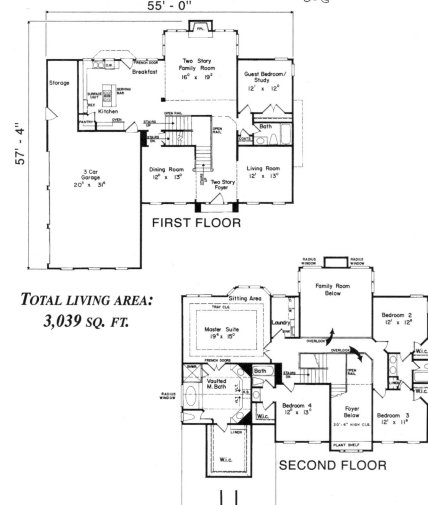

TOTAL LIVING AREA:
3,039 SQ. FT.

FIRST FLOOR

SECOND FLOOR

55' - 0"

57' - 4"

To order your Blueprints, call 1-800-235-5700

Traditional Elegance
PRICE CODE: F

PLAN NO. 92504

This plan features:
- Four bedrooms
- Three full and one half baths

A elegant entrance leading into a two-story Foyer with an impressive staircase highlighted by a curved window

Floor to ceiling windows in both the formal Living and Dining Rooms

A spacious Den with a hearth fireplace, built-in book shelves, a wetbar and a wall of windows viewing the backyard

A large, efficient Kitchen, equipped with lots of counter and storage space, a bright Breakfast area, and access to the Dining Room, Utility Room, walk-in Pantry and Garage

A grand Master Suite with decorative ceilings, a private Porch, an elaborate Bath and two walk-in closets

Three additional Bedrooms on the second floor with walk-in closets, sharing adjoining, full Baths and an ideal Children's Den

An optional crawl space or slab foundation — please specify when ordering

FIRST FLOOR — 2,553 SQ. FT.
SECOND FLOOR — 1,260 SQ. FT.
GARAGE — 714 SQ. FT.

**TOTAL LIVING AREA:
3,813 SQ. FT.**

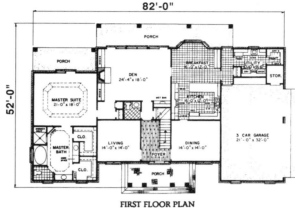

FIRST FLOOR PLAN

SECOND FLOOR PLAN

Elegant Stone Two-Story
PRICE CODE: E

PLAN NO. 99149

This plan features:
- Four bedrooms
- Two full and one half baths

The two-story entry leads directly into the Great Room

The Kitchen has a center island and is open to the large Nook

The Master Bedrooms has an access door to the rear Deck

Upstairs are two Bedrooms that are serviced by a full Bath

Also upstairs is a large Game Room for all the kid's toys

A three-season Porch with a cathedral ceiling rounds out this plan

No materials list is available for this plan

MAIN FLOOR — 2,039 SQ. FT.
SECOND FLOOR — 613 SQ. FT.

**TOTAL LIVING AREA:
2,652 SQ. FT.**

SECOND FLOOR

MAIN FLOOR

Tradition Combined with Contemporary

PRICE CODE: A

■ This plan features:
— Three bedrooms
— Two full baths
■ A vaulted ceiling in the Entry
■ A formal Living Room with a fireplace and a half-round transom
■ A Dining Room with sliders to the Deck and easy access to the Kitchen
■ A main floor Master Suite with corner windows, a closet and private Bath access
■ Two additional Bedrooms that share a full hall Bath

MAIN FLOOR — 858 SQ. FT.
UPPER FLOOR — 431 SQ. FT.
BASEMENT — 858 SQ. FT.
GARAGE — 400 SQ. FT.

TOTAL LIVING AREA:
1,289 SQ. FT.

MAIN FLOOR

UPPER FLOOR

Lots of Space in this Small Package

PRICE CODE: A

■ This plan features:
— Two or three bedrooms
— Two full baths
■ A Living Room with dynamic, soaring angles and a fireplace
■ A first floor Master Suite with full Bath and walk in closet
■ Walk-in closets in all Bedrooms

MAIN FLOOR — 878 SQ. FT.
UPPER FLOOR — 405 SQ. FT.

TOTAL LIVING AREA:
1,283 SQ. FT.

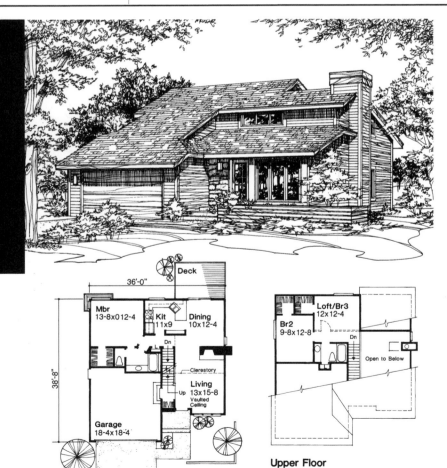

Main Floor

Upper Floor

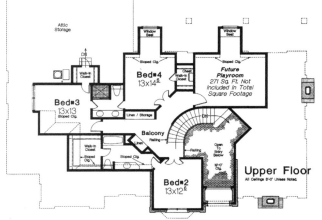

Upper Floor
All Ceilings 8'-0" Unless Noted.

Attic Storage

Bed#4
13x14⁹

Future Playroom
271 Sq. Ft. Not Included In Total Square Footage

Bed#3
13x13
Sloped Clg.

Balcony

Bed#2
13x12⁶

Country Estate Home
Price Code: F

■ This plan features:
— Four bedrooms
— Three full and one half baths

■ Impressive two-story Entry with a lovely curved staircase

■ Formal Living and Dining rooms have columns and decorative windows

■ Wood plank flooring, a large fireplace and Veranda access accent Great Room

■ Hub Kitchen with brick pavers, extended serving counter, bright Breakfast area, and nearby Utility/Garage entry

■ Private Master Bedroom suite offers a Private Lanai and plush dressing area

■ Future Playroom offers many options

■ No materials list is available for this plan

MAIN FLOOR — 2,441 SQ. FT.
SECOND FLOOR — 1,039 SQ. FT.
GARAGE — 660 SQ. FT.
FUTURE PLAYROOM — 271 SQ. FT.

TOTAL LIVING AREA:
3,480 SQ. FT.

73'-0"
56'-6 1/2"

3-Car Gar
30x22

Covered Veranda

Kit
Din
10x14

GreatRm
19x19

Utll

MstrBed
15x18

Study
12x11

FmlDin
13x13

Ent

FmlLiv
17x14

Private Lanai

Main Floor
All Ceiling Heights 10'-0" Unless Noted.
Future Playroom Not Included In Total Sq. Ft.

Drive Under Garage

Price Code: A

■ This plan features:

— Three bedrooms

— Two full baths

■ Porch shelters Entry into Living Area with an inviting fireplace topped by a vaulted ceiling

■ Convenient Dining Area opens to Living Room, Kitchen and Sundeck

■ Efficient, U-shaped Kitchen serves Dining Area and Sun Deck beyond

■ Pampering Master Bedroom with a vaulted ceiling, two closets and a double vanity Bath

■ Two additional Bedrooms share a full Bath and convenient Laundry Center

MAIN FLOOR — 1,208 SQ. FT.
BASEMENT — 728 SQ. FT.
GARAGE — 480 SQ. FT.

**TOTAL LIVING AREA:
1,208 SQ. FT.**

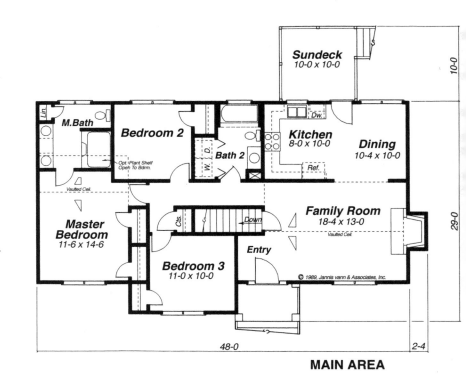

MAIN AREA

To order your Blueprints, call 1-800-235-5700

Brick and Stucco
PRICE CODE: F

- This plan features:
  - Four bedrooms
  - Two full, two three-quarter and one half baths
- The brick, stucco wing walls, and dual chimneys add elegant eye appeal to this home
- A large front Courtyard adds intrigue to front of the home
- The spider beamed Den with French doors includes arched transom windows
- The formal Dining Room opens to a dramatic high ceiling in the entry
- The Great Room features a fireplace wall with entertainment center, bookcases and wetbar
- Informal areas include the gazebo shaped Dinette, Kitchen with wrapping counters, large island/snack bar, walk-in Pantry, and private stairs accessing the second floor
- Each secondary Bedroom includes a walk-in closet, a built-in desk and a private Bath
- The exquisite first floor Master Suite includes a Sitting Room with a built-in bookcase and a fireplace

FIRST FLOOR — 2,603 SQ. FT.
SECOND FLOOR — 1,020 SQ. FT.
BASEMENT — 2,603 SQ. FT.
GARAGE — 801 SQ. FT.

TOTAL LIVING AREA:
3,623 SQ. FT.

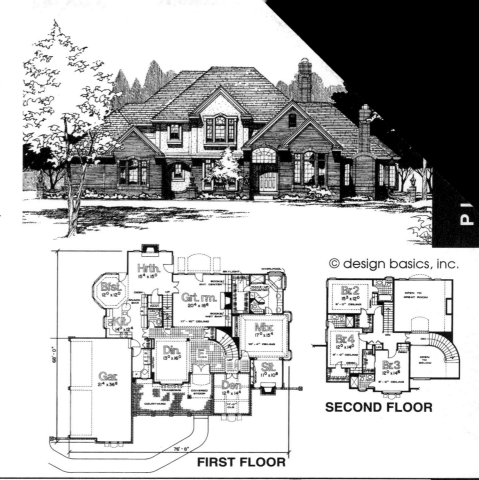

© design basics, inc.

SECOND FLOOR

FIRST FLOOR

Three Porches Offer Outdoor Charm
PRICE CODE: A

- This plan features:
  - Three bedrooms
  - Two full baths
- An oversized log burning fireplace in the spacious Living/Dining Area which is two stories high with sliding glass doors
- Three Porches offering the maximum in outdoor living space
- A private Bedroom located on the second floor
- An efficient Kitchen including an eating bar and access to the covered Dining Porch

FIRST FLOOR — 974 SQ. FT.
SECOND FLOOR — 300 SQ. FT.

TOTAL LIVING AREA:
1,274 SQ. FT.

PLAN NO. 90048

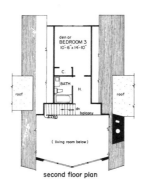

second floor plan

first floor plan

To order your Blueprints, call 1-800-235-5700

Lovely Second Home
PRICE CODE: A

■ This plan features:
— Three bedrooms
— One full and one three-quarter baths
■ Firedrum fireplace warming both entryway and Living Room
■ Dining and Living rooms opening onto the Deck, which surrounds the house on three sides

MAIN FLOOR — 808 SQ. FT.
UPPER FLOOR — 288 SQ. FT.

TOTAL LIVING AREA: 1,096 SQ. FT.

MAIN FLOOR PLAN

UPPER FLOOR PLAN

Old Fashioned With Contemporary Interior
PRICE CODE: C

■ This plan features:
— Four bedrooms
— Three full baths
■ A two-story Foyer is flanked by the Living Room and the Dining Room
■ The Family Room features a fireplace and a French door
■ The bayed Breakfast Nook and Pantry are adjacent to the Kitchen
■ The Master Suite with a trayed ceiling has an attached Bath with a vaulted ceiling and radius window
■ Upstairs are two additional Bedrooms, a full Bath, a Laundry closet and a Bonus Room
■ An optional basement, crawl space or slab foundation available — please specify when ordering this plan

FIRST FLOOR — 1,135 SQ. FT.
SECOND FLOOR — 917 SQ. FT.
BONUS — 216 SQ. FT.
BASEMENT — 1,135 SQ. FT.
GARAGE — 452 SQ. FT.

TOTAL LIVING AREA: 2,052 SQ. FT.

© Frank Betz Associates

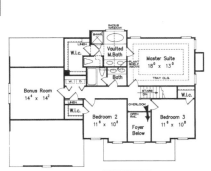

FIRST FLOOR PLAN

SECOND FLOOR PLAN

To order your Blueprints, call 1-800-235-5700

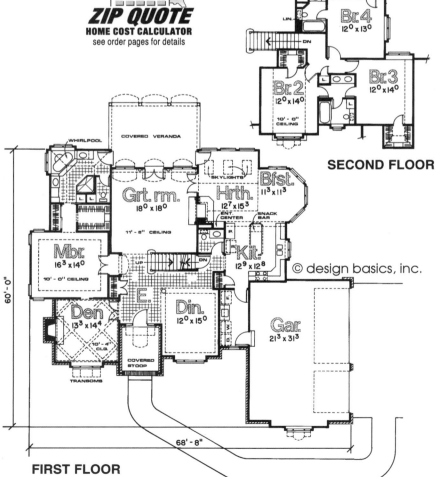

ZIP QUOTE
HOME COST CALCULATOR
see order pages for details

SECOND FLOOR

Br. 4
12⁰ x 13⁰

Br. 2
12⁰ x 14⁰

Br. 3
12⁰ x 14⁰

10' - 0"
CEILING

BOOKS

LIN.

DN

FIRST FLOOR

WHIRLPOOL

COVERED VERANDA

SKYLIGHTS

Grt. rm.
18⁰ x 18⁰

Hrth.
12⁷ x 15³

Bfst.
11³ x 11³

ENT.
CENTER

SNACK
BAR

11'- 8" CEILING

Mbr
16³ x 14⁰

10' - 0" CEILING

Kit.
12⁹ x 12⁸

UP

DN

© design basics, inc.

Den
13³ x 14⁴

10' - 4"
CLG.

Din.
12⁰ x 15⁰

Gar.
21³ x 31³

COVERED
STOOP

TRANSOMS

60'-0"

68' - 8"

Stucco, Brick and Elegant Details

Price Code: E

■ This plan features:
— Four bedrooms
—Three full and one half baths

■ Majestic Entry opens to Den and Dining Room

■ Expansive Great Room shares a see-thru fireplace with the Hearth Room

■ Lovely Hearth Room enhanced by three skylights above triple arched windows

■ Hub Kitchen has a work island/snack bar

■ Sumptuous Master Bedroom Suite with corner windows and two closets

FIRST FLOOR — 2,084 SQ. FT.
SECOND FLOOR — 848 SQ. FT.
BASEMENT — 2,084 SQ. FT.
GARAGE — 682 SQ. FT.

TOTAL LIVING AREA:
2,932 SQ. FT.

Gorgeous

Price Code: E

■ This plan features:

— Four bedrooms

— Two full and one half baths

■ A bay window that enhances the Living Room with natural light

■ A Breakfast Room with an incredible shape

■ An island Kitchen in close proximity to both the formal Dining Room and the informal Breakfast Room

■ A fantastic Master Suite with a decorative ceiling, private Master Bath and a large walk-in closet

■ Three additional Bedrooms share a full hall Bath

FIRST FLOOR — 1,273 SQ. FT.
SECOND FLOOR — 1,477 SQ. FT.
BASEMENT — 974 SQ. FT.
GARAGE — 852 SQ. FT.

TOTAL LIVING AREA: 2,750 SQ. FT.

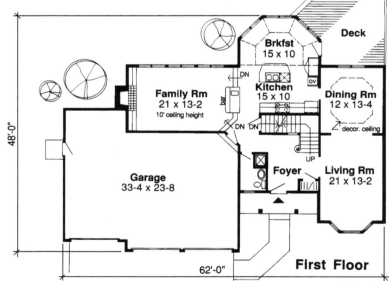

First Floor

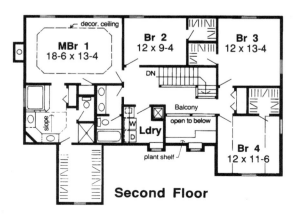

Second Floor

To order your Blueprints, call 1-800-235-5700

Easy Living One-Level

PRICE CODE: A

This plan features:
- Three bedrooms
- Three baths and two half baths

The Great Room, combined with the Dining area, creates an open spacious effect

Triple doors lead to a raised Deck creating a favorable indoor/outdoor relationship

The Master Bedroom has a large walk-in closet and a deluxe Bath

The rear walkout basement creates the opportunity of increasing square footage

No materials is list available for this plan

MAIN FLOOR — 1,488 SQ. FT.
BASEMENT — 1,488 SQ. FT.
GARAGE — 417 SQ. FT.

TOTAL LIVING AREA:
1,488 SQ. FT.

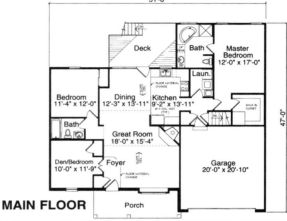

MAIN FLOOR

Lap of Luxury

PRICE CODE: D

This plan features:
- Four bedrooms
- Three full and one half baths

Entertaining in grand style in the formal Living Room, the Dining Room, or under the covered Patio in the backyard

A Family Room crowned in a cathedral ceiling, enhanced by a center fireplace, and built-in book shelves

An efficient Kitchen highlighted by a wall oven, plentiful counter space and a Pantry

A Master Bedroom with a Sitting Area, huge walk in closet, private Bath, and access to a covered Lanai

A secondary Bedroom wing containing three additional Bedrooms with ample closet space, and two full Baths

No materials list is available for this plan

MAIN FLOOR — 2,445 SQ. FT.
GARAGE — 630 SQ. FT.

TOTAL LIVING AREA:
2,445 SQ. FT.

FLOOR PLAN

ZIP QUOTE
HOME COST CALCULATOR
see order pages for details

To order your Blueprints, call 1-800-235-5700

373

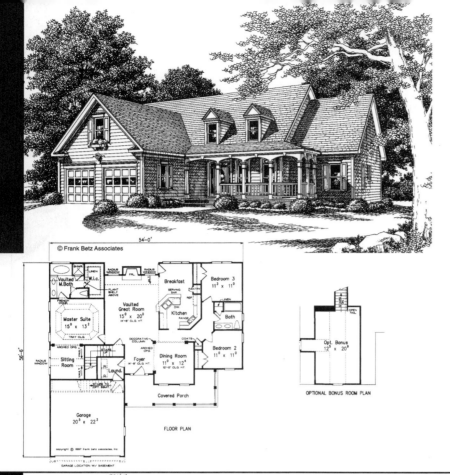

© Frank Betz Associates

FLOOR PLAN

OPTIONAL BONUS ROOM PLAN

Elegant Ceiling Treatments
PRICE CODE: B

- This plan features:
— Three bedrooms
— Two full baths
- A cozy wrapping front Porch sheltering entrance
- Dining Room defined by columns at the entrances
- Kitchen highlighted by a peninsula counter/serving bar
- Breakfast Room flowing from the Kitchen
- Vaulted ceiling highlighting the Great Room which also includes a fireplace
- Master Suite crowned in a tray ceiling over the Bedroom, a Sitting Room and plush Master Bath
- Two additional Bedrooms are located at the other side of the house
- An optional basement or crawl space foundation — please specify when ordering
- No materials list is available for this plan

MAIN FLOOR — 1,692 SQ. FT.
BONUS ROOM — 358 SQ. FT.
BASEMENT — 1,705 SQ. FT.
GARAGE — 472 SQ. FT.

TOTAL LIVING AREA:
1,692 SQ. FT.

Main floor

Outstanding Family Home
PRICE CODE: C

- This plan features:
— Three bedrooms
— Two full baths
- Split-bedroom layout, perfect floor plan for a family with older children
- Great Room including a cozy fireplace, access to the rear porch and an open layout with the Nook and Kitchen
- Extended counter in the Kitchen providing a snack bar for meals or snacks
- Formal Dining Room directly accessing the Kitchen
- Bright Nook with a built-in Pantry
- Master Suite includes access to rear Porch and a pampering Bath and walk-in closet

MAIN FLOOR — 2,162 SQ. FT.
GARAGE — 498 SQ. FT.

TOTAL LIVING AREA:
2,162 SQ. FT.

To order your Blueprints, call 1-800-235-5700

Computer Center

Price Code: B

- This plan features:
  — Three or four bedrooms
  — Three full baths
- The Great Room includes a gas fireplace and computer center
- The Dining Room has columns accenting its entrance
- The Kitchen/Breakfast Room is efficiently designed and has direct access to the Grilling Porch
- There are two suites located on the first floor a Master Suite and a Guest Suite
- An optional basement, crawl space or slab foundation — please specify when ordering
- No materials list is available for this plan

FIRST FLOOR — 1,558 SQ. FT.
SECOND FLOOR — 429 SQ. FT.
GARAGE — 445 SQ. FT.

TOTAL LIVING AREA:
1,987 SQ. FT.

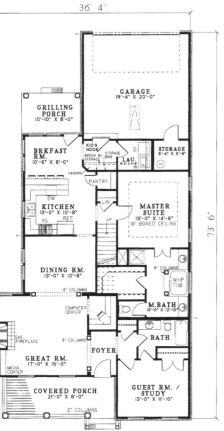

FIRST FLOOR

SECOND FLOOR

Open Plan Accented By Loft, Windows and Decks

Price Code: C

■ This plan features:

— Three bedrooms

— Two full and one half baths

■ A fireplaced Family Room and Dining Room

■ A large Kitchen sharing a preparation/eating bar with Dining Room

■ A first floor Master Bedroom featuring two closets and a five-piece bath

■ An ample Utility Room designed with a pantry and room for a freezer, a washer and dryer, plus a furnace and a hot water heater

MAIN FLOOR — 1,280 SQ. FT.
UPPER LOFT — 735 SQ. FT.
GREENHOUSE — 80 SQ. FT.

**TOTAL LIVING AREA:
2,015 SQ. FT.**

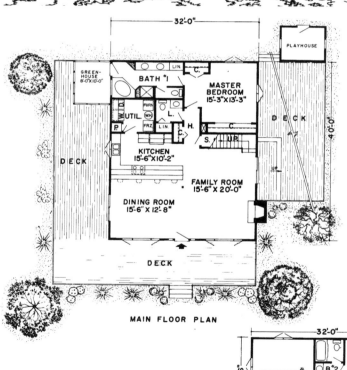

MAIN FLOOR PLAN

UPPER LOFT PLAN

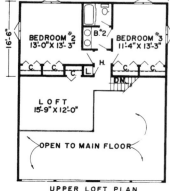

ZIP QUOTE
HOME COST CALCULATOR
see order pages for details

To order your Blueprints, call 1-800-235-5700

Fieldstone Facade
PRICE CODE: D

This plan features:
- Four bedrooms
- Two full and one half baths
- Covered porch shelters entrance into Gallery and Great Room with a focal point fireplace and Patio access topped by a vaulted ceiling
- Formal Dining Room conveniently located for entertaining
- Cooktop island, built-in Pantry and a bright Breakfast Area highlight Kitchen
- Secluded Master Bedroom with Patio access, large walk-in closet and corner spa tub
- Three additional Bedrooms with ample closets, share a double vanity Bath
- No materials list is available for this plan

MAIN FLOOR — 2,261 SQ. FT.
GARAGE — 640 SQ. FT.

TOTAL LIVING AREA:
2,261 SQ. FT.

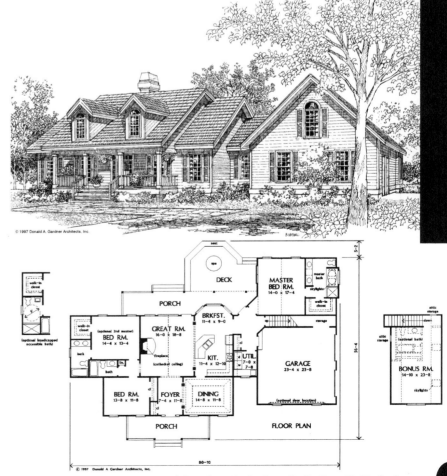

MAIN FLOOR

Grace and Style
PRICE CODE: E

This plan features:
- Three bedrooms
- Three full baths
- Foyer accented by columns provides Entry into the formal Dining Room
- Angled island Kitchen is open to the Breakfast Bay
- Great Room with cathedral ceiling is enhanced by a fireplace
- Secluded Master Suite with a skylit Bath
- Two secondary Bedrooms with an alternate Bath design create a wheel chair accessible option for the disabled
- Bonus Room possibilities include a terrific fourth Bedroom and Bath

MAIN FLOOR — 2,057 SQ. FT.
GARAGE & STORAGE — 622 SQ. FT.
BONUS ROOM — 444 SQ. FT.

TOTAL LIVING AREA:
2,057 SQ. FT.

To order your Blueprints, call 1-800-235-5700

Traditional Ranch
PRICE CODE: B

- This plan features:
— Three bedrooms
— Two full baths
- A large front palladium window that gives this home great curb appeal, and allows a view of the front yard from the Living Room
- A vaulted ceiling in the Living Room, adding to the architectural interest and the spacious feel of the room
- Sliding glass doors in the Dining Room that lead to a wood Deck
- A built-in Pantry, double sink and breakfast bar in the efficient Kitchen
- A Master Suite that includes a walk-in closet and a private Bath with a double vanity
- Two additional Bedrooms that share a full hall Bath

MAIN AREA — 1,568 SQ. FT.
GARAGE — 509 SQ. FT.
BASEMENT — 1,568 SQ. FT.

TOTAL LIVING AREA:
1,568 SQ. FT.

MAIN AREA

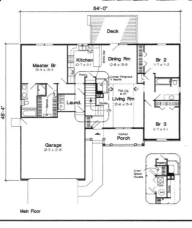

ZIP QUOTE
HOME COST CALCULATOR
see order pages for details

Tailored for a View to the Side
PRICE CODE: D

- This plan features:
— Three or four bedrooms
— Three full and one half baths
- A designed for a homesite with a view to the side, perfect for entertaining and everyday living
- A sheltered entrance with windows over the door and a side light
- A large entry Foyer highlighted by a ceiling dome and French doors leading to the private Study or Guest Bedroom with a vaulted ceiling
- An elegant formal Dining Room with a high ceiling and a columned and arched entrance
- A sunken Great Room with a tray ceiling, arched and columned openings and a cozy fireplace
- A Breakfast Room, with an optional planning desk, opens to the Kitchen via the eating bar
- An island and walk-in Pantry adding to the Kitchen's efficiency
- A tray ceiling and lavish bath pamper the owner in the Master Suite
- Two additional Bedrooms that share a split vanity Bath
- No materials list is available for this plan

MAIN FLOOR — 2,579 SQ. FT.
GARAGE — 536 SQ. FT.

TOTAL LIVING AREA:
2,579 SQ. FT.

To order your Blueprints, call 1-800-235-5700

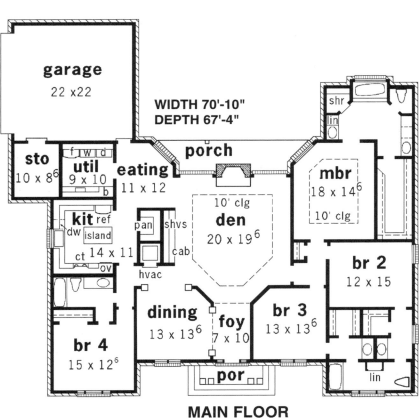

WIDTH 70'-10"
DEPTH 67'-4"

garage
22 x22

sto
10 x 8⁶

util
9 x 10

eating
11 x 12

porch

shr
lin

mbr
18 x 14⁶
10' clg

10' clg

den
20 x 19⁶

kit
ref
dw island
ct 14 x 11
ov

pan shvs
cab

hvac

br 2
12 x 15

dining
13 x 13⁶

foy
7 x 10

br 3
13 x 13⁶

br 4
15 x 12⁶

por

lin

MAIN FLOOR

Lavish Accommodations

Price Code: F

■ This plan features:

— Four bedrooms

— Three full baths

■ A central Den with a large fireplace, built-in shelves and cabinets and a decorative ceiling

■ An island Kitchen that has been well thought out and includes a walk-in Pantry

■ An informal Breakfast Room that is directly accessible from either the Kitchen or the Den

■ A Master Bedroom enhanced by a decorative ceiling and a walk-in closet as well as a luxurious Master Bath

■ An optional crawl space or slab foundation — please specify when ordering

MAIN FLOOR — 2,733 SQ. FT.
GARAGE AND STORAGE — 569 SQ. FT.

TOTAL LIVING AREA:
2,733 SQ. FT.

Balcony Porch

Price Code: B

- This plan features:
- — Four bedrooms
- — Two full and a half baths
- The Great Room includes a built-in media center next to the cozy fireplace
- The Dining Room and the Kitchen adjoin with a breakfast bar between them
- The Master Bedroom is topped by a boxed ceiling and includes a lavish Bath
- An optional basement, crawl space or slab foundation — please specify when ordering
- No materials list is available for this plan

FIRST FLOOR — 1,295 SQ. FT.

SECOND FLOOR — 664 SQ. FT.
GARAGE — 498 SQ. FT.

**TOTAL LIVING AREA:
1,959 SQ. FT.**

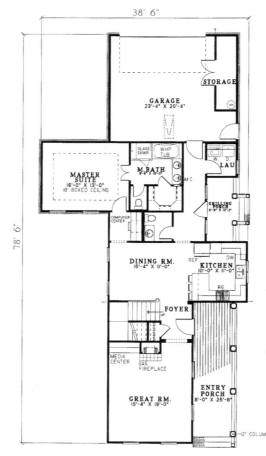

FIRST FLOOR

SECOND FLOOR

Country Style Charm

PRICE CODE: C

This plan features:
- Three bedrooms
- Two full baths
- Brick accents, front facing gable, and railed wrap-around covered Porch
- A built-in range and oven in a L-shaped Kitchen
- A Nook with garage access for convenient unloading of groceries and other supplies
- A bay window wrapping around the front of the formal Living Room
- A Master Suite with French doors opening to the Deck

MAIN AREA — 1,857 SQ. FT.
GARAGE — 681 SQ. FT.

TOTAL LIVING AREA:
1,857 SQ. FT.

WIDTH 51'-6"
DEPTH 65'-0"

Symmetrical and Stately

PRICE CODE: E

This plan features:
- Four bedrooms
- Two full and one half baths
- Double column Porch leads into the open Foyer, the Dining Room accented by an arched window and pillars, and a spacious Den
- Decorative ceiling crowns the Den with a hearth fireplace, built-in shelves and window access to the rear Porch
- Large, efficient Kitchen with a peninsula serving counter, a Breakfast Area, adjoining the Utility and the Garage
- Master Bedroom suite with a decorative ceiling, two vanities and a large walk-in closet
- Three additional Bedrooms with double closets share a full Bath
- An optional slab or crawl space foundation — please specify when ordering

MAIN AREA — 2,387 SQ. FT.
GARAGE — 505 SQ. FT.

TOTAL LIVING AREA:
2,387 SQ. FT.

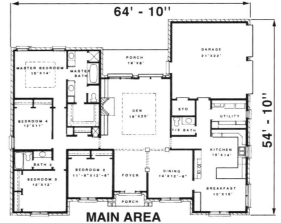

MAIN AREA

To order your Blueprints, call 1-800-235-5700

PLAN NO. 93048

WIDTH 49-10

© Larry E. Belk

MAIN AREA

For First Time Buyers
PRICE CODE: A

- This plan features:
  - Three bedrooms
  - Two full baths
- An efficiently designed Kitchen with a corner sink, ample counter space and a peninsula counter
- A sunny Breakfast Room with a convenient hide-away Laundry Center
- An expansive Family Room that includes a corner fire place and direct access to the Patio
- A private Master Suite with a walk-in closet and a dou ble vanity Bath
- Two additional Bedrooms, both with walk-in closets, that share a full hall Bath
- No materials list is available for this plan

MAIN AREA — 1,310 SQ. FT.
GARAGE — 449 SQ. FT.

TOTAL LIVING AREA:
1,310 SQ. FT.

PLAN NO. 91418

FLOOR PLAN

Carefree Comfort
PRICE CODE: B

- This plan features:
  - Three bedrooms
  - Two full baths
- A dramatic vaulted Foyer
- A range top island Kitchen with a sunny eating Nook surrounded by a built-in planter
- A vaulted ceiling in the Great Room with a built-in ba and corner fireplace
- A bayed Dining Room that combines with the Great Room for a spacious feeling
- A Master Bedroom with a private reading Nook, vault ceiling, walk-in closet, and a well-appointed private Ba
- Two additional Bedrooms sharing a full hall Bath
- An optional basement, slab or crawl space foundation please specify when ordering

MAIN FLOOR — 1,665 SQ. FT.

TOTAL LIVING AREA:
1,665 SQ. FT.

To order your Blueprints, call 1-800-235-5700

Elegant and Efficient
PRICE CODE: D

This plan features:
– Three bedrooms
– Two full baths

Covered entrance into the Foyer leads to a spacious Den with a decorative ceiling above a hearth fireplace and French doors to the Patio area

Decorative window and ceiling highlight the formal Dining Room

Large, Country Kitchen with double ovens, a cooktop and a peninsula snackbar serving the bright Breakfast Area

Large Master Bedroom suite with a decorative ceiling, a walk-in closet and a plush Bath with a double vanity and a whirlpool tub

Two additional Bedrooms with walk-in closets share a full Bath

An optional slab or crawl space foundation — please specify when ordering

MAIN FLOOR — 1,959 SQ. FT.
GARAGE — 512 SQ. FT.

TOTAL LIVING AREA:
1,959 SQ. FT.

WIDTH 65'-0"
DEPTH 51'-0"

br 2 12 x 12
living 19 x 18 10' clg 9' clg
eating 12 x 10
mbr 18 x 16 10' clg 9' clg
kit 12 x 12
util
sto
br 3 12 x 12
foy
por
dining 12 x 13 11' clg 10' clg
garage 22 x 22

MAIN FLOOR

Grace and Style
PRICE CODE: D

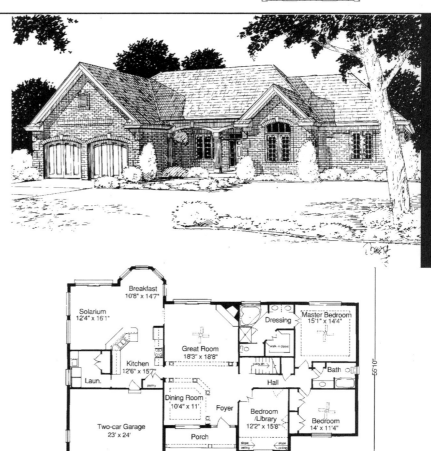

This plan features:
– Three bedrooms
– Three full baths

Foyer accented by columns provides Entry into the formal Dining Room

Angled island Kitchen is open to the Breakfast Bay

Great Room with cathedral ceiling is enhanced by a fireplace

Secluded Master Suite with a skylit Bath

Two secondary Bedrooms with an alternate Bath design create a wheel chair accessible option for the disabled

Bonus Room possibilities include a terrific fourth Bedroom and Bath

No materials list is available for this plan

MAIN FLOOR — 2,283 SQ. FT.
GARAGE — 545 SQ. FT.

TOTAL LIVING AREA:
2,283 SQ. FT.

Solarium 12'4" x 16'1"
Breakfast 10'8" x 14'7"
Master Bedroom 15'1" x 14'4"
Dressing
Kitchen 12'6" x 15'7"
Great Room 18'3" x 18'8"
Laun.
Bath
Dining Room 10'4" x 11'
Foyer
Hall
Bedroom /Library 12'2" x 15'8"
Bedroom 14' x 11'4"
Two-car Garage 23' x 24'
Porch

MAIN FLOOR

©1997Donald A. Gardner Architects, Inc.

Wrapping Front Porch and Gabled Dormers

Price Code: F

- ■ This plan features:
- — Four bedrooms
- — Three full baths

- ■ Generous Great Room with a fireplace, cathedral ceiling, and a balcony above

- ■ Flexible Bedroom/Study having a walk-in closet and an adjacent full Bath

- ■ Master Suite with a sunny bay window and a private Bath topped by a cathedral ceiling and highlighted by his-n-her vanities, and a separate tub and shower

- ■ Two additional Bedrooms, each with dormer windows, share a full bath with a cathedral ceiling, palladian window and a double vanity

- ■ Bonus room over the Garage for future expansion

FIRST FLOOR — 1,939 SQ. FT.
SECOND FLOOR — 657 SQ. FT.
GARAGE & STORAGE — 526 SQ. FT.
BONUS ROOM — 386 SQ. FT.

TOTAL LIVING AREA:
2,596 SQ. FT.

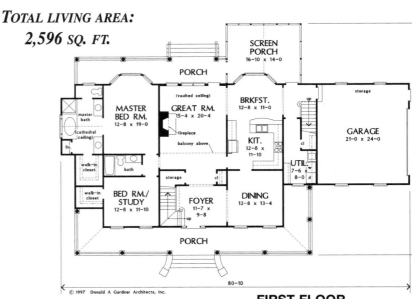

© 1997 Donald A Gardner Architects, Inc.

FIRST FLOOR
No. 96411

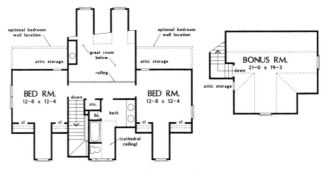

SECOND FLOOR

To order your Blueprints, call 1-800-235-5700

Attractive Exterior

PRICE CODE: C

- This plan features:
  — Three bedrooms
  — Two full baths
- In the gallery columns separate space into the Great Room and the Dining Room
- Access to backyard covered Patio from bayed Breakfast Nook
- The large Kitchen is a chef's dream with lots of counter space and a Pantry
- The Master Bedroom is removed from traffic areas and contains a luxurious Master Bath
- A hall connects the two secondary Bedrooms which share a full skylit Bath
- No materials list is available for this plan

MAIN FLOOR — 2,167 SQ. FT.
GARAGE — 690 SQ. FT.

TOTAL LIVING AREA:
2,167 SQ. FT.

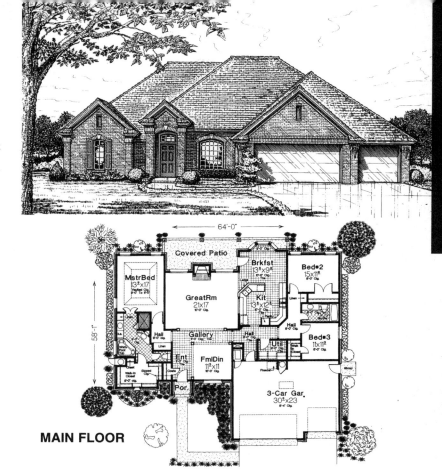

MAIN FLOOR

Demonstrative Detail

PRICE CODE: C

- This plan features:
  — Three bedrooms
  — Two full and one half baths
- Keystone arched windows, stone and stucco combine with shutters and a flower box to create an eye-catching elevation
- The Foyer accesses the Dining Room, Family Room or the Master Suite
- The Family Room has a sloped ceiling and is accented by a fireplace with windows to either side
- The Kitchen/Breakfast Area has easy access to the rear Porch
- Two roomy Bedrooms on the second floor share the full hall Bath
- An optional Bonus Area over the Garage offers possibilities for future expansion

FIRST FLOOR — 1,317 SQ. FT.
SECOND FLOOR — 537 SQ. FT.
BONUS — 312 SQ. FT.
BASEMENT — 1,317 SQ. FT.

TOTAL LIVING AREA:
1,854 SQ. FT.

Classically Appointed
PRICE CODE: D

- This plan features:
  — Three bedrooms
  — Two full baths
- The recessed front entry leads into a formal Foyer
- The Dining room has a bright front window and directly accesses the Kitchen
- The Kitchen is U-shaped and features a wall oven, and an angled counter eating bar
- There is an Eating Bay that overlooks the back Porch and is open to the Kitchen
- The Den has a 12-foot raised ceiling and a fireplace
- The Master Suite features a raised ceiling, a full Bath, and a walk-in closet
- Two large secondary Bedrooms share a Bath in the hall
- This plan is available with a slab or a crawl space foundation — please specify when ordering

MAIN FLOOR — 1,856 SQ. FT.
GARAGE — 521 SQ. FT.

TOTAL LIVING AREA:
1,856 SQ. FT.

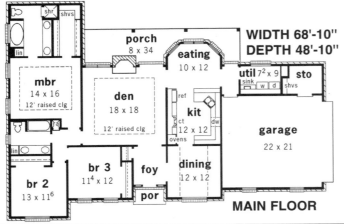

WIDTH 68'-10"
DEPTH 48'-10"

MAIN FLOOR

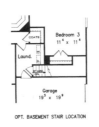

Covered Porch with Columns
PRICE CODE: C

- This plan features:
  — Three bedrooms
  — Two full baths
- The Foyer with 12' ceiling leads past decorative columns into the Family Room with a center fireplace
- The Living Room and Dining Room are linked by the Foyer and have windows overlooking the front Porch
- The Kitchen has a serving bar and is adjacent to the Breakfast Nook which has a French door that opens to the backyard
- The private Master Suite has a tray ceiling, a vaulted Bath with a double vanity, and a walk-in closet
- The two other Bedrooms share a full Bath
- An optional basement, slab, or crawl space foundation — please specify when ordering

MAIN FLOOR — 1,856 SQ. FT.
GARAGE — 429 SQ. FT.

TOTAL LIVING AREA:
1,856 SQ. FT.

To order your Blueprints, call 1-800-235-5700

Country Front Porch

Price Code: A

■ This plan features:

— Three bedrooms

— Two full baths

■ A ten-foot high ceiling and a cozy fire-place accent the expansive Great Room.

■ The Kitchen and the Dining Room adjoin for a feeling of more space.

■ The split Bedroom floor plan is perfect for families with older children.

■ The Master Suite is near the garage entrance for a quick change of clothes after work.

■ A rear Porch expands living space to the outside.

MAIN FLOOR — 1,458 SQ. FT.
GARAGE — 452 SQ. FT.

TOTAL LIVING AREA:
1,458 SQ. FT.

MAIN FLOOR

67'

40'

BATH

MASTER SUITE
12 × 16
FAN

CLOSET

STO

A/C

GARAGE
21 × 21

UTIL

DRY   WASH

KITCHEN
9 × 12
10' CEILING

REFG   RANGE

D/W

BAR

PORCH

DINING
12 × 12
10' CEILING

DIVIDER

GREAT RM
14 × 22
10' CEILING
FAN

F/P

PORCH

LIN   CLO

BATH

CLO   CLO

BEDRM
11 × 12

BEDRM
11 × 12

Opulence and Grandeur

Price Code: F

■ This plan features:

— Four bedrooms

— Three full and one half baths

■ Dramatic two-story glass Entry with a curved staircase

■ Both Living and Family rooms offer high ceilings, decorative windows and large fireplaces

■ Large, but efficient Kitchen with a cook-top serving island, walk-in pantry, bright Breakfast area and Patio access

■ Lavish Master Bedroom with a cathedral ceiling, two walk-in closets, and large bath

■ Two additional bedrooms with ample closets, share a double vanity bath

■ A materials list is not available for this plan

FIRST FLOOR — 2,506 SQ. FT.
SECOND FLOOR — 1,415 SQ. FT.
GARAGE — 660 SQ. FT.

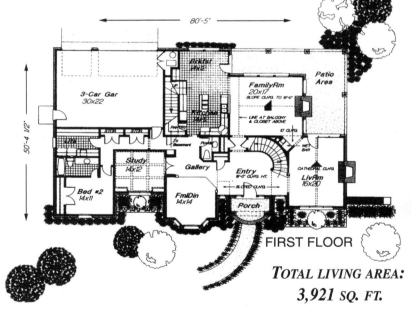

FIRST FLOOR

TOTAL LIVING AREA:
3,921 SQ. FT.

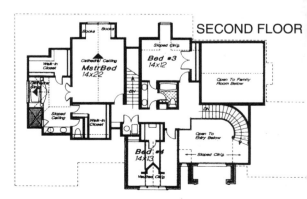

SECOND FLOOR

To order your Blueprints, call 1-800-235-5700

Spectacular Traditional

PRICE CODE: B

This plan features:
- Three bedrooms
- Two full baths
- The use of gable roofs and the blend of stucco and brick to form a spectacular exterior
- A high vaulted ceiling and a cozy fireplace, with built-in cabinets in the Den
- An efficient, U-shaped Kitchen with an adjacent Dining Area
- A Master Bedroom, with a raised ceiling, that includes a private Bath and a walk-in closet
- Two family Bedrooms that share a full hall Bath
- An optional slab or crawl space foundation — please specify when ordering

MAIN AREA — 1,237 SQ. FT.

GARAGE — 436 SQ. FT.

TOTAL LIVING AREA: 1,237 SQ. FT.

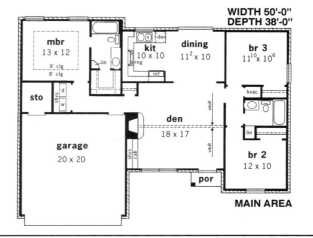

Enhanced by a Columned Porch

PRICE CODE: C

This plan features:
- Three bedrooms
- Two full baths
- A Great Room with a fireplace and decorative ceiling
- A large efficient Kitchen with Breakfast Area
- A Master Bedroom with a private Master Bath and walk-in closet
- A formal Dining Room conveniently located near the Kitchen
- Two additional Bedrooms with walk-in closets and use of full hall Bath
- An optional slab or crawl space foundation — please specify when ordering

MAIN FLOOR — 1,754 SQ. FT.

GARAGE — 552 SQ. FT.

TOTAL LIVING AREA: 1,754 SQ. FT.

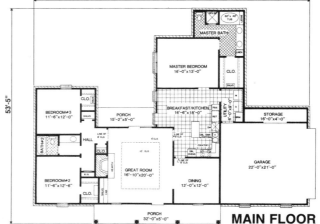

Family Friendly

Price Code: C

■ This plan features:

— Three bedrooms

— Two full baths

■ The combination Great Room and Dining Room have eight inch columns visually separating the rooms.

■ The Kitchen/Breakfast Nook has easy access to the Grilling Porch

■ The Laundry Room is located in proximity to the Kitchen

■ The Computer Center is located close the secondary Bedrooms

■ An optional crawl space or slab foundation — please specify when ordering

■ No materials list is available for this plan

Main floor — 1,934 sq. ft.
Garage — 489 sq. ft.

Total living area:
1,934 sq. ft.

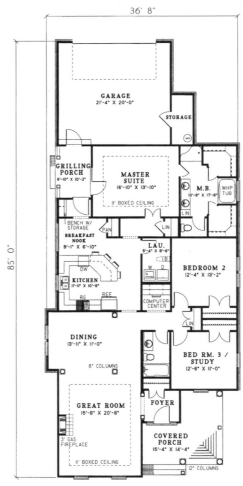

MAIN FLOOR

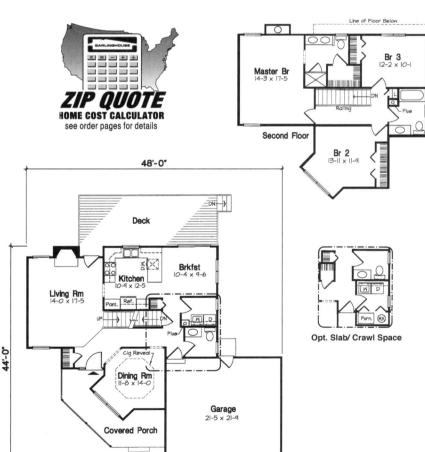

Second Floor

Master Br
14-3 x 17-5

Br 3
12-2 x 10-1

Br 2
13-11 x 11-9

Line of Floor Below

DN

Railing

Flue

Opt. Slab/ Crawl Space

Furn.

W D

Covered Porch on Farm Style Traditional

Price Code: B

■ This plan features:

— Three bedrooms

— Two full and one half baths

■ A Dining Room with bay window and elevated ceiling

■ A Living Room complete with gas light fireplace

■ A two-car Garage

■ Ample storage space throughout the home

FIRST FLOOR — 909 SQ. FT
SECOND FLOOR — 854 SQ. FT.
BASEMENT — 899 SQ. FT.
GARAGE — 491 SQ. FT.

TOTAL LIVING AREA:
1,763 SQ. FT.

48'-0"

44'-0"

Deck

DN

Brkfst
10-4 x 9-6

Kitchen
10-4 x 12-5

Pant. Ref.

Living Rm
14-0 x 17-5

UP DN

Flue

Clg Reveal

Dining Rm
11-8 x 14-0

Garage
21-5 x 21-9

Covered Porch

First Floor

© 1994 Donald A. Gardner Architects, Inc.

The Great Outdoors

Price Code: F

■ This plan features:

— Four bedrooms

— Two full and one half baths

■ Bay windows and a long, skylit, screened Porch make this four Bedroom country home a haven for outdoor enthusiasts

■ Foyer is open to take advantage of the light from the central dormer with palladian window

■ Vaulted ceiling in the Great Room adds vertical drama to the room

■ Contemporary Kitchen is open to the Great Room creating a feeling of additional space

■ Master Suite is privately tucked away with a large luxurious Bath complete with a bay window, corner shower, and a garden tub

FIRST FLOOR — 1,907 SQ. FT.
SECOND FLOOR — 656 SQ. FT.
BONUS ROOM — 467 SQ. FT.
GARAGE & STORAGE — 580 SQ. FT.

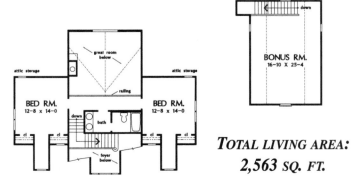

FIRST FLOOR PLAN

© 1994 Donald A Gardner Architects, Inc.

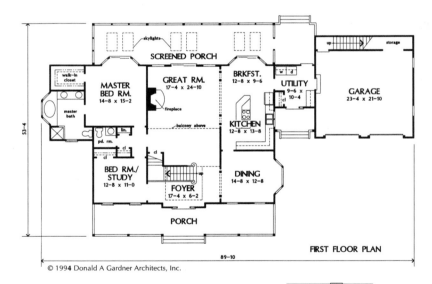

SECOND FLOOR PLAN

TOTAL LIVING AREA:
2,563 SQ. FT.

To order your Blueprints, call 1-800-235-5700

An Open Concept Home

PRICE CODE: A

This plan features:

- Three bedrooms
- Two full baths
- An angled Entry creating the illusion of space
- Two square columns that flank the bar and separate the Kitchen from the Living Room
- A Dining Room that may service both formal and informal occasions
- A Master Bedroom with a large walk-in closet
- A large Master Bath with double vanity, linen closet and whirlpool tub/shower combination
- Two additional Bedrooms that share a full Bath
- No materials list is available for this plan

MAIN FLOOR — 1,282 SQ. FT.

GARAGE — 501 SQ. FT.

TOTAL LIVING AREA:
1,282 SQ. FT.

WIDTH 48-10

DEPTH 52-6

MAIN FLOOR

© Larry E. Belk

Four Bedroom Favorite

PRICE CODE: F

This plan features:

- Four bedrooms
- Two full and one half baths
- The Hearth Room is a warm family retreat
- The open plan between the Kitchen and Breakfast Nook encourages interaction
- A box bay window and decorative ceiling beautifies the Dining Room
- The split-bedroom plan has the Master Bedroom on the first floor
- Secondary Bedrooms are located upstairs
- No materials list is available for this plan

FIRST FLOOR — 2,543 SQ. FT.

SECOND FLOOR — 1,072 SQ. FT.

BASEMENT — 2,543 SQ. FT.

GARAGE — 915 SQ. FT.

TOTAL LIVING AREA:
3,615 SQ. FT.

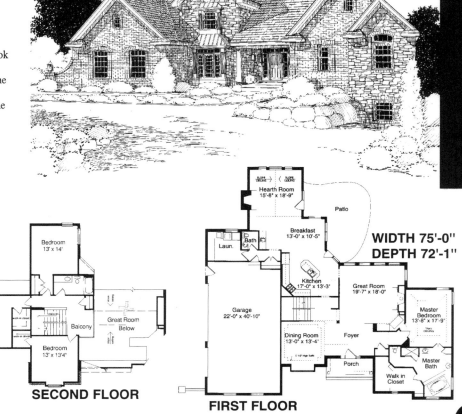

WIDTH 75'-0"
DEPTH 72'-1"

SECOND FLOOR

FIRST FLOOR

To order your Blueprints, call 1-800-235-5700

Cabin in the Country
PRICE CODE: A

- This plan features:
  — Two bedrooms
  — One full and one half baths
- A screened porch for enjoyment of your outdoor surroundings
- A combination Living and Dining area with cozy fireplace for added warmth
- An efficiently laid out Kitchen with a built-in Pantry
- Two large Bedrooms located at the rear of the home
- An optional slab or crawl space foundation — please specify when ordering

FIRST FLOOR — 928 SQ. FT.
SCREENED PORCH — 230 SQ. FT.
STORAGE — 14 SQ. FT.

TOTAL LIVING AREA:
928 SQ. FT.

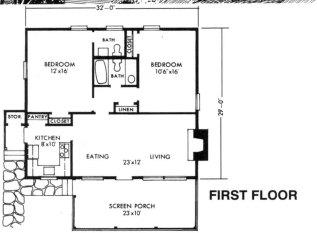

FIRST FLOOR

Cute and Compact
PRICE CODE: A

- This plan features:
  — Three bedrooms
  — One full and one half baths
- Walk-in closets are in all of the Bedrooms
- The Master Bedroom has a Sitting Area
- The Living Room has a clean burning gas fireplace
- The Kitchen is arranged in a convenient U-shape
- The Garage has an option for one or two bays

FIRST FLOOR — 732 SQ. FT.
SECOND FLOOR — 667 SQ. FT.
BASEMENT — 732 SQ. FT.
GARAGE — 406 SQ. FT.

TOTAL LIVING AREA:
1,399 SQ. FT.

WIDTH 46'-9"
DEPTH 43'-6"

FIRST FLOOR PLAN

SECOND FLOOR PLAN

To order your Blueprints, call 1-800-235-5700

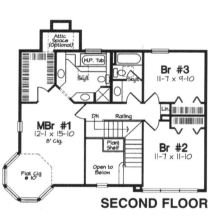

MBr #1
12-1 x 15-10

8' Clg.

Flat Clg
@ 10'

Br #3
11-7 x 9-10

Attic Space (Optional)

W.P. Tub

Skylt

Skylt

DN   Railing

Plant Shelf

Open to Below

Lin.

Br #2
11-7 x 11-10

SECOND FLOOR

ZIP QUOTE
HOME COST CALCULATOR
see order pages for details

D

W

LT

Fum

Br.

Alternate Crawl/Slab Plan

Gingerbread Charm

Price Code: D

- ■ This plan features:
- — Three bedrooms
- — Two full and one half baths

- ■ A wrap-around Porch and rear Deck adding lots of outdoor living space

- ■ A formal Parlor and Dining Room just off the central entry

- ■ A Family Room with a fireplace

- ■ A Master Suite complete with a five-sided Sitting Nook, walk-in closets and a sunken tub

FIRST FLOOR — 1,260 SQ. FT.
SECOND FLOOR — 1,021 SQ. FT.
BASEMENT — 1,186 SQ. FT.
GARAGE — 851 SQ. FT.

TOTAL LIVING AREA:
2,281 SQ. FT.

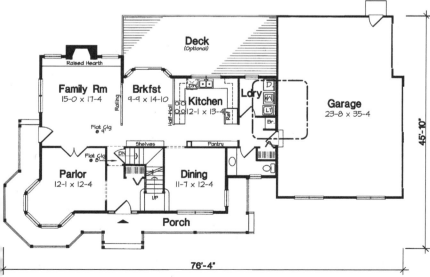

Deck
(Optional)

Raised Hearth

Family Rm
15-0 x 17-4

Railing

Flat Clg @ 8'

Brkfst
9-9 x 14-10

DN

Kitchen
12-1 x 13-4

Ldry

D

W

LT

Br.

Garage
23-8 x 35-4

45'-10"

Shelves

Pantry

Flat Clg @ 8'

DN

Parlor
12-1 x 12-4

UP

Dining
11-7 x 12-4

Porch

76'-4"

FIRST FLOOR

Charming Brick Ranch

Price Code: B

■ This plan features:

— Three bedrooms

— Two full baths

■ Sheltered entrance leads into open Foyer and Dining Room defined by columns

■ Vaulted ceiling spans Foyer, Dining Room, and Great Room with corner fireplace and atrium door to rear year

■ Central Kitchen with separate Laundry and pantry easily serves Dining Room, Breakfast Area and Screened Porch

■ Luxurious Master bedroom offers tray ceiling and French doors to double vanity, walk-in closet and whirlpool tub

■ No materials list is available for this plan

MAIN AREA —1,782 SQ. FT.
GARAGE — 406 SQ. FT.

TOTAL LIVING AREA:
1,782 SQ. FT.

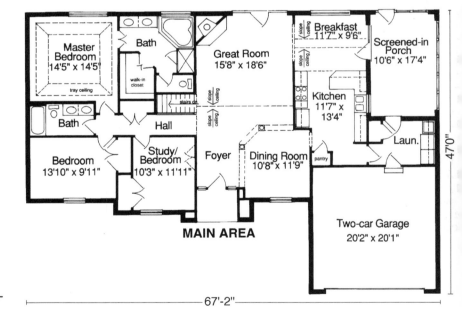

ZIP QUOTE
HOME COST CALCULATOR
see order pages for details

PLAN NO. 92630

To order your Blueprints, call 1-800-235-5700

Comfortable Design
Encourages Relaxation

PRICE CODE: E

This plan features:
- Four bedrooms
- Three full bathrooms

A wide front Porch providing a warm welcome

Center dormer lighting Foyer, as columns punctuate the entry to the Dining Room and Great Room

Spacious Kitchen with angled countertop and open to the Breakfast Bay

Tray ceilings adding elegance to the Dining Room and the Master Bedroom

Master Suite, privately located, features an arrangement for physically challenged

Two Bedrooms share a third full Bath with a linen closet

Skylit bonus room is located over the Garage

MAIN FLOOR — 2,349 SQ. FT.
BONUS — 435 SQ. FT.
GARAGE — 615 SQ. FT.

TOTAL LIVING AREA:
2,349 SQ. FT.

© 1997 Donald A. Gardner Architects, Inc.

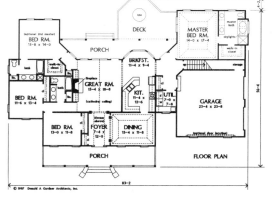

ZIP QUOTE
HOME COST CALCULATOR
see order pages for details

Your Classic Hideaway

PRICE CODE: B

This plan features:
- Three bedrooms
- Two full baths

A lovely fireplace in the Living Room which is both cozy and a source of heat for the core area

An efficient country Kitchen, connecting the large Dining and Living Rooms

A lavish Master Suite enhanced by a step-up sunken tub, more than ample closet space, and separate shower

A screened Porch and Patio Area for outdoor living

An optional basement, slab or crawl space foundation — please specify when ordering

MAIN AREA — 1,773 SQ. FT.
SCREENED PORCH — 240 SQ. FT.

TOTAL LIVING AREA:
1,773 SQ. FT.

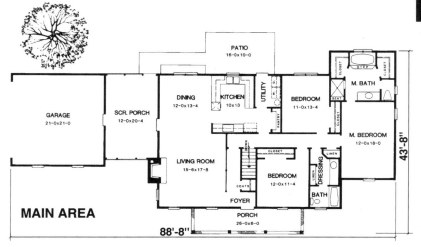

MAIN AREA

To order your Blueprints, call 1-800-235-5700

Classically Detailed
PRICE CODE: D

- ■ This plan features:
  - — Four bedrooms
  - — Two full and one half baths
- ■ Keystones and columns accent the front triple arched Porch
- ■ On either side of the two-story Foyer are arched openings to the formal areas
- ■ The Family room has a rear wall fireplace set between bank of windows
- ■ The Kitchen has a convenient center island and is open to the Nook
- ■ The Master Suite has a tray ceiling and an optional Sitting Room
- ■ Bedroom number two has a window seat in the front of the room
- ■ An optional basement, slab or crawl space foundation please specify when ordering

FIRST FLOOR — 1,200 SQ. FT.
SECOND FLOOR — 1,168 SQ. FT.
BASEMENT — 1,200 SQ. FT.
GARAGE — 527 SQ. FT.

TOTAL LIVING AREA:
2,368 SQ. FT.

SECOND FLOOR PLAN

© Frank Betz Associates

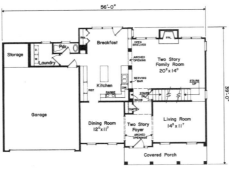

FIRST FLOOR PLAN

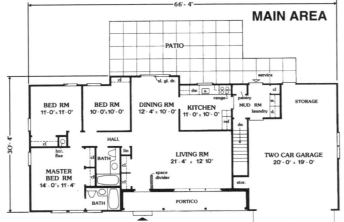

Inviting Porch Adorns Affordable Home
PRICE CODE: A

- ■ This plan features:
  - — Three bedrooms
  - — Two full baths
- ■ A large and spacious Living Room that adjoins the Dining Room for ease in entertaining
- ■ A private Bedroom wing offering a quiet atmosphere
- ■ A Master Bedroom with his-n-her closets and a private Bath
- ■ An efficient Kitchen with a walk-in Pantry

MAIN AREA — 1,243 SQ. FT.
BASEMENT — 1,103 SQ. FT.
GARAGE — 490 SQ. FT.

TOTAL LIVING AREA:
1,243 SQ. FT.

MAIN AREA

To order your Blueprints, call 1-800-235-5700

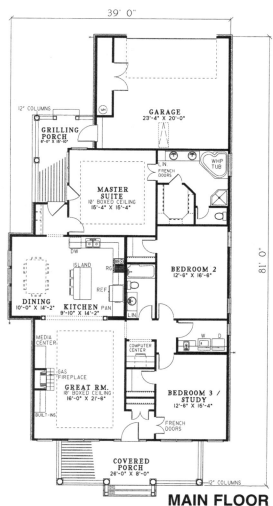

MAIN FLOOR

Garage to the Rear

Price Code: C

■ This plan features:

— Three bedrooms

— Two baths

■ The Great Room includes a box ceiling and built-ins around the gas fireplace

■ The Kitchen has a central island and a Dining Area adjoining

■ There is a built-in Computer Center making efficient use of space

■ The front Bedroom could easily become a Study

■ An optional crawl space or slab foundation — please specify when ordering

■ No materials list is available for this plan

MAIN FLOOR — 1,832 SQ. FT.
GARAGE — 492 SQ. FT.

TOTAL LIVING AREA:
1,832 SQ. FT.

ZIP QUOTE
HOME COST CALCULATOR
see order pages for details

Distinctive Brick with Room to Expand

Price Code: E

■ This plan features:

— Four bedrooms

— Two full and one half baths

■ Arched entrance with decorative glass leads into two-story Foyer

■ Formal Dining Room with tray ceiling above decorative window

■ Kitchen with island cooktop and built-in desk and Pantry

■ Master Bedroom wing topped by tray ceiling with French door to Patio, and a lavish Bath

■ Second Floor optional space for Storage and future Bedroom with full Bath

■ An optional basement, slab or crawl-space foundation — please specify when ordering

FIRST FLOOR — 2,577 SQ. FT.
BRIDGE — 68 SQ. FT.
OPTIONAL SECOND FLOOR — 619 SQ. FT.
BASEMENT — 2,561 SQ. FT.
GARAGE — 560 SQ. FT.

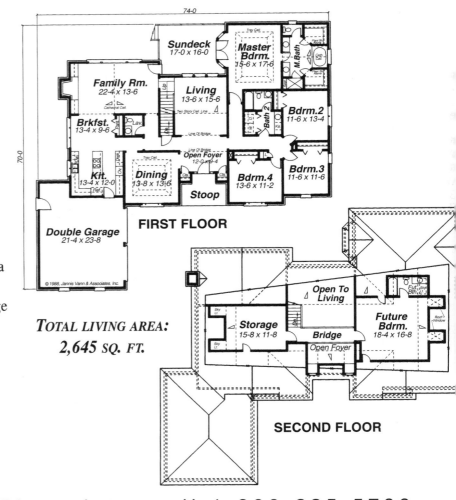

FIRST FLOOR

SECOND FLOOR

TOTAL LIVING AREA:
2,645 SQ. FT.

400

Tandem Garage

PRICE CODE: B

This plan features:
- Three bedrooms
- Two full baths

■ Open Foyer leads into spacious Living highlighted by a wall of windows

Country-size Kitchen with efficient, U-shaped counter, work island, eating Nook with back yard access, and nearby Laundry/Garage entry

French doors open to pampering Master Bedroom with window alcove, walk-in closet and double vanity Bath

Two additional Bedrooms with large closets, share a full Bath

MAIN FLOOR — 1,761 SQ. FT.
GARAGE — 658 SQ. FT.
BASEMENT — 1,761 SQ. FT.

TOTAL LIVING AREA: 1,761 SQ. FT.

ZIP QUOTE
HOME COST CALCULATOR
see order pages for details

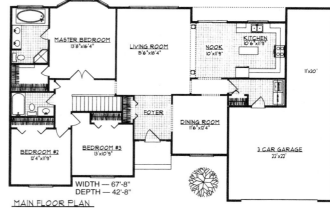

MASTER BEDROOM 13'8"x16'4"
LIVING ROOM 15'6"x18'4"
NOOK 10'x11'9"
KITCHEN 10'6"x11'9"
11'x20'
FOYER
DINING ROOM 11'6"x12'4"
3 CAR GARAGE 22'x22'
BEDROOM #2 12'4"x11'9"
BEDROOM #3 13'x10'9"
WIDTH — 67'-8"
DEPTH — 42'-8"
MAIN FLOOR PLAN

PLAN NO. 93133

Wide Open and Convenient

PRICE CODE: B

This plan features:
- Three bedrooms
- Two full baths

Vaulted ceilings in the Dining Room and Master Bedroom

A sloped ceiling in the fireplaced Living Room

■ A skylight illuminating the Master Bath

A large Master Bedroom with a walk-in closet

MAIN FLOOR — 1,737 SQ. FT.
BASEMENT — 1,727 SQ. FT.
GARAGE — 484 SQ. FT.

TOTAL LIVING AREA: 1,737 SQ. FT.

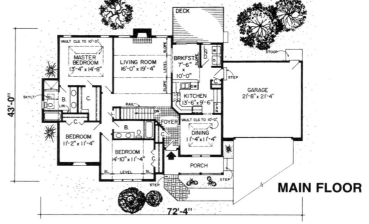

ZIP QUOTE
HOME COST CALCULATOR
see order pages for details

DECK
VAULT CLG. TO 10'-0"
MASTER BEDROOM 13'-4" x 14'-8"
LIVING ROOM 16'-0" x 19'-4"
BRKFST. 7'-6" x 10'-0"
KITCHEN 13'-6" x 9'-6"
GARAGE 21'-8" x 21'-4"
SKYLT.
43'-0"
BEDROOM 11'-2" x 11'-4"
BEDROOM 14'-10" x 11'-4"
FOYER
VAULT CLG. TO 10'-0"
DINING 11'-4" x 11'-4"
PORCH
STOOP
STEP
MAIN FLOOR
72'-4"

PLAN NO. 20100

To order your Blueprints, call 1-800-235-5700

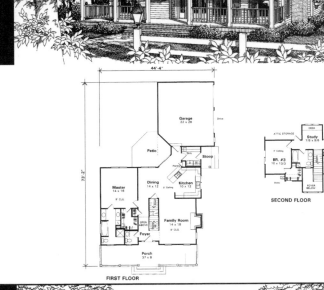

Open & Airy
PRICE CODE: C

■ This plan features:
— Three bedrooms
— Two full and one half baths
■ The Foyer is naturally lit by a dormer window above
■ Family Room is highlighted by two front windows and fireplace
■ Kitchen includes an angled extended counter/snack bar and an abundance of counter/cabinet space
■ Dining Area opens to the Kitchen, for a more spacious feeling
■ The roomy Master Suite is located on the first floor and has a private five-piece Bath plus a walk-in closet
■ Laundry Room doubles as a Mudroom from the side entrance
■ No materials list is available for this plan

FIRST FLOOR — 1,271 SQ. FT.
SECOND FLOOR — 537 SQ. FT.
BASEMENT — 1,271 SQ. FT.
GARAGE — 555 SQ. FT.

TOTAL LIVING AREA:
1,808 SQ. FT.

Quaint Starter Home
PRICE CODE: A

■ This plan features:
— Three bedrooms
— Two full baths
■ A vaulted ceiling giving an airy feeling to the Dining and Living Rooms
■ A streamlined Kitchen with a comfortable work area, a double sink and ample cabinet space
■ A cozy fireplace in the Living Room
■ A Master Suite with a large closet, French doors leading to the Patio and a private Bath
■ Two additional Bedrooms sharing a full Bath
■ No materials list is available for this plan

MAIN AREA — 1,050 SQ. FT.
GARAGE — 261 SQ. FT.

TOTAL LIVING AREA:
1,050 SQ. FT.

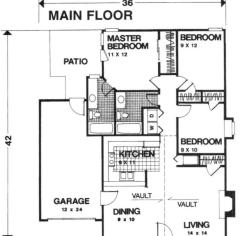

To order your Blueprints, call 1-800-235-5700

© 1994 Donald A. Gardner Architects, Inc.

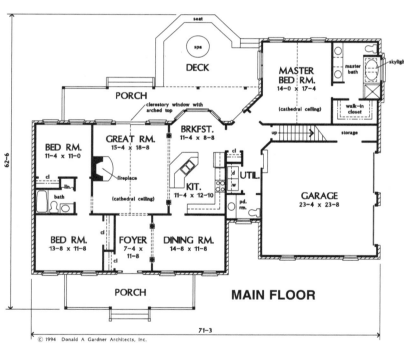

seat

spa

DECK

PORCH

MASTER
BED RM.
14-0 x 17-4

master
bath

skylights

(cathedral ceiling)

walk-in
closet

clerestory window with
arched top

BRKFST.
11-4 x 8-8

up

storage

BED RM.
11-4 x 11-0

GREAT RM.
15-4 x 18-8

62-6

cl

GARAGE
23-4 x 23-8

fireplace

KIT.
11-4 x 12-10

UTIL.

d
w

cl

(cathedral ceiling)

bath

lin.

pd.
rm.

BED RM.
13-8 x 11-8

FOYER
7-4 x
11-8

DINING RM.
14-8 x 11-8

cl

PORCH

MAIN FLOOR

71-3

© 1994 Donald A Gardner Architects, Inc.

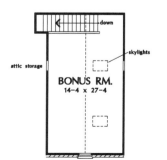

down

skylights

attic storage

BONUS RM.
14-4 x 27-4

GARLINGHOUSE

ZIP QUOTE
HOME COST CALCULATOR
see order pages for details

Mixture of Traditional and Country Charm

Price Code: D

■ This plan features:

— Three bedrooms

— Two full and one half baths

■ Stairs to the skylit bonus room located near the Kitchen and Master Suite

■ Master Suite crowned in cathedral ceilings has a skylit Bath that contains a whirlpool tub and dual vanity

■ Great Room, topped by a cathedral ceiling and highlighted by a fireplace, is adjacent to the country Kitchen

■ Two additional Bedrooms share a hall Bath

MAIN FLOOR — 1,954 SQ. FT.
GARAGE — 649 SQ. FT.
BONUS ROOM — 436 SQ. FT.

TOTAL LIVING AREA:
1,954 SQ. FT.

Country Style For Today

Price Code: D

- This plan features:
— Three bedrooms
— Two full and one half baths

- A wide wrap-around porch for a farmhouse style

- A spacious Living Room with double doors and a large front window

- A garden window over the double sink in the huge, country Kitchen with two islands, one a butcher block, and the other an eating bar

- A corner fireplace in the Family Room enjoyed throughout the Nook and Kitchen, thanks to an open layout

- A Master Suite with a spa tub, and a huge walk-in closet as well as a shower and double vanities

FIRST FLOOR — 1,785 SQ. FT.
SECOND FLOOR — 621 SQ. FT.

TOTAL LIVING AREA:
2,406 SQ. FT.

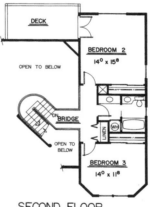

SECOND FLOOR

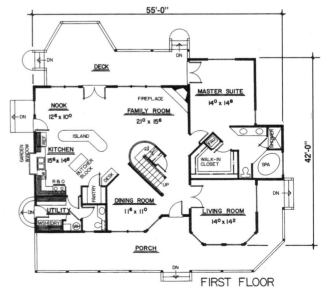

FIRST FLOOR

To order your Blueprints, call 1-800-235-5700

Skylight Brightens Master Bedroom

PRICE CODE: B

This plan features:
– Three bedrooms
– One full and one three-quarter baths
■ A covered Porch entry
■ A foyer separating the Dining Room from the Breakfast Area and Kitchen
■ A Living Room enhanced by a vaulted beam ceiling and a fireplace
■ A Master Bedroom with a decorative ceiling and a skylight in the private Bath
■ An optional Deck accessible through sliding doors off the Master Bedroom

MAIN AREA — 1,686 SQ. FT.
GARAGE — 484 SQ. FT.
BASEMENT — 1,676 SQ. FT.

TOTAL LIVING AREA:
1,686 SQ. FT.

ZIP QUOTE
HOME COST CALCULATOR
see order pages for details

MAIN AREA

Rocking Chair Living

PRICE CODE: B

This plan features:
– Three bedrooms
– Two full baths
■ A massive fireplace separating Living and Dining Rooms
■ An isolated Master Suite with a walk-in closet and compartmentalized Bath
■ A galley-type Kitchen between the Breakfast Room and Dining Room
■ An optional basement, slab or crawl space foundation — please specify when ordering

MAIN AREA — 1,670 SQ. FT.
BASEMENT — 1,670 SQ. FT.
GARAGE — 427 SQ. FT.

TOTAL LIVING AREA:
1,670 SQ. FT.

MAIN AREA

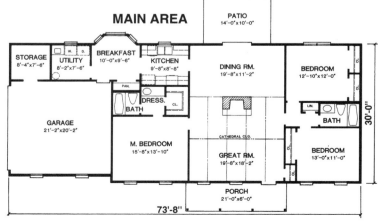

To order your Blueprints, call 1-800-235-5700

© 1992 Donald A. Gardner Architects, Inc.

Stately Home
Price Code: F

- This plan features:
— Four bedrooms
— Two full and one half baths
- An elegant brick exterior and careful detailing
- Light floods through the arched window in the clerestory dormer above the Foyer
- Great Room topped by a cathedral ceiling boasts built-in cabinets and bookshelves
- Through glass doors capped by an arched window the Sun Room is accessed from the Great Room
- Both the Dining Room and the Bedroom/Study have tray ceilings
- Master Suite includes a fireplace, access to the Deck, his and her vanities and a whirlpool tub

MAIN FLOOR — 2,526 SQ. FT.
GARAGE — 611 SQ. FT.

TOTAL LIVING AREA:
2,526 SQ. FT.

ALTERNATE PLAN FOR BASEMENT

FLOOR PLAN

© Donald A. Gardner Architects, Inc.

French Country Styling
Price Code: F

- This plan features:
— Four bedrooms
— Three full and one half baths
- Brick and stone blend masterfully for an impressive French Country exterior
- Separate Master Suite has an expansive Bath and closet
- Study contains a built-in desk and a bookcase
- Angled island Kitchen is highlighted by a walk-in Pantry
- Fantastic Family Room includes a brick fireplace and a built-in entertainment center
- Three additional Bedrooms have private access to a full Bath
- No materials list is available for this plan

MAIN FLOOR — 3,352 SQ. FT.
GARAGE — 672 SQ. FT.

TOTAL LIVING AREA:
3,352 SQ. FT.

MAIN FLOOR

ZIP QUOTE
HOME COST CALCULATOR
see order pages for details

To order your Blueprints, call 1-800-235-5700

MAIN FLOOR

Floor plan dimensions: 39' 0" × 72' 0"

- WHP TUB
- GLASS SHWR
- M. BATH 16'-6" X 13'-0"
- GARAGE 19'-4" X 19'-0"
- MASTER SUITE 16'-8" X 15'-0"
- 11' BOXED CEILING
- GRILLING PORCH 8'-4" X 8'-11"
- LAU. 7'-0" X 6'-5"
- W   D
- KID'S NOOK
- PANTRY
- BENCH W/ STORAGE
- BEDROOM 2 13'-4" X 12'-1"
- KITCHEN 13'-2" X 12'-1"
- REF
- RG
- DW
- DINING 11'-6" X 11'-9"
- 8" COLUMNS
- LIN
- COMPUTER AREA
- MEDIA CENTER
- GREAT ROOM 17'-8" X 17'-0"
- FOYER
- 3' GAS FIREPLACE
- BEDROOM 3 / STUDY 13'-4" X 12'-0"
- 8" COLUMNS
- COVERED PORCH 25'-0" X 8'-0"
- 12" COLUMNS

Easy Living
Price Code: C

- ■ This plan features:
- — Three bedrooms
- — Two full baths
- ■ This home includes a built-in computer area and a media center in the Great Room
- ■ The Dining Room and the Kitchen adjoin with a peninsula counter/snack bar between them
- ■ A decorative ceiling and a five-piece bath add to the elegance and convenience of the Master Suite
- ■ An optional crawl space or slab foundation — please specify when ordering
- ■ No materials list is available for this plan

MAIN FLOOR — 1,915 SQ. FT.
GARAGE — 401 SQ. FT.
PORCH — 279 SQ. FT.

TOTAL LIVING AREA:
1,915 SQ. FT.

Discriminating Buyers

Price Code: B

■ This plan features:

— Three bedrooms

— Two full baths

■ A sheltered entrance into the Foyer

■ A sloped ceiling adding elegance to the formal Dining Room

■ A sloped ceiling and a corner fireplace enhancing the Great Room

■ A peninsula counter joins the Kitchen and the Breakfast Room in an open layout

■ A Master Suite, equipped with a large walk-in closet and a private Bath with an oval corner tub

■ Two additional Bedrooms that share a full hall Bath

MAIN AREA — 1,746 SQ. FT.
BASEMENT — 1,560 SQ. FT.
GARAGE — 455 SQ. FT.

**TOTAL LIVING AREA:
1,746 SQ. FT.**

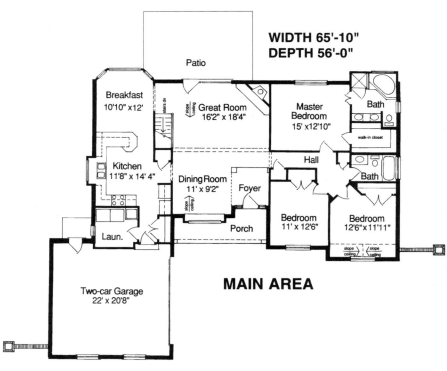

WIDTH 65'-10"
DEPTH 56'-0"

MAIN AREA

ZIP QUOTE
HOME COST CALCULATOR
see order pages for details

To order your Blueprints, call 1-800-235-5700

Definitely Detailed

PRICE CODE: C

This plan features:

- Three bedrooms
- Two full baths

An artistically detailed brick exterior adds to the appeal of this home

The Foyer is separated from the Great room by columns

The Great Room has a wall of windows and a warming fireplace

The Dining Room has a sloped ceiling and is adjacent to the Kitchen

The Kitchen is arranged in a U-shape and features a center island plus a walk-in Pantry

The Bedrooms are all on one side of the home for privacy

An optional plan for the basement includes a Recreation Room, an Exercise Room, and a Bath

No materials list is available for this plan

FIRST FLOOR — 1,963 SQ. FT.

LOWER LEVEL — 1,963 SQ. FT.

TOTAL LIVING AREA:
1,963 SQ. FT.

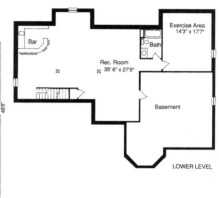

For an Established Neighborhood

PRICE CODE: A

This plan features:

- Three bedrooms
- Two full baths

A covered entrance sheltering and welcoming visitors

An expansive Living Room enhanced by natural light streaming in from the large front window

A bayed formal Dining Room with direct access to the Sun Deck and the Living Room for entertainment ease

An efficient, galley Kitchen, convenient to both formal and informal eating areas, and equipped with a double sink and adequate counter and storage space

An informal Breakfast Room with direct access to the Sun Deck

A large Master Suite equipped with a walk-in closet and a full private Bath

Two additional Bedrooms that share a full hall Bath

MAIN FLOOR — 1,276 SQ. FT.

FINISHED STAIRS — 16 SQ. FT.

BASEMENT — 392 SQ. FT.

GARAGE — 728 SQ. FT.

TOTAL LIVING AREA:
1,292 SQ. FT.

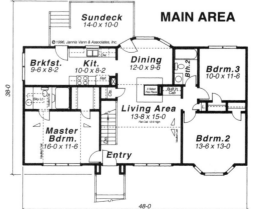

ZIP QUOTE
HOME COST CALCULATOR
see order pages for details

To order your Blueprints, call 1-800-235-5700

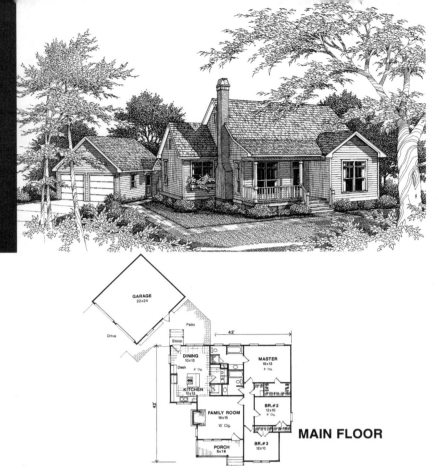

Cute Cottage
PRICE CODE: A

- This plan features:
— Three bedrooms
— Two full baths
- A cute covered front Porch adds character to this cottage plan
- The large Living Room has a 10-foot ceiling and a side wall fireplace
- The Kitchen is open to the Dining Room
- The Kitchen is equipped with a center island, a planning desk, and a cooktop
- A convenient Laundry Room is located off of the Kitchen
- The Master Bedroom has a walk in closet and a full Bath
- Two secondary Bedrooms are identical in size and share a Bath in the hall
- There is a detached two-car Garage with this plan
- No materials list is available for this plan

MAIN FLOOR — 1,393 SQ. FT.
GARAGE — 528 SQ. FT.

TOTAL LIVING AREA:
1,393 SQ. FT.

MAIN FLOOR

Cozy Front and Back Porches
PRICE CODE: B

- This plan features:
— Three bedrooms
— Two full baths
- A spacious Great Room is highlighted by a corner fireplace and access to the rear porch
- The Dining area with views of the front yard is separated from the Kitchen by an eating bar
- The private Master Suite is tucked into the rear left corner of the home
- A tray ceiling, a whirlpool tub and a walk-in closet highlight the Master suite
- Two additional Bedrooms are located on the opposite side of the home, a full Bath is between the Bedrooms

MAIN FLOOR — 1,652 SQ. FT.
GARAGE — 497 SQ. FT.

TOTAL LIVING AREA:
1,652 SQ. FT.

MAIN FLOOR

© 1996 Donald A Gardner Architects, Inc.

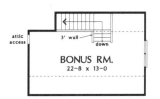

attic access

3' wall

down

BONUS RM.
22-8 x 13-0

DECK

MASTER BED RM.
14-0 x 16-0

skylight

master bath

lin.

UTILITY
7-0 6-4

down

walk-in closet

d w

BED RM.
12-0 x 13-0

GREAT RM.
16-8 x 19-6

(cathedral ceiling)

fireplace

cl

bath

lin.

cl

BRKFST.
12-0 x 9-8

up

storage

GARAGE
22-8 x 19-8

KIT.
12-0 x 12-2

cl

FOYER
8-2 x 6-8

cl

BED RM./ STUDY
12-0 x 11-4

PORCH

DINING
12-0 x 12-4

(optional door location)

FLOOR PLAN

55-2

65-8

© 1996 Donald A Gardner Architects, Inc.

Easy, Economical Building

Price Code: D

■ This plan features:

— Three bedrooms

— Two full baths

■ Many architectural elements offer efficient and economical design

■ Great Room vaulted ceiling gracefully arches to include arched window dormer

■ Open Kitchen with angled counter easily serves Breakfast Area

■ Tray ceilings enhance Dining Room, front Bedroom and Master Bedroom

■ Private Master Bath includes garden tub, double vanity and skylight

MAIN FLOOR — 1,959 SQ. FT.
BONUS ROOM — 385 SQ. FT.
GARAGE & STORAGE — 484 SQ. FT.

TOTAL LIVING AREA:
1,959 SQ. FT.

Elegant Brick Two-Story

Price Code: D

- ■ This plan features:
- — Four bedrooms
- — Two full and one half baths
- ■ A large two-story Great Room with a fireplace and access to a wood Deck
- ■ A secluded Master Suite with two walk-in closets and a private, lavish, Master Bath
- ■ A large island Kitchen serving the formal Dining Room and the sunny Breakfast Nook with ease
- ■ Three additional Bedrooms, two with walk-in closets, sharing a full hall Bath
- ■ An optional bonus room with a private entrance from below
- ■ An optional basement or crawl space foundation — please specify when ordering

FIRST FLOOR — 1,637 SQ. FT.
SECOND FLOOR — 761 SQ. FT.
BONUS — 453 SQ. FT.

SECOND FLOOR PLAN

TOTAL LIVING AREA:
2,398 SQ. FT.

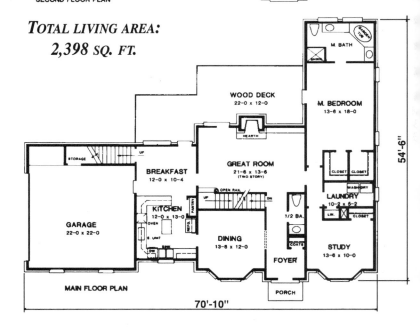

MAIN FLOOR PLAN

To order your Blueprints, call 1-800-235-5700

Traditional Ranch

PRICE CODE: D

This plan features:
- Three bedrooms
- Two full baths
- A tray ceiling in the Master Suite that is equipped with his and her walk-in closets and a private Master Bath with a cathedral ceiling
- A formal Living Room with a cathedral ceiling
- A decorative tray ceiling in the elegant formal Dining Room
- A spacious Family Room with a vaulted ceiling and a fireplace
- A modern, well-appointed Kitchen with snack bar and bayed Breakfast Area
- Two additional Bedrooms that share a full hall Bath each having a walk-in closet

MAIN FLOOR — 2,275 SQ. FT.
GARAGE — 512 SQ. FT.
BASEMENT — 2,207 SQ. FT.

TOTAL LIVING AREA:
2,275 SQ. FT.

MAIN FLOOR

Elegant Brick Veneer

PRICE CODE: E

This plan features:
- Three bedrooms
- Two full and one half baths
- Arched and oval windows enhance the elegance of this home
- Open, formal Dining Room defined by columns and topped with tray ceiling
- Expansive Great Room offers a tray ceiling, Porch access and a cozy fireplace with windows all around
- Curved serving counter, vaulted ceiling and bright Breakfast Area highlight Kitchen
- Separate Master Bedroom accented by a vaulted ceiling, roomy walk-in closet and lavish Bath
- Two secondary Bedrooms, with roomy closets, near laundry and double vanity Bath
- Bonus Room offers attic storage and cozy window seat

MAIN FLOOR — 2,198 SQ. FT.
BONUS ROOM — 325 SQ. FT.
GARAGE — 588 SQ. FT.

TOTAL LIVING AREA:
2,198 SQ. FT.

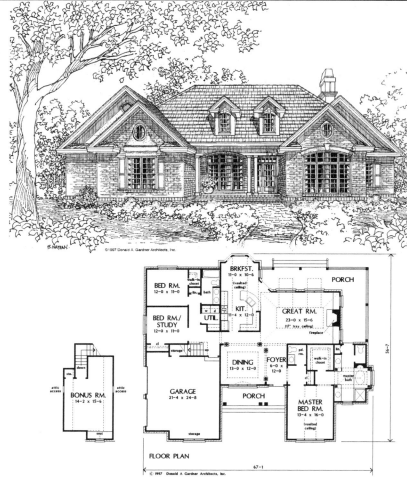

FLOOR PLAN

Romantic Second Floor Porch

Price Code: C

■ This plan features:

— Three bedrooms

— Two full and one half baths

■ The first floor Master Suite is tucked into the rear of the home allowing for the maximum in privacy

■ The Great Room includes a gas fireplace for a cozy atmosphere

■ The Dining Room is accented by columns at its entrance

■ An optional basement, crawl space or slab foundation — please specify when ordering

■ There is no material list available for this plan

FIRST FLOOR — 1,298 SQ. FT.
SECOND FLOOR — 624 SQ. FT.
GARAGE — 431 SQ. FT.
PORCH — 353 SQ. FT.

TOTAL LIVING AREA:
1,922 SQ. FT.

FIRST FLOOR

36' 4"

64' 10"

WHP TUB
M. BATH
14'-8" X 10'-4"
LIN
GLASS SHWR

GARAGE
20'-8" X 20'-0"

MASTER SUITE
14'-8" X 16'-1"

LAU.
7'-2" X 5'-6"

GRILLING PORCH
11'-2" X 10'-8"

FRENCH DOORS

REF
PAN

KITCHEN
10'-0" X 13'-0"

OPT. COURT YARD

DW
RG

GREAT ROOM
14'-8" X 16'-5"

3' GAS FIREPLACE

DINING
9'-8" X 16'-10"

8' COLUMNS

COVERED PORCH
16'-4" X 9'-0"

8X8 BOXED COL.

SECOND FLOOR

LIN
COMPUTER DESK
LIN

BEDROOM 2
12'-8" X 14'-1"
8' CEILING

BEDROOM 3
12'-0" X 16'-1"
8' CEILING

PORCH
16'-6" X 8'-4"

To order your Blueprints, call 1-800-235-5700

© Frank Betz Associates

61'-0"

Den / Bedroom 4
13⁵ x 11⁰

Two Story
Family Room
14⁵ x 18²

Breakfast

Laund.

Storage

Bath

LINEN

Living Room
13⁵ x 14⁰

Two Story
Foyer

Dining Room
13⁵ x 11⁰

Kitchen

Garage
20⁸ x 20⁵

FIRST FLOOR
No. 98410

TOTAL LIVING AREA:
2,389 SQ. FT.

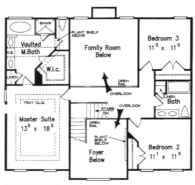

Vaulted
M.Bath

W.I.c.

Family Room
Below

Bedroom 3
11⁰ x 11⁰

Bath

Master Suite
13⁵ x 18⁵

Foyer
Below

Bedroom 2
11¹ x 11⁰

SECOND FLOOR

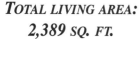

Bedroom 3
11⁰ x 12⁴

Bath

Bonus Room
12¹⁰ x 20⁵

Bedroom 2
13⁵ x 12³

SECOND FLOOR WITH BONUS ROOM

A Magnificent Manor
Price Code: D

- This plan features:
  — Three bedrooms
  — Three full baths
- The two-story Foyer is dominated by a lovely staircase
- The formal Living Room is located directly off the Foyer
- An efficient Kitchen accesses the Dining Room for ease in serving
- The Breakfast Area is separated from the Kitchen by an extended counter/serving bar
- The two-story Family Room is highlighted by a fireplace that is framed by windows
- A tray ceiling crowns the Master Bedroom while a vaulted ceiling tops the Master Bath
- An optional basement or crawl space foundation — please specify when ordering

FIRST FLOOR — 1,428 SQ. FT.
SECOND FLOOR — 961 SQ. FT.
BONUS — 472 SQ. FT.
BASEMENT — 1,428 SQ. FT.
GARAGE — 507 SQ. FT.

For a Golf Course

Price Code: D

- This plan features:
— Three bedrooms
— Three full and one half baths

- A combination of exterior textures and a built-in window box gives a warm curb presence to this home

- Great care has been given to enhance the rear views created by living on a golf course by allowing a terrific sight line through many windows

- A second floor verandah provides a quiet spot and added living space

- No materials list is available for this plan

FIRST FLOOR — 1,661 SQ. FT.
SECOND FLOOR — 882 SQ. FT.
GARAGE — 497 SQ. FT.

TOTAL LIVING AREA:
2,543 SQ. FT.

WIDTH 59'-0"
DEPTH 58'-11"

FIRST FLOOR

FAIRWAY DINING 15'-0" X 10'-0"
GATHERING ROOM 18'-2" X 19'-2"
TERRACE
KITCHEN 15'-0" X 13'-2"
MASTER SUITE 13'-8" X 16'-2"
DINING ROOM 12'-0" X 15'-6"
FOYER
HIS
HERS
LAUN.
STOOP
PDR.
MASTER BATH
GARAGE 21'-6" X 21'-10"

SECOND FLOOR

SUITE 2 12'-2" X 14'-0"
LINKSIDE RETREAT 19'-4" X 14'-10"
FAIRWAY VERANDA
SUITE 3 12'-0" X 12'-0"
BATH
OPEN TO BELOW
STOR.
W.I.C.
BATH
ATTIC

To order your Blueprints, call 1-800-235-5700

Backyard Views
PRICE CODE: B

This plan features:
- Three bedrooms
- Two full baths
- Front Porch accesses open Foyer, and spacious Dining Room and Great Room with sloped ceilings
- Corner fireplace, windows and atrium door to Patio enhance Great Room
- Convenient Kitchen with a Pantry, peninsula serving counter for bright Breakfast Area and nearby Laundry/Garage entry
- Luxurious Bath, walk-in closet and backyard view offered in Master Bedroom
- Two additional Bedrooms, one with an arched window, share a full Bath

MAIN AREA — 1,746 SQ. FT.
BASEMENT — 1,697 SQ. FT.
GARAGE — 480 SQ. FT.

TOTAL LIVING AREA:
1,746 SQ. FT.

ZIP QUOTE
HOME COST CALCULATOR
see order pages for details

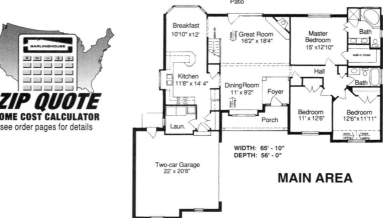

WIDTH: 65' - 10"
DEPTH: 56' - 0"

MAIN AREA

Compact Country Cottage
PRICE CODE: C

This plan features:
- Three bedrooms
- Two full baths
- Foyer opening to a large Great Room with a fireplace and a cathedral ceiling
- Efficient U-shaped Kitchen with peninsula counter extending work space and separating it from the Dining Room
- Two front Bedrooms, one with a bay window, the other with a walk-in closet, sharing a full Bath in the hall
- Master Suite located to the rear with a walk-in closet and a private Bath with a double vanity
- Partially covered Deck with skylights accessible from the Dining Room, Great Room and the Master Bedroom

MAIN FLOOR — 1,310 SQ. FT.
GARAGE & STORAGE — 455 SQ. FT.

TOTAL LIVING AREA:
1,310 SQ. FT.

91 Donald A. Gardner Architects, Inc.

FLOOR PLAN

To order your Blueprints, call 1-800-235-5700

A Nest for Empty-Nesters
PRICE CODE: A

- This plan features:
  — Two bedrooms
  — One full bath
- An economical design
- A covered Sun Deck adding outdoor living space
- A Mudroom/Laundry area inside the side door, trapping dirt before it can enter the house
- An open layout between the Living Room with fireplace Dining Room and Kitchen

MAIN FLOOR — 884 SQ. FT.

TOTAL LIVING AREA:
884 SQ. FT.

MAIN FLOOR

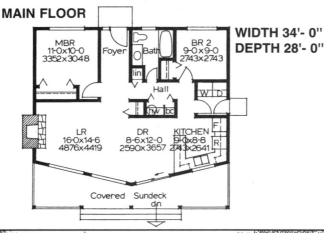

WIDTH 34'- 0"
DEPTH 28'- 0"

An
EXCLUSIVE DESIGN
By Westhome Planners, Ltd.

Style and Convenience
PRICE CODE: A

- This plan features:
  —Three bedrooms
  —Two full baths
- Large front windows, dormers and an old-fashioned Porch giving a pleasing style to the home
- A vaulted ceiling topping the Foyer flowing into the Family Room which is highlighted by a fireplace
- A Formal Dining Room flowing from the Family Room crowned in an elegant vaulted ceiling
- An efficient Kitchen enhanced by a Pantry, a pass through to the Family Room and direct access to the Dining Room and Breakfast Room
- A decorative tray ceiling, a five-piece private Bath and walk-in closet in the Master Suite
- Two additional Bedrooms, roomy in size, share the full Bath in the hall
- An optional basement or crawl space foundation — please specify when ordering

MAIN FLOOR — 1,373 SQ. FT.
BASEMENT — 1,386 SQ. FT.

TOTAL LIVING AREA:
1,373 SQ. FT.

WIDTH 50'-4"
DEPTH 45'-0"

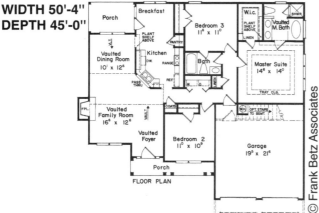

© Frank Betz Associates

To order your Blueprints, call 1-800-235-5700

B. NATHAN.

First Floor Plan

DECK

GREAT RM.
19-4 x 15-10
(cathedral ceiling)
fireplace

KIT.
13-8 x 15-4

PORCH

BRKFST.
9-11 x 10-0

MASTER
BED RM.
15-4 x 13-4

lin.

walk-in
closet

pd.
rm.

FOYER
6-0 x

cl

UTIL.
8-0 x 6-2
d   w

storage

pan.

master
bath

DINING
12-0 x 12-4

up

stor.

PORCH

GARAGE
22-4 x 21-0

FIRST FLOOR PLAN

59-8

10-0

48-0

© 1998 Donald A Gardner Architects, Inc.

Second Floor Plan

great room
below

BED RM.
11-0 x 12-0

cl

down

lin. walk-in
closet

BED RM.
11-0 x 12-0

BED RM.
14-4 x 11-0

cl

bath

down

storage

attic storage

attic storage

BONUS RM.
12-0 x 16-8

© 1998 Donald A Gardner Architects, Inc.

SECOND FLOOR PLAN

Brimming With Comfort

Price Code: E

■ This plan features:

— Four bedrooms

— Two full and one half baths

■ The Great Room offers convenience and storage with dual built-ins on either side of the fireplace

■ Graceful tray ceiling caps both the Master Bedroom and Bath on the first floor.

■ Three second floor Bedrooms are in close proximity to a full Bath in the hall.

■ The Bonus Room stands ready for future expansion.

FIRST FLOOR — 1,520 SQ. FT.
SECOND FLOOR — 743 SQ. FT.
BONUS ROOM — 259 SQ. FT.

TOTAL LIVING AREA: 2,263 SQ. FT.

© 1995 Donald A Gardner Architects, Inc.

Great Room With Columns

Price Code: D

TOTAL LIVING AREA:
1,879 SQ. FT.

ZIP QUOTE
HOME COST CALCULATOR
see order pages for details

- ■ This plan features:
- — Three bedrooms
- — Two full baths
- ■ Great Room crowned with a cathedral ceiling and accented by columns and a fireplace
- ■ Tray ceilings and arched picture windows accent front Bedroom and the Dining Room
- ■ Secluded Master Suite highlighted by a tray ceiling and contains a Bath with skylight, a garden tub and spacious walk-in closet
- ■ Two additional Bedrooms share a full Bath

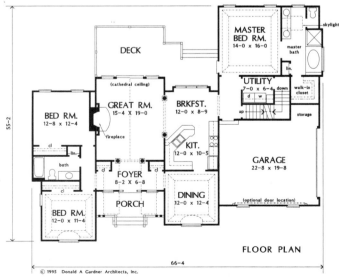

FLOOR PLAN

© 1995 Donald A Gardner Architects, Inc.

MAIN FLOOR — 1,879 SQ. FT.
GARAGE — 485 SQ. FT.
BONUS — 360 SQ. FT.

To order your Blueprints, call 1-800-235-5700

Brick Beauty

PRICE CODE: B

■ This plan features:
— Three bedrooms
— Two full baths

■ The Great Room includes a ten foot boxed ceiling and a fireplace

■ The Dining Room adjoins with the Kitchen for a more spacious feel

■ The Kitchen includes a peninsula counter/breakfast bar for meals on the go

■ The Dining Room and the Master Bedroom have access to the Court Yard

■ An optional crawl space or slab foundation — please specify when ordering

■ No materials list is available for this plan

FIRST FLOOR - 1,660 SQ. FT.
GARAGE - 390 SQ. FT.
PORCH - 143 SQ. FT.

TOTAL LIVING AREA:
1,660 SQ. FT.

MAIN FLOOR

Plush Master Bedroom Wing

PRICE CODE: C

■ This plan features:
— Three bedrooms
— Two full baths

■ A raised, tile Foyer with a decorative window leads into an expansive Living Room, accented by a tiled fireplace and framed by French doors

■ An efficient Kitchen with a walk-in Pantry and serving bar adjoins the Breakfast and Utility Areas

■ A private Master Bedroom, crowned by a stepped ceiling, offering an atrium door to outside, a huge, walk-in closet and a luxurious Bath

■ Two additional Bedrooms with walk-in closets, share a full hall Bath

■ No materials list is available for this plan

MAIN FLOOR — 1,849 SQ. FT.
GARAGE — 437 SQ. FT.

TOTAL LIVING AREA:
1,849 SQ. FT.

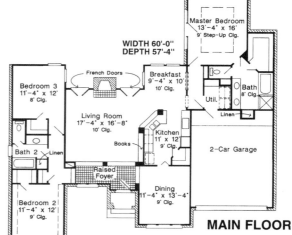

WIDTH 60'-0"
DEPTH 57'-4"

Master Bedroom
13'-4" x 16'
9' Step-Up Clg.

Bedroom 3
11'-4" x 12'
8' Clg.

French Doors

Breakfast
9'-4" x 10'
10' Clg.

Bath
8' Clg.

Util.

Linen

Living Room
17'-4" x 16'-8"
10' Clg.

Kitchen
11' x 12'
9' Clg.

2-Car Garage

Bath 2

Linen

Books

Raised Foyer

Bedroom 2
11'-4" x 12'
9' Clg.

Dining
11'-4" x 13'-4"
9' Clg.

MAIN FLOOR

Multiple Gables

Price Code: B

■ This plan features:

— Three bedrooms

— Two full and one half baths

■ A Foyer area that leads to a bright and cheery Great Room capped by a sloped ceiling and highlighted by a fireplace

■ The Dining Area includes double hung windows and angles adding light and dimension to the room

■ A functional Kitchen providing an abundance of counter space with additional room provided by a breakfast bar

■ A Master Bedroom Suite including a walk-in closet and private Bath

■ Two additional Bedrooms share a full Bath in the hall

MAIN FLOOR — 1,508 SQ. FT.
BASEMENT — 1,439 SQ. FT.
GARAGE — 440 SQ. FT.

TOTAL LIVING AREA:
1,508 SQ. FT.

MAIN FLOOR

ZIP QUOTE
HOME COST CALCULATOR
see order pages for details

To order your Blueprints, call 1-800-235-5700

©1993 Donald A. Gardner Architects, Inc.

B. NATHAN

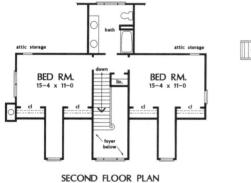

attic storage   attic storage

BED RM.
15-4 x 11-0

down

lin.

BED RM.
15-4 x 11-0

cl   cl   cl   cl

foyer
below

SECOND FLOOR PLAN

down

BONUS RM.
13-4 x 25-8

Perfect for the Growing Family

Price Code: E

■ This plan features:

— Three bedrooms

— Two full and one half baths

■ Natural light fills the two-story Foyer through a palladian window in dormer above

■ Dining Room and Great Room adjoin for entertaining possibilities

■ U-shaped Kitchen with a curved counter opens to a large Breakfast Area

■ Master Suite, situated downstairs for privacy with generous walk-in closet, double vanity, separate shower and a whirlpool tub

FIRST FLOOR — 1,484 SQ. FT.
SECOND FLOOR — 660 SQ. FT.
BONUS ROOM — 389 SQ. FT.
GARAGE — 600 SQ. FT.

TOTAL LIVING AREA:
2,144 SQ. FT.

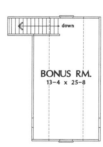

spa

DECK

covered porch   covered porch

DINING
12-0 x 12-8

KIT.
10-6 x 16-4

BRKFST.
10-7 x 9-8

pd. rm.

up

storage

walk-in closet

d   w   cl

GARAGE
23-4 x 22-0

GREAT RM.
15-4 x 19-8

master bath

fireplace

MASTER BED RM.
15-4 x 14-4

up

FOYER
7-0 x 6-0

PORCH

54-4

72-8

FIRST FLOOR PLAN

© Donald A. Gardner Architects, Inc.

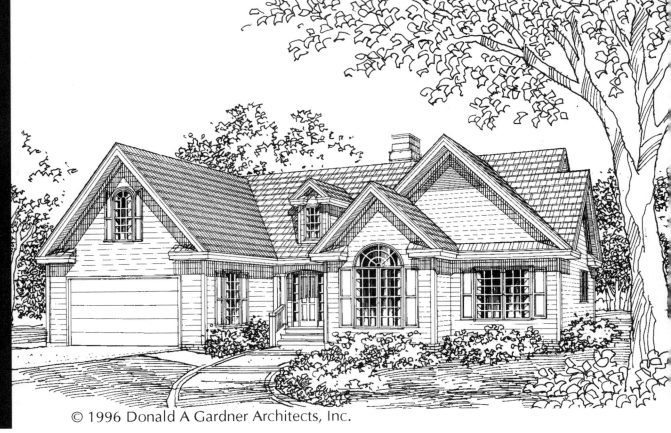

© 1996 Donald A Gardner Architects, Inc.

Sunny Dormer Brightens Foyer

Price Code: C

■ This plan features:

— Three bedrooms

— Two full baths

■ Today's comforts with cost effective construction

■ Open Great room, Dining Room, and Kitchen topped by a cathedral ceiling emphasizing spaciousness

■ Adjoining Deck providing extra living or entertaining room

■ Front Bedroom crowned in cathedral ceiling and pampered by a private Bath with garden tub, dual vanity and a walk-in closet

■ Skylit bonus room above the garage offering flexibility and opportunity for growth

MAIN FLOOR — 1,386 SQ. FT.

GARAGE — 517 SQ. FT.

BONUS ROOM — 314 SQ. FT.

ZIP QUOTE
HOME COST CALCULATOR
see order pages for details

TOTAL LIVING AREA:
1,386 SQ. FT.

BONUS RM.
12-0 x 20-8
(cathedral ceiling)

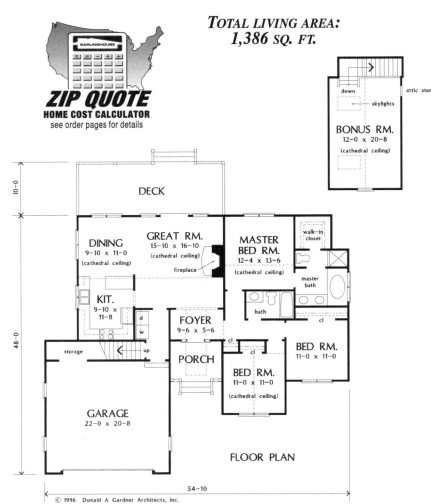

FLOOR PLAN

© 1996 Donald A Gardner Architects, Inc.

To order your Blueprints, call 1-800-235-5700

Ranch Provides Great Kitchen Area

PRICE CODE: A

This plan features:
- Three bedrooms
- Two full baths
- A Dining Room with sliding glass doors to the backyard
- Access to the Garage through the Laundry Room
- A Master Bedroom with a private full Bath
- A two-car Garage

MAIN FLOOR — 1,400 SQ. FT.
BASEMENT — 1,400 SQ. FT.
GARAGE — 528 SQ. FT.

TOTAL LIVING AREA:
1,400 SQ. FT.

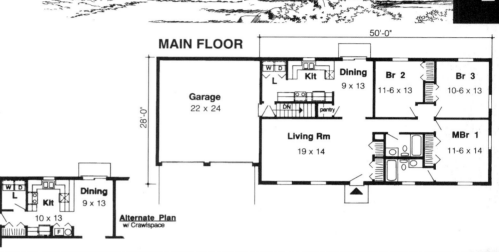

MAIN FLOOR

50'-0"

28'-0"

Garage 22 x 24

W D L Kit Dining 9 x 13 Br 2 11-6 x 13 Br 3 10-6 x 13

DN pantry

Living Rm 19 x 14 MBr 1 11-6 x 14

W D L Kit 10 x 13 Dining 9 x 13 F

Alternate Plan
w/ Crawlspace

Mind Your Manor

PRICE CODE: F

This plan features:
- Five bedrooms
- Two full, one three-quarter and one half baths

From the front covered Porch enter into the Entry/Gallery which features a grand spiral staircase

In the front of the house find the formal Living Room and Dining Room, each with two palladian windows

The Study has built in book cases centered between a window

The large Family Room has a fireplace and a built in stereo cabinet

The bayed Breakfast Nook has a door that leads into the backyard covered Patio

The first floor Master Bedroom has two walk in closets with a built-in chest of drawers and a Bath with a cathedral ceiling

An optional slab or a crawl space foundation — please specify when ordering

No materials list is available for this plan

FIRST FLOOR — 2,208 SQ. FT.
SECOND FLOOR — 1,173 SQ. FT.
BONUS — 224 SQ. FT.
GARAGE — 520 SQ. FT.

TOTAL LIVING AREA:
3,381 SQ. FT.

72'-0"

63'-10"

MstrBed 14x18 Covered Patio Brkfst 12x10 FamilyRm 16 x 17 Kit 14x12

Study 14x11 Gallery Util Gar 20x26

LivRm 15x12 Ent FmlDin 15x12

Cov Porch

Main Floor

Bed 5 12x13 Bed 4 14x11 Balcony Bonus Room Bed 3 15x12 Bed 2 15x12

Upper Floor

To order your Blueprints, call 1-800-235-5700

Family Favorite
PRICE CODE: A

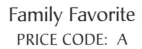

■ This plan features:
— Three bedrooms
— Two full baths
■ An open arrangement with the Dining Room that combines with ten foot ceilings to make the Living Room seem more spacious
■ Glass on three sides of the Dining Room which overlooks the deck
■ An efficient, compact Kitchen with a built-in pantry and peninsula counter
■ A Master Suite with a romantic window seat, a compartmentalized private bath and a walk-in closet
■ Two additional bedrooms that share a full hall closet
MAIN FLOOR — 1,359 SQ. FT.
GARAGE — 501 SQ. FT.

MAIN FLOOR

TOTAL LIVING AREA:
1,359 SQ. FT.

ZIP-QUOTE
HOME COST CALCULATOR
see order pages for details

No Wasted Space
PRICE CODE: A

■ This plan features:
— Three bedrooms
— Two full baths
■ A centrally located Great Room with a cathedral ceiling, exposed wood beams, and large areas of fixed glass
■ The Living and Dining areas separated by a massive stone fireplace
■ A secluded Master Suite with a walk-in closet and private Master Bath
■ An efficient Kitchen with a convenient laundry area
■ An optional basement, slab or crawl space foundation — please specify when ordering
MAIN AREA — 1,454 SQ. FT.

TOTAL LIVING AREA:
1,454 SQ. FT.

MAIN AREA

To order your Blueprints, call 1-800-235-5700

Deck

Breakfast
10'10" x 17'2"

Kitchen
13'6" x 16'7"

Laun.

Bath

Sunken
Great Room
15'2" x 21'1"

Hall

Hall

Hall

stairs up

stairs dn

Three-car Garage
22' x 38'

Dining Room
14'3" x 14'11"

Foyer

Library
11'10" x 12'9"

Porch

FIRST FLOOR

55'8"

72'6"

Bath

Bedroom
12'4" x 13'3"

walk-in closet

Bath

Dressing

Bedroom
12'1" x 12'7"

Balcony

walk-in closet

stairs dn

Foyer
Below

Master Bedroom
14'2" x 17'6"

walk-in closet

Bath

Bedroom
14'3" x 16'5"

SECOND FLOOR

The Ultimate in Style

Price Code: F

■ This plan features:

— Four bedrooms

— Three full and one half baths

■ A variety of exterior materials combine with a well planned interior for impeccable style

■ The Kitchen is open, has ample counter space and features a center island

■ Upstairs find the Master Bedroom, which has a walk-in closet and a sumptuous Bath

■ Three additional Bedrooms all have access to Baths

■ No materials list is available for this plan

FIRST FLOOR — 1,678 SQ. FT.
SECOND FLOOR — 1,766 SQ. FT.
BASEMENT — 1,639 SQ. FT.
GARAGE — 761 SQ. FT.

TOTAL LIVING AREA:
3,444 SQ. FT.

Ceiling Treatments
Add Interest

Price Code: B

- ■ This plan features:
  - — Three bedrooms
  - — Two full baths

- ■ A vaulted ceiling over the Family Room and a tray ceiling over the Master Suite

- ■ Decorative columns accenting the entrance into the Dining Room

- ■ Great Room with a pass through from the Kitchen and a fireplace framed by a window to one side and a French door

- ■ A built-in Pantry and desk adding convenience to the Kitchen

- ■ An optional basement, crawl space or slab foundation — please specify when ordering

MAIN FLOOR — 1,553 SQ. FT.
BASEMENT — 1,605 SQ. FT.
GARAGE — 434 SQ. FT.

TOTAL LIVING AREA :
1,553 SQ. FT.

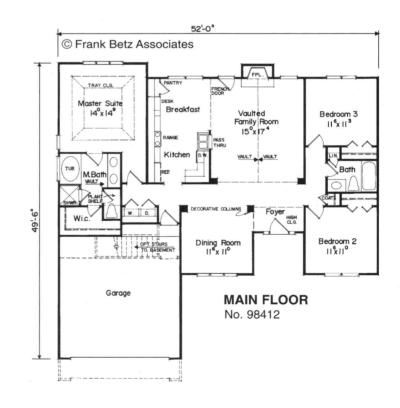

© Frank Betz Associates

52'-0"

49'-6"

TRAY CLG.

Master Suite
14⁰ x 14⁹

PANTRY

DESK

Breakfast

FRENCH
DOOR

FPL.

Vaulted
Family Room
15⁶ x 17⁴

Bedroom 3
11⁶ x 11³

RANGE

Kitchen

PASS
THRU

D.W.

VAULT   VAULT

LIN.

Bath

TUB

M.Bath
VAULT

REF.

COATS

SHWR.

PLANT
SHELF

Wic.

W   D.

DECORATIVE COLUMNS

Foyer

HIGH
CLG.

Bedroom 2
11⁶ x 11⁰

OPT. STAIRS
TO. BASEMENT

Dining Room
11⁶ x 11⁰

Garage

MAIN FLOOR
No. 98412

To order your Blueprints, call 1-800-235-5700

Impeccable Style
PRICE CODE: C

This plan features:

Three bedrooms

Two full and one half baths

Brick, stone, and interesting rooflines showcase the impeccable style of this home

Inside a deluxe staircase highlights the Foyer

The Dining Room has a bay window at one end and columns at the other

The U-shaped Kitchen has an island in its center

The two-story Great Room has a warm fireplace

The shape of the Master Bedroom adds to its character

Upstairs find two Bedrooms and a full Bath

No materials list is available for this plan

FIRST FLOOR — 1,706 SQ. FT.

SECOND FLOOR — 492 SQ. FT.

BASEMENT — 1,706 SQ. FT.

TOTAL LIVING AREA:
2,198 SQ. FT.

PLAN NO. 97710

Expansion Ready
PRICE CODE: B

This plan features:

Three bedrooms

Two full and one half baths

Columns accent the entrance into the Dining Room

The efficient Kitchen includes an island/snack bar and a Nook area

Bonus area for future expansion is located next to the secondary Bedrooms

No material list is available for this plan

An optional basement, slab, or crawl space foundation — please specify when ordering

FIRST FLOOR — 1,155 SQ. FT.

SECOND FLOOR — 529 SQ. FT.

BONUS — 380 SQ. FT.

GARAGE — 400 SQ. FT.

TOTAL LIVING AREA:
1,684 SQ. FT.

PLAN NO. 82010

Delightful, Compact Home

PRICE CODE: A

■ This plan features:
— Three bedrooms
— Two full baths
■ A fireplaced Living Room brightened by a wonderful picture window
■ A counter island featuring double sinks separating the Kitchen and Dining areas
■ A Master Bedroom that includes a private Master Bath and double closets
■ Two additional bedrooms with ample closet space that share a full bath

MAIN FLOOR — 1,146 SQ. FT.

TOTAL LIVING AREA:
1,146 SQ. FT.

44'-0"

28'-0"

Br 2
10 x 12-8

Br 3
10 x 9-4

Kit
10 x 11

Dining
9 x 11

linen

MBr 1
13-4 x 12

Living Rm
19 x 12-4

Deck

Floor Plan

slab/crawlspace option

W

D

ZIP QUOTE
HOME COST CALCULATOR
see order pages for details

© 1998 Donald A. Gardner, Inc.

Economical Home

PRICE CODE: D

■ This plan features:
— Three bedrooms
— Two full baths
■ Practical to build design offers appealing character with gables, pediments and inviting front Porch
■ Tray ceiling and columns define Dining area from Great Room for comfortable gatherings
■ Great Room features a cathedral ceiling, fireplace with built-in shelves, Deck and Kitchen access
■ Open Kitchen keeps cook part of all activities
■ Corner Master Bedroom offers two walk-in closets and double vanity Bath
■ Two additional Bedrooms with ample closets, share a full Bath in the hall
■ Bonus room over Garage provides options for growing families

MAIN FLOOR — 1,544 SQ. FT.
BONUS ROOM — 320 SQ. FT.
GARAGE & STORAGE — 478 SQ. FT.

TOTAL LIVING AREA:
1,544 SQ. FT.

DECK

8-0

BED RM.
12-0 x 11-0

shelves
fireplace

KIT.
9-8 x
12-4

master
bath

MASTER
BED RM.
12-0 x 15-8

GREAT RM.
18-0 x 12-0
(cathedral ceiling)

walk-in
closet

BED RM.
11-0 x 11-0

FOYER
5-6 x
11-4

DINING
12-6 x 11-4

UTIL.

walk-in
closet

43-0

bath

PORCH

GARAGE
21-0 x 21-0

storage

BONUS
RM.
10-6 x 21-0

attic storage

down

attic storage

FLOOR PLAN

63-0

© 1998 Donald A Gardner, Inc.

Terrific Kid's Nook
PRICE CODE: C

- This plan features:
  — Three bedrooms
  — Two full baths
- There is a combination Dining, Kitchen and Nook living space that encourage family interaction
- The Great Room includes a fireplace with built-in shelves to either side and a boxed ceiling
- A terrific kid's Nook to store the sport paraphernalia, hats and gloves or outdoor toys
- The Master Suite incorporates a Sitting Area, Bedroom, and a private Bath with a walk-in closet
- An optional basement, crawl space or slab foundation — please specify when ordering
- No materials list is available for this plan

MAIN FLOOR — 1,848 SQ. FT.
GARAGE — 429 SQ. FT.
PORCHES — 430 SQ. FT.

TOTAL LIVING AREA:
1,848 SQ. FT.

MAIN FLOOR

Gathering Room
PRICE CODE: B

- This plan features:
- Three bedroom
- Two full and one half baths
- An optional door from the front Porch leads to the Master Suite
- A gas fireplace is located in the corner of the Living Room
- A Shop or Storage Space is in the rear of the Garage
- The Gathering Room is perfect for the kids to play in
- All of the upstairs rooms have vaulted ceilings
- No materials list is available for this plan

FIRST FLOOR — 1,112 SQ. FT.
SECOND FLOOR — 672 SQ. FT.
BASEMENT — 1,112 SQ. FT.
GARAGE — 406 SQ. FT.

TOTAL LIVING AREA:
1,784 SQ. FT.

WIDTH 51'-0"
DEPTH 50'-9"

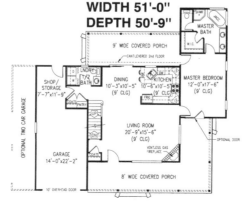

FIRST FLOOR PLAN

SECOND FLOOR PLAN

© 1996 Donald A. Gardner Architects, Inc.

B. NATHAN

Dramatic Dormers

Price Code: D

TOTAL LIVING AREA:
1,685 SQ. FT.

ZIP QUOTE
HOME COST CALCULATOR
see order pages for details

■ This plan features:

— Three bedrooms

— Two full baths

■ A Foyer open to the dramatic dormer, defined by columns

■ A Dining Room augmented by a tray ceiling

■ A Great Room expanded into the open Kitchen and the Breakfast Room

■ A privately located Master Suite, topped by a tray ceiling in the Bedroom and pampered by a garden tub with a picture window as the focal point of the Master Bath

■ Two additional Bedrooms, located at the opposite side of the home from the Master Suite, sharing a full Bath and linen closet

MAIN FLOOR — 1,685 SQ. FT.
GARAGE & STORAGE — 536 SQ. FT.
BONUS — 331 SQ. FT.

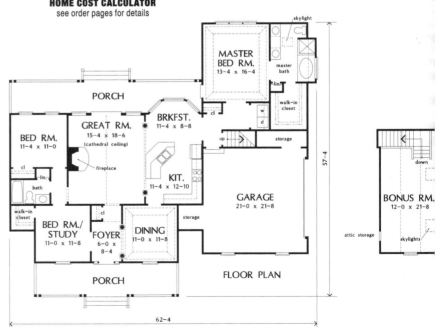

© 1996 Donald A Gardner Architects, Inc.

To order your Blueprints, call 1-800-235-5700

A Great Idea

PRICE CODE: D

■ This plan features:
— Three bedrooms
— Two full and one half baths
■ French doors lead from the Dining Room to the Porch
■ The Kitchen has plenty of counter space
■ The Master Suite features a tray ceiling
■ A Loft upstairs would make a great play area for the kids
■ A Deck in the rear makes for wonderful entertaining
■ No materials list is available for this plan

FIRST FLOOR — 1,670 SQ. FT.
SECOND FLOOR — 763 SQ. FT.
GARAGE — 502 SQ. FT.

**TOTAL LIVING AREA:
2,433 SQ. FT.**

**WIDTH 53'-0"
DEPTH 54'-0"**

FIRST FLOOR

SECOND FLOOR

Rustic Simplicity

PRICE CODE: C

■ This plan features:
— Three bedrooms
— Two full and one half baths
■ The central living area is large and boasts a cathedral ceiling, exposed wood beams and a clerestory
■ A long screened Porch has a bank of skylights
■ The open Kitchen contains a convenient serving and eating counter
■ The generous Master Suite opens to the screened Porch, and is enhanced by a walk-in closet and a whirlpool tub
■ Two more Bedrooms share a second full Bath

MAIN FLOOR — 1,426 SQ. FT.

**TOTAL LIVING AREA:
1,426 SQ. FT.**

© 1987 Donald A. Gardner Architects, Inc.

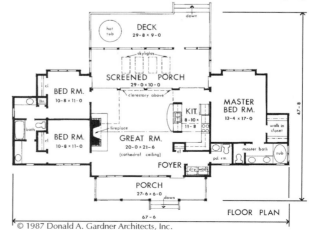

FLOOR PLAN

© 1987 Donald A. Gardner Architects, Inc.

©1994 Donald A. Gardner Architects, Inc.

Sense of Spaciousness
PRICE CODE: D

■ This plan features:
— Three bedrooms
— Two full and one half baths
■ Creative use of natural lighting gives a feeling of spaciousness to this Country home
■ Traffic flows easily from the bright Foyer into the Great Room which has a vaulted ceiling and skylights
■ The open floor plan is efficient for Kitchen/Breakfast Area and the Dining Room
■ Master Bedroom Suite features a walk-in closet and a private Bath with whirlpool tub
■ Two second floor Bedrooms with storage access share a full Bath

FIRST FLOOR — 1,180 SQ. FT.
SECOND FLOOR — 459 SQ. FT.
BONUS ROOM — 385 SQ. FT.
GARAGE & STORAGE — 533 SQ. FT.

TOTAL LIVING AREA:
1,639 SQ. FT.

FIRST FLOOR PLAN

© 1994 Donald A Gardner Architects, Inc.

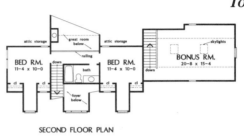

SECOND FLOOR PLAN

Elegant Victorian
PRICE CODE: D

■ This plan features:
— Three bedrooms
— Two full and one half baths
■ Sit and relax on the front Porch at the end of the day with family and friends
■ Serve guests dinner in the bayed Dining Room and then gather in the Living Room which features a cathedral ceiling
■ There is plenty of space for activities in the Family Room which is accented by a fireplace
■ The Master Bedroom has a Sitting Area, walk-in closet and a private Bath
■ Two additional Bedrooms share a full Bath, and there is a bonus room upstairs for future expansion
■ This plan features a three car Garage with space for storage
■ A basement or a slab foundation — please specify when ordering
■ No material list is available for this plan

FIRST FLOOR — 1,447 SQ. FT.
SECOND FLOOR — 1,008 SQ. FT.
GARAGE — 756 SQ. FT.

TOTAL LIVING AREA:
2,455 SQ. FT.

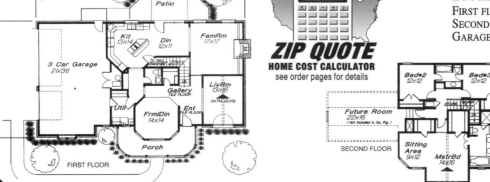

ZIP QUOTE
HOME COST CALCULATOR
see order pages for details

FIRST FLOOR

SECOND FLOOR

To order your Blueprints, call 1-800-235-5700

Compact Country Home
PRICE CODE: D

- This plan features:
  — Three bedrooms
  — Two full baths
- Economical squared off design still stylish with gables and arches
- Comfortable gathering area created by open layout of Great Room, Dining area and Kitchen
- Master Bedroom Suite provides privacy, an elegant tray ceiling, walk-in closet and lavish Bath with two vanities
- Two more Bedrooms, with ample closets, share a double vanity Bath, Laundry facilities and access to Bonus Room with skylight

MAIN FLOOR — 1,517 SQ. FT.
BONUS ROOM — 287 SQ. FT.
GARAGE — 447 SQ. FT.

TOTAL LIVING AREA:
1,517 SQ. FT.

©1997 Donald A. Gardner Architects, Inc.

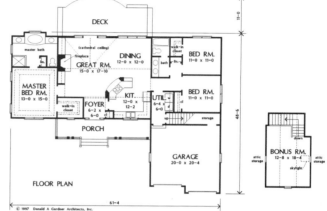

Farmhouse with a Modern Flair
PRICE CODE: D

- This plan features:
  — Three bedrooms
  — Two full and one half baths
- Covered Porch, a two-level Foyer and a bank of clerestory windows add modern flair to this farmhouse
- Columns between the Great Room and the island Kitchen
- Large rear Deck expands your living space to the backyard
- Second floor Master Suite with a walk-in closet, double vanity, shower and a garden tub
- Two additional upstairs Bedrooms share a full, skylit Bath

FIRST FLOOR — 943 SQ. FT.
SECOND FLOOR — 840 SQ. FT.
GARAGE & STORAGE — 510 SQ. FT.
BONUS ROOM — 323 SQ. FT.

TOTAL LIVING AREA:
1,783 SQ. FT.

© Donald A. Gardner Architects, Inc.

To order your Blueprints, call 1-800-235-5700

Comfortable and Relaxed Environment
Price Code: A

- This plan features:
  — Three bedrooms
  — Two full and one half baths
- An easy flow traffic pattern crating step saving convenience in the interior
- An open stairway adding elegances to the Foyer
- A spacious Great Room and Breakfast Area
- A U-shaped Kitchen with ample counter and storage space
- A Master Suite with a walk-in closet plus a compartmented Bath
- Two additional Bedrooms sharing use of a Bath with skylight
- No materials list is available for this plan

FIRST FLOOR — 748 SQ. FT.
SECOND FLOOR — 705 SQ. FT.
GARAGE — 744 SQ. FT.

TOTAL LIVING AREA:
1,453 SQ. FT.

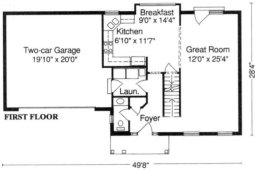

Option to Expand
PRICE CODE: C

- This plan features:
  — Three bedrooms
  — Two full baths
- There is an optional Bonus Room on the second floor to expand the home
- The Great Room has a fireplace and easy access to the formal Dining Room
- The Kitchen has ample cabinet space and a peninsula counter/snack bar
- Columns accent the entrance of the Dining Room
- An optional crawl space or slab foundation — please specify when ordering
- No materials list is available for this plan

MAIN FLOOR — 1,845 SQ. FT.
BONUS — 1,191 SQ. FT.
GARAGE — 496 SQ. FT.
PORCH — 465 SQ. FT.

TOTAL LIVING AREA:
1,845 SQ. FT.

SECOND FLOOR

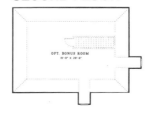

MAIN FLOOR

To order your Blueprints, call 1-800-235-5700

Small Yet Stately
PRICE CODE: A

■ This plan features:
- Two bedrooms
- Two full baths
  The Living Room has a ten-foot ceiling and a fireplace
  The Dining Room has a ten-foot ceiling and eight-inch boxed columns defining it from the Living Room
  The Kitchen include wrapping counters a breakfast bar to the Dining Room
■ The Master Suite incorporates a private Bath and a walk-in closet
  An optional crawl space or slab foundation — please specify when ordering
  No materials list is available for this plan

MAIN FLOOR — 1,172 SQ. FT.

GARAGE — 213 SQ. FT.

TOTAL LIVING AREA:
1,172 SQ. FT.

MAIN FLOOR

Mixture of Styles
PRICE CODE: E

■ This plan features:
- Three bedrooms
- Two full and one half baths
  Built-ins flank the fireplace in the Great Room while a soaring cathedral ceiling expands the room visually
■ The Kitchen has an angled counter and opens to the Breakfast Bay and the Great Room
  The large screened porch has access to the Great Room and the Master Suite
  A Bonus Room stands ready for future expansion

MAIN FLOOR — 2,042 SQ. FT.

BONUS ROOM — 475 SQ. FT.

GARAGE — 660 SQ. FT.

PORCH — 514 SQ. FT.

TOTAL LIVING AREA:
2,042 SQ. FT.

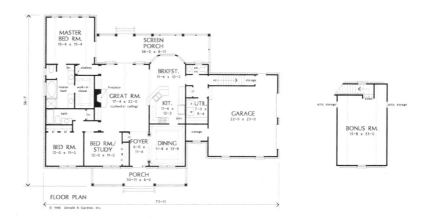

FLOOR PLAN

"How to obtain a construction cost calculation based on labor rates and building material costs in <u>your</u> Zip Code area!"

ZIP-QUOTE!
HOME COST CALCULATOR

ZIP QUOTE
HOME COST CALCULATOR

WHY?

Do you wish you could quickly find out the building cost for your new home without waiting for a contractor to compile hundreds of bids? Would you like to have a benchmark to compare your contractor(s) bids against? *Well, Now You Can!!,* with **Zip-Quote** Home Cost Calculator. Zip-Quote is only available for zip code areas within the United States.

HOW?

Our new **Zip-Quote** Home Cost Calculator will enable you to obtain the calculated building cost to construct your new home, based on labor rates and building material costs within your zip code area, without the normal delays or hassles usually associated with the bidding process. Zip-Quote can be purchased in two separate formats, an itemized or a bottom line format.

"How does **Zip-Quote** actually work?" When you call to order, you must choose from the options available, for your specific home, in order for us to process your order. Once we receive your **Zip-Quote** order, we process your specific home plan building materials list through our Home Cost Calculator which contains up-to-date rates for all residential labor trades and building material costs in your zip code area. "The result?" A calculated cost to build your dream home in your zip code area. This calculation will help you (as a consumer or a builder) evaluate your building budget. This is a valuable tool for anyone considering building a new home.

All database information for our calculations is furnished by Marshall & Swift, L.P. For over 60 years, Marshall & Swift L.P. has been a leading provider of cost data to professionals in all aspects of the construction and remodeling industries.

OPTION 1

The **Itemized Zip-Quote** is a detailed building material list. Each building material list line item will separately state the labor cost, material cost and equipment cost (if applicable) for the use of that building material in the construction process. Each category within the building material list will be subtotaled and the entire Itemized cost calculation totaled at the end. This building materials list will be summarized by the individual building categories and will have additional columns where you can enter data from your contractor's estimates for a cost comparison between the different suppliers and contractors who will actually quote you their products and services.

OPTION 2

The **Bottom Line Zip-Quote** is a one line summarized total cost for the home plan of your choice. This cost calculation is also based on the labor cost, material cost and equipment cost (if applicable) within your local zip code area.

COST

The price of your **Itemized Zip-Quote** is based upon the pricing schedule of the plan you have selected, in addition to the price of the materials list. Please refer to the pricing schedule on our order form. The price of your initial **Bottom Line Zip-Quote** is $29.95. Each additional **Bottom Line Zip-Quote** ordered in conjunction with the initial order is only $14.95. **Bottom Line Zip-Quote** may be purchased separately and does NOT have to be purchased in conjunction with a home plan order.

FYI

An **Itemized Zip-Quote** Home Cost Calculation can ONLY be purchased in conjunction with a Home Plan order. The **Itemized Zip-Quote** can not be purchased separately. The **Bottom Line Zip-Quote** can be purchased separately and doesn't have to be purchased in conjunction with a home plan order. Please consult with a sales representative for current availability. If you find within 60 days of your order date that you will be unable to build this home, then you may exchange the plans and the materials list towards the price of a new set of plans (see order info pages for plan exchange policy). The **Itemized Zip-Quote** and the **Bottom Line Zip-Quote** are NOT returnable. The price of the initial **Bottom Line Zip-Quote** order can be credited towards the purchase of an **Itemized Zip-Quote** order only. Additional **Bottom Line Zip-Quote** orders, within the same order can not be credited. Please call our Customer Service Department for more information.

Itemized Zip-Quote is available for plans where you see this symbol.

Bottom Line Zip-Quote is available for all plans under 4,000 square feet.

SOME MORE INFORMATION

Itemized and Bottom Line Zip-Quotes give you approximated costs for constructing the particular house in your area. These costs are not exact and are only intended to be used as a preliminary estimate to help determine the affordability of a new home and/or as a guide to evaluate the general competitiveness of actual price quotes obtained through local suppliers and contractors. However, Zip-Quote cost figures should never be relied upon as the only source of information in either case. Land, sewer systems, site work, landscaping and other expenses are not included in our building cost figures. Garlinghouse and Marshall & Swift L.P. can not guarantee any level of data accuracy or correctness in a Zip-Quote and disclaim all liability for loss with respect to the same, in excess of the original purchase price of the Zip-Quote product. All Zip-Quote calculations are based upon the actual blueprints and do not reflect any differences or options that may be shown on the published house renderings, floor plans, or photographs.

Seismic Engineering
...for California!

The Garlinghouse Company has teamed with Parker Resnick Structural Engineering, a premiere Engineering firm in Southern California, to provide structural engineering services to the Southwestern Sunbelt market. We are now able to provide structural and seismic engineering for any plan that appears in this publication. Seismic engineering can be provided with, or without, specific soils information, depending on your local building needs.

Our extensive engineering packages will come to you complete with 3 sets of stamped and signed blueprints, 1 set of reproducible vellums, and 3 sets of stamped and signed structural calculations!

Parker Resnick Structural Engineering, located in Los Angeles California will help make building your dream home a reality. Through this exclusive offer, we are able to provide these services at very reasonable prices.

Price Code	Without Specific Soils Information	With Specific Soils Information
A	$1020	$1500
B	$1080	$1590
C	$1160	$1720
D	$1250	$1840
E	$1360	$2000
F	$1490	$2200
G	$1620	$2400
H	$1760	$2600

NOTE: Seismic engineering pricing is in addition to the cost of a reproducible vellum.

You will be required to provide all applicable soils reports (if they are required in your area) before any specific foundation engineering can begin. Once we have received your order or approved soils reports, please allow 10-14 additional business days for delivery. Check with your local building department to find out your exact requirements before placing your order.

The above pricing includes shipping from Parker Resnick Structural Engineering to you. All plan check revisions, site visits or field questions will be billable at $100.00 per hour. Site visit billing will include travel time. Seismic engineering is a custom professional service and is locally specific. Please note that all fees for this service are non-refundable upon commencement of any engineering.

We are proud to offer these engineering services to you at these very competitive rates.

INDEXINDEXINDEX

ML *Materials List Available* **ZIP** *Zip Quote Available* **RRR** *Right Reading Reverse* **DUP** *Duplex Plan*

Plan#	Page	Price Code	Sq. Ft.	
10274	132	B	1783	ML/RRR
10507	263	C	2194	ML/ZIP
10515	376	C	2015	ML/ZIP
10531	21	F	3576	ML
10686	232	F	3276	ML/ZIP
10690	395	D	2281	ML/ZIP
10698	86	F	4741	ML/ZIP
10839	291	B	1738	ML/ZIP/RRR
19422	31	B	1695	ML/ZIP
20071	187	E	3169	ML
20087	297	B	1568	ML/ZIP
20093	314	C	2001	ML
20100	401	B	1737	ML/ZIP/RRR
20156	426	A	1359	ML/ZIP/RRR
20161	302	A	1307	ML/ZIP/RRR
20164	304	A	1456	ML/ZIP/RRR
20195	353	A	1427	ML
20196	372	E	2750	ML
20198	362	B	1792	ML/ZIP
20209	66	D	2387	ML
20220	378	B	1568	ML/ZIP
20507	88	E	2927	
22004	95	C	2070	ML
24245	1	C	2083	ML/ZIP/RRR
24265	77	E	2672	ML
24268	98	D	2244	ML/ZIP
24302	155	A	988	ML/ZIP
24304	105	A	993	ML
24307	118	A	1038	ML
24319	65	B	1710	ML/ZIP
24400	200	C	1978	ML/ZIP/RRR
24403	64	E	2647	ML/ZIP
24404	225	D	2356	ML/ZIP
24405	96	C	2064	ML/ZIP
24594	28	E	2957	ML/ZIP
24610	35	B	1785	ML/ZIP
24653	42	D	2578	
24654	57	B	1554	ML/ZIP
24700	114	A	1312	ML/ZIP
24701	135	B	1625	ML/ZIP
24706	324	A	1470	ML/ZIP
24708	138	B	1576	ML/ZIP
24711	159	A	1434	
24714	144	B	1771	
24717	143	B	1642	
24718	146	A	1452	
24723	259	A	1112	
24735	50	D	2426	
26112	266	A	1487	ML/ZIP
32006	47	F	5288	ML/ZIP
32032	280	C	1881	ML/ZIP
32046	63	F	4292	ML/ZIP
32063	6	F	4283	ML/ZIP/RRR
32101	32	B	2764	ML/ZIP
32109	78	C	2038	ML/ZIP
32122	286	A	1112	ML/ZIP
32146	102	F	3895	ML/ZIP
32291	172	B	1852	
34003	430	A	1146	ML/ZIP/RRR
34011	274	B	1672	ML/ZIP/RRR
34029	405	B	1686	ML/ZIP/RRR
34031	279	C	1831	ML/ZIP/RRR
34043	67	B	1583	ML/ZIP/RRR
34054	425	A	1400	ML/ZIP/RRR
34150	22	A	1492	ML/ZIP/RRR
34154	294	A	1486	ML/ZIP/RRR
34600	29	A	1328	ML/ZIP/RRR
34601	53	A	1415	ML/ZIP/RRR
34602	323	B	1560	ML/ZIP
34603	314	B	1560	ML/ZIP
34679	311	C	1994	ML/ZIP
34901	391	B	1763	ML/ZIP/RRR
35001	307	B	1609	ML/RRR
35002	293	B	1712	ML/RRR

Plan#	Page	Price Code	Sq. Ft.	
35003	325	A	1373	ML/RRR
35007	338	A	1027	ML
35009	344	A	1003	ML/RRR
81005	350	E	2998	
81006	345	C	2120	
81007	361	C	2180	ML
82010	429	B	1684	
82014	375	B	1987	
82015	380	B	1959	
82016	390	C	1934	
82017	399	C	1832	
82018	414	C	1922	
82019	407	C	1915	
82020	436	C	1845	
82021	431	C	1848	
82039	421	B	1660	
82040	437	A	1172	
82041	440	C	1892	
82043	66	A	1425	
82045	75	A	1289	
82046	90	B	1541	
82047	86	B	1771	
82048	70	B	1595	
82049	96	A	1447	
82050	126	B	1746	
82051	101	C	1921	
83000	106	D	2463	
83001	118	F	3205	
86012	136	D	2415	
86013	152	D	2300	
86014	144	B	1582	
90007	164	C	1830	ML
90025	169	A	1309	ML
90048	369	A	1274	ML
90356	323	A	1351	ML
90378	366	A	1283	ML
90406	249	B	1737	ML
90409	405	B	1670	ML
90412	426	A	1454	ML
90420	175	D	2473	ML
90423	397	B	1773	ML
90433	394	A	928	ML
90436	74	C	2181	ML
90441	189	C	1811	ML
90443	39	E	2759	ML
90450	412	D	2398	ML
90451	179	C	2068	ML
90454	160	D	2218	ML
90458	192	D	2263	ML
90467	213	D	2290	ML
90476	213	C	1804	ML
90502	220	B	1642	ML
90601	185	B	1613	ML
90630	193	A	1207	ML
90671	141	B	1587	ML
90682	398	A	1243	ML
90684	211	B	1590	ML
90689	168	A	1476	ML
90844	330	B	1552	ML
90865	217	A	1313	ML
90870	245	B	1755	
90871	230	C	2182	
90930	329	B	1702	ML
90934	418	A	884	ML
90986	237	B	1731	ML
90990	72	A	1423	ML
91002	370	A	1096	ML
91026	357	A	1354	ML
91033	12	A	1249	ML/ZIP
91053	238	C	2099	ML
91091	226	A	1250	ML
91102	255	B	1701	
91109	247	E	2747	
91129	252	C	1983	

Plan#	Page	Price Code	Sq. Ft.	
91133	34	E	2786	
91149	260	A	1370	
91153	267	C	1959	
91157	278	C	1862	
91160	284	A	1473	
91163	257	B	1561	
91165	267	B	1589	
91319	181	E	3192	ML
91343	13	C	2162	ML
91346	289	C	2185	ML/RRR
91418	382	B	1665	ML
91436	300	D	2591	ML
91512	85	D	2432	ML/RRR
91514	58	B	1707	ML/RRR
91518	99	D	2550	ML/RRR
91545	109	A	1420	ML
91588	122	E	2913	
91592	157	E	2287	ML
91700	404	D	2406	ML
91704	307	C	1837	ML
91731	381	C	1857	ML
91746	310	B	1717	ML
91901	158	D	2212	
92048	5	F	3500	ML
92156	334	E	2608	ML
92160	350	C	1995	ML
92219	15	F	3335	ZIP
92220	344	C	1830	ML/ZIP
92237	16	F	3783	ML/ZIP
92238	191	B	1664	ML/ZIP
92243	337	E	2858	
92248	388	F	3921	ZIP
92265	342	F	3818	
92273	182	F	3254	ZIP
92277	20	E	3110	ZIP
92283	354	B	1653	
92284	377	D	2261	
92400	402	A	1050	
92404	413	D	2275	ML
92501	188	F	2727	ML
92502	389	B	1237	ML
92504	365	F	3813	ML
92515	383	D	1959	ML
92523	76	B	1293	ML
92527	71	C	1680	ML
92531	389	C	1754	ML
92535	52	F	2965	ML
92538	379	F	2733	ML
92546	381	E	2387	ML
92549	315	E	2490	ML
92550	196	F	2735	ML
92552	207	D	1873	ML
92557	210	B	1390	ML
92560	219	C	1660	ML
92561	386	D	1856	ML
92576	227	E	2858	ML
92609	49	B	1768	ZIP
92610	23	C	2101	ZIP
92625	408	B	1746	ML/ZIP
92630	396	B	1782	ZIP
92631	19	C	2157	ZIP
92639	436	A	1453	
92642	301	C	2082	ZIP
92643	25	D	2209	
92644	33	C	1897	ML/ZIP
92646	11	D	2320	
92649	422	B	1508	ML/ZIP
92651	9	D	2403	ZIP
92655	417	B	1746	ML/ZIP
92666	427	F	3444	
92671	3	F	3445	
92674	316	C	1876	
92692	251	D	2388	ZIP
92695	265	B	1704	

Plan#	Page	Price Code	Sq. Ft.	
92697	68	C	2017	
92705	421	C	1849	
93017	270	A	1142	
93018	79	A	1142	
93021	393	A	1282	
93034	27	E	2838	
93048	382	A	1310	
93075	94	A	1170	
93080	87	C	1890	
93095	80	D	2409	ML
93107	99	C	1868	RRR
93118	271	F	3397	ML/ZIP/RRR
93133	401	B	1761	ML/ZIP/RRR
93143	121	C	1802	
93161	100	B	1540	ML/ZIP
93165	106	A	1472	
93171	137	B	1642	
93200	115	F	5730	
93202	135	A	1447	ML
93206	400	E	2645	ML/ZIP
93212	183	C	2091	ML/ZIP
93219	4	B	1668	ML/ZIP
93222	409	A	1292	ML/ZIP/RRR
93241	97	E	2640	ML/ZIP
93254	317	D	2509	
93261	150	B	1778	ML/ZIP
93265	306	A	1325	ML/ZIP
93269	146	B	1735	ML
93279	131	A	1388	ML/ZIP
93298	329	B	1683	
93333	151	E	3198	
93340	159	D	2462	
93344	162	D	2259	
93349	363	C	1961	
93354	277	C	2102	
93410	385	C	1854	ML
93413	402	C	1808	
93414	410	A	1393	
93432	26	C	1833	ML
93442	84	C	2148	
93447	91	A	1474	
93453	191	A	1333	
93609	37	C	2771	
93708	378	D	2579	
93716	178	E	2698	
94109	205	C	2013	
94112	18	E	2733	
94116	113	C	1546	ML
94124	116	E	2459	
94135	223	C	1493	
94138	305	C	1576	
94202	132	F	2376	ML
94204	139	B	1764	
94220	195	F	3477	ML
94222	208	F	4565	
94230	149	F	4759	
94231	156	E	2891	ML
94239	163	F	4106	ML
94242	214	E	2978	
94248	197	C	1853	
94259	203	C	2520	
94260	218	C	2068	
94265	231	E	2879	
94307	252	A	786	
94611	239	D	2406	
94613	246	D	2357	
94614	243	D	2533	
94615	256	E	2665	
94622	258	E	3149	
94640	264	D	2558	
94641	253	D	2400	
94644	269	E	2673	
94801	161	C	1300	ML
94804	234	C	1855	ML

Plan#	Page	Price Code	Sq. Ft.	
94810	276	E	2690	ML
94811	281	D	2165	ML
94900	287	C	1999	ML
94904	202	C	1998	ML/ZIP
94911	299	C	1858	ML/ZIP/RRR
94923	262	B	1666	ML
94933	349	F	3306	ML/ZIP
94944	313	C	1933	ML/ZIP
94956	322	D	2303	ML/ZIP/RRR
94965	330	E	2715	ML/ZIP/RRR
94966	335	C	1911	ML
94967	268	D	2355	ML
94971	278	C	2172	ML
94972	284	B	1580	ML
94973	340	D	2512	ML
94986	347	B	1604	ML
94994	352	E	2957	ML/ZIP
94995	361	E	3172	ML/ZIP
94999	369	F	3623	ML
96402	110	E	2027	ML/RRR
96403	259	F	2832	ML/RRR
96404	201	E	2301	ML/ZIP/RRR
96405	153	D	1903	ML/RRR
96406	263	E	2023	ML/RRR
96407	241	F	2772	ML/RRR
96408	283	E	2164	ML/RRR
96411	384	F	2596	ML/RRR
96413	397	E	2349	ML/RRR
96417	298	D	1561	ML/ZIP/RRR
96418	130	C	1452	ML/ZIP/RRR
96421	229	E	2045	ML/RRR
96423	299	E	2218	ML/RRR
96435	406	F	2526	ML/RRR
96436	312	D	1622	ML/RRR
96438	305	E	2130	ML/RRR
96440	288	D	1713	ML/RRR
96442	261	E	2182	ML/RRR
96443	54	G	3352	ML/RRR
96446	423	E	2144	ML/RRR
96452	321	C	1475	ML/RRR
96453	318	D	1807	ML/RRR
96456	434	D	1639	ML/RRR
96457	339	D	1843	ML/RRR
96458	348	D	1512	ML/RRR
96459	334	E	2370	ML/RRR
96461	351	D	1838	ML/RRR
96462	147	D	1846	ML/RRR
96463	69	D	1633	ML/RRR
96468	87	D	1864	ML/RRR
96471	92	E	2190	ML/RRR
96472	356	D	1989	ML/RRR
96474	103	D	1883	ML/RRR
96476	108	D	1823	ML/RRR
96479	115	D	1883	ML/RRR
96480	124	D	1991	ML/RRR
96483	377	E	2057	ML/RRR
96484	199	C	1246	ML/RRR
96487	236	D	1669	ML/RRR
96489	357	D	1609	ML/RRR
96490	44	F	2682	ML/RRR
96491	81	E	2250	ML/RRR
96493	134	D	1770	ML/RRR
96494	140	E	2201	ML/RRR
96498	155	E	2048	ML/RRR
96503	170	D	2256	ML
96504	374	C	2162	ML
96505	180	D	2069	ML
96506	186	B	1654	ML
96509	197	A	1438	ML
96511	206	A	1247	ML
96513	212	B	1648	ML
96516	387	A	1458	ML/RRR
96519	221	A	1243	
96522	227	B	1515	ML

ML Materials List Available   **ZIP** Zip Quote Available   **RRR** Right Reading Reverse   **DUP** Duplex Plan

Everything You Need...
...to Make Your Dream Come True

You pay only a fraction of the original cost for home designs by respected professionals.

You've Picked Your Dream Home!

You can imagine your new home situated on your lot in the morning sunlight. You can visualize living there, enjoying your family, entertaining friends and celebrating holidays. All that remains are the details. That's where we can help. Whether you plan to build it yourself, act as your own general contractor or hire a professional builder, your Garlinghouse Co. home plans will provide the perfect design and specifications to help make your dream home a reality.

We can offer you an array of additional products and services to help you with your planning needs. We can supply materials lists, construction cost estimates based on your local material and labor costs and modifications to your selected plan if you would like.

For over 90 years, homeowners and builders have relied on us for accurate, complete, professional blueprints. Our plans help you get results fast... and save money, too! These pages will give you all the information you need to order. So get started now... We know you'll love your new Garlinghouse home!

Sincerely,

President   Chief Executive Officer

EXTERIOR ELEVATIONS

Elevations are scaled drawings of the front, rear, left and right sides of a home. All of the necessary information pertaining to the exterior finish materials, roof pitches and exterior heig dimensions of your home are defined.

CABINET PLANS

These plans, or in some cases elevations, will detail the layout of the kitchen and bathroom cabinets at a larger scale. This gives you an accurate layout for your cabinets or an ideal starti point for a modified custom cabinet design. Available for most plans in our collection. You may also show the floor plan without a cabinet layout. This will allow you to start from scratch and design your own dream kitchen.

TYPICAL WALL SECTION

This section is provided to help your builder understand the structural components and materi used to construct the exterior walls of your home. This section will address insulation, roof components, and interior and exterior wall finishes. Your plans will be designed with either 2x4 2x6 exterior walls, but most professional contractors can easily adapt the plans to the wall thickness you require. Available for most plans in our collection.

FIREPLACE DETAILS

If the home you have chosen includes a fireplace, the fireplace detail will show typical method. to construct the firebox, hearth and flue chase for masonry units, or a wood frame chase for a zero-clearance unit. Available for most plans in our collection.

FOUNDATION PLAN

These plans will accurately dimension the footprint of your home including load bearing points and beam placement if applicable. The foundation style will vary from plan to plan. Your local climatic conditions will dictate whether a basement, slab or crawlspace is best suited for your area. In most cases, if your plan comes with one foundation style, a professional contractor ca easily adapt the foundation plan to an alternate style.

ROOF PLAN

The information necessary to construct the roof will be included with your home plans. Some plans will reference roof trusses, while many others contain schematic framing plans. These framing plans will indicate the lumber sizes necessary for the rafters and ridgeboards based o the designated roof loads.

TYPICAL CROSS SECTION

A cut-away cross-section through the entire home shows your building contractor the exact correlation of construction components at all levels of the house. It will help to clarify the load bearing points from the roof all the way down to the basement.

DETAILED FLOOR PLANS

The floor plans of your home accurately dimension the positioning of all walls, doors, windows, stairs and permanent fixtures. They will show you the relationship and dimensions of rooms, closets and traffic patterns. The schematic of the electrical layout may be included in the plan. This layout is clearly represented and does not hinder the clarity of other pertinent information shown. All these details will help your builder properly construct your new home.

STAIR DETAILS

If stairs are an element of the design you have chosen, the plans will show the necessary information to build these, either through a stair cross section, or on the floor plans. Either way, the information provides your builders the essential reference points that they need to build the stairs.

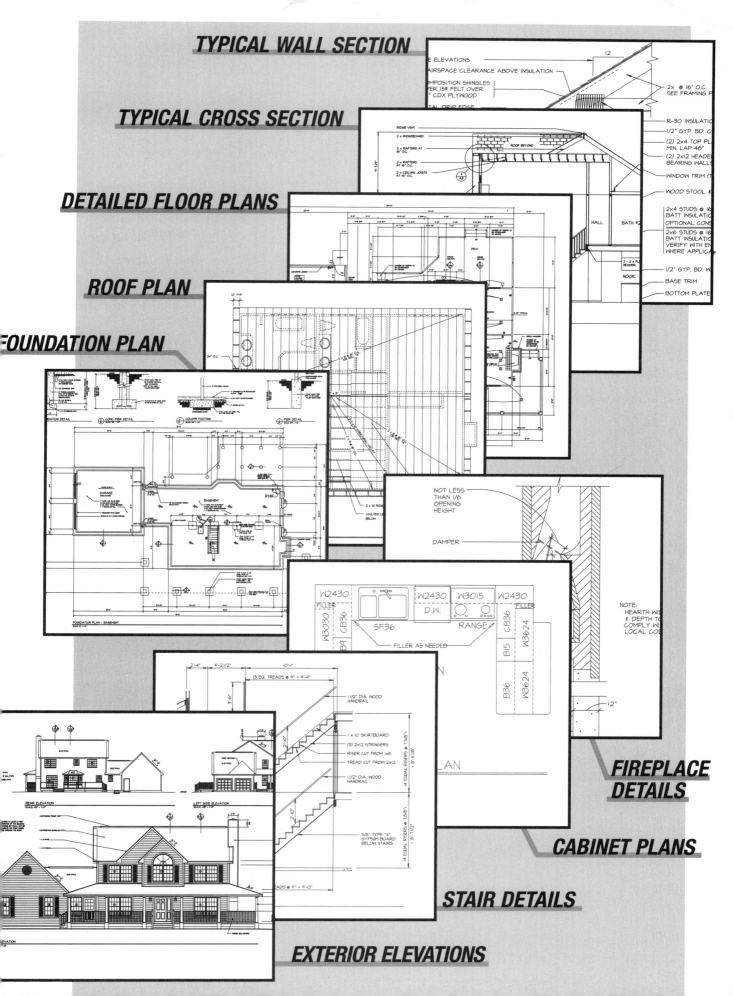

TYPICAL WALL SECTION

TYPICAL CROSS SECTION

DETAILED FLOOR PLANS

ROOF PLAN

FOUNDATION PLAN

FIREPLACE DETAILS

CABINET PLANS

STAIR DETAILS

EXTERIOR ELEVATIONS

Garlinghouse Options & Extras ...Make Your Dream A Home

Reversed Plans Can Make Your Dream Home Just Right!

"That's our dream home...if only the garage were on the other side!"

You could have exactly the home you want by flipping it end-for-end. Check it out by holding your dream home page of this book up to a mirror. Then simply order your plans "reversed." We'll send you one full set of mirror-image plans (with the writing backwards) as a master guide for you and your builder.

The remaining sets of your order will come as shown in this book so the dimensions and specifications are easily read on the job site...but most plans in our collection come stamped "REVERSED" so there is no construction confusion.

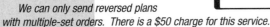

As Shown   Reversed

We can only send reversed plans with multiple-set orders. There is a $50 charge for this service.

Some plans in our collection are available in Right Reading Reverse. Right Reading Reverse plans will show your home in reverse, with the writing on the plan being readable. This easy-to-read format will save you valuable time and money. Please contact our Customer Service Department at (860) 343-5977 to check for Right Reading Reverse availability. (There is a $150 charge for plan series 964, 980, & 998. $125 for all other plans.)

Specifications & Contract Form

We send this form to you free of charge with your home plan order. The form is designed to be filled in by you or your contractor with the exact materials to use in the construction of your new home. Once signed by you and your contractor it will provide you with peace of mind throughout the construction process.

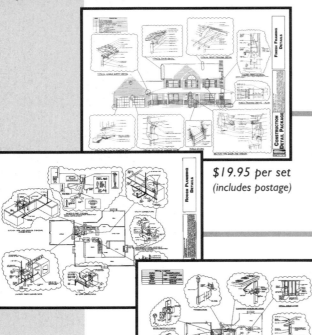

$19.95 per set
(includes postage)

Remember To Order Your Materials List

It'll help you save money. Available at a modest additional charge, the Materials List gives the quantity, dimensions, and specifications for the major materials needed to build your home. You will get faster, more accurate bids from your contractors and building suppliers — and avoid paying for unused materials and waste. Materials Lists are available for all home plans except as otherwise indicated, but can only be ordered with a set of home plans. Due to differences in regional requirements and homeowner or builder preferences... electrical, plumbing and heating/air conditioning equipment specifications are not designed specifically for each plan. However, non-plan specific detailed typical prints of residential electrical, plumbing and construction guidelines can be provided. Please see below for additional information. If you need a detailed materials cost you might need to purchase a Zip Quote. (Details follow)

Detail Plans Provide Valuable Information About Construction Techniques

Because local codes and requirements vary greatly, we recommend that you obtain drawings and bids from licensed contractors to do your mechanical plans. However, if you want to know more about techniques — and deal more confidently with subcontractors — we offer these remarkably useful detail sheets. These detail sheets will aid in your understanding of these technical subjects. **The detail sheets are not specific to any one home plan and should be used only as a general reference guide.**

RESIDENTIAL CONSTRUCTION DETAILS

Ten sheets that cover the essentials of stick-built residential home construction. Details foundation options — poured concrete basement, concrete block, or monolithic concrete slab. Shows all aspects of floor, wall and roof framing. Provides details for roof dormers, overhangs, chimneys and skylights. Conforms to requirements of Uniform Building code or BOCA code. Includes a quick index and a glossary of terms.

RESIDENTIAL PLUMBING DETAILS

Eight sheets packed with information detailing pipe installation methods, fittings, and sized. Details plumbing hook-ups for toilets, sinks, washers, sump pumps, and septic system construction. Conforms to requirements of National Plumbing code. Color coded with a glossary of terms and quick index.

RESIDENTIAL ELECTRICAL DETAILS

Eight sheets that cover all aspects of residential wiring, from simple switch wiring to service entrance connections. Details distribution panel layout with outlet and switch schematics, circuit breaker and wiring installation methods, and ground fault interrupter specifications. Conforms to requirements of National Electrical Code. Color coded with a glossary of terms.

Modifying Your Favorite Design, Made *EASY!*

OPTION #1

Modifying Your Garlinghouse Home Plan

Simple modifications to your dream home, including minor non-structural changes and material substitutions, can be made between you and your builder by marking the changes directly on your blueprints. However, if you are considering making significant changes to your chosen design, we recommend that you use the services of The Garlinghouse Co. Design Staff. We will help take your ideas and turn them into a reality, just the way you want. Here's our procedure!

When you place your Vellum order, you may also request a free Garlinghouse Modification Kit. In this kit, you will receive a red marking pencil, furniture cut-out sheet, ruler, a self addressed mailing label and a form for specifying any additional notes or drawings that will help us understand your design ideas. Mark your desired changes directly on the Vellum drawings. NOTE: Please use only a **red pencil** to mark your desired changes on the Vellum. Then, return the redlined Vellum set in the original box to The Garlinghouse Company at, 282 Main Street Extension, Middletown, CT 06457. **IMPORTANT**: Please **roll** the Vellums for shipping, **do not fold** the Vellums for shipping.

We also offer modification estimates. We will provide you with an estimate to draft your changes based on your specific modifications before you purchase the vellums, for a $50 fee. After you receive your estimate, if you decide to have The Garlinghouse Company Design Staff do the changes, the $50 estimate fee will be deducted from the cost of your modifications. If, however, you choose to use a different service, the $50 estimate fee is non-refundable. (Note: Personal checks cannot be accepted for the estimate.)

Within 5 days of receipt of your plans, you will be contacted by a member of The Garlinghouse Co. Design Staff with an estimate for the design services to draw those changes. A 50% deposit is required before we begin making the actual modifications to your plans.

Once the design changes have been completed to your vellum plan, a representative will call to inform you that your modified Vellum plan is complete and will be shipped as soon as the final payment has been made. For additional information call us at 1-860-343-5977. Please refer to the Modification Pricing Guide for estimated modification costs.

OPTION #2

Reproducible Vellums for Local Modification Ease

If you decide not to use the Garlinghouse Co. Design Staff for your modifications, we recommend that you follow our same procedure of purchasing our Vellums. You then have the option of using the services of the original designer of the plan, a local professional designer, or architect to make the modifications to your plan.

With a Vellum copy of our plans, a design professional can alter the drawings just the way you want, then you can print as many copies of the modified plans as you need to build your house. And, since you have already started with our complete detailed plans, the cost of those expensive professional services will be significantly less than starting from scratch. Refer to the price schedule for Vellum costs. Again, please call for Vellum availability for plan numbers 85,000 and above.

IMPORTANT RETURN POLICY: Upon receipt of your Vellums, if for some reason you decide you do not want a modified plan, then simply return the Kit and the unopened Vellums. Reproducible Vellum copies of our home plans are copyright protected and only sold under the terms of a license agreement that you will receive with your order. Should you not agree to the terms, then the Vellums may be returned, **unopened,** for a full refund less the shipping and handling charges, plus a 15% restocking fee. For any additional information, please call us at 1-860-343-5977.

MODIFICATION PRICING GUIDE

CATEGORIES	ESTIMATED COST
KITCHEN LAYOUT — PLAN AND ELEVATION	$175.00
BATHROOM LAYOUT — PLAN AND ELEVATION	$175.00
FIREPLACE PLAN AND DETAILS	$200.00
INTERIOR ELEVATION	$125.00
EXTERIOR ELEVATION — MATERIAL CHANGE	$140.00
EXTERIOR ELEVATION — ADD BRICK OR STONE	$400.00
EXTERIOR ELEVATION — STYLE CHANGE	$450.00
NON BEARING WALLS (INTERIOR)	$200.00
BEARING AND/OR EXTERIOR WALLS	$325.00
WALL FRAMING CHANGE — 2X4 TO 2X6 OR 2X6 TO 2X4	$240.00
ADD/REDUCE LIVING SPACE — SQUARE FOOTAGE	QUOTE REQUIRED
NEW MATERIALS LIST	QUOTE REQUIRED
CHANGE TRUSSES TO RAFTERS OR CHANGE ROOF PITCH	$300.00
FRAMING PLAN CHANGES	$325.00
GARAGE CHANGES	$325.00
ADD A FOUNDATION OPTION	$300.00
FOUNDATION CHANGES	$250.00
RIGHT READING PLAN REVERSE	$575.00
ARCHITECTS SEAL (Available for most states)	$300.00
ENERGY CERTIFICATE	$150.00
LIGHT AND VENTILATION SCHEDULE	$150.00

Questions?

Call our customer service department at **1-860-343-5977**

IMPORTANT INFORMATION TO READ BEFORE YOU PLACE YOUR ORDER

How Many Sets Of Plans Will You Need?

The Standard 8-Set Construction Package

Our experience shows that you'll speed every step of construction and avoid costly building errors by ordering enough sets to go around. Each tradesperson wants a set — the general contractor and all subcontractors; foundation, electrical, plumbing, heating/air conditioning and framers. Don't forget your lending institution, building department and, of course, a set for yourself.
* Recommended for Construction *

The Minimum 4-Set Construction Package

If you're comfortable with arduous follow-up, this package can save you a few dollars by giving you the option of passing down plan sets as work progresses. You might have enough copies to go around if work goes exactly as scheduled and no plans are lost or damaged by subcontractors. But for only $50 more, the 8-set package eliminates these worries. * Recommended for Bidding *

The Single Study Set

We offer this set so you can study the blueprints to plan your dream home in detail. They are stamped "study set-not for construction", and you cannot build a home from a them. In pursuant to copyright laws, it is illegal to reproduce any blueprint.

An Important Note About Building Code Requirements:

All plans are drawn to conform to one or more of the industry's major national building standards. However, due to the variety of local building regulations, your plan may need to be modified to comply with local requirements — snow loads, energy loads, seismic zones, etc. Do check them fully and consult your local building officials.

A few states require that all building plans used be drawn by an architect registered in that state. While having your plans reviewed and stamped by such an architect may be prudent, laws requiring non-conforming plans like ours to be completely redrawn forces you to unnecessarily pay very large fees. If your state has such a law, we strongly recommend you contact your state representative to protest.

The rendering, floor plans, and technical information contained within this publication are not guaranteed to be totally accurate. Consequently, no information from this publication should be used either as a guide to constructing a home or for estimating the cost of building a home. Complete blueprints must be purchased for such purposes.

Order Form

Plan prices guaranteed until 3/1/01—After this date call for updated pricing

Order Code No. **HOBS**

____ set(s) of blueprints for plan #_____ $_____

____ Vellum & Modification kit for plan #_____ $_____

____ Additional set(s) @ $35 each for plan #_____ $_____

____ Mirror Image Reverse @ $50 each $_____

____ Right Reading Reverse $_____

____ Materials list for plan #_____ $_____

____ Detail Plans @ $19.95 each

    ❏ Construction ❏ Plumbing ❏ Electrical $_____

____ Bottom line ZIP Quote @ $29.95 for plan #_____ $_____

____ Additional Bottom Line Zip Quote

    @ $14.95 for plan(s) #_____

_____ $_____

____ Itemized ZIP Quote for plan(s) #_____ $____

Shipping (see charts on opposite page) $____

Subtotal $____

Sales Tax (CT residents add 6% sales tax, KS residents add 6.15% sales tax) (Not required for other states) $____

TOTAL AMOUNT ENCLOSED   **$____**

Send your check, money order or credit card information to:
(No C.O.D.'s Please)
Please submit all orders to:
Garlinghouse Company
P.O. Box 1717
Middletown, CT. 06457

ADDRESS INFORMATION:

NAME: _____

STREET: _____

CITY: _____ STATE: _____ ZIP: _____

DAYTIME PHONE: _____ EMAIL ADDRESS: _____

Credit Card Information

Charge To: ❏ Visa   ❏ Mastercard

Card # |__|__|__|__|__|__|__|__|__|__|__|__|__|__|__|__|

Signature _____ Exp. ____/____